PQ
4053
A7
G3
1971

Gardner, Edmund
Garratt, 1869-1935.

The Arthurian legend
in Italian
literature

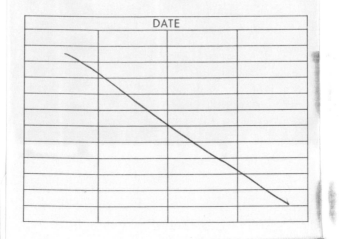

DATE			

THE ARTHURIAN LEGEND
IN ITALIAN LITERATURE

ARTHUR AND MORDRED

From Boccaccio, *De casibus virorum illustrium* (French translation by Laurent de Premierfait). B.M., Royal MS. 14 E, V

THE ARTHURIAN LEGEND IN ITALIAN LITERATURE

BY

EDMUND G. GARDNER

In him that should say or think that there was
never such a king called Arthur might well be
aretted great folly and blindness. For . . .
ye shall see also in the history of Bochas, in
his book *De Casu Principum,* part of his noble
acts and also of his fall.—CAXTON.

1971

OCTAGON BOOKS

New York

First published in 1930

Reprinted 1971
by special arrangement with J. M. Dent & Sons Ltd.

OCTAGON BOOKS
A DIVISION OF FARRAR, STRAUS & GIROUX, INC.
19 Union Square West
New York, N. Y. 10003

LIBRARY OF CONGRESS CATALOG CARD NUMBER: 78-120255

ISBN 0-374-92999-8

Manufactured by Braun-Brumfield, Inc.
Ann Arbor, Michigan

Printed in the United States of America

To
EDWARD HUTTON

PREFACE

The present work originated in a course of lectures delivered in University College at a time when I only partially realised the complexity of the subject and the richness of Italy with respect to the Arthurian legend. Even after six years' subsequent study and research, I cannot but recognize that much remains to be done in the elucidation of sources and the investigation of texts. In offering the results in this volume, I have tried to keep in mind two classes of readers: students of Italian literature who have not always any special knowledge of the Arthurian story; Arthurian students who, not unfrequently, do not read Italian with ease. For the benefit of the former, I have frequently repeated matter that is quite elementary to the professed Arthurian; while, for the aid of the latter, I have, as a general rule, appended translations of the passages in Italian quoted in the text. English readers who know the subject mainly through the medium of Malory will, perhaps, be struck by the somewhat different aspect that the Arthurian legend assumes in Italy: how, for instance, in contrast with the *Morte Darthur*, Tristan, rather than Lancelot, is the more significant figure, and certain knights unknown to English literature, such as Guiron the Courteous and Segurant the Knight of the Dragon, appear among the leading heroes. In the treatment of proper names, I have usually adopted forms corresponding to the French as these are the more generally accepted, but have occasionally retained those given by Malory; it would be, for instance, intolerable to call the mysterious sister of Arthur anything else than "Morgan le Fay," or spell the name of the seneschal otherwise than "Kay." But I have duly recorded the Italian and other chief alternative forms in an index which, in humble imitation of the admirable example set by M. Löseth, I have endeavoured to make a sort of rudimentary Arthurian "Who's Who."

I owe an inestimable debt of gratitude to the Italian scholars who have dealt with the subject of the "matière de Bretagne" in Italy; above all to the late Ernesto Giacomo Parodi, Pio Rajna, Giulio Bertoni, and Ezio Levi. I am also deeply indebted to M. Löseth's fundamental work on the prose *Tristan* and the *Palamède*; to the late J. D. Bruce in his *Evolution of Arthurian Romance*; and to Miss Lucy Allen Paton in her recent volumes on the *Prophecies de Merlin*. For English readers, Dr. Paget Toynbee has been a pioneer with his essay, *Dante and the Lancelot Romance*. My grateful thanks are due to Professor Roger Sherman Loomis and Professor A.

Kingsley Porter, who have placed at my disposal
their photographic reproductions of the Arthurian
archivolt at Modena.

Antonio Panizzi was, I believe, the first to indicate
that Dante's episode of Paolo and Francesca should
be connected with the prose *Tristan*. It is as
the unworthy holder of the chair that was his at
University College that I would thus close this brief
preface with his name.

EDMUND G. GARDNER.

UNIVERSITY COLLEGE, LONDON
July, 1930

CONTENTS

CHAP.   PAGE

I. EARLY REFERENCES TO ARTHUR IN ITALY: MERLIN THE PROPHET: THE HOLY GRAIL 1

II. THE "MATTER OF BRITAIN" IN THE POETS OF THE THIRTEENTH CENTURY 21

III. THE "PALAMÈDE" AND RUSTICIANO DA PISA . . 44

IV. THE "TRISTANO RICCARDIANO" 64

V. ARTHURIAN MATTER IN THE "NOVELLE" . . . 85

VI. ARTHURIAN MATTER IN THE "MARE AMOROSO" AND IN THE "INTELLIGENZA" 101

VII. SOME "TRISTAN" AND "LANCELOT" FRAGMENTS . 114

VIII. DANTE AND THE ARTHURIAN LEGEND . . . 130

IX. THE "TAVOLA RITONDA" 152

X. THE ITALIAN ROMANCES OF MERLIN . . . 191

XI. THE "MATTER OF BRITAIN" IN THE POETS OF THE TRECENTO AND BOCCACCIO 217

XII. THE "MATTER OF BRITAIN" IN THE "CANTARI" . 239

XIII. THE ARTHURIANISM OF BOIARDO AND ARIOSTO . . 273

XIV. LATER TREATMENT OF ARTHURIAN MATTER IN ITALY 295

APPENDIX: AN UNPUBLISHED ROMANCE OF THE OLD TABLE 331

INDEX I: ARTHURIAN NAMES AND MATTERS . . 337

INDEX II: SUBSIDIARY AND GENERAL . . . 346

ABBREVIATIONS

M.L.R. . . . *Modern Language Review* (Cambridge)

M.L.A.A. . . Modern Language Association of America (Baltimore)

M.L.N. . . . *Modern Language Notes* (Baltimore)

G.S.L.I. . . . *Giornale Storico della Letteratura Italiana* (Turin)

Zs. f. rom. Phil. . *Zeitschrift für romanische Philologie* (Halle)

LIST OF ILLUSTRATIONS

ARTHUR AND MORDRED. From Boccaccio, *De casibus virorum illustrium* (French translation by Laurent de Premierfait). B.M., Royal MS. 14 E, V . *Frontispiece*

THE MODENA ARCHIVOLT (Porta della Pescheria, Modena) . . . . *facing page* 4

DETAILS OF THE MODENA ARCHIVOLT: I. "Galvaginus" (Gawain); II. "Galvariun" . . . ,, 6

TRISTAN AND ISEULT EMBARK FOR CORNWALL; THE DRINKING OF THE LOVE POTION. Florence, Biblioteca Nazionale, Cod. Pal. 556 . . . ,, 26

KING ARTHUR WELCOMES THE GOOD KNIGHT WITHOUT FEAR; KING MELIADUS WITH THE CHILD TRISTAN. *Palamède*; B.M., Add. MS. 12228 . . . ,, 52

TRISTAN MORTALLY WOUNDED BY KING MARK. Florence, Biblioteca Nazionale, Cod. Pal. 556. . ,, 112

THE COMING OF GALAHAD; GALAHAD AT THE TOURNAMENT. Florence, Biblioteca Nazionale, Cod. Pal. 556 . . . . ,, 122

TRISTAN AND LANCELOT IN THE HOUSE OF THE LADY OF THE LAKE. Florence, Biblioteca Nazionale, Cod. Pal. 556 . . . . ,, 174

LANCELOT AT THE CASTLE OF CORBENIC. Florence, Biblioteca Nazionale, Cod. Pal. 556 . . . ,, 178

GALAHAD, BORS, AND PERCEVAL; THE SISTER OF PERCEVAL. Florence, Biblioteca Nazionale, Cod. Pal. 556 . . . . ,, 180

JOSEPH OF ARIMATHEA; THE REVELATION OF THE HOLY GRAIL. Florence, Biblioteca Nazionale, Cod. Pal. 556 . . . . ,, 190

PERCEVAL DELIVERS THE YOUNG LION FROM THE SERPENT (Malory, XIV, 7). Florence, Biblioteca Nazionale, Cod. Pal. 556 . . . . . ,, 208

THE ROUND TABLE. From Boccaccio, *De casibus virorum illustrium* (French translation by Laurent de Premierfait). B.M., Add. MS. 35321 . . *facing page* 234

THE DEATH OF GUINEVERE; LANCELOT ENTERS THE HERMITAGE. Florence, Biblioteca Nazionale, Cod. Pal. 556 . . . .   „   268

THE PASSING OF ARTHUR. Florence, Biblioteca Nazionale, Cod. Pal. 556 . . . . . .   „   272

TRISTAN AND KAHEDYN AT THE FOREST OF DAR-NANTES; TRISTAN AND THE HERMIT. Florence, Biblioteca Nazionale, Cod. Pal. 556 . . .   „   286

CHAPTER I

THE *Morte Darthur* of Sir Thomas Malory—finished
in 1469 or 1470—has been called our national prose
epic. It is at least our gospel and treasury of high
romance which, with the quest and achievement of
the Holy Grail, attains a mystical significance not
without analogies with the *Divina Commedia* itself.
In his preface Caxton appeals to Italian sources for
the historicity of the Arthurian legend. Among the
many evidences against "him that should say or
think that there was never such a king called Arthur"
is the testimony of Boccaccio: "Ye shall see also in
the history of Bochas, in his book *De Casu Principum*,
part of his noble acts and also of his fall." And there
are "books made of his noble acts" in Italian. To
Italy this particular romantic cycle, the *materia di
Brettagna*, came as a subject more foreign and
esoteric than the rival Carolingian cycle, the *materia
di Francia*.[1] Unlike Charlemagne, Arthur had no
connection with Italian history, real or legendary;
the story of his conquest of Italy, and how "he came
into Rome, and was crowned emperor by the pope's

---

[1] Cf. P. Rajna, in *Romania*, IV, p. 178.

hand, with all the royalty that could be made," told in the fifth book of the *Morte Darthur*, and that of his expedition to Sicily for the relief of Palermo, which appears in *Floriant et Florete*, were unknown to or ignored by Italians. Nevertheless, echoes of the various legends, whether of mythic origin or artistic finding, which we read woven into that somewhat confused dramatic unity of the Arthuriad which is mainly Malory's own creation,[1] are heard from the very beginnings of Italian literature.

M. Bédier has observed that, between the conquest of England by the Normans in 1066 and the first extant romances of Chrétien de Troyes (about 1168), there is a century in which there was probably an initial flowering of Arthurian poems which have not come down to us.[2] It will be borne in mind that it was between 1134 and 1139 that Geoffrey of Monmouth wrote his *Historia Regum Britanniae*, which for us is practically the starting point of the Arthurian legend.[3] Now it is in these years, before any reflection in literature, that some sort of acquaintance with Arthurian story may be argued from the names borne by Italians. Pio Rajna first showed that the name of Arthur is frequently found in documents from the first half of the twelfth century onwards, more particularly in north and north-eastern Italy; especially

[1] Cf. E. Vinaver, *Le Roman de Tristan et Iseut dans l'œuvre de Thomas Malory* (Paris, 1925), p. 14.

[2] J. Bédier, *Le Roman de Tristan par Thomas* (Paris, 1903–5), II, p. 154.

[3] Cf. E. K. Chambers, *Arthur of Britain* (London, 1927), pp. 41–6.

Mr. Acton Griscom, in his recent edition, *The Historia Regum Britanniae of Geoffrey of Monmouth* (London, 1929), chap. vi, holds that it was first published in April 1136.

at Pavia, Padua, and in the March of Treviso.[1] It occurs as Artusius (Artuxius) or Artusus; agreeing with the French vernacular form, "Artus," rather than with the Latin, "Arthurius" or "Arthurus." The earliest Italian of whom we have record as bearing the name is an Artusius, brother of Count Ugo of Padua, in a document of 1114—who must obviously have been so christened in the previous century. We find other persons of this name in documents at Venice, Pavia (where they are abundant after 1151), Monselice, Cremona, Chioggia, Este; and, passing southwards, at Ravenna, and in Tuscany at Altopascio in 1169 or 1170. Together with the name of Arthur, but more sparingly, occurs that of his nephew Gawain: "Galvanus," "Walwanus"; at Padua in 1136, at Genoa in 1158, at Feltre in 1182. A Pavian document of 1198 gives the name *Gradalis*, which Rajna tentatively associates with the Grail. To these may be added the name of Merlin, discovered in a Pistoian document of 1128; he, too, was probably born in the previous century as he is spoken of as dead: *quondam Merlinus*.[2] This early acquaintance with Arthur, at least by name, is presumably due to the wandering minstrels, "jongleurs" or "giullari," who came from France; Pavia was an important station on the great road that brought them into

---

[1] *Gli eroi brettoni nell' onomastica italiana del secolo xii*, in *Romania*, XVII (1888). But the identification of these names, as well as the significance of their occurrence, is disputed. Cf. especially E. Faral, *Recherches sur les sources latines des contes et romans courtois du moyen âge* (Paris, 1913), pp. 393–7, and E. K. Chambers, *op. cit.*, p. 133.

[2] I. Sanesi, *Storia di Merlino di Paolino Pieri* (Bergamo, 1898), pp. xi–xiii.

Italy, and the March of Treviso one of their favourite resorts.

But, even more significant than the occurrence of Arthurian names in baptism, we have contemporaneously an Arthurian document in stone. Over the north door, the Porta della Pescheria, of the cathedral at Modena, is a bas-relief representing the attack upon a castle, the central tower of which is surrounded with water. The actors in the scene, with one exception, have names inscribed above them. From the battlements a man and woman, "Mardoc" and "Winlogee," are watching the progress of the assault; on the left, a combatant on foot, "Burmaltus," is contending the passage with a knight on horseback, above whose figure is inscribed "Artus de Bretania." Behind Arthur are two others; the first, without helmet or hauberk, "Isdernus," is turning to speak with the knight who follows and who is unnamed. On the other side, a mounted knight, "Carrado," issues to engage in battle with the first of three similarly armed and mounted opponents, "Galvaginus," who is followed by "Galvariun" and "Che." It is tempting to assume that "Winlogee" is Guinevere, though the name suggests Queen Guenloie, beloved by the hero in the thirteenth-century Norman romance of *Yder*. "Galvaginus" can hardly be other than Gawain; "Che" is obviously the personage familiar to us as Sir Kay the Seneschal; while "Mardoc" appears to be playing a part suggestive of Meliagrance or Mordred. Professor Loomis claims to have identified—or, rather, reconstructed—the story as a Breton tale of the abduction of Guinevere

THE MODENA ARCHIVOLT
(Porta della Pescheria, Cathedral, Modena)

and her rescue by Gawain—a story including elements
to be found later in the thirteenth-century romance
of *Durmart le Gallois* and the episode of Carados of
the Dolorous Tower in the prose *Lancelot*. "Isdernus" would reappear as the Yder of *Durmart*, "Galvariun" as the Galeschin of the *Lancelot*, while
"Burmaltus" is an earlier representative of the
Celtic tradition which will produce the Bercilak of
Gawain and the Green Knight. Further, from the
similarity between this sculpture and a corresponding one at Bari, and the fact that a party of
Bretons passed through Bari for the first Crusade,
Professor Loomis would definitely assign the work to
a date between 1099 and 1106, the period of the
first building of the cathedral. In support of this
view, he points out that twelfth-century iconography
seems to show that the helmets of the knights are of
a style that went out soon after the beginning of the
twelfth century. Alluring though this theory is, I
cannot feel entirely convinced; but it is at least
probable (though some authorities like M. Mâle would
place it later) that the Modena bas-relief was executed
before Geoffrey of Monmouth wrote, and perhaps by
Wiligelmus or Niccolò, who are known to have been
working on the cathedral in the first part of the
twelfth century. In any case, we may regard this
bas-relief as a concrete example of the productions
of the minstrels and reciters celebrating Arthur
and his companions in arms, before the "materia
di Brettagna" had received its definite form in
the work of the courtly poets, and belonging
to the period of preparation in which the Celtic

tradition was being diffused among the Latin peoples.[1]

The earliest literary allusions to the Arthurian legend in Italy occur towards the end of the twelfth century, and are naturally in Latin.

Godfrey of Viterbo, an ecclesiastic in the imperial service who had been one of the secretaries of Frederick Barbarossa, wrote—between 1186 and 1191 —his *Pantheon*, a kind of universal history in prose and verse. He concludes the section on the Angles and Saxons with the story of Vortigern and the building of the tower of which the foundations are perpetually swallowed up, until the wizards bid the king seek and sacrifice the boy who never had a father, the finding of Merlin, his prophecies, the love of Uther

---

[1] Cf. B. Colfi, *Di una recente interpretazione data alle sculture dell'archivolto nella porta settentrionale del duomo di Modena*, in *Atti e memorie della R. Deputazione di Storia Patria per le provincie modenesi*, Series IV, vol. ix (Modena, 1899); W. Foerster, *Ein neues Artus-dokument*, in *Zs. f. rom. Phil.*, XXII (1898), pp. 526–9; G. Bertoni, *Atlante storico paleografico del duomo di Modena* (Modena, 1909), tav. x, and second part (Modena, 1921), pp. xvii, xviii, 46–7; J. D. Bruce, *Evolution of Arthurian Romance* (Göttingen and Baltimore, 1923–4), I, pp. 14–17; A. K. Porter, *Bari, Modena, and St. Giles*, in *Burlington Magazine*, XLIII (1923), pp. 58–67; R. S. Loomis, *Story of the Modena Archivolt and its Mythological Roots*, in *Romanic Review*, XV (1924), *The Date, Source, and Subject of the Arthurian Sculpture at Modena*, in *Medieval Studies in Memory of G. S. Loomis* (Paris and New York, 1927), pp. 109–228, and *Celtic Myth and Arthurian Romance* (Columbia University Press, 1927), chap. i. Miss Jessie L. Weston, in what was the last Arthurian note published by her before her death, remarks: "It seems far more probable that we have here, as Professor Singer has suggested, the representation of two separate and distinct stories: that on the right being, so far, unidentified; while that on the left represents an incident drawn from the *Yder* story, which certainly formed a very early part of the Arthurian *corpus*" (*M.L.R.*, XXIII, p. 245). The *Yder* story has no trace in Italian literature.

Details of the Modena Archivolt
I. "Galvaginus" (Gawain); II. "Galvarium"

Pendragon for Hierna (Igerna, Igraine, the episode with which Malory will begin the *Morte Darthur*). Godfrey's source is manifestly Geoffrey of Monmouth, but he handles his matter freely, the Uther Pendragon and Hierna story being considerably elaborated in a dramatic fashion, not without echoes from Ovid.[1] He ends at the point where Arthur is about to be born, and Merlin foretells his future greatness:

> Laetus ait vates: "En gaudia magna parate.
> Currite primates, caeloque resolvite grates,
> nam quae ventre latent mira futura patent.
> Hic erit Arturus rex summus in orbe futurus,
> praelia gesturus, loca Gallica rex habiturus,
> nomine magnus erit, vulneribusque perit.
> Nec perit omnino, maris observabitur imo,
> vivere perpetuo poterit rex ordine primo:
> ista tibi refero, caetera claudo sinu." [2]

---

[1] *Godefridi Viterbiensis Pantheon sive Universitatis libri qui Chronici appellantur XX* (Basle, 1559), pars xviii: "de Anglis et Saxonibus." Reprinted in Muratori, *R.I.S.*, VII, and Migne, *Pat. Lat.*, CXCVIII (the Arthurian portions omitted in *M.G.H.S.* XXII). The passages mentioned are based upon Geoffrey of Monmouth, VI, 17–19, VIII, 19–20. The identification of Merlin by the quarrel between the two boys (which we shall find presently in Italian literature) is omitted, and his prophecies merely cover the reign of Aurelius. The story of Vortigern's tower is first found in the *Historia Brittonum*, attributed to Nennius and the ninth century (ed. Mommsen, *M.G.H.*, *Chronica minora Saec.* iv–vii, III, pp. 181–6), but there the boy, supposed to have had no father, is not Merlin, but Ambrosius Aurelianus, the future king.

[2] "Joyously speaks the prophet: 'Lo, prepare great rejoicing. Hasten, ye nobles, and give thanks to Heaven, for the future will reveal the wonders hidden in the womb. This will be Arthur, the supreme king to come in the world, wars will he wage, in Gaul will he dwell as king, he will be great in renown, and will perish of his wounds. Yet not perish utterly, he will be preserved within the sea, to live for ever a king as before. These things I tell thee, the rest I keep shut in my breast.'" Here the survival of Arthur is more definitely expressed than in Geoffrey's *Historia*. Cf. Chambers, *op. cit.*, pp. 49, 89, and Griscom, *op. cit.*, pp. 501, 546.

A little later, probably about 1193, a priest in Tuscany—Henricus of Settimello—wrote a famous poem, the *Elegia de diversitate fortunae et philosophiae consolatione*, a work of far greater literary merit than the *Pantheon* of Godfrey of Viterbo. Here we find the first literary mention of Tristan—though not expressly as a lover—in Italy:

> Quis ille
> Tristanus qui me tristia plura tulit?

Who is that Tristan who bore more sorrows than I?

Arthur is to him a type of human greatness and felicity:

> Quot sub sole vigent fateor me tot meliores:
> sim licet Arturus, qualis habebor ero.
> Omnibus invideo, nullus mihi;

All who thrive under the sun I confess better than myself; even if I am Arthur, I shall be what I am deemed; I envy every one, no one envies me.

And he twice refers to the legend of Arthur's expected return:

> Et prius Arturus veniet vetus ille Britannis,
> quam ferat adversis falsus amicus opem;

That old Arthur shall come to the Britons before a false friend brings aid in adversity;

> Qui cupit auferre naturam seminat herbam,
> cuius in Arturi tempore fructus erit; [1]

He who desires to take away nature sows grass whose fruit shall be in the time of Arthur.

---

[1] *Elegia*, 97–8, 119–21, 157–8, 537–8. *Henrici Septimellensis Elegia sive de Miseria*, ed. A. Marigo (Padua, 1926). The tone of the allusion to Tristan curiously suggests the recitations of the "histriones" recorded at about the same time in the *De Consolatione* of Peter of Blois (cf. the passage quoted by E. K. Chambers, *op. cit.*, p. 267).

There are other allusions to "the hope of Britain" in the Latin literature of Italy in the early part of the thirteenth century. The first Florentine chronicler, Sanzanome, who wrote his *Gesta Florentinorum* about 1231, speaks of the Sienese looking for a victory over the Florentines "like the Britons who are said still to expect King Arthur": "tamquam Brittoni qui regem adhuc expectare dicuntur Arturum." [1] A few years later an anonymous poet of Parma, celebrating the defeat of Frederick II in 1248, adopts a similar image for the vain threats of the Emperor:

> Conminatur impius, dolens de iacturis,
> cum suo Britonibus Arturo venturis; [2]

The ruthless man, bewailing his overthrow, threatens the Britons coming with their Arthur.

A literary source is hardly needed; the tradition was so widely spread that "Arturum expectare" had become a proverbial phrase for expecting the impossible. But, earlier than this, we meet what appears to be an allusion to the Round Table itself. The famous master of rhetoric, Boncompagno da Signa, in his *Cedrus* (composed between 1194 and 1203), speaks of societies of young men formed in many parts of Italy, with names like the "fellowship of the falcons," the "fellowship of the lions," or "the fellowship of the Round Table"—*de tabula rotonda societas*.[3] And, according to Brother Leo, St. Francis

---

[1] *Sanzanomis Gesta Florentinorum*, in Hartwig, *Quellen und Forschungen zur ältesten Geschichte der Stadt Florenz*, I, p. 33.

[2] *Carmina triumphalia*, ed. Jaffé, in Pertz, *M.G.H.S.*, XVIII, p. 796.

[3] In Rockinger, *Briefsteller und Formelbücher des eilften bis vierzehnten Jahrhunderts* (in *Quellen zur Bayerischen und Deutschen Geschichte*, IX, i, Munich, 1863), p. 122. The whole passage is

of Assisi used to say of his first followers: "These
are my brethren, the knights of the Round Table";
"Isti sunt mei fratres, milites tabulae rotundae, qui
latitant in remotis et in desertis locis, ut diligentius
vacent orationi et meditationi." [1]   Boncompagno
is also the first writer in Italy who mentions Iseult.
In his *De Amicitia* (about 1205), her name is coupled
with that of Helen. The infatuated lover, "orbatus
amicus," so idealises his mistress that, even if de-
formed or ill-favoured, she is transfigured into a
Helen or an Iseult.[2]   And he can make humorous
use of the Arthurian story. Among his models for
letters is one from a lecturer to a student who
has been playing truant, telling him that he will
complete his academic course when Arthur returns
to Britain.[3]

So far we have been keeping to north and central
Italy, to which the knowledge of Arthurian stories
came first on the lips of the minstrels and reciters:
"histriones," "jongleurs," "giullari"; and then with

interesting as bearing upon the "brigata nobile e cortese" of the
sonnets of Folgore da San Gimignano and Betto Brunelleschi's
"brigata" in the *Decameron*.

[1] *Intentio Regulae*, in *Documenta Antiqua Franciscana*, ed. L.
Lemmens (Quaracchi, 1901), p. 90. Also in *Speculum Perfectionis*,
ed. P. Sabatier, cap. 72. The Round Table is first mentioned in
Wace's *Brut* (1155).

[2] "Nec est distinctio inter despectibilem et formosam, quoniam ex
quo placet orbato, gibbosa vel nasicurva convertitur in Elenam vel
Ysottam." *Amicitia di maestro Boncompagno da Signa*, ed. S.
Nathan (Rome, 1909), p. 71.

[3] "Credo firmiter quod cum Arturo in Britanniam reverteris et
cum eo tuum studium celebrabis."   I owe this quotation, from an
unpublished portion of the *Rhetorica antiqua*, to my friend and
former student, Miss Helen M. Briggs, who is preparing what promises
to be an exhaustive monograph on Boncompagno.

the Provençal troubadours, the written French poems and romances following later, though we must always take into account a probable early circulation of the history of Geoffrey of Monmouth. To the south they were probably brought in the first instance by the Normans. From the middle of the eleventh century, personages bearing names suggestive of the "materia brettone" begin to appear in Campanian and Apulian documents. We hear of a Norman soldier "Torstainus" in southern Italy in 1022, who is probably the same as a "Tristainus" who received Monte Peloso in Apulia in 1042. There is record of a Robertus, son of "Trostenus" or "Tristaynus," in 1096 and 1109, and again in 1122 of a "Trostaynus cum familia sua." [1] A "Trustanius de Unfrido" has been found in documents of 1149 and 1151, referring to the church of San Pietro di Vico. [2] These are presumably variants of "Tristan," a name not hitherto met with in the "onomastica" of northern Italy at so early a date. At Bari, over a side doorway of the church of San Nicola, is what is probably an Arthurian scene resembling that of Modena (but without names), executed in the early part of the twelfth century. On the mosaic pavement of the cathedral at Otranto, executed by a priest named Pantaleone between 1163 and 1166, we find the figure of King Arthur, "Rex Arturus," riding what M. Bertaux calls "une sorte de

[1] *Leonis Marsicani et Petri Diaconi Chronica monasterii Casinensis*, ed. W. Wattenbach, in *M.G.H.S.*, VII, pp. 655, 676, 766, 778, 799. Cf. F. M. Warren, *Tristan on the Continent before 1066*, in *M.L.N.*, XXIV (Baltimore, 1909), pp. 37–8; Bruce, *op. cit.*, I, p. 177, n. 35.

[2] R. Ortiz, *La materia epica di ciclo classico nella lirica italiana delle origini*, in *G.S.L.I.*, LXXIX (Turin, 1922), p. 8, n. 1.

bouc énorme," but which may perhaps be intended to represent a horse.[1]

We next meet the curious legend of Arthur in Etna, which was first investigated by Arturo Graf.[2] Gervaise of Tilbury, an Englishman who had been in the service of the Norman king of Sicily, William II, in his *Otia imperialia* (written at the beginning of the thirteenth century), tells how a hostler of the Bishop of Catania in the search for a lost horse comes to a wonderful palace within "Mongibel," Mongibello, or Mount Etna, where he finds King Arthur reclining upon a royal couch. He has been here since the battle with Mordred and Childeric, the Saxon, his wounds breaking out afresh every year. The servant is sent back to the bishop with the horse and with gifts.[3] The same story, in a somewhat different form, is told a few years later by the German monk, Caesarius of Heisterbach, in the *Dialogus miraculorum*. At the time when the Emperor Henry conquered Sicily, a certain deacon at Palermo lost a valuable palfrey and sent his servant to look for it. An old man meets him, tells him that his lord King Arthur has the horse in Mons Gyber, and sends a summons to the deacon to come to the king's court within

---

[1] Émile Bertaux, *L'Art dans l'Italie méridionale*, I (Rome, 1904), pp. 483–91. What remains of the figure is shown on p. 491.

[2] *Artù nell' Etna*, in his *Miti, leggende e superstizioni del medio evo* (Turin, 1893), II, pp. 303–25.

[3] *Otia imperialia*, ed. Leibnitz, in *Script. rerum Brunsvicensium*, I, p. 921. Richard Cœur de Lion is said to have given Arthur's sword, Excalibur, to William's successor, Tancred, the last Norman king of Sicily: "gladium optimum Arcturi, nobilis quondam regis Britonum, quem Britones vocaverunt *Caliburnum*" (Benedict of Peterborough, *Chronicle*, ed. Stubbs, II, p. 159).

fourteen days. The deacon mocks at the message, but falls ill and dies on the appointed day.[1] Arthur is again brought into connection with Sicily in a French poem, probably of the third quarter of the thirteenth century: *Floriant et Florete*. Morgan le Fay—the "Fata Morgana" of later Italian poetry—and her sisters have their palace on Mongibel, and Arthur makes an expedition to the island to relieve Palermo, which is besieged by the Emperor of Constantinople. Floriant, when about to die, is led by a white stag to Mongibel (where he had been brought up in childhood), and Morgan tells him that she will ultimately bring her brother Arthur himself there when mortally wounded.[2] Another version of the same myth appears in *La Faula*, a poem in Catalan-Provençal composed by Guillem de Torrella, or Torroella, of Majorca, between 1350 and 1380. The poet is conveyed to an island, which we may take as Sicily, though represented as far more distant from Majorca. In a splendid palace he sees King Arthur lying ill on a rich couch, tended by Morgan le Fay. Arthur has been brought here by Morgan after receiving his mortal wound, and is kept young in aspect by recurrent visits of the Holy Grail.[3]

The local traditions of Etna are classical, not romantic, and the story—though Gervaise attributes

---

[1] *Dialogus miraculorum*, ed. Strange (Cologne, 1851), dist. xii, cap. 12.

[2] *Floriant et Florete*, ed. F. Michel (Edinburgh, 1873), II, ll. 8241-6. Cf. Bruce, *op. cit.*, II, pp. 254-9.

[3] Manuel Milá y Fontanals, *Poëtes Catalans, les noves rimades—la codolada* (Paris, 1876), pp. 8-22. Cf. W. J. Entwistle, *The Arthurian Legend in the Literatures of the Spanish Peninsula* (London, 1925), pp. 81-4.

it to the natives—could only have originated with
the Norman conquerors who, in some way, identified
Sicily with the legendary island or vale of Avalon,
the "insula pomorum quae fortunata vocatur" of
Geoffrey of Monmouth.[1] A trace of the story seems
to linger in the name "Fata Morgana" applied to a
kind of mirage in the Strait of Messina, which is
occasionally visible from the coast of the mainland.

No allusion to this pleasing fable has been found
in the poetry of Sicily itself, where the only romantic
traditions that took any root among the people were
those of the Carolingian cycle.[2] The single trace of
it in early Italian vernacular literature is in a
Tuscan poem of the latter part of the thirteenth
century: the *Detto del Gatto Lupesco*. The "gatto
lupesco" is apparently a wandering minstrel, who in
his travels has strayed from the right path—like
Brunetto Latini in the *Tesoretto*, and Dante himself at
the beginning of the *Divina Commedia*—and meets

[1] *Vita Merlini*, ed. J. J. Parry (University of Illinois Press, 1925),
l. 908.

[2] Cf. G. Pitrè, *Le tradizioni cavalleresche popolari in Sicilia*, in
Romania, XIII (1884), p. 391: "Solo la splendida epopea carolingia è
quella che tra noi ha favore e diffusione per via di rappresentazioni
teatrali, di racconti, di poesia, di tradizioni topografiche e paremio-
grafiche. Le leggende del ciclo brettone mancano quasi del tutto."
The same applies to the scenes painted upon the Sicilian carts. Cf.
G. Capitò, *Il Carretto Siciliano* (Milan, 1923), pp. 43-52. But Sicily
has given notable contributions to Arthurian iconography. There
is the famous quilt or coverlet, Sicilian workmanship of the latter
part of the fourteenth century, with scenes from the story of Tristan,
a portion of which is at South Kensington, and a ceiling of the
Palazzo Chiaramonte at Palermo has paintings of Arthurian subjects,
executed by Simone da Corleone and Cecco di Naro (1377-80). Cf.
P. Rajna, *Intorno a due antiche coperte con figurazioni tratte dalla
storia di Tristano*, in *Romania*, XLII (1913), and R. S. Loomis, in
Burlington Magazine, XLI (1922).

two knights from England who are returning home
from a pilgrimage to Sicily:

> Cavalieri siam di Bretangna,
> ke veniamo de la montangna
> ke ll'omo apella Mongibello.
> Assai vi semo stati ad ostello
> per apparare ed invenire
> la veritate di nostro sire,
> lo re Artù, k' avemo perduto
> e· non sapemo che ssia venuto.
> Or ne torniamo in nostra terra,
> ne lo reame d'Inghilterra.[1]

This is not quite the only instance of an attempt to
link the *materia di Brettagna* geographically with
Italy; but the other two examples are later and come
from the north of the peninsula. The Angevin kings
of England prided themselves on possessing the sword
of Tristan, which is said to be still among the regalia
in the Tower of London [2]; but the Lombard chronicler,
Galvano Fiamma (himself bearing an Arthurian
name), writing in the early part of the fourteenth
century, declares that at Seprio, near Milan, a tomb
was discovered, in which lay the body of a Langobard
king—one Galdanus, a personage unknown to history
—and by its side a sword with the inscription: *Cel
est l'espée de Meser Tristant, un il ocist l'Amoroyt de
Yrlant*; "This is the sword of Sir Tristan with which

---

[1] "We are knights of Britain, who come from the mountain that
men call Mongibello. Long have we stayed there to learn and find
the truth concerning our lord, King Arthur, whom we have lost
and know not what has befallen. Now we are returning to our native
land, to the realm of England." In Monaci, *Crestomazia italiana dei
primi secoli* (Città di Castello, 1912), p. 449, and V. De Bartholomaeis,
Rime giullaresche e popolari d'Italia (Bologna, 1926), p. 24.

[2] Cf. R. S. Loomis, *Tristram and the House of Anjou*, in *M.L.R.*,
XVII (1922), p. 29.

he slew the Morholt of Ireland."[1] The Morholt —"l'Amoroldo"—is, of course, "the queen's brother of Ireland," perhaps originally a sea monster, but transformed by romance from Thomas onwards into the knight whom Tristan slew to deliver Cornwall from the truage. Again, at Verona, there are traces of legends that Lancelot fought a duel in the arena or amphitheatre with "Malgaretes"—who is obviously the Meleagant of Chrétien's poem and the prose *Lancelot*, the Meliagrance of the *Morte Darthur*, the abductor and accuser of Guinevere, who was ultimately slain by Lancelot—and that the amphitheatre itself had been built by the magic art of Merlin.[2]

In the middle of the thirteenth century, Merlin acquired a significance for Italians quite unconnected with the Arthurian legend. He was regarded as a prophet, but the prophecies that passed under his name bear no resemblance to those given by Geoffrey of Monmouth; they relate to the emperors of the house of Hohenstaufen, more particularly to Frederick II, and include the latter's whole career. The Franciscan followers of the Abbot Joachim greedily seized upon them. Fra Salimbene of Parma, in his famous chronicle, tells us how a certain Friar Hugh, disputing concerning the doctrines of Joachim with the Dominican Peter of Apulia, hurled at the latter's head texts from Isaiah and from Merlin (*anglicus vates*) on the subject of Frederick; but the Dominican answered:

---

[1] *Opusculum de rebus gestis Azonis Vicecomitis*, in Muratori, *R.I.S.*, XII, coll. 1027-8. The same story is told in the *Flos florum*, also of the fourteenth century, attributed to Ambrogio Bossi. See Graf, *op. cit.*, pp. 353-6.

[2] Cf. Graf, *op. cit.*, pp. 356-9.

"This is heretical talk, to take the words of an infidel like Merlin as testimony." Salimbene quotes at length the supposed prophecies of Merlin, associating them with those attributed to Michael Scott. Describing events in Italy in 1284, he says: "These things were done that the scripture of Merlin, the English prophet, might be fulfilled," and cites a long composition in verse in which the vicissitudes of the cities of Lombardy, Tuscany, Romagna, and the Marches "are fully and truly contained." [1] There was also current, and is still extant, an *Expositio Sibyllae et Merlini*, supposed to have been addressed in 1196 to Henry VI, the father of Frederick, by Joachim himself; in reality, of course, it is a later fabrication, devoid of all connection with the Calabrian abbot and his authentic doctrines.

In the still somewhat dim morning of Arthurian studies, Paulin Paris fancied that the "sagro catino" in the cathedral at Genoa might be the starting point of the romances of the Holy Grail. This famous relic, an hexagonal dish of green glass, is said to have been received by the Genoese as their share in the spoils at the taking of Caesarea from the Saracens in 1101. The story is told, in the latter part of the same century, by William of Tyre:

There was found a vessel of greenest colour, formed in the shape of a dish, which the Genoese, deeming it to be of emerald,

---

[1] *Cronica Fratris Salimbene de Adam*, ed. O. Holder-Egger, *M.G.H.S.*, XXXII, pp. 241-7, 359, 539. The Cistercian, Caesarius of Heisterbach, would have agreed with Hugh against the Dominican: "Merlinus vero homo rationalis et Christianus fuit; multa futura praedixit, quae quotidie implentur" (*Dialogus Miraculorum*, dist. iii, cap. 12).

c

and receiving it in lot instead of a great sum of money, offered to their church as a most excellent ornament. Wherefore, even to this day, when great persons pass through their city, they are wont to show that vessel, as though it were a miracle, maintaining that it truly is an emerald as its colour indicates.[1]

At what precise date popular devotion began to connect this vessel with the Last Supper or the Precious Blood, we do not know; but the identification with the Holy Grail appears to be due to the Archbishop, Jacopo da Voragine, towards the end of the thirteenth century:

That vessel is made in the likeness of a dish, whence it is commonly said that it was that dish out of which Christ with His disciples ate at the Last Supper, concerning which Christ said: *He that dippeth his hand with Me in the dish, the same shall betray Me.* Now whether this be true, we know not; but, since with God nothing is impossible, therefore we neither firmly assert, nor obstinately deny it. . . . This, however, must not be passed over in silence; that in certain books of the English it is found that, when Nicodemus took down the Body of Christ from the Cross, he collected His blood, which was still fresh and had been shamefully scattered, in a certain vessel of emerald miraculously presented to him by God, and that vessel the said English in their books call *Sanguinalia.* That vessel Nicodemus guarded with much reverence. Now in course of time it was translated to Caesarea, and at last brought to Genoa. Fitting, then, it was that that vessel should be precious, in which the precious treasure, to wit the Blood of Jesus Christ, was to be preserved.[2]

---

[1] *Hist. rerum in partibus transmarinis gestarum*, X, xvi (Migne, *P.L.*, CCI, col. 469). Cf. P. Paris, *Guillaume de Tyr et ses continuateurs* (Paris, 1879), I, p. 353 n.

[2] *Chronica de civitate Januensi*, XI, xviii (Muratori, *R.I.S.*, IX, (coll. 32–3). Cf. the elaborate work of Fra Gaetano da S. Teresa, *Il Catino di smeraldo orientale*, etc. (Genoa, 1726); J. D. Bruce, *op. cit.*, I, pp. 360–2. In 1319, during the struggle between Robert

This vague allusion to "certain books of the English"—the writer being, perhaps, led by the legend of the Santo Volto at Lucca, or the Saint-Sang relic at Fescamp, to substitute Nicodemus for Joseph of Arimathea—is not the first reference to the Holy Grail by an Italian. Between 1215 and 1216, Tomasino de' Cerchiari, of Cividale in the Friuli, wrote a German poem, *Der Wälsche Gast*. Here he holds up various characters of the Arthurian cycle as examples for youth; Arthur himself and Gawain, Erec and Ivain, Tristan, Sagramour, and Calogrenant. Let them look at the knights of the Round Table, how they rivalled each other in prowess, but avoid the evil example of Sir Kay whose spirit, rather than that of Perceval, is still living, and who would not seek the Holy Grail if it still existed in our days.[1] The existence of the supposed relic at Genoa seems to have had no influence upon the development of the story in Italy. Among the frequent allusions to Arthurian names and matters in the lyrics of the thirteenth century, and the fuller treatment of such themes and motives in fourteenth-century poetry,

---

of Naples and the Visconti for the possession of Genoa, the Commune pawned the "sagro catino" to Cardinal Luca de' Fieschi. Cf. R. Davidsohn, *Geschichte von Florenz*, III, pp. 625–6. The document relating to this transaction, in *Hist. Patriae Monumenta*, XVIII (*Leges Genuenses*, Turin, 1901, coll. 236 sq.), speaks "de illo pretiosissimo vase, qui scutela seu Parasis vocatur."

[1] "Ouwê, wâ bistu Parzivâl? | wan waer noch inder dehein grâl | und stüende er umb einn phenninc phant, | in erlôst niht Keyes hant." *Der Wälsche Gast des Thomasin von Zirclaria*, ed. H. Rückert (Quedlinburg, 1852, p. 30), ll. 1075–78. Cf. G. Grion, *Tomasino de' Cerchiari poeta cividalese del Duecento* (Udine, n.d.), p. 99. With the exception of Tristan, the poet's choice of names is evidently due to the poems of Chrétien de Troyes.

the Grail and its questers seldom appear. In Italian prose we shall indeed find one Grail text of singular importance, but the story of the Holy Grail took no root in Italian soil; its mysticism was of a kind alien to the Italian genius.

CHAPTER II

It is with the poets of the "scuola siciliana"—that
first phase of courtly lyrical poetry in Italy that
centred round the court of Frederick II, and may
be taken as running approximately from 1220 to 1250
—that we begin to find allusions to the "matière de
Bretagne" in Italian vernacular literature. But the
only branch of the "matter" with which these poets
seem acquainted is the story of Tristan and Iseult.
Here—and the remark applies generally to the reflections of Arthurianism in thirteenth-century Italian
poetry—it is frequently hazardous to decide whether
we are dealing with direct knowledge of French
literary sources or with independent circulation of the
legends in Italy.

Whatever may be its remote origin, the story of
Tristan first appears in the *Tristan* of the Anglo-
Norman poet, Thomas, usually held to have been
written between 1155 and 1170, though a somewhat
later date is sometimes assigned to it. It has come
down to us in fragments, but its missing parts are
preserved, and the matter of the entire poem has
been tentatively reconstructed from them (first by
M. Bédier), in several early thirteenth-century works
based upon it: chiefly the old Norse prose *Tristrams*

Saga and the German poem of Gottfried von Strassburg.[1] We are accustomed to think of the Tristan
story as part of the Arthurian legend, but there can
be no doubt that it was originally entirely independent.
Nothing is known of the lost poem "del roi Marc
et d'Iseut la blonde" of Chrétien de Troyes. Thomas
brought the name of Arthur incidentally into the
story; the Norman poet, Béroul, of whose *Tristan*
only a large fragment exists and who wrote probably
a little later than Thomas, connected Arthur more
directly with the course of the narrative;[2] the
complete Arthurianising of Tristan, the linking up
of the protagonists with the main lines of Arthurian
legend, is due to the author of the French prose
romance, the prose *Tristan*, now generally supposed
to have been written between 1225 and 1230, but of
which the elaborate versions that have come down
to us do not represent the primitive form.[3]

The earliest of these allusions is probably contained
in the "discordo" or "caribo," *Donna audite como*,
a kind of dance song showing the influence of the

---

[1] J. Bédier, *Le Roman de Tristan par Thomas* (Paris, 1903–5);
R. S. Loomis, *The Romance of Tristan and Ysolt, translated from the
Old French and Old Norse* (New York, 1923). The Middle English
poem, *Sir Tristrem*, is likewise a derivative from Thomas.

[2] Béroul, *Le Roman de Tristan*, édité par Ernest Muret (Paris, *Les
Classiques français du moyen âge*).

[3] The prose *Tristan* has not yet been edited, but we have a full
analysis in the fundamental work of E. Löseth, *Le roman en prose
de Tristan, le roman de Palamède et la compilation de Rusticien de Pise*
(Paris, 1890). It is, of course, later than the *Lancelot, Queste del
Saint Graal*, and *Mort Artu*—the branches of the Vulgate cycle of
prose romances—and purports to be the work of Luce de Gast and
Hélie de Boron (both now regarded as probably fictitious personages).
Cf. E. Vinaver, *Études sur le Tristan en prose* (Paris, 1925), pp. 24–5.

French *lais*, which may, perhaps, be assigned to an earlier date than the other extant lyrics of the school. In the only manuscript in which it occurs, the famous Codice Vaticano 3793, it is attributed to "Messer lo Re Giovanni," who is usually identified with the Emperor's father-in-law, Jean de Brienne, titular King of Jerusalem; the great warrior from whom, Salimbene says, "the Saracens fled as though they saw the devil."[1] Into its tripping measure is introduced a lyrical summary of the story, based on the drinking of the love potion by Tristan and Iseult on the ship that is bringing them from Ireland to Cornwall:

> Fino amore m' à comandato
> ch'io m'allegri tutavia,
> faccia sì ch' io serva a grato
> a la dolze donna mia,
> quella c'amo più 'n cielato
> che Tristano non faciea
> Isotta como contato,
> ancora che le fosse zia;
> lo re Marco era 'ngannato,
> perch' el lui si confidia.
> Ello n'era smisurato,
> e Tristano se ne godea
> de lo bello viso rosato
> ch' Isaotta blond' avia:

---

[1] No. 24 in the manuscript, published as *Le antiche rime volgari secondo la lezione del Codice Vaticano*, ed. A. D'Ancona and D. Comparetti (Bologna, 1875–88), and as *Il libro de varie romanze volgare, Cod. Vat.* 3793, ed. S. Satta and F. Egidi (Rome, 1902–08). Cf. M. Casella, in *Bullettino della Società Dantesca Italiana*, N.S., XIX (Florence, 1912), pp. 277 sq. In the present chapter I refer to the manuscript where the poems quoted are not included in Monaci, *Crestomazia italiana*, or have not been critically edited elsewhere. The numeration in the two editions is, of course, identical.

ancora che fosse peccato,
altro fare non ne potea:
c'a la nave li fui dato
onde ciò li dovenia.[1]

The motive of the ship and the love-potion would, no doubt, have been common to every version of the story. It will be remembered that the episode in question is not included in the extant portions of the French text of the *Tristan* of Thomas;[2] but that this was probably here the source seems indicated by the fact that a direct and manifest echo of the Anglo-Norman poet may be detected in the lyrics of Giacomo da Lentino, "il Notaro," the most representative and one of the earliest poets of the Sicilian school. In his canzone, *Madonna mia, a voi mando,* he sings:

In gran dilectanza era,
madonna, in quello giorno
quando vi forma' in cera
le belleze d'intorno.
Più bella mi parete
ke Isolda la bronda;
amorosa, gioconda,
flor de le donne sete.[3]

---

[1] "Fine love has commanded me that I ever rejoice; may it make me serve acceptably my sweet lady, she whom I love more secretly than Tristan did Iseult, as is told, albeit she was his aunt; King Mark was deceived, for he trusted him. He was excessive therein, and Tristan enjoyed the fair rosy face that gold-haired Iseult had; albeit it was sin, nought else could he do; for on the ship was given them whence this befell them" (Monaci, *Crestomazia*, pp. 70–1). In the seventh line of the quotation, it is doubtful whether the word in the manuscript is *contato* or *cantato*.

[2] Cf. Bédier, I, pp. 142–7; R. S. Loomis, *op. cit.,* p. 133.

[3] "In great delight was I, my lady, on that day when I shaped in wax your beauteous form. More beautiful you seem to me than fair-haired Iseult; full of love and pleasure, you are the flower of women" (Monaci, p. 46).

Here Giacomo seems inspired by the episode in the *Tristan* which M. Bédier calls "la salle aux images," where Tristan in Brittany, after his marriage with the other Iseult, "Iseult of the White Hands," has a hall built with various images and in the midst one of Queen Iseult, "so lifelike as it had been on live":

> Por iço fist il ceste image
> que dire li volt son corage,
> son bon penser, sa fole error,
> son paigne, sa joie d'amor,
> car ne sot vers cui descovrir
> ne son voler, ne son desir.[1]

The same motive, though here the waxen image is transformed to a picture, occurs in another of the lyrics of the Notary, the famous canzone, *Meravilliosamente*:

> Avendo gran disio
> dipinsi una pintura,   bella, voi somigliante;
> E quando voi non vio,
> guardo in quella figura   e par k' eo v' agia avante,
> Sì kom om ke si crede
> salvarsi per sua fede,   ancor non vegia inante.[2]

In yet another of his poems, the discordo, *Dal core mi vene*, he declares that the love between him and his lady is stronger than that of Tristan and Iseult:

> Dal vostro lato
> alungato,
> bel l' ò provato,
> mal è che non salda.

---

[1] "For this he made that image that he wished to speak his heart, his good thought, his mad error, his pain, his joy of love, for he knew not to whom to discover his will or his desire" (Bédier, I, p. 317).

[2] "Having great desire, I painted a picture, fair one, resembling you; and when I see you not, I look upon that figure and it seems that I have you before me, even as a man who believes to be saved by his faith, albeit he sees not beyond" (Monaci, p. 43).

> Tristano ed Isalda
> non amar sì forte.
> Ben mi pare morte
> non vedervi fiore.[1]

These passages exemplify the way in which the poets of this school use the story: simply to illustrate their own loves. Apart from the supposed King John and the Notary, they show no special knowledge of the legend; Tristan and Iseult are for them merely types of famous lovers. Thus in a sonnet, later than the Notary, but sometimes erroneously attributed to him:

> Chè fino amore non tiene sospecione,
> e nom poria cangiar la sua 'ntendanza
> chi sente forza d' amorosa sprone.
> E di ciò porta la testimonanza
> Tristano ed Isaotta co' ragione,
> che nom partir giamai di loro amanza.[2]

So, too, Filippo da Messina:

> Poi non son meo ma vostro, amor meo fino;
> preso m'avete como Alena Pari,
> e non amò Tristano tanto Isolda
> quanto amo voi per cui penar non fino.[3]

Similarly Inghilfredi—who, however, should perhaps be regarded not as a Sicilian, but as a follower

[1] "To be far from your side, in sooth I have felt, is an ill that does not heal. Tristan and Iseult loved not so mightily. In sooth it seems to me death, not to see aught of you" (Monaci, p. 48).

[2] "For noble love admits not doubt, and he who feels the force of loving spur could not change his devotion. And of this Tristan and Iseult rightly bear witness, for they never departed from their loving" (In E. F. Langley, *The Poetry of Giacomo da Lentino*, Harvard University Press, 1915, p. 89). It is anonymous in the Cod. Vat. 3793 (no. 338), but was attributed to the Notary by Trucchi.

[3] "For I am not mine but yours, my noble love; you have taken me as Helen did Paris, and Tristan loved not Iseult so much as I love you for whom I cease not to suffer" (Monaci, p. 215).

TRISTAN AND ISEULT EMBARK FOR CORNWALL
Florence, Biblioteca Nazionale, Cod. Pal. 556

THE DRINKING OF THE LOVE POTION
Florence, Biblioteca Nazionale, Cod. Pal. 556

of the school of Fra Guittone—compares his loyalty
in love with that of Tristan:

> La mia fede è più casta   e più diritta c' asta;
> chè 'n sengnoria s' è recata a serva,
> e più lealtà serva   che 'l suo dir non conserva
> lo bon Tristano, al cui pregio s' adasta.[1]

Other examples might be cited, but they present
little variation, and it has been pointed out that the
allusions to Tristan and Iseult in the poetry of the
Sicilian school closely resemble those found in that
of the Provençal troubadours.[2]

In the second phase of this early lyrical poetry, the
mainly Tuscan phase represented by the "rimatori
Siculo-Toscani," who flourished from the fifties to
the eighties of the century, the field is widened.
Allusions to Tristan and Iseult still prevail, but
others appear as well, and the purpose is no longer
exclusively erotic. In particular, Lancelot now enters
Italian poetry as a type of chivalry. Thus Guittone
d'Arezzo, the acknowledged leader and master of all
this group of poets, has a sonnet in which his lady
is the paragon of firmness against the assaults of love
as Lancelot is the paragon of valour:

> Siccome a Lancelotto omo simiglia
> un prode cavaler, simil se face
> a lei, di fera donna a maraviglia.
> Manti baron d' alto valor verace

---

[1] "My faith is more pure and more straight than a spear; for it has
become a servant in lordship, and maintains more loyalty than the
good Tristan keeps his word for his honour's sake" (Monaci, p. 205).

[2] Cf. L. Sudre, in *Romania*, XV (1886), pp. 534 sq. The Catalan
troubadours similarly "point their verses with Arthurian names"
(Entwistle, *op. cit.*, pp. 80–1).

> l' ànno saggiata assai; ma sì lor piglia,
> che mai tornar ver ciò non ànno face.[1]

There has been some discussion as to the possible source of a phrase in one of Guittone's canzoni, where he says to his lady: "You are my God and my life and my death":

> Fede e speranza aggiate, amore meo,
> ch'en amar voi sempr' eo cresco e megliuro:
> così v' ò 'l core, el senno e 'l voler puro,
> che 'n ubrianza ò meve stesso e Deo.
> Voi me' Deo sete e mea vita e mea morte:
> chè s' eo so en terra o 'n mare
> en periglioso afare,
> voi chiamo com' altri fa Deo
> tantosto liber mi veo;
> mia vita sete ben, dolze amor, poi
> sol mi pasco de voi:
> e mia morte anco sete,
> chè, s' amar me sdicete,
> un giorno in vita star mi fora forte.[2]

The whole stanza reads like an elaboration of the famous couplet in the *Tristan* of Gottfried von Strassburg, which in all probability was taken from a lost portion of Thomas; the words that Tristan often sang in his songs when in Brittany:

> Isot ma drue, Isot m'amie,
> en vus ma mort, en vus ma vie.

---

[1] "Even as a man compares a valiant knight to Lancelot, so a wondrously austere lady is likened to her. Many barons of right high worth have often assayed her; but she deals with them so that they never dare to return to it" (*Rime di Fra Guittone d'Arezzo*, ed. F. Pellegrini, son. lxii, p. 93).

[2] "Have faith and hope, my love, that I ever increase and advance in loving you; I have heart, mind and will so pure to you that I forget myself and God. You are my God and my life and my death: for if I am on land or on sea in perilous plight, I call on you as others upon God, straightway I see myself free; in sooth you are my life, sweet love, since I feed on you alone; and you are my death too, for, if you deny you love me, to stay a day in life to me were hard" (canz. viii, p. 240).

It may be that the motive, "en vus ma mort, en vus ma vie," which is found elsewhere in early French and Provençal poets (including Sordello), hardly needs a literary source.[1] But, in the Italian poetry of the epoch we are considering, it occurs in a form more closely resembling the immortal French line in a sonnet of Rustico di Filippo (whose sonnets, for the rest, have no allusions to the "matter of Britain," excepting a passing reference to Merlin):

> In voi è la mia morte e la mia vita.[2]

The names of Tristan and Iseult do not occur in Guittone's poetry. An exceedingly interesting reference to Perceval seems to show that the poet had some knowledge, though manifestly superficial, of the version of the Grail story of which "the widow's son" is the hero. Should the lover tell his lady or be content to serve on in silence?

> Fallenza era demando
> far lei, senza ragione:
> poi veggio che, sì stando,
> m' à sovra meritato el meo servire.
> Però 'n tacer m' asservo,
> per che già guiderdone

---

[1] Cf. E. Levi, *I lais brettoni e la leggenda di Tristano* (Perugia, 1918, reprinted from *Studi romanzi*, XIV), pp. 22–27; G. Bertoni, *Guittone d'Arezzo e il così detto "lai Tristan"* (*Studi su vecchie e nuove poesie e prose d'amore e di romanzi* (Modena, 1921), pp. 125–9.

[2] *Sonetti burleschi e realistici dei primi due secoli*, ed. A. F. Massèra (*Scrittori d'Italia*), I, p. 19. Cf. Dante's canzone, *La dispietata mente che pur mira*:

> chè 'l sì e 'l no di me in vostra mano
> ha posto Amore ;

and Sennuccio del Bene (Volpi, *Rime di Trecentisti minori*, p. 29):

> mie vita e morte sta nel tuo disporre.

non dea cheder bon servo:
bisogna no ch 'el cheri al suo servire,
se no atendendo, lasso:
poi, m' avenisse, lasso!
che mi trovasse in fallo
sì come Prenzevallo a non cherere;
verrei a presente morto! [1]

I tentatively understand this perplexing stanza thus: "It were wrong to demand aught of her without reason, since I see that, abiding so, she has excessively rewarded my service. Therefore I remain silent, because a good servant should not indeed ask for guerdon; he need ask nought for his service save wearily to wait; then, if it befell me, alas, that she found me in fault like Perceval in not asking, straightway should I die." The allusion is clearly to the episode in the poem of Chrétien de Troyes, the earliest extant version of the story of the Holy Grail, where Perceval visits the Grail Castle, the castle of the "Maimed King" or "King Fisherman," sees the solemn procession in which the Bleeding Lance and the Grail are borne past, but, in consequence of the advice of an old knight against asking questions, does not inquire the meaning of the pageant. When Perceval has left the castle, he is questioned by a damsel and told of the evils which will result from his having refrained from asking, and more sternly rebuked later on by "la laide damoisele," the "loathly damsel" who appears before Arthur at

[1] Canz. *Amor tant' altamente*, in *Rime di Fra Guittone d'Arezzo*, ed. F. Pellegrini, canz. xxi (p. 341). In line 8, I read "bisogna" and "al" (instead of "bisognai" and "el"), and take "trovasse" in line 11 as third person singular (though it might be the archaic form of the first). Cf. Pellegrini's note, *op. cit.*, p. 344.

Carleon, when the evil consequences of his silence appear more extensive.[1] This is the only allusion that I have been able to find in Italian literature to Perceval's failure to ask the fateful question; the episode which has been traced back to the initiation into a pagan rite or mystery, and which has been suppressed in the Galahad version of the Grail story. The Venetian troubadour, Bartolomeo Zorzi (a contemporary of Guittone), alludes to the episode of Perceval confessing to his uncle.[2] There is no evidence of direct acquaintance on Guittone's part with the significance of Perceval's silence in Chrétien's poem or either of the prose versions of the Perceval legend. But another of Chrétien's poems, probably the earliest extant Arthurian romance, was known to one of his friends and admirers, an anonymous poet who ends a sonnet addressed to him with the line:

> Vostro son piò non fu d'Enida Erecche;
> I am yours more than Erec was Enide's;

an obvious allusion to the *Erec et Enide* of Chrétien, that story of fidelity in love, echoed elsewhere in Italian literature, and retold by Tennyson from the Welsh version in the *Mabinogion*.[3]

The only specific mention of the Holy Grail that I have found among these early poets is in the

---

[1] *Perceval le Gallois*, ed. C. Potvin, ll. 4421–31, 4744–68, 5981–6061.

[2] In his (Provençal) sestina *En tal dezir mos cors intra* (Emil Levy, *Der Troubadour Bertolome Zorzi*, Halle, 1883, p. 68). Cf. *Perceval le Gallois, ed cit.*, ll. 7734 sq.

[3] *Il Canzoniere Laurenziano Rediano* 9, ed. T. Casini, no. 274 (p. 285); *piò* is a not uncommon dialectical form for *più*.

curious "vaunt" of the Sienese giullare, Ruggieri
Apuliese:

> Et so ben la lancia
> et lo gradale.
> De Merlin sapiria tractare
> quando fece bene et male,
> comunque Artuso al temporale;
> la mia materia è cutale
> che de senno abunda.
> So de la Taula Rotonda
> et Tristan et d' Isota la blonda.[1]

But here it is probable that the poet's vaunted
knowledge of "the Lance and the Grail," whatever
it may amount to, comes from the Galahad version
in the Vulgate *Queste*, rather than from the *Perceval*
of Chrétien.

Brunetto Latini compares the "valente signore,"
to whom he dedicates the *Tesoretto*, to Lancelot and
Tristan as well as to the heroes of antiquity, for he
bears the crown and mantle of valour and prowess:

> Sì ch' Achiles lo prode
> ch' aquistò tante lode,
> e 'l buono Ettor troiano,
> Lancelotto e Tristano
> non valse me' di vue,
> quando bisogno fue.[2]

---

[1] "And I know well the Lance and the Grail. Of Merlin I could
treat, when he wrought good and evil, as soon as Arthur stood in
need; my matter is such that it abounds in wisdom. I know about
the Round Table and Tristan and Iseult the Fair" (ed. V. De Bartholomaeis, *Rime giullaresche e popolari d'Italia*, p. 20). Cf. Rajna,
Il Cantare dei Cantari e il Serventese del Maestro di tutte l'Arti (II),
in *Zs. f. rom. Phil.*, V (1881), pp. 30–40, and F. Torraca, *Studi di
Storia Letteraria* (Florence, 1923), pp. 38–42. The tenzone with
Provenzano Salvani shows that Ruggieri was living in 1262.

[2] "So that the brave Achilles who won such renown, and the good
Trojan Hector, Lancelot and Tristan were not worth more than you
when there was need" (*Tesoretto*, ed. B. Wiese, ll. 37–42).

Two early lyrics allude to definite episodes in the French prose *Lancelot*. One of these—the canzone, *Donna senza pietanza*, by Lapuccio Belfradelli—contains the earliest mention in Italian of Galehaut, "the haut prince," whose submission to Arthur for love of Lancelot, after his victory over the king, is cited as an example of faithful fulfilment of a rash promise:

> Pensate a Galeotto,
> di ciò c'a Lancelotto
> promise in sua volglienza,
> che no volle mentire:
> poi ch'ebe dato il botto
> ad Artu re d' u' motto
> li si diede in servenza.[1]

In the other—an anonymous canzone, beginning "Per gioiosa baldanza, lo meo cor torna a vita"—the poet declares that the return of joy will make him persevere in fidelity:

> E (in) breve il mosteragio
> che sì faragio
> com fece Lanccallotto   ver Morgana,
> quando il tenea in salvagio
> del bel visagio,
> che tornò per corrotto   la catena vana.[2]

I understand this to refer to the episode in the French romance where Morgan has been holding Lancelot captive, and attempting to make him disloyal to

---

[1] "Think of Galehaut, of what he promised Lancelot at his will, which he would not gainsay; after he had overthrown King Arthur, at a word he yielded to him in allegiance" (Cod. Vat. 3793, no. 296). Cf. below, p. 87.

[2] "And soon shall I show it, for I will act as did Lancelot towards Morgan, when she held him in estrangement from the fair visage, for the chain became useless through sorrow" (*ibid.*, no. 290).

D

Guinevere. She allows him temporary liberty to achieve an adventure, after which, faithful to his word, he returns to her prison. By means of a philtre, she makes him see a dream of the queen in the arms of a young knight, and hear her bid him never see her again. Morgan then releases him.

The name of Guinevere occurs rarely in comparison with that of Morgan. One of the earliest references to her is particularly charming. Among the lyrics of the second half of the thirteenth century are three sonnets by a young woman, whom the only manuscript that preserves them (the Vat. 3793) calls "la compiuta donzella di Firenze," Compiuta being probably her real name. To her Maestro Torrigiano, a Florentine who taught medicine at Bologna, addressed a sonnet in which he declares that to be a girl poet, "donzella di trovare dotta," is such a wonder that she eclipses Guinevere and Iseult:

> Essere donzella di trovare dotta
> sì grand' è meravilglia per antendre,
> che se Ginevra fosse od Isaotta,
> ver loro di lei se ne poria contendre.[1]

An anonymous sonnet, probably by another Florentine, Monte Andrea, similarly assures her that she has surpassed Morgan le Fay, the Lady of the Lake, and Constance:

> Gentil donzella somma ed insengnata,
> poi c' agio inteso di voi tant' oranza
> che non credo che Morgana la fata

---

[1] "That there is a damsel skilled in composing is so great a wonder to hear that, were Guinevere or Iseult on live, we could set her up as a rival to them" (Monaci, p. 281).

nè la Donna de Lago nè Gostanza
ne ffesse alchuna come voi prescata,
e di trovare avete nominanza.[1]

Morgan le Fay is seldom presented under the
sinister, or at least ambiguous aspect, that she wears
for English readers; more frequently, she is the type
of beauty. Thus, in an anonymous lyric:

Flore sovr' ongne sovrana,
conta e gaja ed adorna,
in chui l'amore sogiorna,
tu c'avanzi Morgana,
merzè, che m' ài conquiso.[2]

Similarly, Guido delle Colonne:

Chè, se Morgana fosse infra la giente,
in ver Madonna non paria neiente.[3]

Chiaro Davanzati, the first true poet that Florence
produced, has a similar allusion to Morgan:

Ringrazio Amore de l' aventurosa
gioia ed allegrezza che m' à data,
chè mi donò a servir la più amorosa
che non fue Tisbia o Morgana la fata.[4]

In an anonymous sonnet, Morgan is associated

[1] "Gentle damsel high and wise, I have heard of you such honour
that I deem not that Morgan the Fay nor the Lady of the Lake nor
Constance wrought anything so glorious as you, and you have the
renown of composing" (Cod. Vat. 3793, no. 909). Cf. the association
of the three names in the *Tavola Ritonda*, p. 13, where "Gostanza"
is the mother of Lancelot.

[2] "Flower supreme above all, beauteous and gay and adorned, in
whom love dwells, thou that dost surpass Morgan, be pitiful, for thou
hast conquered me" (Monaci, p. 99).

[3] "For, if Morgan were among the people, she would seem nought
in comparison with my lady" (Cod. Vat. 3793, no. 22).

[4] "I thank Love for the fortunate joy and gladness that he has
given me, for he gave me to serve one more worthy of love than was
Thisbe or Morgan the Fay" (*ibid.*, no. 352).

with Iseult and Blanchefleur, though all three must
yield to the poet's lady:

> Più mi rilucie che stella diana
> a voi sotana e tutto valimento,
> nè Blanziflor nè Isaotta nè Morgana
> non eber quanto voi di piacimento.[1]

Similarly, Dante da Maiano:

> Nulla bellezza in voi è mancata;
> Isotta ne passate e Blanziflore.[2]

Romance knows more than one Blanchefleur. In
the Thomas version of the story, Blanchefleur, the
rose of the world, is the sister of King Mark, the
mother of Tristan by Rivalen; in Chrétien de Troyes,
we meet "Blanceflour, s'amie, la bele," the beloved
of Perceval. But here the allusion is probably to the
heroine of the old French poem, *Floire et Blanchefleur*, which seems to have been known at an early
date in Italy.

Merlin appears under two aspects; coupled with
Samson as an example of the wise or strong man
deluded by a woman; and, again, as the political
prophet. Thus, in a serventese of the Pisan poet,
Leonardo del Guallacca:

> Se lo scritto non mente,
> per femmina treccera
> si ffo Merlin derizo;
> e Senson malamente
> tradil una leccera.[3]

---

[1] "Your face shines on me more than the morning star, surpassed
by you and all your worth, neither Blanchefleur nor Iseult nor Morgan
had as much loveliness as you" (Cod. Vat. 3793, no. 393).

[2] "No beauty is lacking in you; you surpass Iseult therein and
Blanchefleur" (*Rime di Dante da Maiano*, ed. Bertacchi, son. vi).

[3] "If the script lies not, by a treacherous woman was Merlin beguiled,
and in evil fashion a wanton betrayed Samson" (Monaci, p. 199).

In the French prose of his *Trésor* (written about 1263), Brunetto Latini associates Merlin under this aspect with Aristotle in accordance with the well-known mediaeval legend. But he also affirms: "If Merlin or the Sibyl speaks sooth, we find in their books that the imperial dignity is to end" with the second Frederick; though he adds that he knows not if this means only his lineage, or the Germans, or if it refers to the Empire in general.[1] However, some years later, in a tenzone on the expected descent of Rudolf of Hapsburg into Italy against Charles of Anjou in 1274, in which Chiaro Davanzati, Monte Andrea, and other Florentine rhymers take part, "il profeta Merlino" is cited as foretelling the advent of the new Emperor.[2]

Among the Florentine poets taking part in this disputation, was one who himself drew his name from the Arthurian cycle: Pallamidesse di Bellindote; a friend of Brunetto, who had fought at Montaperti in 1260. It was he, apparently, who had brought Merlin into the discussion. In a previous tenzone on a similar political theme, he and a certain Orlanduccio Orafo had exchanged compliments upon their heroic names,[3] and Pallamidesse evidently rejoiced in bearing that of Tristan's rival for the love of Iseult, that pathetic and attractive figure of the pagan knight from Babylon whom the author of the prose *Tristan* had brought into the story. In his only extant

[1] *Li Livres dou Trésor*, ed. Chabaille, pp. 91 (I, ii, 94), 432 (II, ii, 89).
[2] *Sonetti burleschi e realistici dei primi due secoli*, ed. A. F. Massèra, I, pp. 46, 48.
[3] *Ibid.*, I, pp. 46, 39, 40.

canzone, Pallamidesse identifies himself with his prototype in an amorous lamentation:

> Amore, gran peccato
> faciesti del mio core,
> di meterllo in servagio
> la ov' io nom sono amato
> e amat' ò a tuttore
> e stato a vassallagio.[1]

After a series of fantastic images from the bestiaries, he finally sends his song to Tristan at Joyous Gard:

> A la Guardia Giojosa
> ten va al mio Tristano,
> mia canzone dolorosa,
> e dí che Speranvano
> a lei tosto verrà.
> E, com 'io credo, forse
> n' avrà doglia e paura:
> chè, s' una lonze fosse,
> si perderia natura
> ed avriane pietanza.[2]

We read in the prose *Tristan* of the "chansons" and "lais" in which Palamede poured out his hopeless passion. In particular, at the fountain in the forest (an episode familiar to readers of Malory), he sang a new "lai" which he had himself composed, "the which was marvellously and wonderfully well said, and full dolefully and piteously made"; it is

[1] "Love, great wrong hast thou done my heart, to set it in bondage there where I am not loved and have ever loved and been in vassalhood."

[2] "Wend thee to Joyous Gard, my mournful song, to my Tristan, and say that Hope-in-Vain will soon come to her. And, as I believe, perchance she will have grief and fear thereat; for, if she were a leopard, she would lose her nature and would have compassion" (Cod. Vat. 3793, no. 188; Monaci, pp. 250–1). Or does the "lei" refer to "la Guardia Giojosa," and is it Tristan himself who will change nature?

overheard by Tristan, with the result that the two
rivals agree to meet and do battle in fifteen days'
time, either at the fountain or in the meadow under
Joyous Gard. It would seem that the Italian poet is
composing a new "lai de Palamède," to replace the
one given in the French romance, perhaps supposing
it sung after the reconciliation with Tristan, as the
coming of the singer to Joyous Gard hardly here
suggests the purpose of combat.[1]

This reference to the hero at Joyous Gard is the
first distinct reflection of the prose *Tristan* in Italian
poetry. But Brunetto Latini, probably some few
years before, had introduced an elaborate description
of the beauty of Iseult into his *Trésor*, as an example of
"rhetorical colour." The Scriptures, he says, adopted
this device in the description of the virtues of Job:

The like did Tristan when he described the beauty of Queen
Iseult. Her hair, he said, shines like threads of gold, her forehead surpasses the lily, her black eyebrows are curved like
little bows, and a little milky way divides them in the centre
above her nose in so meet a measure that it is neither excess
nor defect; her eyes surpass all emeralds and glow in her face
like two stars; her countenance imitates the beauty of the
dawn, for it is of rose and white together, in such wise that
the one colour blends harmoniously with the other; her mouth
is small, her lips full and glowing with beauteous hue, and her
teeth whiter than ivory, set in order and measure; neither
panther nor any spicery could compare with her most sweet
breath; her chin is far more bright than marble, her neck

---

[1] Cf. Löseth, sect. 384 (p. 275); Malory, X, 86, 80. There are
several versions of the "lai," "D'amours viennent li douz pensser,"
given in the French manuscripts of the *Tristan*. One of these
(from a manuscript in the Biblioteca Estense, Modena) was edited
by P. Heyse, *Romanische Inedita auf italiënischen Bibliotheken*
(Berlin, 1856), pp. 169–71. It naturally bears no resemblance to
the Italian poem.

whiter than milk, her throat more gleaming than crystal. From her shoulders descend two slender and long arms, and white hands with soft and tender flesh; her fingers are large and round, and on them the beauty of her nails glows; her beautiful breast is adorned with two apples of Paradise, which are as white as a mass of snow; and so slender is she at her waist that a man could clasp it between his hands. But I will be silent on the rest that is hid within, of which the heart speaks better than the tongue.[1]

This remarkable piece of eloquence does not seem to occur in the extant French texts of the *Tristan*, but is found in a Spanish version at the end of *Don Tristan de Leonis*.[2] There is a close connection between the Spanish and Italian renderings of the Tristan story, and it may well be that both the Spanish translator and Brunetto drew from a French redaction of the prose romance containing this passage. But the way in which it occurs in the Spanish, added as a kind of appendix, suggests that it may come direct from the author of the *Trésor*.

The allusions to the "matter of Britain" run on through the lyrics of the thirteenth, more sparingly in the early years of the following century, without much novelty. Bonagiunta Orbicciani, the poet of Lucca, whose question touching the "nuove rime" in the *Purgatorio* prompts Dante's definition of poetry, has the conventional reference to Tristan and Iseult in a ballata ("Donna, vostre belleze"):

Ed io similemente
'nnamorato son di vue

---

[1] *Li Livres dou Trésor*, ed. cit., pp. 488–9 (III, i, 13); *Il Tesoro volgarizzato da Bono Giamboni*, VIII, 14 (part iii).

[2] *Don Tristan de Leonis*, ed. A. Bonilla y San Martín in *Libros de Caballerías*, I (Nueva Biblioteca de Autores Españoles, VI, Madrid, 1907). Cf. Entwistle, *op. cit.*, p. 120.

> assai più che non fue   Tristan d' Isolda;
> meo cor non solda   se non vostr' altura; [1]

but, in his discordo ("Oi, amadori, intendete l' affanno"), a fresh figure appears:

> E messire Ivano
> e 'l dolze Tristano
> ciascun fue sotano
> ver' me di languire.[2]

"Ivano" is doubtless Ivain, son of King Uriens, the hero of Chrétien's *Chevalier au Lion*; an important character in Arthurian romance who figures in Malory as Sir Uwaine. In a popular poem, found in a Bolognese notary's *Memoriale* of 1282, a girl tells her mother, who is dissuading her from getting married, that she is more resolute than in arms were Roland and the "cavalier sens paura"; an allusion to one of the heroes of the *Palamède*, "the Good Knight without Fear," the rival of Meliadus and father of the japing Dinadan (familiar to readers of the *Morte Darthur*):

> Matre, de flevel natura
> te ven, che me vai sconfortando
> de quello ch' eo sun plu segura
> non fo per arme Rolando,
> nè 'l cavalier sens paura,
> nè lo bon duso Morando.[3]

---

[1] "And I likewise am enamoured of you far more than Tristan of Iseult; nought contents my heart save your nobleness" (*Rimatori siculo-toscani*, ed. Zaccagnini and Parducci, p. 74).

[2] "And Sir Ivain and the gentle Tristan, each fell short of me in languishing" (*ibid.*, p. 70).

[3] "Mother, it is because of thy feeble nature that thou keepest discouraging me from that for which I am more resolved than were in arms Roland or the Knight without Fear or the good duke Morando" (Monaci, p. 291). Morando, like Roland, belongs to the Carolingian cycle.

Cecco Angiolieri of Siena, the "scamp" of Dante's circle as Rossetti called him, is true to himself in his romantic allusions:

> In una ch'e danar mi danno meno,
> anco che pochi me n' entrano 'n mano,
> son come vin, ch' è du' part' acqua, leno,
> e son più vil, che non fu pro' Tristano; [1]

and Folgore da San Gimignano dedicates his sonnets of the month to the spendthrift club of young Sienese nobles with a fine Arthurian compliment:

> Prodi e cortesi più che Lancilotto;
> se bisognasse, con le lance in mano,
> farian torneamenti a Camelotto. [2]

With these last two examples I have, perhaps, slightly passed the chronological limit which I have set myself for this chapter. I will just add one pleasing stanza from an anonymous Bolognese serventese, found in a *Memoriale* of 1309:

> Per te patisco doloroso affano,
> più che non fe' per Isotta Tristano,
> imaginando, quando m' è lontano,
> lo tuo vedere. [3]

The poets of the "dolce stil nuovo," who followed in the footsteps of Guido Guinicelli, for the most part abandoned this conventional use of names from the

---

[1] "When my money falls low, though little of it comes into my hand, I am more weak than wine that is two parts water, and more cowardly than Tristan was brave" (Massèra, I, p. 105).

[2] "Valiant and courteous more than Lancelot, if need were, with lance in hand, they would make tournaments at Camelot" (*ibid.*, I, p. 157).

[3] "For thee I suffer grievous pang, more than Tristan did for Iseult, imagining thy aspect when it is far from me" (Monaci, p. 295, corrected with T. Casini, *Le rime dei poeti bolognesi del secolo xiii*, p. 167).

"matter of Britain." In their spiritual ideal of love, Tristan and Iseult had less place.[1] There are no references to any part of the Arthurian cycle in the authentic poems of Guido Guinicelli or Guido Cavalcanti, nor (so far as I have observed) in those of Cino da Pistoia. Indeed, it would seem that, towards the end of the thirteenth century, such mere allusions—with nothing behind them — were beginning to be regarded as an antiquated convention.

[1] Cf. E. Sommer-Tolomei, *La leggenda di Tristano in Italia*, in *Rivista d'Italia*, XIII (Rome, 1910), pp. 113-14.

CHAPTER III

THE "PALAMÈDE" AND RUSTICIANO DA PISA

THERE is extant a letter[1] in which the Emperor Frederick II thanks one of his officials, the "secretus" of Messina, for sending him the "book of Palamede." This is the first known allusion to the French romance entitled *Palamède*, a work later in date than the *Lancelot* and the *Tristan*, but which goes back to the exploits of knights of a generation previous to that of the Round Table, representing a supposed earlier period, the heroes being the fathers or predecessors of the knights of King Arthur. Conspicuous among them are Meliadus, King of Liones and father of Tristan, and his rival, the "Good Knight without Fear," King of Estrangorre and father of Dinadan; Guiron le Courtois and his friend, Danain le Roux; Esclabor ("Scalabrone"), the father of Palamede; Lac, the father of Erec and Brandelis; and various members of the great family of Brun, notably Galehaut, the son of the mighty Hector le Brun "who surpassed all the knighthood of his time," and Segurant (or "Segurades"), the "Knight of the Dragon."[2] Although the *Palamède*

[1] Letter dated Foligno, 5 February, 1240. In Huillard-Breholles, *Friderici secundi Historia diplomatica*, V, p. 772.

[2] Galehaut le Brun, the son of Hector, is not to be confused with Galehaut the "haut prince," the son of Brunor and the Giantess. There was also a younger Hector, nephew of the first and father of Segurant. The *Palamède* has not been preserved as an organic whole,

—which purports to be the work of the problematical Hélie de Boron—may not have been of Italian origin, it became one of the chief sources of the "matière de Bretagne" in Italy.

The *Palamède* is not the only Arthurian book associated with the name of the second Frederick. We have, written in French, but unquestionably composed in Italy and by an Italian, *Les Prophecies de Merlin*, which purports to have been produced in Sicily at the Emperor's bidding by a certain "Maistre Richart d'Irlande." It is, perhaps, possible that there was such a person as Richard of Ireland, and that Frederick, on the principle of not letting the devil have all the best tunes, thought to promulgate prophecies in the imperial interest, attributed to Merlin, as a counterblast to those such as we read later in Salimbene on the ecclesiastical side; but Miss Paton has conclusively shown that the greater part of the book, as we now have it, was composed at Venice, or by a Venetian, between 1274 and 1279. It is a curious medley of historical and apocalyptic prophecies delivered by Merlin to successive scribes, prophecies in which the Venetians — "les bons mariniers"—and the March of Treviso figure prominently, with romantic elements and Arthurian matter. This Arthurian matter largely consists of

and the only portions printed are the *Meliadus* and *Guiron* volumes. Cf. the analysis in Löseth, *op. cit.*, pp. 435 sq., and his later *Le Tristan et le Palamède des manuscrits de Rome et de Florence* (Christiania, 1924). The manuscripts differ very considerably among themselves. Several of the more important—for instance, the Turin L. I. 7-9 and the B.M. Add. 12228 (with miniatures executed for Louis of Taranto about 1352)—may be the work of Italian scribes.

adventures in continuation of the *Lancelot* and not found elsewhere, but the *Tristan* and the *Palamède* have also been laid under contribution. From the last-named romance, the figure of Segurant le Brun is elaborated to appear as a hero second only to Lancelot in valour and knightly achievement; he follows his quest, the pursuit from land to land of a mysterious dragon, eventually goes upon a crusade, and becomes King of "Abiron." [1] The account of Merlin's deception by the Lady of the Lake, whether the author's own invention, or drawn from a more primitive source than the continuations of Robert de Boron,[2] differs from all other known versions, and, with the striking motive of the prophet continuing to utter his predictions from the tomb, was ultimately to pass to Ariosto.

Prince Edward of England, afterwards King Edward I, disembarked at Trapani at the end of October 1270, and stayed in Sicily until the following spring, when he took ship for the Holy Land. He returned in the autumn of 1272, and was in the island when he heard of the death of his father, after which he slowly made his way home through Italy in the spring of 1273. From a "book of King Edward of England," "in that time when he passed beyond the sea in the service of Our Lord God to

---

[1] *Les Prophecies de Merlin edited from MS. 593 in the Bibliothèque Municipale of Rennes*, by Lucy Allen Paton (2 vols., London and New York, 1926-7). Miss Paton regards "Richard of Ireland" as a purely fictitious character. For Segurant, see II, pp. 279-92, where evidence is shown that much material of which he was the hero has been lost. Galehaut is here represented as the younger brother of Hector le Brun.

[2] Cf. Miss Paton, II, pp. 296-300, and see below, pp. 207-8.

conquer the Holy Sepulchre," Rusticiano or Rustichello da Pisa—the same man who afterwards took
down from Marco Polo's lips the account of his
travels when they were prisoners together at Genoa—
"translated" or "compiled" what is, perhaps, the
earliest Arthurian romance written by an Italian.
Drawn mainly from the *Tristan* and the *Palamède*,
it is a compilation in French to contain "all the
great adventures that befell among the knights-
errant of the time of King Uther Pendragon to the
time of King Arthur his son, and of the companions
of the Round Table," and was entitled *Meliadus*,
"le livre du roy Meliadus de Leonnois," "because
King Meliadus did more noble deeds at that time
than any other of the knights of whom we have
spoken."[1]

This Franco-Italian compilation of Rusticiano has
come down to us only in a fragmentary form. It
mainly consists of a large excerpt from the *Palamède*,
which became divided (probably at an early date)
into two portions of which printed editions appeared
at Paris in the first half of the sixteenth century:
Gyron le Courtoys (Verard, undated, but probably
1501) and *Meliadus de Leonnoys* (Galliot du Pré,
1528, and Denis Janot, 1532). These two romances

---

[1] See Rusticiano's introduction and epilogue, in Löseth, *Le roman
en prose de Tristan*, pp. 423, 472. L. F. Benedetto—in his edition of
the *Milione* of Marco Polo (Florence, 1928) and a polemical pamphlet,
Filologia e Geografia (Florence, n.d.), pp. 55–68—has recently shown
strong reasons for believing that the right form of the name was
Rustichello (French, "Rusticiaus"), and not Rusticiano ("Rus-
ticians," "Rusticiens"). I have, however, retained "Rusticiano"
in the present work, as it has become traditional in Arthurian
literature.

are closely interlaced, with frequent references from one to the other for elucidation of the matter, or for episodes omitted. They were translated into Italian as *Girone il Cortese* and *Il gran Re Meliadus*: "Gli egregi fatti del gran Re Meliadus," and "Le prodezze et aspre guerre del gran Meliadus, Re di Leonis, et il suo innamoramento con la morte." [1] The scene is laid in the early years of Arthur's reign, when, instead of Guinevere and Iseult, the beauties of the world are the Queen of Scotland and the Lady of Malehaut—the latter drawn from the *Lancelot*, and destined to be immortalised by Dante for a cough. But there is much retrospective narrative (especially in the *Girone*) introduced, going back to the time of Uther Pendragon or even earlier, when knights were of larger stature and greater prowess, and the heroes of the house of Brun were performing mighty feats of arms. The *Girone* is better

---

[1] The two volumes of the Italian *Meliadus* are translated from the French printed edition, and were published by Aldus (Venice, 1558-9). *Girone il Cortese* (ed. F. Tassi, Florence, 1855) is likewise a sixteenth-century translation, apparently from the Verard edition, but there is another unpublished translation of the same period extant, and a fragmentary earlier version. Cf. P. Rajna, *Le Fonti dell' Orlando Furioso* (2nd edition, Florence, 1900), pp. 61-2. Löseth (*op. cit.*, p. 435) notes that the French prints are in the main faithful reproductions of Rusticiano manuscripts. The Italian versions closely follow the French, and may, therefore, for our purpose be treated here as thirteenth-century matter. Tassi's translator of the *Girone* sometimes borrows phrases and images from Dante in his rendering. Thus (p. 317), for "comme homme qui demande paix" (Verard, f. ccviii), he has "come messaggier che porta ulivo," and (p. 420), where the French says that it would be shame to allow "que cestuy qui fut roy demourast ainsi au vent et a la pluye comme il est orendroit" (Verard, f. ccl), we read: "Sarebbe scritto a scortesia di lasciar le ossa d'un re cavaliere, come sono ora, che la pioggia le bagni e muova il vento."

constructed and a more harmonious whole; for the
Meliadus, at least towards the end of the book, professedly "non riguardando a l'ordine de' tempi,"
introduces adventures of knights "who flourished a
long time after the death of King Meliadus."[1] To get
a consecutive narrative, it is necessary to take the
two works as a single romance.

Girone il Cortese opens with the story with which
Rusticiano begins his compilation, and which he calls
"the most beauteous adventure and the most marvellous that is written in all the romances of the
world"; chronologically it belongs to a later stage of
the work, but he puts it first because he found it at
the beginning of "the book of the King of England."[2]
King Arthur is holding high court at Camelot, on the
feast of Pentecost, when a knight of huge stature,
who is more than a hundred years old, appears with
a beautiful and richly attired lady, attended by
two squires, and challenges all the best knights of
the kingdom to joust with him, the lady's person
and possessions to be the prize of the victor. Twelve
knights, including Palamede, Gawain, and Lamorat,
are overthrown by merely tilting at him as at the
quintain. With Tristan and Lancelot he employs
his lance, and they fall in like manner. Arthur
himself and fourteen kings, his guests, share the
same fate. The old knight, who will only tell the
king that he was of the household of his father Uther
Pendragon, and that he has not borne arms for
forty years, now departs. His prowess is only
equalled by his piety. He makes his way home to

---

[1] Aldus *Meliadus*, II, p. 326.   [2] *Girone il Cortese, ed. cit.,* p. 21.

E

Northumberland, discomfiting evil knights and re-
dressing wrongs as he goes, and finally sends a message to Arthur to the effect that he is Branor le
Brun, the uncle of Segurades (Segurant), and that the
lady is his niece; he has jousted with Arthur and
his knights, merely "to test the prowess of the knights
of this time, and to know which were the better,
the old or the young." Arthur and his knights are
amazed, as they had supposed that Branor was dead.
The adventure is duly recorded in the annals of the
Round Table, and is the last of Branor's exploits.[1]

The *Meliadus* brings the knight of Babylon,
Esclabor, with his young son, Palamede, to the
court of Arthur at the beginning of his reign. We
are given various adventures of Meliadus himself and
the Good Knight without Fear, the two supreme
knights of the day, of King Pharamond of Gaul,
the Morholt of Ireland, and King Pellinor of Listenois,
the father of Lamorat. But the chief interest lies
in the second part of the romance. Meliadus—his
wife is dead, and Tristan is not yet three years old—
becomes enamoured of the Queen of Scotland, and
pours out his love in a lay which is sung to the harp
by a knight of Liones in the presence of Arthur and
the lady herself. Meliadus comes to Camelot. Morgan reveals the matter to the King of Scotland, who

---

[1] *Girone il Cortese*, capp. i–vi. The source of the story is unknown.
For a fourteenth century Greek poem based upon it, cf. Bruce,
Evolution of Arthurian Romance, II, p. 28. A Tristan episode, the
combat at the Rock of Merlin (cf. below, p. 262), now follows as an
independent episode (cap. vii), after which, in the printed text, we
plunge into the story of Guiron. The MSS. of Rusticiano continue
adventures of Tristan (Löseth, pp. 429–30).

lays a trap and surprises the lovers in the queen's chamber, but dares not lay hands on Meliadus. The king is taking her back to Scotland, when Meliadus assails the party, while still on Arthur's territory, and carries the queen off to Liones.

Arthur promptly adopts the cause of the King of Scotland, and is joined by the Good Knight without Fear, the Morholt, Pellinor, and other kings. In the "parliament" Uriens compares the fall of Meliadus with that of Adam, but Arthur very properly prefers a Homeric simile for the situation: "He is in Liones like Hector in Troy, but we have Achilles outside in the person of the King of Estrangorre." In the meantime, Meliadus has obtained the support of Pharamond (who advised him to give back the lady to her husband) and of King Claudas of the "terra diserta," as also of Mark of Cornwall. He shows the little Tristan to Claudas, who repeats what he has heard from Merlin of his future greatness, but the father has a dream in which he sees his son's death at the hands of his present ally, King Mark.[1] There are two tremendous battles outside the city, in which Meliadus performs heroic feats against overwhelming odds, but, in the second, he is stunned in an encounter with the Good Knight without Fear, and taken prisoner by Gawain. The city now surrenders. Arthur, though he has lost a fourth part of his men, makes the people of Liones swear allegiance to the child Tristan, whom he commends to the care of Gouvernal, and there is a pathetic scene where Meliadus bids farewell to his

[1] Aldus *Meliadus*, II, pp. 68, 68 v°. Cf. below, pp. 112, 113.

little son before he himself is conveyed as a prisoner
to Camelot. The unfortunate Queen of Scotland,
whose husband is compelled by Arthur to spare
her life, is condemned to perpetual imprisonment—
from which, we are told, she was delivered in after
years by Tristan, who found her still "one of the
marvellous beauties of the world."

King Arthur is now taken grievously ill. There is
anarchy in Logres, and his vassal kings make war
upon each other. Pellinor conquers Galles, and,
while he is there, Perceval is born. Uriens invades
Ireland, the dispossessed king fleeing to invoke the
aid of the Saxons, who assemble a great host under
Ariohan, the father of Frolle, whom Arthur had
slain in single combat before Paris, and prepare to
reconquer Britain. Arthur, who has recovered his
health, summons the Good Knight without Fear to
his aid; but the King of Estrangorre refuses to come,
on account of the dishonour done to knighthood in
the person of Meliadus who has been languishing for
a year in his dungeon, and demands his release:
"Even though he was my mortal foe, he does not
cease to be the honour and glory of all earthly
chivalry." Gawain adding his intercession, Meliadus
is set free and himself writes to urge his deliverer to
come to Arthur's succour.[1] With the aid of the Good

---

[1] A peculiar feature of the *Meliadus* (both French and Italian texts)
is the insertion of inscriptions, *lais*, and letters in verse. Three of
these, including a previous letter from Pharamond to Meliadus and
the two now interchanged between Meliadus and the Good Knight
(French edition, cap. cxvi; Aldus, II, pp. 162, 165 v°), are contained
in a Franco-Italian text of the fourteenth century, and edited by
G. Bertoni in his *Studi su vecchie e nuove poesie e prose d'amore e di*

KING ARTHUR WELCOMES THE GOOD KNIGHT WITHOUT FEAR
Palamède; B.M., Add. MS. 12228

KING MELIADUS WITH THE CHILD TRISTAN
Palamède; B.M., Add. MS. 12228

Knight and Pellinor, Arthur gives battle to the
Saxons. After the struggle has raged all day and
neither army proved victorious, Ariohan proposes
that the matter should be decided by single combat,
himself against a knight on Arthur's side. The
Good Knight without Fear promptly offers himself
as champion, but chivalrously withdraws his claims
when Arthur's kings unanimously declare that
Meliadus is the best knight of the world and that
their cause must be committed to his arms. Meliadus,
after a combat pronounced unequalled in the annals
of chivalry, conquers Ariohan, but spares his life,
the Saxons taking an oath never again to return
to the kingdom of Logres. Arthur has a chapel in
honour of St. John built upon the scene of the
battle, with brazen images of Meliadus and Ariohan
on the doors, and appropriate verses celebrating the
event. Ariohan stays an honoured guest in Arthur's
palace until his wounds are healed, when he departs,
and, after various adventures in which he is
associated with King Leodegrance of Cameliard (the
father of Guinevere, who, however, is not mentioned),
makes his way to Denmark. There he marries the
king's daughter, succeeds to the crown, and becomes
the ancestor of Ogier the Dane.

A peerless knight now comes into the kingdom of
Logres, who will not reveal his name. This is Guiron
le Courtois, mirror of courtesy and loyal friendship.[1]

romanzi, pp. 183–206, as "Le lettere franco-italiane di Faramon e
Meliadus." Bertoni makes the curious error of supposing them to
be fragments of a narrative poem now lost. Cf. M.L.R., XXIV, p. 204.

[1] The Aldus Meliadus links up with Girone at II, cap. lxx, and,
after some adventures and narratives, II, cap. lxxx, where the

He is descended from Clovis, "the first king of
France of the Christian religion," and, on his mother's
side, is of the lineage of Joseph of Arimathea, the
guardians of the Grail. Although younger, he is
of the mighty mould and temper of the Brun heroes;
he had been the chosen companion of Galehaut and
bears the sword of Hector le Brun. Guiron had
already gained fame in the days of Uther Pendragon, but had unjustly incurred disgrace through
excess of chivalry; he had then disappeared from
view, and was believed to be dead, though in reality
a prisoner in the hands of a giant, from whom he had
regained his liberty shortly after the death of Uther.[1]
The Lady of Malehaut, Maloaut, or Maloant, the
wife of his beloved friend Danain le Roux, is enamoured of him, but has vainly sought a return of
love. At the tournament of the Castle of the Two
Sisters, Guiron and Danain disguised are the victors
over King Meliadus and Lac. Here the lady's
beauty overwhelms both Guiron himself, in spite
of a struggle with his loyalty to his friend, and Lac,
who makes a vaunt that he will carry her off from
the twenty-six knights who guard her. Danain,
summoned elsewhere to avenge the death of a kins-

tournament at the Castle of the Two Sisters is introduced. *Girone il
Cortese* begins (after the Branor and Tristan episodes) with a combat
between the hero and the Good Knight without Fear (cap. viii). I
take up the narrative with the tournament (cap. x).

[1] The episode of Guiron being placed upon the cart of shame by
Uther Pendragon is not here given. Cf. *Tavola Ritonda*, cap. i, and
Löseth, *Le Tristan et le Palamède des manuscrits de Rome et de Florence*,
pp. 89–94. The same disgrace, likewise through the treachery of a
woman, befell Meliadus in his youth at the hands of the King of
Northumberland, as he himself relates (Aldus *Meliadus*, II, cap. lxxv)

man, commits his wife to Guiron's care to be escorted
back to Malehaut. Lac intercepts the cortège and
routs the twenty-six knights, but the lady is promptly
rescued by Guiron, who now reveals his love. They
rest at a fountain; Guiron has disarmed, and is about
to betray his friend, when his sword—the sword that
had belonged to his great kinsman, Hector le Brun—
falls into the water. He recovers it, draws it out of
the sheath to dry, and reads again the words that its
first owner had inscribed upon it: "Loyalty conquers
everything, and treachery shames and deceives all
men in whom it finds harbourage." [1] In the past
these words had inspired him to noble deeds, and they
now seem to him as though he had never seen them
before. He realises the baseness of his intention;
in his remorse, he runs himself through with the
sword, and is only prevented from killing himself by
the lady. Danain hears from a knight, who had
attempted to rob the wounded man of his sword, a
false account of what had happened. Coming to
the fountain, he is about to slay his wife and his
friend, when the lady, to save Guiron, tells the whole
truth, and Guiron himself confesses his disloyal
thought. There is mutual forgiveness, and Guiron
is conveyed to Malehaut to be healed.

Their friendship is broken by Danain abducting
Bloia, the damsel of whom Guiron is now enamoured.
Guiron is seeking them when he liberates a treacherous
lady, whose story—she has entrapped the man who
scorned her love into slaying his companion and
becoming her lover—is told with some tragic power. [2]

[1] *Girone il Cortese*, capp. xvi–xvii.   [2] *Ibid.*, cap. xxxv.

She falls into the hands of Breus sans Pitié, who becomes so enamoured of her that, for the only time in his life, he acts with courtesy. To rid herself of him, she contrives to hurl him down into a cavern. Here we come to the famous episode of the romance. In the cavern are a series of chambers. In one lies the body of a gigantic knight, clad in the armour of a bygone age, with a scroll in his hand: "Febus was my name, and rightly, for, as Febus illumines all the world, so was I the light of chivalry whilst I could wield sword." In an adjoining room is the body of a beautiful maiden, round whom are trees of silver with silver birds that break into song when the bed is touched. In another room are the tombs of the four sons of Febus, and in another an altar with two burning torches. An old knight hermit of superhuman stature, another son of Febus, reveals himself as the grandfather of Guiron (who is rightful king of France, Pharamond being a usurper), and tells the story. Febus resigned the throne of France to a younger brother, and with forty companions passed into the realm of Logres, where he defeated three pagan kings almost single-handed, and became enamoured of the beautiful daughter of the King of Northumberland, the maiden whose body Breus has just seen. Hating him in her heart, she imposed adventures upon him in the hope that he would lose his life, and at last, after he had performed amazing feats of strength and valour, sent him to slay the giants who had made their home in this cave, bidding him, when this was done, to await her there. He awaited her coming in vain, until the news reached the princess that the best knight of the world was thus dying of love. She relented, and came in time for him to die in her arms, she herself then choosing to remain by his body till her death. The sons of Febus found the place, and four of them died there. The speaker, twenty years later, took up his abode in the cave, joined afterwards by others of his house, of whom only his son, Guiron's 'father, and a cousin (formerly King of Gaunes) now remain alive with him. Guiron's father gives a proof of strength still surpassing that of the knights of the present day, and Breus, after promising to reveal to no one save Guiron what he has seen, is shown the way by which to return to the world.[1]

Guiron achieves the adventure of the Perilous Pass, culminating in a fight with the lord of the castle, who is revealed as a namesake of the great Febus and a son of Galehaut le Brun. He comes upon Danain with Bloia at a fountain in Sorelois. The combat between the two former friends is one of the finer things of the romance.[2] Moved by his repentance and appeal to chivalry, Guiron spares Danain's life, delivers him presently from a giant, but renounces his companionship. Pursuing his way with Bloia, who suffers grievously from the cold, the courteous hero is deceived by the protested innocence of Helin le Roux, a murderous knight born in incest, whom he liberates from two. knights who have bound him and his paramour naked to a tree over a frozen lake. Helin retaliates by treacherously seizing Guiron and Bloia, and exposing

---

[1] *Girone il Cortese*, capp. xxxix–xlix.   [2] *Ibid.*, cap. lx.

them to the snow in like manner. Danain appears
upon the scene, defeats Helin, and, after testing the
love of Guiron and Bloia (that, at least, seems the
purpose of his threat to slay one of them with
Guiron's sword), sets both at liberty, and obtains
from Guiron both forgiveness and the renewal of their
old friendship. They come to a forked road, with a
threatening inscription, the one branch being that
of "false pleasure," the other that of "wrath." The
two knights separate, to follow these different
adventures, and both fall into captivity. Bloia dies
in prison, after giving birth to a son, to whom the
lord of the castle gave his own name Galinan, who
grew up with the valour of Guiron, but the bad
qualities of his foster-father, and was ultimately
killed by Palamede.[1]

In the meantime, the Good Knight without Fear,
accompanied by a single squire, has entered the
valley of the Servage, a smiling and outwardly
peaceful region, but ruled by the giant Nabon le
Noir, in which more than a thousand knights-errant
with many others are held in shameful captivity.
They have been forced to swear allegiance to the
tyrant, and can, therefore, take no steps to liberate
themselves. Among them is Ludinas, the "Good
Knight of Norgalles," whom the King of Estrangorre has come especially to deliver. Ludinas is
compelled by his oath to give battle to the new-comer

---

[1] *Girone il Cortese*, capp. lxxxv–lxxxvi. In the prologue to the
Palamède, published by Rajna (in *Romania*, IV, pp. 264–6), the
line of the Bruns ends with the son of Guiron. Löseth (p. 434,
n. 3) regards the relationship of Guiron with the Bruns as a later
invention.

on behalf of Nabon; but the king, when he discovers with whom he is fighting, breaks off the combat, and goes on his way with a defiance to the tyrant. An old hermit, once himself a knight of Logres, but now a subject of Nabon, tells him of an inscription promising that the evil custom will be destroyed at the coming of the flower of Liones, whose valour will transform servitude into liberty. The Good Knight without Fear supposes that Meliadus must be meant. He defeats Nabon's son Nathan and his company, but is deluded and betrayed by a treacherous damsel, and goes mad in his prison in the castle of Lothan. Released at Nabon's orders, he takes a dire revenge upon the damsel (which Nabon remarks is only what she deserves), and is allowed to wander freely in his madness, the passes being closely guarded to prevent information reaching King Arthur.[1]

We are referred to the *Meliadus* for subsequent happenings in the Servage. But this latter romance, in the printed text, becomes now a confused series of adventures, professedly interpolated without respect to chronology, in which Galehaut le Brun is represented as still living and Segurant (here called Segurades), leaving for a while the pursuit of the dragon, is victor at the tournament of Winchester, matches himself with Tristan and Palamede, but, at the bidding of the Lady of the Lake, refuses Lancelot's challenge, and, from a later epoch, Perceval

---

[1] *Girone il Cortese*, capp. lxiii–lxxi. The Servage episode is, of course, borrowed and modified from the prose *Tristan*. Cf. below, pp. 77, 115, 227.

and Galahad appear upon the scenes.[1] The text
returns to the main story with Meliadus seeking for
Guiron, and persuading the Lady of Malehaut to allow
him to release Lac, whom she holds prisoner. The
search proves ineffectual; for Guiron, after delivering
Danain from his imprisonment, has himself in some
unexplained way passed into the valley of the Servage, and is among the captives of Nabon.[2] Meliadus
overthrows ten knights, including Danain and Palamede, with a single lance; and when, at a high
festival at Camelot, a crown is brought by a
mysterious damsel and placed upon his head by
Arthur himself, he courteously resigns it to
Guinevere. Later on he returns to Liones, Tristan
being then ten years old, and is murdered by
two kinsmen of the Morholt at the bidding of King
Mark.[3]

Danain has fallen prisoner in the Servage. Between the last exploits of Meliadus and his death,
the printed romance introduces a peculiar account
of the ending of that evil custom; it is apparently
an invention of Rusticiano himself, an attempt to
combine the *Tristan* and the *Palamède* by redupli-
cating the original episode given in the former, in
accordance with which the Servage is now (as in

[1] Aldus *Meliadus*, II, capp. lxxvi–xcvi. For the place of these
episodes in the manuscripts, cf. Löseth, p. 432.

[2] Guiron had been delivered by Lancelot from the prison in which
Bloia died, but this is not mentioned in the printed texts of the
Girone and *Meliadus*. Cf. Löseth, p. 464.

[3] At the end of the Aldus *Meliadus*, II, cap. cxii. Elsewhere (cf.
Löseth, p. 471), Tristan is inconsistently represented as old enough
to have adventures and to joust with his father.

Malory) an island.[1] A rumour of Tristan's exploit
having reached Arthur's court, Lancelot and Palamede set out to find him. Shortly before Tristan
came to the Servage, Nabon had sent a letter to
Arthur, bidding him come to a festival for the knighting of his son and do homage to him, in which case
he will give back his knights — Guiron, the Good
Knight without Fear, and Danain—whom he holds
in a secret prison; otherwise, he will have them put
to death, as he has already done with Menion il
Piccolo (Mecion le Petit, Malory's Sir Nanowne le
Petite), one of the companions of the Round Table.
Lancelot and Palamede meet Nabon's two messengers,
are insulted by them, kill them both, and read the
letter. They join Tristan at a castle of King Hoel's,
and hear from him that he has already killed Nabon
and liberated the Servage, which he has left in charge
of Segurades (Malory's Segwarides, not Segurant),
but has heard nothing of Guiron and the others,
though he has seen the tomb of Menion. The three
heroes now go again to the Servage; without further
difficulty, they find Guiron, the Good Knight,
Danain, as also Lac, in separate dungeons of the
castle of Mormonda, and the liberation is finally
accomplished.[2]

The salt of the old romance, to borrow a phrase
from Charles Lamb, is in the character of Guiron, the
scenes between him and Danain, and the episode of

[1] Aldus *Meliadus*, II, capp. cvii-cxi. Cf. Löseth, sects. 640, 641,
and p. 469, n. 4.

[2] It is stated in the *Girone* (cap. lxxi) that, when the Good Knight
without Fear recovered his senses, Nabon had him imprisoned in a
place of which no one but the custodian knew.

the cavern of Febus with its white-robed hermits. Febus, we are told, was "of the lineage of those of Brun, of whom many books were made of old." [1] It is probable that the compiler of the *Palamède* drew from some lost romance of the Bruns,[2] and also from some genuine Celtic tradition for the story of Guiron and his ancestors. It has been conjectured that the name Guiron may have been taken from the "Guirun" of the "lai pitus d'amur" that Iseult sings to her harp in the poem of Thomas;[3] but, in that case, we should have expected some resemblance in the two stories. More alluring is the suggestion of Professor Loomis that Guiron should be associated with Gwron, who is named among the three original bards of Britain in the *Mabinogion*, and that the cavern episode is ultimately a Welsh myth, the dead warrior being a god of the sun, the tale having passed into the hands of a Breton or French *conteur*.[4] Rusticiano does not give the end of the story of Guiron. It is found, however, in manuscript continuations of the *Palamède*. After Danain has died of wounds received in a tournament, Guiron, who

[1] *Girone il Cortese*, p. 53.
[2] Cf. Löseth, p. 434, n. 3.
[3] *Le Roman de Tristan par Thomas*, ed. Bédier, I, p. 295. Cf. below, p. 131.
[4] *Celtic Myth and Arthurian Romance*, pp. 305–8. On the other hand, the name "Febus" may have been suggested by the prose *Tristan*, where there is an Apollo, King of Liones, among the ancestors of the hero. Guiron composed the "Lai des Deux Amants," and his son Galinan was also a musician. But Professor Loomis surely overstates the case in saying that "such accomplishments are by no means common among heroes of French romance." Besides Guiron, Meliadus, Palamede, and Tristan are represented as poets and musicians.

has now borne arms for sixty years, seeks the cavern of his ancestors, to devote the rest of his life to the service of God. He finds his grandfather dead. After one brief and reluctant return to the world to succour a kinsman, he goes back to the cavern. His father dies, and, fifteen years later, "Messer Guiron ended his days full holily." [1]

[1] Löseth, sect. 639a (pp. 466–8).

CHAPTER IV

THE "TRISTANO RICCARDIANO"

SOME few years later than Rusticano's compilation, but well before the end of the thirteenth century, we have what is probably the earliest Arthurian romance in Italian: the admirable work which has come down to us incomplete, and was edited by Parodi as the *Tristano Riccardiano*.[1] Written originally in a Tuscan-Umbrian dialect, perhaps that of Cortona, it is the earliest representative of a special group of Italian and Spanish versions of the Tristan story, which differ in various particulars from any extant French redaction of the prose romance, and show remarkable points of mutual resemblance in order of episodes, modification and substitution of proper names.[2] It is questionable whether, in the omission of extraneous matter and accretions, the author or translator is using independent judgment of selection, or harking back to the more primitive form of the prose *Tristan* through his presumed, but unidentified, French source.

[1] *Il Tristano Riccardiano* edito e illustrato da E. G. Parodi (Bologna, 1896). Parodi shows that the manuscript, the Codice Riccardiano 2543, written at the end of the thirteenth, or in the first years of the fourteenth century, is not to be regarded as the original.

[2] Cf. G. T. Northup, *Italian Origin of Spanish prose Tristan versions*, in *Romanic Review*, III (New York, 1912), and *El Cuento de Tristan de Leonis*, edited from the unique MS. Vaticano 6428 (Chicago, 1928).

The matter of the *Tristano Riccardiano* corresponds roughly with portions of the Tristan romance included in the eighth and earlier chapters of the ninth book of Malory. It ignores the introductory sections of the fuller prose *Tristan*, plunging straightway into the story: "Lo re che Filicie iera chiamato avea tre figliuoli e quattro figliuole"; "The king that hight Felix had three sons and four daughters." Here, at once, we have a deviation from the orthodox French version: the sons are Meliadus, King of Liones; Mark, King of Cornwall; and Pernam. Thus Meliadus and Mark are brothers, instead of the former wedding Mark's sister. After the death of Felix, the Morholt, "l' Amoroldo d' Irlanda," comes for the truage. Pernam urges that it should not be paid, but Mark asks what knight will dare fight with the Morholt, who is the best knight of the world. Pernam retorts that Mark is not worthy to reign; the latter orders the truage to be paid for seven years, and, shortly afterwards, treacherously murders Pernam at the "Fontana del Leone."[1] The lineage of the wife of Meliadus, the beautiful queen Eliabel, is not indicated. Meliadus, going to hunt in the desert, is met by a damsel, who, promising to show him an adventure, takes him to a tower, and brings him into an enchanted room where he forgets everything except herself. First the barons of Liones, then the queen, seek him in vain. The queen is met by the disguised Merlin, who tells her that the king will be found, but that

[1] Cap. i (cf. Löseth, sects. 19, 21). In Malory, Pernam becomes Sir Boudwin, who is slain by Mark at a later stage and for a different reason; he is the father of Alisander le Orphelin (*Morte Darthur*, X, 32 sq. Cf. Löseth, sect. 282 e).

F

she will never see him again; she gives birth to a
male child, whom she names Tristan in memory of
her sorrows, and dies. Two knights, kinsmen of the
king, think to slay the child, who is saved by the
queen's gentlewoman promising to take him away
with her. On their bringing the body of the queen
to the city, the knights are imprisoned by Merlin's
orders, and Meliadus is delivered from the tower.
Merlin will entrust the future lord of Liones to
Gouvernal, the son of the King of Gaul, who had
left his native land because he had slain a knight.[1]
Merlin and he go to find Tristan, and come to the
"fontana del petrone," on which letters speak of a
future meeting of the three best knights of the
world: Lancelot, Galahad (Galeas), and Tristan.
Merlin brings the child to the king, and reveals his
own identity: "Some folk call me Merlin the prophet."

In the events of Tristan's childhood, the Italian
romance differs slightly from the French version and
from Malory. Meliadus takes a second wife, who is
not "King Howell's daughter of Brittany," but
simply "una gentile donna." In spite of Gouvernal's
precautions, the new queen attempts to poison the
boy, the plot being discovered when the king is about
to drink of the cup. At Tristan's entreaty, she is
spared from the fire; but renews the attempt, her
own little son falling victim. At a hunt, Meliadus is
ambushed and slain by eight knights, Gouvernal
saving Tristan. No motive is given for the deed.

[1] Cap. ii (cf. Löseth, sect. 20). In the French, Gouvernal has
accidentally killed his own brother, and is not the son of a king.
In the Italian text, the King of Gaul does not appear to recognise
him in any way as his son.

Later, after he has become a knight, Tristan avenges
the death of his father; but "this adventure does not
belong to our matter."[1] The queen continuing her
practices upon his life, Gouvernal advises Tristan
to leave Liones and go to King Pharamond in Gaul.
To the same court comes the Morholt, with a great
company from the realm of Logres. He is struck
by Tristan's beauty; a jester, who has a prophetic
gift, says: "His beauty will cost thee dear"; but, in
spite of the king's warning, the Irish knight laughs
and departs next day. Bellicies, the king's daughter,
has become madly enamoured of Tristan, who will
give her nought but loyal and chivalrous love. She
accuses him of attempted violence, and he is imprisoned. Convinced by Gouvernal of his innocence,
the king bids her choose between Tristan and a
cousin, who is under sentence of death, and, when
she professes to prefer the latter, extorts her confession by threatening to strike off Tristan's head.
Tristan decides to go to King Mark in Cornwall,
revealing his identity before his departure. Bellicies,
by a squire, sends him a letter, a brachet, and a horse,
and then kills herself. The letter reaches him on
his way to Tintagel, where, without betraying who
he is, he offers his service to Mark.[2]

Tristan is about fifteen, when the Morholt comes

---

[1] Capp. iii, iv (cf. Löseth, sects. 22, 23). In the French text, the
murderers are two knights of the Count of Norhout instigated by
King Mark. The conversion of the queen to love of Tristan seems
peculiar to Malory, who represents Meliadus as himself sending
Tristan to France and being still alive when he returns (*Morte
Darthur*, VIII, 3).
[2] Capp. v–xiv.

again to demand the truage, with Gaheris and other knights. At his own request Tristan is knighted by Mark, reveals himself, and undertakes the battle on the "Isola sanza Aventura." The Morholt is at first unwilling to fight so young a knight. Mortally wounded, he asks Tristan to help him into the boat, and, as he does so, wounds him with a poisoned dart in the thigh—an act of treachery peculiar to the Italian versions and alien to the chivalrous character of the knight of Ireland.[1]

We have then—as in the orthodox prose *Tristan*— the hero's voyage over sea with his harp, his arrival in Ireland at the court of King Languis (Hanguin, Anguish), the father of Iseult, who consigns him to the maiden's care to be healed of his wound; the meeting with Gawain and the squire of Bellicies, whom Tristan charges not to reveal his identity; the tournament of the King of Scotland and the King of the Hundred Knights, and the beginning of the rivalry with Palamede, the pagan knight who bore two swords; the discovery by the queen that the unknown guest is the slayer of her brother the Morholt, and Tristan's enforced return to Cornwall.[2] A dwarf, the son of a king and with power of divination, who has been banished by his father on account of his ungainly appearance, comes to King Mark, and warns him against a nephew of his who will do him great dishonour, but whom, nevertheless, he may not slay because of the many knights and ladies who will

[1] Capp. xv–xviii.
[2] Capp. xix–xxxviii. Tristan's visit to his father (Malory, VIII, 13) naturally does not occur, as Meliadus is already dead.

escape death through his valour. Mark bids him
stay at his court, but, when the dwarf has looked upon
Tristan and heard his name, he instantly takes leave
of the king: "I have remembered a message that I
must deliver." [1] There are changes in the names
in the story of the rivalry between Mark and Tristan
for the love of a knight's wife; she is "la damigiella
dell' Agua della Spina," and her husband is Lambegues (instead of Segurades); [2] the knight-errant
who takes her from the court, and fights Tristan
for her, is not Blioberis, but his brother Blanor.
This is clearly an error, as Tristan and Blanor
presently meet as strangers.

Tristan is now sent by Mark to Ireland to obtain
Iseult in marriage for the king. Driven to shore
near Camelot, he overthrows Breus sans Pitié who has
taken the divided shield from the damsel of the Lady
of the Lake, [3] and, in the combat with Blanor, delivers
the King of Ireland from the accusation of treason.
When they have come to Ireland, Tristan asks the
king for his promised gift, which he makes the hand
of Iseult for King Mark. Languis would fain give

---

[1] Cap. xxxix. In the prose *Tristan* (Löseth, sect. 23), the episode
is less dramatic and occurs earlier.

[2] In the French, Tristan's love is the lady of the "Fontaine du
Pin" (Löseth, sect. 34). For the changes in the name, by which
she has become the "Lady of the Water of the Thorn," cf. Northup's
introduction to *El Cuento de Tristan de Leonis*, p. 19. Following
the French, Malory calls the husband Segwarides, who is apparently
not the same person as Sagwarides or Segurides, the "christened"
brother of Palamede.

[3] Cf. Löseth, sect. 37. Vinaver, *Le Roman de Tristan et Iseut dans
l'œuvre de Thomas Malory* (pp. 221–5), points out the curious error
by which the "shield" has become a "child" in the *Morte Darthur*
(VIII, 21).

her to Tristan himself, but the latter will abide by his word:

> Then said the king: "Ask all that you please." And Tristan said: "I would have you give my lady Iseult the Fair as wife to King Mark." And the king said: "Dost thou ask her for thyself or for King Mark?" And Tristan said: "I want her in sooth for King Mark." But King Languis said: "I would fain give her only to thee and not to another." And Tristan said: "I want her indeed for King Mark, because I have promised her to him." [1]

The queen entrusts to Gouvernal and Brangwain (Braguina) the love potion that Iseult and Mark are to drink together on their wedding night. They embark and have fair weather:

> It chanced one day that they were playing at chess, and neither was thinking of the other aught save all honour, and as yet in their hearts they were not thinking any fault of mad love. And, having played two games together, they were beginning the third game, and it was very hot, and Tristan said to Gouvernal: "I have a great thirst." Then went Gouvernal and Brangwain to fetch drink, and they took the flasks of the love potion, not witting that they were these. Gouvernal washed a goblet and Brangwain poured out, and Gouvernal gave first to Sir Tristan to drink, and Tristan first drank the contents of the goblet because he was very thirsty, and he filled the other goblet and gave it to Lady Iseult. And she threw the dregs of the cup on to the deck, and then her little dog licked them up for the great thirst that it had. And, as soon as the little dog had licked it, straightway Tristan changed his heart, and was no longer in that wise mind that he was at first. And Lady Iseult fared the same, and they began to think and to gaze upon each other. Before they had finished that game, they rose and both went

---

[1] Cap. lvi. Cf. Löseth, sect. 38; Malory, VIII, 24; Vinaver, *Le Roman de Tristan et Iseut dans l'œuvre de Thomas Malory*, p. 163. Both the Italian text and Malory make Tristan's loyalty under temptation more emphatic than in the French.

below into a cabin, and there began that game together that they played desirously until the end of their life.[1]

The ship is driven by a storm to the Island of the Giants, upon which is the Castle of Pleur (Proro), "that is to say, the Weeping Castle," as Malory has it. At the shore, Tristan is compelled with his company to surrender, and they are imprisoned in the castle, where two knights come to explain the conditions of release and the history of the "evil custom." When Joseph of Arimathea preached Christianity on the island, the giant Dialicies cut off the heads of his ten sons who had been converted, slew all Joseph's adherents, built the castle over their bones, and established the custom that all strangers arriving should be cast into prison, never to come forth unless among them is a knight so strong as to conquer the lord of the island, with a lady more beautiful than the said lord's lady. The victor must cut off the head of the lady who is the less beautiful, remain lord of the island with the same condition, and never depart from it. The challenge is accepted. "What think you of my lady?" asks Tristan. "She can pass, but it would need a Lancelot to meet our lord." The knights inform their lord, who is Brunor,[2] "the father of the good Galehaut." He is somewhat

---

[1] Cap. lvii. The motive of the dog, the "little brachet," thus sharing in the love potion, is peculiar to the Italian versions and the English poem, Sir Tristrem. Thus, in the latter (ed. Kölbing, ll. 1673–6):

> "An hounde there was beside,
> That was ycleped Hodain;
> The coupe he licket that tide,
> Tho doun it sett Bringwain."

[2] He is alternatively called "Blanor" in the text.

reluctant, but the knights insist: "By God, in the morning at the sound of the horn you shall be outside the castle with your lady." Morning comes; Tristan and Iseult are on the field, and, at the sound of the horn, Brunor and his lady appear. "The tale tells that the lady of Brunor was tall and beautiful as a lady who was descended from a giant, but she could not match or compare with the beauties of Lady Iseult. And the wife of Brunor became all pale with fear, so that sentence was given that Lady Iseult was the more beautiful." They fight; Brunor is mortally wounded and dies, upon which Tristan is compelled, under protest, to behead the wife. Tristan and Iseult are lord and lady of the island from which, with their company, they may not depart, and they are content with the situation.[1]

But the daughter of the slain man takes his body and the head of her mother, and passes over to the kingdom of Norgalles which belongs to Galehaut. After long search, near a castle where the King of the Hundred Knights is staying, she meets her brother. Having arranged his plan of campaign with the said king (who is his vassal), Galehaut with two squires embarks on a ship, and compels the crew to convey him to the island, slaying the captain who tries to resist. He is not recognised by the knights who arrest him on landing, and Tristan, under the impression that he is Lancelot, offers peace. "My name is Galehaut, Lord of the Distant Isles, whose

[1] Capp. lvii–lx. Cf. Löseth, sect. 40, and the somewhat different version in the *Morte Darthur*, VIII, 24–6. Malory seems to imply that Brunor was the originator of the evil custom, but, in fact, he was a knight from Ireland who had himself conquered his predecessor.

father and mother he has slain, and therefore am I
come here to take vengeance upon him." On hearing who his challenger is, Tristan says to himself:
"Now am I the most fortunate knight in the world,
since I am to fight with so high a prince." The
combat is abruptly ended by the advent of the
King of the Hundred Knights and his men, who have
captured the castle, and now sweep down upon
Tristan. Overcome by the courtesy of Galehaut,
who forbids his vassal to interpose, Tristan gives up
his sword, and the two become friends. Galehaut
makes Tristan promise that, as soon as he can leave
Mark, he will join him in Gaul, "for the greatest desire that I have is to see you and Lancelot together." [1]
To Arthur and Guinevere he despatches a letter:

To you King Arthur and to my lady, Queen Guinevere,
and to all the knights-errant of Logres and other lands, I,
Galehaut, Lord of the Distant Isles, send salutation. By my
letters I inform you that I with my knights passed to the
Island of the Giants, to abolish the evil custom which was in
that place, and I have abolished it and destroyed the Castle
of Pleur, and freed all the prisoners who were there. And, to
avenge me for the wrong that Tristan had done me, I fought
him heart to heart. Know ye therefore, my lord King Arthur
and my lady Queen Guinevere and all the other knights of
your realm, that in the world are only two knights and two
ladies, and in these two knights is all the goodness and all
the valour of the world, and in the two ladies is all the gentleness and all the beauty of the world; nor in other knights do
I see valour, nor in other ladies do I see beauty, save in them. [2]

But the adventure has cost Galehaut his life:

After Sir Galehaut had destroyed the evil custom of the
Island of the Giants, he stayed in the island until he deemed

---

[1] Capp. lxi–lxii. Cf. Löseth, sect. 41, and Malory, VIII, 27.
[2] Cap. lxiv.

that he was healed of the wounds he had received. And thereafter he returned into his kingdom with his folk, and within a short time after his return he died. Great damage was there in his kingdom, and great was the grief thereat among the knights of King Arthur. And when Tristan heard that Galehaut was dead, he grieved greatly for what had befallen, because he was preparing to go to him in Gaul as he had promised.[1]

In the meantime Tristan and Iseult have reached Cornwall, and we have the marriage of Mark with Iseult, the substitution of Brangwain on the wedding night, Iseult's projected murder of her maid by the two serfs, her remorse, and the restitution of Brangwain by Palamede.[2] The story follows the lines of the usual French prose; but the knight who, in the absence of Tristan, rebukes the cowardice of the Cornish knights, and pursues Palamede to rescue the queen, is here called Sigris, a knight-errant of the kingdom of Logres who had come to be healed by Iseult of a wound received in a battle in a foreign land.[3] Tristan ultimately defeats the would-be ravisher, and, at her own bidding, brings Iseult back to Mark. A pathetic motive in the romance (as also in the French) is the way the king's growing suspicion and jealousy struggle in his mind with his

[1] Cap. lxv. This entirely unorthodox version of the death of Galehaut seems peculiar to the present text and the Spanish versions.

[2] Malory (VIII, 29) omits the substitution, and lays the attempted murder to the account of two of Iseult's ladies.

[3] Cap. lxxii. In the French (Löseth, sect. 43), it is Lambegues, a character from the prose *Lancelot* where he is associated with the story of the youth of Bors and Lionel. Here he has been wounded in a combat with Andred and another knight of Cornwall. Malory (VIII, 30) makes him Lambegus, "a knight of Sir Tristram." Sigris is unknown in the French romance; but he appears at intervals (Sagris) in the *Tavola Ritonda*, where he is killed during the quest of the Grail.

admiration for his nephew's prowess and valour—
a motive due, in part, to the fact that the nobler
figure of Mark in Thomas has never become quite
concealed in the baser character presented by the
writer of the prose *Tristan*.[1] The order of the events
that lead to Tristan's departure from Cornwall
differs considerably in the Italian text from the orthodox French version. A damsel whose love Tristan
has rejected (the Basille of the French romance),
and who has become the mistress of Mark's other
nephew, Andred (here called Ghedin), first perceives
the relations between Tristan and the queen, and
informs her lover, who—to convince the reluctant
king—sets the trap of the two scythes near Iseult's
bed. Lamorat (Amoratto), coming to the festivity by
the sea, overthrows the Cornish knights, but, when
he and his horse are wearied, receives a fall from
Tristan whom the king, against knighthood, has
compelled to joust with him. In revenge, Lamorat
sends to Mark the horn (intended by Morgan le Fay
for the destruction of Guinevere) out of which no lady
who is false to her husband can drink without spill-
ing the contents. Tristan, forbidden access to the
queen's apartment, mounts by a tree in the garden;
denounced by the false damsel and surprised by
Mark, he strikes the king down with the flat of his
sword and leaves the court. There is a temporary
reconciliation, but Tristan is again surprised in the
queen's chamber. Iseult is imprisoned in a tower,
to which Tristan makes his way disguised as a damsel
from Ireland, and he is apprehended by Andred and a

[1] Cf. Vinaver, *Études sur le Tristan en prose*, pp. 16–19.

band of knights. Tristan is sentenced to death,
Iseult to be handed over to the lepers; he breaks his
bonds and leaps into the sea, while she is rescued by
his four companions, after which they stay together
in the forest in the "mansion of the wise damsel." [1]
Here, while Tristan is out hunting, they are traced
by Mark and Andred, Iseult is carried off and imprisoned in a tower. In the meantime, Tristan has
been wounded by a poisoned arrow by a man whose
father he had slain in the tourney in Ireland. He
returns to be healed by Iseult, finds the place all
trampled, and calls upon her in vain. The faithful
Gouvernal conveys him towards Tintagel, where he
learns from Brangwain that the only cure for his
wound is to be sought from a damsel in Brittany,
whom, however, she does not name.

The damsel is Iseult of the White Hands, the
daughter of the King of Brittany, and he consigns
Tristan to her care. Tristan delivers the king from
the assault of the hostile count, and reveals his
name. Iseult has become innocently enamoured of
him, and her brother Kahedyn (here called Ghedin),
who has become his inseparable friend, hearing him
sigh for "bella Isotta," "not knowing that there was
another Iseult in the world," supposes his sister is
meant. Tristan, thinking thus to free himself from

[1] Capp. lxxv–lxxxi. Cf. Löseth, sects. 45–51; Malory, VIII, 32–5;
and see G. T. Northup, *Italian Origin of Spanish prose Tristan
versions*. In our text, Tristan's four companions appear as Sigris,
Sagramour, Oddinello (Dodinel), and another knight unnamed.
The *Tavola Ritonda* (cap. xliv) strangely substitutes Lionel and
Agravaine for the last two. Malory (following a French text) has
only Gouvernal, Lambegues, and Sentraille (Sentaille), "that were
Sir Tristram's men."

his guilty passion, consents to the marriage, but, when it comes to the point, maintains loyalty to the first Iseult, and the second in her innocence asks no more than she receives, but holds herself "the most fortunate damsel in the world."[1] King Mark is in the hall of his palace with many barons and knights of Cornwall, when a knight, fully armed, appears and asks to be allowed to tell of great adventures that will please the king. He relates the whole story of Tristan's exploits in Brittany, ending with the marriage with Iseult and her father giving him all the kingdom. "Know, therefore, that he will never return to Cornwall; whereat I am right glad, for I hate him with all my heart, for he has too much offended me." This knight is Lambegues, who was the husband of the "Damsel of the Water of the Thorn."[2] This striking episode is not found in the extant French redactions of the prose *Tristan*; but it may well be primitive, as it closely resembles the motive in the poem of Thomas, where Cariados, likewise a jealous rival of Tristan, tells Queen Iseult of her lover's marriage with the daughter of the Duke of Brittany.[3]

Brangwain brings the news to Iseult in her tower. If it is true, the queen will kill herself, but she cannot believe that Tristan has really abandoned her. When

---

[1] Capp. ciii–cxxx.   [2] Cap. cxxxviii.

[3] Cf. Bédier, *Le Roman de Tristan par Thomas*, I, pp. 295–9. In the French (Löseth, sect. 62) and Malory (VIII, 38), Tristan and the lady's husband (Segurades, Segwarides) are reconciled in the adventure of the Servage. It cannot, however, be assumed from this that the reconciliation is a part of the original version, as the Servage is admittedly a later interpolation in the primitive romance.

visited by Mark, she professes to be glad: "But I know that you will never conquer any kingdom or town or castle by your own prowess." She sends Brangwain to Brittany with a letter summoning Tristan to return. Tristan and Kahedyn are riding by the sea shore when they meet Brangwain, and she delivers the letter:

Friend, friend Tristan, loved with the whole heart and with loyal love above all other lovers, I, Iseult, constrained to many sufferings and sorrows, send you all salutations that could be uttered or written or sent. Know, friend, that since you departed from me, as you know, I have endured much sorrow; but, when I bethink me how you have abandoned me, I would fain die a hundred times the day. For in no wise did I deem that you could abandon me for any dame or damsel that was in the world or could be, so did I trust in you. But now I see and know for certain that you have Iseult of the White Hands for your lady, and I know well that with her you have right great solace and disport, at your full will, and I, hapless and sorrowful, cease not to weep and make great grief, beminding me of you. Wherefore know, friend, that I cannot send to tell you the hundredth part of my sufferings and my sorrows, for my heart fails to think and my tongue to utter and my eyes fail to see and my hands fail to write. And all this befalls me through the great grief which I feel for your sake. Therefore know, friend, that I have written this letter with ink that was made of the many tears that I shed night and day for you. And, therefore, I send you Brangwain, who will tell you all my sufferings, because I cannot signify them all to you by my letters, albeit I have many times rewritten this note because of the many tears that I have shed for you. And therefore, my sweet love, I send to pray you to come to me. Come before I die for you, since you know, friend, that, if you do not come to me, straightway I shall slay myself for your sake.[1]

---

[1] Cap. cxliii. Our text does not contain the episode of Iseult writing to Guinevere and the indignation of Lancelot at Tristan's marriage (Löseth, sects. 57, 59, and Malory, VIII, 36, 37). Cf. Bruce,

Having sworn him to secrecy, Tristan reveals the
truth to Kahedyn, and tells him that he can give him
back his sister as he gave her to him, but that, if he
does not return to his own country to see his lady,
he will die. The king is told that Brangwain has
brought Tristan news that his presence is needed in
his own land, to make peace among his barons.
During the night Iseult bathes Tristan with her tears,
and implores to be allowed to come with him. He
promises to return as soon as possible. Next day
from a high tower she watches the ship depart,
consoling herself a little with the thought that
Kahedyn is with Tristan as a pledge of his fidelity
and return. When the ship has disappeared, she
goes down and embraces the bed.[1] Tristan has been
a year in Brittany.

The remainder of the *Tristano Riccardiano* is
occupied with Tristan's adventures in the desert or
forest of Darnantes (here called "Nerlantes," Malory's
"Forest Perilous"), and his deliverance of King
Arthur.[2]

A storm has diverted Tristan and his company
from their course to Cornwall, and the ship enters
a harbour in the land of Arthur, the sailors declaring
that "this is the finest desert that there is, and the

I, p. 493. In Malory (VIII, 38, 39), Iseult first learns of Tristan's
marriage through the deliverance of the Servage, which is not
included in the *Tristano Riccardiano*. Cf. Löseth, sects. 61–3.

[1] Capp. cxliv–cxlix. In the usual French version, the revelation
to Kahedyn takes place before the reception of the letter (Löseth,
sect. 58).

[2] Capp. cl–ccxviii. Cf. Löseth, sects. 71a–74a, and Malory, IX,
10–16. The order of events and some of the motives are different
in the Italian.

one where more adventures are found than in any part of the world, nor did any knight go there without finding adventure." Gouvernal and Brangwain with the servants are to wait at a certain castle, while Tristan goes to seek adventures. Kahedyn, who is a mere youth and agog for excitement, insists on accompanying him, "for I want to see the wondrous feats of arms of the knights-errant." A hermit tells them that Arthur is lost in this desert, and all the knights-errant are seeking him in vain. Tristan exults in such good fortune, "as to find in this desert all the knights-errant, and to enter into adventure to deliver the noblest king that there is in the world." They encounter Lamorat ; he overthrows and seriously wounds Kahedyn, but is himself worsted by Tristan, who burns to slay him for the matter of the magic horn, but ultimately agrees that they should be friends. Kahedyn is left at the house of the forester, while Tristan and Lamorat, riding through the forest together, see the Questing Beast ("Bestia Grattisante") come to drink at a fountain and pursued by a knight, who defeats them both and disappears. The knight is Sir Perceval.[1] At a parting of the ways, Tristan separates from his companion, to meet again at the fountain on the third day, bidding him tell Lancelot, if he finds him, that he desires to see him more than anything in the

[1] The pursuer of the Questing Beast in the French romance, and in Malory (excepting in I, 19-20, where it has previously been followed by Pellinor, the father of Perceval), is always Palamede. It is only the Italian and Spanish group that associates Perceval with this quest, but it may be observed that Lamorat does not here recognise his brother.

world. Lamorat encounters and is overthrown by King Arthur, who is wandering through the forest under a spell, overthrowing all his own knights and unable to speak. Next Lamorat meets Lancelot, who is equally desirous of seeing Tristan. At a ruined chapel Lamorat meets Meliagus (Meliagrance) lamenting—at great length—his unrequited love for Queen Guinevere, the most beautiful and courteous lady of the world. Lamorat challenges him on behalf of the Queen of Orkney, but Lancelot, coming upon the scene with Estore (Hector de Maris), takes the quarrel upon himself and furiously attacks Lamorat, in spite of the latter's protests, until checked by the remonstrances of his companion, after which he apologises.[1] The series of humorous episodes (excellently told) in which Tristan, concealing his identity, fools Sir Kay the Seneschal and two other knights of Arthur over the supposed cowardice of the knights of Cornwall, differs somewhat from the French and the brief summary in Malory; the two companions of the Round Table are here Arthur's nephews, Gareth and Gaheris, and the former, who had seen Tristan at the tournament in Ireland, and vaguely remembers his face, suspects from the outset that he is in reality a gallant knight.[2]

In a deep valley, where the forest is thickest,

[1] In the French and Malory, this companion is not Hector, but Blioberis, and his remonstrance is based on higher grounds than (as here) that Lancelot's conduct may lead to Arthur learning of his relations with Guinevere. Lamorat, throughout the Italian text, is an inferior character to that of "Sir Lamorak" in Malory, and Queen Morgause of Orkney in Italian romance is not the tragic figure that we know from the *Morte Darthur* and Swinburne.

[2] In the French and in Malory, the knights are Brandelis and Tor.

G

Tristan meets a damsel on a sorrel palfrey, with dishevelled hair and lamenting bitterly, for that to-day all barons and knights and dames and damsels "will have the greatest damage and the greatest sorrow that ever befell in the world." Only the best knight in the world can avert the misfortune; but, though Tristan declares that not every man can be of the strength and prowess of Lancelot, she accepts him, and they come to a palace with a green sward in front of it, where an unhorsed knight is lying on the ground attacked by four others; a damsel has already taken off his helmet and is calling upon the others to kill him, when the first damsel tells Tristan that it is King Arthur and bids him deliver him. Tristan kills the four knights, the damsel who was holding Arthur to the ground flying towards the palace. But his guide calls out that, if he lets her escape, he will have done nothing; in spite of her tears and promises, he takes her by the hair and brings her to Arthur, who strikes off her head. Tristan is grieved and amazed at Arthur's action, thinking "it not befitting him or any king to cut off the head of a damsel." But he says nothing, and bears Arthur company on the way to the house of the forester, while the first damsel fastens the head of the slain woman to her saddlebow by the hair (which was so beautiful that few damsels in the world, save Iseult, had the like), and brings it to Camelot to Queen Guinevere, who thinks that the deliverer must be Lancelot.

In the meantime, as they ride together, Tristan begs Arthur not to ask his name, "as his lady has

forbidden him to reveal it," and the king, knowing
that he would be shamed if knights heard that he had
killed a damsel, tells his story. A year ago he left
Camelot, and set himself in adventure in this desert
alone. At the "adventurous fountain," a damsel
with wonderful hair besought him to come with
her, promising him the most high adventures that
ever were seen in the world. They rode together
to a great palace, where she made him disarm, and
gave him an enchanted ring. When he had put it
on his finger, he straightway forgot Queen Guinevere
and all else, caring only for the damsel: "And she
made me fight all day with my own knights, and
every day made me change bearings and horse, so
that I should not be known; and I fought with my
knights and overthrew them all and found not one
that could withstand me, nor had I power to speak
with them in any wise, but went destroying them all.
And at night I returned to her, and, when I was with
her, methought I had all the solace that ever was in
the world." The enchantment lasted until the Lady
of the Lake sent the damsel who brought Tristan
to the palace; the damsel caught Arthur's bridle
and took the ring from him, but the sorceress set her
four cousins (brothers) upon him, and would have
slain him. The king does not think that his deliverer,
or anyone else, can blame him for killing her. The
advent of Hector de Maris enables Tristan to leave
Arthur, now that he has a companion. Arthur comes
to the house of the forester, where Kay and the
others are, and Gareth tells the king of their adventures with Tristan, thus revealing the identity of his

deliverer. Lancelot arrives, and is delighted to hear of Tristan's achievement, "because he is the best knight of whom you ever heard speak." All depart for Camelot, except the seneschal who cannot yet bear arms after his encounter with Tristan. Arthur is reunited to Guinevere, and the head of the enchantress is buried, the king refusing to keep it as a trophy, "because she has done me more shame than any other woman." [1]

Tristan returns to the desert, and, at the fountain, jousts with the unknown knight whom he had previously fought when in pursuit of the Questing Beast, and who now reveals himself as Perceval. They embrace, and are beginning to ride together through the forest to the house of the forester when the text ends. This encounter with Perceval is, again, a peculiarity of the Italian version.

[1] In the somewhat different version given by Malory (IX, 16), the sorceress is called Annowre, and it is the Lady of the Lake herself who comes to the rescue and naturally knows who Tristan is. The story is manifestly the invention of the writer of the prose *Tristan* —or (if we regard the whole episode of the Forest Perilous as an interpolation, though earlier than that of the Servage) one of the first elaborators of the primitive prose romance—for the exaltation of his hero, and was probably suggested by the episode of Camille, the Saxon sorceress from whom Lancelot delivers Arthur in the *Lancelot*. But, for possible earlier sources, cf. Miss Paton, *Studies in the Fairy Mythology of Arthurian Romance* (Boston, 1903), pp. 13-15, 19-22, 97-99.

CHAPTER V

ARTHURIAN MATTER IN THE "NOVELLE"

GALEHAUT, the "haut prince," the "Lord of the Distant Isles," is the creation of the author of the first part of the prose *Lancelot*. The "son of the giantess," who invades Arthur's kingdom, but renounces his dreams of dominion and becomes one of his rival's vassals for love of Lancelot, is among the noblest figures of mediaeval romance. The story of his relations with Lancelot is the great mediaeval example of perfect friendship between man and man, like the classic myth of Orestes and Pylades, or the scriptural tale of David and Jonathan.[1] There is no place for the Castle of Pleur in the earlier legend of Tristan: in the works based on Thomas (the Norse saga, the poem of Gottfried von Strassburg, the English *Sir Tristrem*), and probably in the primitive form of the prose romance, the lovers — after the drinking of the love potion—are conveyed straight to Cornwall.[2] Galehaut was brought into the prose *Tristan* from the *Lancelot* in order that Tristan might be confronted with one of the greatest figures in the cycle, and to serve as the first connecting link with King Arthur.

We learn more about him from one of the earliest collections of short stories in Italian, the *Conti di*

[1] F. Lot, *Étude sur le Lancelot en prose* (Paris, 1918), pp. 65–6.

[2] Cf. Bédier, II, p. 343.

antichi cavalieri, which probably belongs to the end of the thirteenth century. They are twenty in number, only one being Arthurian. Six of these twenty—including the one that concerns us—exist also in a Franco-Italian text.[1]

The story is the "Conto di Brunor e di Galeotto suo figlio." It tells us of the youth and early career of Galehaut. His father, Brunor, driven by tempest to the port of the Castle of Pleur, according to the "malvagia usanza" fights and kills the lord of the island, and takes to wife "la bella gigante," who becomes the mother of Galehaut.[2] Galehaut grows up a model of courtesy and chivalry; in his boyhood he shares equally with his companions, never prevailing over them in their sports. When made a knight, seeing that, if he stayed in that region, he would have to swear to maintain that evil custom, he departs; and, since at that time many kings had usages from which great evils and dishonour resulted to knights and dames and damsels, "he resolved in his heart to overthrow every evil custom." Thinking that he could not cast down that of the Castle of Pleur, because he ought not to set hand upon his own father, he sends to each king "who had an evil custom and usage in his land," bidding him abolish it within a certain time, challenging whoso

---

[1] *Conti di antichi cavalieri,* ed. P. Fanfani (Florence, 1851); with a better text, ed. P. Papa, in *G.S.L.I.,* III (1884); G. Bertoni, *Il testo francese dei "Conti di antichi cavalieri," ibid.,* LIX (1912), where our story is at pp. 82–4.

[2] The story is told slightly differently in the *Tavola Ritonda,* where the "bella gigante" is the wife of a second knight who came to the island and was killed by Brunor. Her name is Bagotta, that of the daughter being Dalis.

would not, and compelling him to do it by force of arms. Knights flock to him. By reason of his great wisdom and valour and liberality, and the good knighthood that follows him, twenty-nine kingdoms submit to him. He is brought into conflict with King Arthur, and, seeing the latter overmatched, grants an armistice for him to be reinforced. In the meantime he has become enamoured of Lancelot, and each has promised to do what the other shall ask. The struggle is renewed, and Arthur is on the point of defeat, when Lancelot calls upon Galehaut to fulfil his promise: to submit to Arthur and swear allegiance. Galehaut consents, convinced that it is a greater honour, with Lancelot and Tristan, to follow Arthur than to rule as a king. Then, one day, he meets his sister, who presents him with the heads of Brunor and his mother, and tells him that Tristan has slain them. He arranges his plan with the King of the Hundred Knights, with the intention, if he conquers Tristan, of destroying the evil custom. The combat and reconciliation follow as in the *Tristano Riccardiano*—the tale ending with Tristan's promise to come, after he has brought Iseult to King Mark, to Galehaut at Sorelois:

Galehaut said: "Whoso had Tristan and Lancelot together, could be said to have all the beauty and goodness of the world." And Galehaut had his mind so noble and great and pure, that he ever strove to love each valiant and good knight as himself or more, and to serve and honour and bring them together. In sum, he had the loftiest and noblest and most debonair heart of any prince or king in the world.[1]

---

[1] Cf. the character of Galehaut given by Galegantis to Arthur in the *Lancelot*, ed. Sommer, *Vulgate Version of the Arthurian Romances*, III, p. 202. But the details of his youth seem peculiar to our *conto*.

We shall meet echoes of other portions of the story of Galehaut later in Italian literature. But —until the translation of the French printed *Lancelot* in the sixteenth century—there is no Italian version of his sheltering Guinevere in Sorelois, nor of the wonderful scene where, content with the love of Lancelot, he watches unmoved the crumbling away of the great castle of the "Orgueilleuse emprise," in which he had thought to imprison Arthur, and himself be crowned, surrounded by conquered kings,[1] nor—save for one or two bare allusions—of how he dies of grief in the erroneous belief that his friend has killed himself.

The "matter of Britain" has naturally penetrated into the delightful collection of stories known as *Il Novellino*, or *Cento novelle antiche*, which were probably selected for verbal narration from a more ample compilation which was originally put together in the thirteenth century.[2]   Here we are dealing with oral tradition rather than literary sources, and when, as in the case of the Arthurian stories, they are ultimately dependent upon French texts, the compiler is not so much translating, as retelling the tale in his own words.

---

[1] Sommer, IV, pp. 5–9. Cf. Lot, *op. cit.*, p. 313. The figure of Galehaut has lost most of its significance in Malory; the plot attributed to him in *Morte Darthur*, X, 50, for the destruction of Lancelot, is utterly inconsistent with his character, and alters an episode in the French *Tristan*, where it is devised by Meleagant, the son of Bagdemagus. Cf. Löseth, sect. 282e.

[2] *Le cento novelle antiche*, ed. E. Sicardi (Bibliotheca romanica, Strasbourg); *Le novelle antiche dei codici Panciatichiano-Palatino 138 e Laurenziano-Gaddiano 193*, ed. G. Biagi (Florence, 1880). The former, from the Cod. Vat. Lat. 3214, is the earlier form of the text.

To what will presently be known as the cycle of
the "Old Table" belongs the story of the "good
King Meliadus and the Knight without Fear":

The good King Meliadus and the Knight without Fear
were mortal enemies in the field. As this Knight without Fear
was going one day in the guise of a knight-errant, disguised,
he met his sergeants who loved him much, but did not recognise
him. And they said: "Tell us, knight-errant, for the honour
of knighthood: Which is the better knight, the good Knight
without Fear or the good King Meliadus?" The Knight
replied: "So may God give me good fortune, King Meliadus
is the best knight that bestrides horse!" Then the sergeants,
who wished ill to King Meliadus for love of their lord,
treacherously surprised this lord of theirs, and, armed as he
was, lifted him from his charger and set him across a nag,
saying among themselves that they would hang him. As
they went their way, they met King Meliadus, in the guise of
a knight-errant who was going to a tournament. He asked
the vassals why they were bringing that knight so shamefully,
and they answered: "Sir, because he well has deserved death,
and, if you knew it, you would drive him quicker than we!
Ask him his misdeed." King Meliadus drew forward, and
said: "Knight, what hast thou done to these men that they
are driving thee so foully?" And the Knight replied: "Nought;
no ill deed have I done them, save that I wished to proclaim
the truth." Said King Meliadus: "That cannot be. Tell
me more fully your misdeed." And he replied: "Willingly.
I was going my way as a knight-errant. I met these sergeants,
and they asked me, by the truth of knighthood, to say which
was the better knight, the good King Meliadus or the Knight
without Fear. And I, as I said before, to proclaim the truth,
said that King Meliadus was the better. And I said it but
to speak the truth, albeit that King Meliadus is my mortal
enemy, and I hate him mortally. I would not lie! No other
misdeed have I done. And for this straightway they do me
shame." Then King Meliadus began to smite the servants,
and made them loose him; and he gave him a fair and rich
charger with the arms covered, and besought him not to
uncover them until he reached his hostelry. So he departed,

and each went his way. King Meliadus, the sergeants, and the Knight came to their hostelries in the evening. The Knight lifted the covering of the saddle; he found the arms of King Meliadus who had wrought his fair deliverance and had made him the gift. And he was his mortal enemy![1]

An episode from the story of Tristan becomes a complete novella. It is that of the moonlight meeting in the garden at the fountain, where Mark spies upon the lovers and is deceived by what he overhears. There are notable differences in the two texts, but the ultimate source appears to be Thomas, with traces of Béroul. Tristan is accustomed to give the signal for Iseult to come out to him, by means of the stream that flows from the fountain past the palace. In the Vatican text, they are denounced to the king by a gardener, instead of the dwarf in the works based on Thomas and in Béroul; in the Panciatichiano, the informer is a "malvagio cavaliere," the Andred of the prose romance. Mark orders a hunt, slips away from his knights, and, at nightfall, conceals himself in a tree above the fountain—which is a pine as in Béroul, not an olive as in Gottfried, nor a laurel as in the prose *Tristan*. Tristan comes to the fountain and gives the signal. In the Vatican text, Iseult comes, and first suspects the king's presence by noticing the unusual denseness of the shadow of the pine.[2] To warn Tristan, she rebukes

[1] Sicardi, no. 63; Biagi, no. 38. The source is presumably some text of the *Palamède*. Cf. Löseth, sect. 631a.

[2] In Béroul, *Le Roman de Tristan*, ed. E. Muret (*Classiques français du Moyen Age*), ll. 351–2, Iseult sees Mark's shadow in the fountain:

"Je vis son onbre en la fontaine.
Dex me fist parler premeraine."

In Gottfried and the Saga, they both see the shadow on the ground; in the prose *Tristan*, they catch sight of the king himself in the tree.

him as a disloyal knight, who has dishonoured her
and the king by saying things of her that would
never have entered her heart, for she would rather
be burned than dishonour so noble a king as Mark.
Tristan protests that, in spite of the evil tongues of
the knights of Cornwall who envy him, he has never
been disloyal to her or to his uncle, and that, at her
command, he will go and end his days elsewhere:
"And perchance, before I die, the malicious knights
of Cornwall will have need of me, as they had in the
time of the Morholt, when I delivered them and
their towns from vile and shameful servitude." In
the Panciatichiano text, it is Tristan who sees the
king's shadow. Iseult comes to the window; he makes
a sign towards the pine, and himself begins the
colloquy by saying that he has come unwillingly, and
asking her not to encourage malicious tongues by
sending for him again. Both versions seem to
depend upon a contamination of Thomas with
Béroul; but the later one, while having the peculiar
detail of Iseult only coming to the window, has
apparently drawn the figure of the "evil knight"
as informer from the prose *Tristan*. The conclusion
is the Italian storyteller's own finale. Mark is
completely reassured by this comedy which has been
played for his benefit. When morning comes, and
Tristan, with much bustling of attendants, makes
a show of departing from the court, the king himself
orders Iseult to join with him in commanding his
nephew to remain.[1]

[1] Sicardi, no. 65; Biagi, no. 45. For another Italian version, in the
Tavola Ritonda (lxiii), see below, p. 165. Cf. Bédier, I, pp. 193–201;

In another tale, a Florentine, to rebuke a man for pride, rehearses a list of the mighty dead, from Saladin and "the young king of England" to St. Francis: "Dead is Lancelot who bore the palm among jousters; dead is Tristan who fought so grimly with the sword."[1]   There are several Lancelot stories or sketches for stories. One is of his combat at a fountain with a knight of Saxony, who professes to be overcome by his name rather than by his prowess.[2]   Another—a mere opening—attributes to him a warning against not taking good advice.[3] A third refers to the famous episode of the cart which, from Chrétien de Troyes, passed into the prose *Lancelot* and thence to Malory, but of which a confused version is here given:

It was the custom through the realm of France that a man who was sentenced to be put to shame or to death went upon a cart; and, if it happened that he did not die, he never found anyone who would consent to associate with him or see him. Lancelot, when he went mad for love of Queen Guinevere, rode upon a cart and had himself drawn through many places.

Löseth, sects. 282, 283; Parodi, *Tristano Riccardiano*, pp. xciv-c; E. Sommer-Tolomei, in *Rivista d'Italia* (XIII), pp. 109-11. In the Borghini edition of the *Novellino* (Florence, 1572), the story of Tristan's madness, "Come Tristano per amore divenne forsennato" (no. 99), is a later addition to the book, and differs somewhat from the normal versions of the episode.

[1] Biagi, no. 34.

[2] Sicardi, no. 45; Biagi, no. 73. In the latter, the Saxon knight's name is G.; in the former, A., which the editor expands as Alibano. In the *Lancelot* (Sommer, III, pp. 141-2), Lancelot fights with a Sir Alibon at the "Queen's ford," but the latter is not a Saxon, and Lancelot refuses to tell his name. In the war with the Saxons, he mortally wounds one of their leaders, the giant Hargodabran, who is taken prisoner (*ibid.*, pp. 422-3), but there is nothing about the effect of his name.

[3] Biagi, no. 63.

From that day onwards the cart was no more scorned; nay, the custom was changed, for dames and damsels and knights of rank now ride thereon for pleasure.[1]

Similarly, Chrétien de Troyes:

> Qui a forfet estoit repris,
> s'estoit an la charrete mis
> et menez par totes les rues,
> s'avoit puis totes lois perdues,
> ne puis n'estoit a cort öiz
> ne enorez ne conjöiz.[2]

It will, of course, be remembered that Lancelot, after a moment's hesitation, mounts the cart, not for madness, but in order to rescue the queen from Meleagant.

But one of the gems of the book is the tale, retold from the *Mort Artu*, of the death of the fair maid of Astolat: "Come la Damigiella di Scalot morì per amore di Lancialotto del Lac"; which W. P. Ker justly called "one of the beautiful small things of mediaeval art":

A daughter of a great baron loved Lancelot of the Lake beyond measure. But he would not give her his love, because he had given it to Queen Guinevere. So much did she love Lancelot that she came to death therefrom. And she bade that, when her soul should be parted from her body, a rich barget should be arrayed covered with red samite, with a rich bed therein, with rich and noble coverings of silk, adorned with rich precious stones, and that her body should be put in that bed,

---

[1] Sicardi, no. 28; Biagi, no. 33.

[2] *Le Chevalier de la Charrette*, ed. W. Foerster, ll. 335-40. "Whoever was convicted of any crime was placed upon a cart and dragged through all the streets, and he lost henceforth all his legal rights, and was never afterwards heard, honoured, or welcomed in any court" (translation by W. W. Comfort in "Everyman's Library"). See "L'épisode de la *Charrette*," in Lot, *op. cit.*, Appendix V.

clad in her noblest clothes, and with a fair crown upon her head, rich with much gold and with many precious stones, and with a rich girdle and purse. In that purse was a letter, of which the intent is written below; but let us first tell of what goes before the letter. The damsel died of the sickness of love, and it was done with her as she had said. The barget, without sails or oars, was set upon the sea with the lady. The sea guided it to Camelot, and it stayed at the shore. The tidings went through the court. Knights and barons went down from the palaces. And the noble King Arthur came thither, and wondered much that it had come there without any guide. The king entered; he saw the damsel and the array. He had the purse opened. They found the letter. He had it read, and it said thus: "To all the knights of the Round Table, this maiden of Astolat sends greetings as to the best folk of the world. And, if you would know for what I have come to my end, it is for the best knight of the world and for the most churlish; to wit, my lord Sir Lancelot of the Lake, whom in sooth I knew not how to beg for love so that he might have pity upon me. And so, woe 's me, I have died through loving well, as ye can see." [1]

Merlin, "il saggio profeta," appears in several of these stories, but in no way associated with the Arthurian cycle. In each case, the direct source appears to be the Franco-Italian *Prophecies de Merlin*. The wife of a French merchant induced her husband, against his will, to lend a sum of money at usury in order to purchase her a new gown with the profit

---

[1] "A tutti i kavallieri della Tavola ritonda manda salute questa damigiella di Scalot, sì chome alla migliore giente del mondo. Et se voi volete sapere perch' io a mia fine sono venuta, si è per lo migliore chavaliere del mondo, e per lo più villano; cioè monsignore messere Lancialotto di Lac, che già no' 'l seppi tanto pregare d' amore, k' elli avesse di me mercede! Et così, lassa! sono morta per ben amare, come voi potete vedere." Sicardi, no. 82; Biagi, no. 119. For another Italian version of the letter, see below, pp. 127-8. Cf. the French text, *Mort Artu*, ed. J. D. Bruce (Halle, 1910, pp. 75-6), which is very similar, whereas in that given in Sommer (VI, pp. 256-7) Lancelot is not named.

on the transaction. Her beauty is praised in the presence of Merlin, who remarks: "If only the enemies of God had no share in her gown!" The woman, converted by his knowledge of what she has done, strips off the offending garment, and begs Merlin to take it and deliver her from danger.[1] When a child, Merlin rebukes the hypocrite Argistres, foretelling that he would be hanged and drowned and burned. Argistres attempts to kill him by setting fire to the house where he lives. The fire spreads to the man's own house; he rushes to the well for water, the chain breaks, entangles itself with his neck and drags him down into the water, where his body is burnt through people throwing in the burning rafters.[2] Merlin's secretary, Maestro Antonio, finds him weeping and expresses his amazement. Merlin bids him write that, in the time of the great dragon of Babylon, one of the latter's ministers in India will destroy "the beautiful palace that Saint Thomas built for King Giddefor of India," a palace all of gold and precious stones.[3]

Another Merlin story—of considerably greater interest—occurs in the *Libro dei Setti Savi di Roma*.

The Book of the Seven Sages, or Seven Wise Masters, of Rome was the first example in Europe of the Oriental device of collecting stories in a frame-

---

[1] Sicardi, no. 26; Biagi, no. 31. Cf. *Prophecies de Merlin*, ed. L. A. Paton, I, pp. 276–8.

[2] Biagi, no. 66. Cf. *Prophecies, ed. cit.*, I, pp. 272–5. It derives ultimately from the *Vita Merlini* of Geoffrey of Monmouth (ed. Parry, ll. 305–41).

[3] Biagi, no. 70. Cf. *Prophecies, ed. cit.*, I, p. 78; Sanesi, *Storia di Merlino*, pp. xxviii sq.

work, which was to bear fruit in the *Decameron* of
Boccaccio. It exists in varying forms and in many
European languages, and was probably originally
written in Latin about the middle of the twelfth
century.[1] It will be remembered that the theme
of the book is that the son of the Emperor of Rome
is falsely accused by his stepmother and sentenced
to death, the Seven Sages day by day — until the
prince can speak on his own behalf—delaying the
execution by a tale illustrating the untrustworthiness
of women, while the empress retorts with one to
confirm her husband in his resolution. The Italian
versions belong to two different groups in the classifi-
cation of the various redactions of the romance.
To the one—which is that into which the French
prose versions and the Middle English poem fall—
belong the well-known text published by Alessandro
D'Ancona, and another in the British Museum, both
of the early fourteenth century.[2] The other is the
group which Mussafia called the "versio italica."
Besides a Latin version published by Mussafia (probably based upon an Italian version and by an Italian),
it includes an Italian prose text of the fourteenth

---

[1] See especially G. Paris, *Deux rédactions du roman des Sept Sages
de Rome* (Paris, 1876); Killis Campbell, *The Seven Sages of Rome*,
edited from the manuscripts, with introduction, notes, and glossary
(Boston, 1907); A. H. Krappe, *Studies on the "Seven Sages of Rome,"*
in *Archivum Romanicum*, VIII (Florence, 1924). Dr. Krappe holds
that "the original version of the *Seven Sages* was composed some time
after 1135 in Northern France or in England." The original version
may have been French rather than Latin.

[2] *Il Libro dei Sette Savi di Roma*, ed. A. D'Ancona (Pisa, 1864);
Eine italienische Prosaversion der Sieben Weisen, ed. Varnhagen
(Berlin, 1881), from B.M. Add. MS. 27429.

century and an artistically insignificant poem of the
fifteenth in twenty-three cantos of ottava rima, the
Storia di Stefano, edited by Rajna.[1]
We are here concerned only with the story known
as *Sapientes*, which is one of those told by the
empress to discredit the counsel of the masters. In
the days of Herod, King or Emperor of Rome, there
was a custom that whoever had a dream should come
before the Seven Sages, bring them a besant, and
have the dream expounded. In this way the Sages
amassed wealth surpassing that of the emperor,
who became temporarily blind whenever he attempted
to leave the city. His Sages are bidden find out the
reason. They ask for fifteen days, and take counsel
with wise folk who tell them that there is a boy in
the country, who never had a father, and who answers
whatever men ask him. Going out of the city, they
find the boy playing with other lads; a quarrel arising,
his companions taunt him with having been born
without a father. He tells the Sages that his name
is Merlin. A man who has had a dream comes with
a besant that he was bringing to Rome to one of the
Sages; Merlin interposes, interpreting the dream as
referring to a hidden treasure, which the man finds

---

[1] A. Mussafia, *Beiträge zur Litteratur der Sieben weisen Meister*
(Vienna Academy, *Sitzungsb.*, *Phil. Hist. Cl.*, LVII, 1868); *Il Libro
dei Sette Savi di Roma*, ed. A. Cappelli (Bologna, 1865), ed. F. Roediger
(Florence, 1883), the two texts practically identical; *La Storia di
Stefano*, ed. Rajna (Bologna, 1880). To this group belong two later
Italian prose texts: *Amabile di Continentia*, ed. A. Cesari (Bologna,
1896), and the romance entitled *Erasto*. According to Campbell,
the parent version of this group was probably not earlier than the
fourteenth century and is derived from some MS. of the previous
group.

H

—sending part to the Sages, part to the boy (who refuses it). The Sages take Merlin with them to Rome, and, as they approach the city, ask him if he can tell Herod why his sight fails him when he would go forth from Rome. Merlin answers that he can. Brought before the emperor on the appointed day, Merlin tells him that under his bed is a cauldron which boils with seven bubbles. As long as these bubbles last, and the cauldron is there, he will not be able to see his way outside the city, and, if he takes the cauldron away without quenching the bubbles, he will lose his sight. The bubbles signify the Seven Sages, who have accumulated wealth by establishing the "evil custom" in the city, whereby folk, rich and poor, are compelled to bring a besant and have their dreams interpreted, and the sight of the emperor becomes darkened, whenever he wishes to leave Rome, because he has permitted this iniquity. As the Sages are beheaded one by one, beginning with the eldest, the bubbles sink, and the water at last lies so cold that the emperor can wash in it if he pleases. With Merlin and his barons, the emperor rides out of the gates, and nothing impedes his sight. In great joy, he embraces Merlin, and retains him as a member of his household.

I have so far followed the version given by D'Ancona.[1] The Italian prose texts of the other group give a somewhat different and shorter story. The king is anonymous and not of Rome, and it is not the philosophers (as they are here called) who

---

[1] *Ed. cit.*, pp. 60–5. In the B.M. manuscript, edited by Varnhagen, the story *Sapientes* is lacking.

first hear of Merlin, who is "uno savio uomo," not a child, and there is no reference to his having been born without a father. The king sends special messengers with gold to fetch him, and, while they are talking together, they see the man who was going to the philosophers to have his dream interpreted. Merlin calls him, tells him what he has dreamed and its significance; the messengers go with him to test the matter, and then bring Merlin to the king. "Said Merlin: 'Wilt thou be healed?' He answered: 'I desire nought else.' Then Merlin said: 'If thou wilt be healed, thou must needs have the heads cut off of those seven philosophers whom thou hast in thy house.'" The king is disturbed, but Merlin convinces him by bidding him dig under his bed, and there he will find a great cauldron full of boiling water with seven bubbles, "and this cauldron thy philosophers have made with magic art." The king cuts off the philosophers' heads, and is cured.[1]

Though considerably modified, it is obvious that the ultimate source of this tale is the story of the Tower of Vortigern in Geoffrey of Monmouth. Vortigern—for safety against the Saxons—is advised by his magicians to build a strong tower, but each day the earth swallows up the foundations as soon as they are laid. He consults the magicians again, who tell him that he must find a youth who has never had a father, kill him, and sprinkle the stones and

[1] *Libro dei Sette Savi*, ed. Roediger, pp. 15–17, ed. Cappelli, pp. 21–3. Mussafia's Latin version, *op. cit.*, pp. 105–6, is almost the same, Merlin there being "homo sapiens." But, in the *Storia di Stefano* (canto vii), he is "uno savio fantino."

mortar with his blood. Messengers are sent to seek
such a victim, and at last come to a city where they
see lads at play, and, a quarrel arising between two
of them, one taunts the other with having had no
father ("de te autem nescitur quis sis, cum patrem
non habeas"). Having learned who the boy is, the
messengers have him sent to the king with his mother
who reveals the story of his daemonic generation.
Confronted with the magicians, Merlin challenges
them to say what lies under the foundations of the
tower. When they keep silence, he bids the king
have workmen dig, and they will find a pond which
prevents the tower standing. This being done, he
challenges the magicians to say what lies under the
pool. They being again silent, he bids the king
have the pond drained, and he will see two hollow
stones and two sleeping dragons. This proves to
be true; but it is not stated that Vortigern put the
magicians to death, though Merlin becomes henceforth his prophet.[1] It will be observed that, while
D'Ancona's text is closer to Geoffrey, the other
version retains different features of the original
story.

[1] *Historia Regum Britanniae*, VI, 17–19. Cf. Krappe, *loc. cit.*,
pp. 398–407, and see above, pp. 6–7.

CHAPTER VI

ARTHURIAN MATTER IN THE "MARE AMOROSO" AND IN THE "INTELLIGENZA"

Il Mare Amoroso is a curious poem of three hundred and thirty-six lines, perhaps the earliest example of blank verse in Italian, and is preserved in a single manuscript which is not the prototype. The date is uncertain; it is more usually assigned to the latter part of the thirteenth century, but may in reality be later. Monaci defined the poem as "a kind of repertory of the similes that were in fashion with the lyrical poets of the old school." A large number of such images and allusions are brought together and woven into an epistle of love, either to supply a useful collection for the would-be poet or possibly with a satirical intention.[1] We are here concerned only with those drawn from the "matter of Britain."

To prove his fidelity to his lady, the poet would be prepared to undertake one of the exploits of Lancelot:

> E sse non fòsse anchora conquistata
> la valle di *Falsamanti* di Morghana,
> io la chonquisterei per Lancialotto;
> chè assai vi sono più leale amante
> che ll' ermellino a la sua bianchezza.[2]

---

[1] *Crestomazia*, pp. 319–27. The poem has obviously something of the nature of a "vaunt."

[2] "And, if it were not yet conquered, Morgan's valley of False Lovers would I conquer instead of Lancelot; for I am a far more loyal lover to you than is the ermine to its whiteness" (ll. 32–6).

I have here ventured upon an obvious emendation of the text: "Falsamanti" for "Falsamonti." The "Val des faux Amants," or "Val-sans-retour," is an adventure to be achieved only by a perfectly loyal lover; the others fall into the power of Morgan le Fay and her paramour; Lancelot alone entered the valley, slew its guardian, and by virtue of his constancy liberated the prisoners.[1]

Nevertheless, the poet is very jealous in his love:

> Ed io vorrei bene, s' esser potesse,
> che voi pareste a tutta l' altra gente,
> e ssichome paria la pulzella laida.[2]

The allusion recalls the episode of "la pucièle laide," the "loathly maiden," in the continuation of the *Perceval* of Chrétien de Troyes by Wauchier de Denain (also in the prose *Perceval*). Perceval meets a knight, Sir Biaus Mauvais, with a most hideous damsel, "la plus laide riens née," who, her lover declares, "seems to me so beautiful that there is no dame or damsel in the world who in beauty can equal her." At Arthur's court, her hideousness inspires general amazement and the jests of Sir Kay, but her knight settles with her at the court and loves her like his life:

> De lui ne vos voel conte faire,
> ne mais por contenir l'afaire,
> vous di que puis fu la pucièle
> si avenans et si très bièle

---

[1] Cf. Sommer, IV, pp. 116–24; Lot, *Étude sur le Lancelot en prose*, pp. 68, 315–16.

[2] "And I were indeed fain, if it could be, that you might appear to all others even as the loathly damsel appeared" (ll. 210–12).

c'on en parla par la contrée;
je ne sai s'ele fu faée.[1]

The context in our Italian poem seems to suggest
this, rather than the episode in Chrétien himself of
the "loathly messenger" who rebukes Perceval for
his silence at the Grail Castle; an episode which,
as far as concerns the hero not asking the fateful
question, was not unknown in early Italian literature,
as we have already found it utilised by Guittone
d'Arezzo. But here the point of the damsel's
apparent ugliness is to protect her lover from
jealousy, and it is not impossible that the allusion
may be, not to the *Perceval*, but to the *Palamède*.
Lac is met bringing a lady of whom Danain says:
"C'est bien la plus laide damoiselle et la plus hideuse
que je oncques veisse en tot mon âge." And, in
another episode, Hermeux de Rûgel has a damsel
with him who is so "laide" that no knight would envy
him her possession: "She hates me with all her heart,
and I love her so much, God help me, that I never
loved damsel more. There is not in all this country
anyone so beautiful for whom I would change her." [2]

---

[1] "Of him I will not tell you the tale, save for what concerns the
matter; I tell you that afterwards the damsel was so charming and
so beautiful that they spoke of it throughout the country. I know
not if she was enchanted." *Perceval le Gallois*, ed. Potvin, ll. 25,
384–6; 25, 739–44. Cf. the prose *Perceval*, ed. Jessie L. Weston, *The
Legend of Sir Perceval*, II, pp. 44 sq.

[2] Quoted by Rajna, *Fonti dell' Orlando Furioso*, 2nd edition,
pp. 317–19. In the final instalment of his *Materia epica nella lirica
italiana delle Origini* (*G.S.L.I.*, LXXXV, pp. 80–1), Ramiro Ortiz
suggests that "laida" is a proper name, Lais appearing with Circe
and Medea in a Latin mediaeval poem, the *Comoedia Lydiae*. I understand the lines as meaning that the poet would have his lady appear
as ugly as the "loathly damsel" to everybody except himself.

But our poet continues to unfold his desires:

> E sse potesse avere una barchetta
> tal, chon fu quella che donò Merlino
> a la valente donna d' Avalona,
> ch' andassi sanza remi e sanza vela
> altressì ben per terra chome per aqua;
> e io sapessi fare una bevanda
> tal chente fu quella che beve Tristaino e Isotta,
> a bere ven daria cielatamente una fiata
> per lo vostro chuore d' una sentenza
> e d' un volere chol mio intendimento . . .
> Poi intrerei chon voi in quella barchetta
> e mai non finirei d' andar per mare,
> infin ch' i' mi vedrei oltre quel braccio
> che fie chiamato il braccio di Saufì per tutta gente,
> ch' à scritto in su la mano: nimo ci passi,
> per ciò che di qua mai non torna chi di là passa.
> Poi mi starei sichuro sanza ranchura
> in giocho e in sollazzo disiato.[1]

A rich combination of romantic motives is here: the enchanted boat, the magic love potion, and with the two the poet, a Ulysses of love, voyaging with his lady over unknown seas beyond the columns of Hercules.[2] But, although we have the drinking of

[1] "And if I could have a small boat, such as was that which Merlin gave to the noble lady of Avalon, that should go without oars and without sail as well over land as over water; and if I could make a potion such as was that which Tristan and Iseult drank, I would give it you secretly to drink just once, to have your heart of one feeling and one wish with my desire. . . . Then would I enter that boat with you, and never end traversing the sea until I saw myself beyond that strait which shall be called the Strait of Saufì by all people, for it has written thereon: 'Let none pass here, for he who passes never thence returns.' Then should I stay safe without wrath in sport and desired joy" (ll. 213-22, 227-34).

[2] Saufì, or Saphis, was supposed to be the Saracen name for the place where Hercules set up his columns, "acciò che l' uom più oltre non si metta" (*Inf.* xxvi, 108-9). Cf. F. Torraca, *Un accenno del "Mare Amoroso"* (*Studi di Storia Letteraria*, pp. 58-9).

the love potion by Tristan and Iseult, the enchanted
boat is obviously not the ship that was bringing those
two lovers from Ireland to Cornwall. Rajna found
its ultimate source in another motive of the prose
Tristan, in "la nef de joie et de deport," which
conveys Tristan and Iseult in their last escape from
Cornwall to the "Island of the Fountain": "Ainssi
s'en vont li dui amant parmi la mer liez et joianz a
grant joie et a grant solaz. Il ne demandent plus
el monde; il ne quierent autre compaignie."[1] It
has been sent by Mabon le Noir, but was originally
made by Merlin for the daughter of the King of
Northumberland and her lover. But "la valente
donna d'Avalona" suggested to Rajna the name of
Morgan le Fay, and he could find no source for our
poet's statement that the boat was given to her by
Merlin. I have hazarded the hypothesis that we
may possibly have here a contamination of the
Tristan with *Floriant et Florete*, where (though Merlin
is not mentioned in the matter) Morgan has a similar
boat which she gives to Floriant.[2] But the *Prophecies de Merlin* offers a more likely source, and
indicates that the allusion may not be to Morgan.
Aglentine, "la Dame d'Avalon," comes to Arthur's
court in a "barge" which sails over the dry land
as over the sea. The barge has been made by Merlin,
"par grant soutillete." She has come from India
whither Merlin had sent her, at the time of the

---

[1] *Dante e i romanzi della Tavola Rotonda*, in *Nuova Antologia*,
1 June, 1920, pp. 242–3. Cf. Löseth, sects. 323–35.
[2] *Floriant et Florete*, ed. cit., ll. 790–8, 802–5. Cf. *M.L.R.*,
XX, p. 332.

foundation of the Round Table in the days of Uther Pendragon, to warn the people of the advent of the Great Dragon of Babylon, but she still seems a young girl. It is this barge that will ultimately convey Arthur himself to Avalon.[1]

Finally, the poet would have an inscription on his tomb that he "died for love in sorrow, even as Adrian and Chaedino died":

> chè per amor son morto in amarore,
> sichom è morto Nadriano e Chaedino.[2]

"Chaedino" is obviously Kahedyn (Ghedino), the brother-in-law of Tristan, who died of love for Iseult, after giving her harper his last lay in her honour. Said Sir Palamede to Sir Tristan (to quote our own Malory): "Well I wot it shall befall me as for her love as befell to the noble knight Sir Kehydius, that died for love of La Beale Isoud."[3]   But who is "Nadriano"?   One thinks of the Emperor Hadrian, but there seems no legend of his dying for love, and it would be far-fetched to suppose some perverted version of the death of Antinous.   Ramiro Ortiz observes that the association with Ghedino recalls the "ciclo brettone," and tentatively suggests the substitution of "Tristano" for "Nadriano."[4]   We could possibly retain "Nadriano" without leaving the Arthurian

---

[1] *Prophecies de Merlin*, ed. *cit.*, I, capp. cclxiii–cclxv. So the Rennes MS., but Miss Paton (I, pp. 415–16) cites another text in which Esglantine (Aglentine) is not the Lady of Avalon, but one of her damsels.   Here, too, the Lady of Avalon and Morgan are different persons.

[2] ll. 333–4. With "Nadriano" for "Adriano," cf. "Nanfosse" (Donno Alfonso), in Brunetto Latini, *Tesoretto*, l. 134.

[3] Löseth, sect. 100; Malory, X, 86.

[4] *Loc. cit.*, pp. 56–8.

cycle. Adriano, or Landriano, is the name under which, in the *Tavola Ritonda*, we meet a well-known figure of the prose *Tristan*: Driant, one of the sons of Pellinor. Like his brother, Lamorat, he falls at the hands of the sons of King Lot in the feud between the two houses.[1] He might here be confused with Lamorat, whose love for the Queen of Orkney was one of the causes that led to his murder. But Santorre Debenedetti has recently shown that the personage intended by the poet was more probably not an Arthurian character, but "Andrieus," the lover of the Queen of France, whose name is frequently cited by the Provençal troubadours as the type of the knight who died for love.[2]

We turn to an allegorical poem in nona rima, composed in the earliest years of the fourteenth, or perhaps even towards the end of the preceding century: the *Intelligenza*, which is questionably attributed to the Florentine chronicler, Dino Compagni.[3]

Here, in the palace of the poet's lady, "la sovrana intelligenza," are carved or painted "le belle ricordanze" of history and romance, and among them are many Arthurian motives. Here are Iseult and Tristan, "even as that vain love surprised them";

---

[1] Cf. Löseth, sect. 307; *Tavola Ritonda*, lxxix, lxxxix. In Malory (XX, 8), Sir Driant is killed in Lancelot's rescue of Guinevere from the fire.

[2] S. Debenedetti, *Nadriano e Caedino*, extract from the *Miscellanea Lucchese di studi storici e letterari in onore di Salvatore Bongi* (Lucca, 1927).

[3] *L' Intelligenza* a cura di V. Mistruzzi (Bologna, 1928). An excellent text is also given by R. Piccoli, *Dino Compagni, la Cronica, le Rime e l'Intelligenza* (Lanciano, 1911). Mistruzzi rejects the traditional attribution to Dino Compagni.

"here is the fair Queen Guinevere and near her Sir Lancelot";[1] here are Erec and Enide, and with them (according to a recent ingenious interpretation of Debenedetti) another pair of lovers from Chrétien de Troyes: Alixandre and Soredamors (here called "Rosenna d'Amore"), the sister of Gawain, from *Cligés*.[2]

> E non fallio, chi fu lo 'ntagliadore,
> e la bella Analida e 'l buon Ivano;
> èv' intagliato Fiore e Blanzifiore,
> e la bell' Isaottà Blanzesmano:
> sì com' ella morio per fin amore,
> cotanto amò Lancialotto sovrano;
> èvi la nobile donna del Lago,
> quella di Maloalto col cuor vago,
> e Palamides cavalier pagano.[3]

Analida is presumably Laudine de Landuc, the bride of Ivain in Chrétien's *Chevalier au Lion*. Iseult of the White Hands, the wife of Tristan, is confused with the fair maid of Astolat,[4] and the Lady of Malehaut, in the company of the Lady of the Lake, has apparently Palamede for her lover instead of Galehaut to whom she was given by Guinevere, and for love of whom she died, in the *Lancelot*! The fate of Merlin is not forgotten:

[1] Stanzas 72, 73.

[2] "Èv' Allessandro e Rosenna d'Amore, | messere Erecco ed Enidia davante" (stanza 74). Cf. S. Debenedetti, in *G.S.L.I.*, XCIV, pp. 144-5.

[3] "And he who was the sculptor did not miss fair Analida and the good Ivain; here is carved Floire and Blanchefleur, and fair Iseult of the White Hands: as she died through fine love, so loved she the supreme Lancelot. Here is the noble Lady of the Lake, she of Malehaut with enamoured heart, and Palamede the pagan knight" (stanza 75).

[4] Although there is no manuscript support, it is tempting to save the poet's orthodoxy by correcting the fifth line of the stanza to "e quella che morio per fin amore," thus ,distinguishing. the two persons.

E la foresta d' Arnante, dov' èe
Merlino 'nchiuso per gran maestria:
èvi la tomba per incantamento,
com' e' medesmo insegnò lo spermento,
a quella che l' avea 'n sua segnoria.[1]

The beauty of Cleopatra surpasses that of Morgan
le Fay.[2] Elsewhere the Arthurian story is depicted
on larger lines:

Dall' altra parte del ricco palazzo
intagliat' è la Tavola Ritonda,
le giostre e 'l torneare e 'l gran sollazzo;
ed èv' Artù e Ginevra gioconda,
per cui 'l pro Lancialotto venne pazzo,
March' e Tristano ed Isolta la blonda;
e sonvi i pini e sonvi le fontane,
le giostre, le schermaglie e le fiumane,
foreste e lande e 'l re di Trebisonda.

E sonvi tutt' i begli accontamenti,
che facevan le donne e' cavalieri;
battaglie e giostre e be' torneamenti,
foreste e rocce, boscaggi e sentieri;
quivi sono li bei combattimenti,
aste troncando e squartando destrieri;
quivi sono le nobili avventure,
e son tutt' a fin oro le figure,
le cacce e' corni, vallett' e scudieri.[3]

---

[1] "And the forest of Darnantes, where Merlin is shut in through great craft; here is the tomb by enchantment, as he himself taught the charm to her who had him beneath her sway" (stanza 76).

[2] Stanza 207.

[3] "On the other side of the rich palace is carved the Round Table, the jousts and the tournaments and the great disport, and there is Arthur and joyous Guinevere, for whom the valiant Lancelot became mad, Mark and Tristan and golden Iseult; there are the pines, there are the fountains, the jousts, the foigning, the rivers, forests, and meadows and the King of Trebisond.

"And there is all the gallant intercourse between the ladies and the knights; battles and jousts and beauteous tourneys; forests and rocks, woods and paths; there are the fair encounters, splintering of

Finally, amidst the music that surrounds the immediate presence of the lady of the palace herself, the poet hears a damsel singing to a harp a lay of the death of Tristan:

> Quiv' era una donzella ch' organava
> ismisurate, dolzi melodie,
> co le squillanti boci che sonava,
> angelicali, dilettose e pie;
> audi' sonar d' un' arpa, e smisurava,
> cantand' un lai come Tristan morie;
> d' una dolze viuola udi' sonante,
> Sonand' una donzella lo' ndormante;
> audivi suon di gighe e ciunfonie.[1]

"Cantando un lai come Tristan morie"! There are essentially two versions of the death of Tristan. In the poem of Thomas, Tristan wounded in Brittany sends Kahedyn to Cornwall for Iseult, with the understanding that, if she comes, a white sail is to be hoisted on the return; if not, a black. Iseult of the White Hands, who is watching by Tristan's couch, falsely tells him that the sail is black; he dies at the word, Queen Iseult landing to hear the church bells ringing and to die upon his body. In the prose *Tristan*, on the other hand, the maiden wife left in Brittany has disappeared from the story; Tristan, back in Cornwall, is in the queen's chamber when

spears and slaying of steeds; there are the noble adventures, and all of fine gold are the figures, the hunts and the horns, the varlets and the squires" (stanzas 287–8).

[1] "There was a damsel who was forming endless sweet melodies with the ringing words that she sang, angelical, delightful, tender; I heard a harp sound with free measure, as she sang a lay of how Tristan died; of a sweet viol I heard the music, as a damsel sang the strain; I heard the sound of lutes and symphonies" (stanza 294). Cf. Bertoni, *Studi su vecchie e nuove poesie*, etc., pp. 126–8, and Levi, *I lais brettoni e la leggenda di Tristano*, p. 25.

Mark mortally wounds him with the stab of a poisoned lance—the two lovers dying locked in each other's arms. One single French manuscript of the prose romance, while following the others in the previous part of the narrative, departs from them in giving a version of the death of Tristan resembling that of the poems—derived, not from Thomas, but from the same source as the German poem of Eilhart von Oberge.[1] Tristan has accompanied Ruvalen, a brother of Kahedyn, in visiting Gargeolain, the wife of a jealous baron, Bedalis. They are pursued by the husband, Ruvalen is killed, and Tristan wounded by a poisoned lance. He sends for Iseult of Ireland, and we have the intervention of the other Iseult with the motive of the black and white sails. From this manuscript, or one akin to it, this version of the death of the lovers passed into the French editions of the prose romance printed in the fifteenth and sixteenth centuries.

Whether the regular texts of the prose *Tristan*, in the account of Tristan's death, present a tradition independent of the poems, or whether it is a deliberate alteration of the end of the story, in correspondence with the change in the nature of the drama (from the conflict between passion and the claims of loyalty in the hearts of the lovers to the material struggle between the two men for the possession of Iseult) and the consequent darkened character of King Mark, is one of the disputed questions in

---

[1] J. Bédier, *La Mort de Tristan et d'Iseut, d'après le manuscrit Fr.* 103 *de la Bibliothèque Nationale comparé au poème allemand d'Eilhart d' Oberg*, in *Romania*, XV (1886), pp. 481 sq.

Arthurian scholarship.[1] If, behind the assumed lost *Estoire Tristan*, there be likewise assumed a legend perhaps of Celtic origin, the slaying of Tristan by Mark might seem a more probable primitive conclusion, than the story of the two sails and the jealousy of the wronged wife, which suggests a literary origin, combining the legend of Oenone and Paris with the black and white sails in the legend of Theseus.[2] But, in any case, we are faced with a curious fact as regards Italy. Although there are echoes of other portions of the poem of Thomas in the lyrics of the Sicilian School and in the *Novelle*, and we shall find a very considerable fragment preserved in the *Tavola Ritonda*, the story of Tristan's death in Brittany, with the episode of the black and white sails, does not appear to have left a trace in Italian literature. As far as our present knowledge extends, the only version of Tristan's death presented in Italian is substantially that of the prose romance.

There is, however, one peculiar exception. In the *Meliadus*, the King of Liones in a dream sees Mark, in the palace of Arthur, standing over the sleeping Tristan with a naked sword, with which he runs him through the body, to the universal lamentation of the world. Awakening, Meliadus thinks that,

---

[1] Cf. Bédier, *Le Roman de Tristan par Thomas*, II, pp. 387–93; Gertrude Schoepperle, *Tristan and Isolt, a Study of the Sources of the Romance* (London, 1913), pp. 439–42; G. Bertoni, *La Morte di Tristano*, in his *Poesie leggende costumanze del medio evo* (2nd edition, Modena, 1927), pp. 231 sq.; E. Vinaver, *Études sur le Tristan en prose*, pp. 17–20.

[2] Cf. Bruce, *Evolution of Arthurian Romance*, I, pp. 187–9; N. Zingarelli, *Tristano e Isotta*, in *Studi medievali*, N.S., I. (Turin, 1928), pp. 52–3.

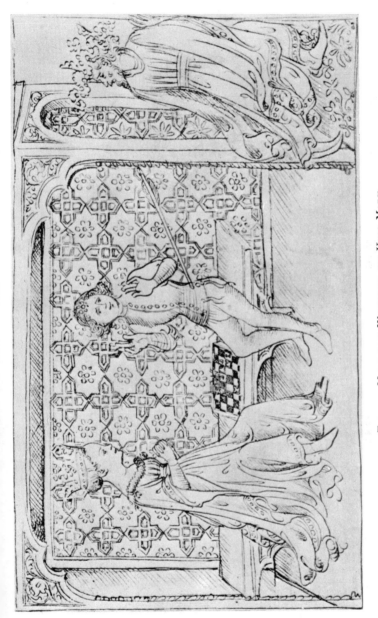

TRISTAN MORTALLY WOUNDED BY KING MARK
Florence, Biblioteca Nazionale, Cod. Pal. 556

if Mark slays Tristan, it will be to gain the kingdom of Liones. The text, however, adds that Mark did kill Tristan, but not as here described,[1] for he gave the occasion for his nephew's death by banishing him from Cornwall, whereby he was compelled to retreat to Brittany with Iseult of the White Hands:

And one day, as he was going for disport with his companion to see the beautiful Gargeolain, the mistress of his companion, he was espied by Bedalis the husband of Gargeolain, and evilly wounded with a poisoned lance, whereof shortly afterwards he died, as is amply recited in the book that treats of Tristan of Liones.[2]

Here the Italian follows what is clearly a clumsy attempt of the French editor of the *Meliadus* (or his source) to reconcile the usual prose version of Tristan's death, implied in the dream, with the one in the printed text of the *Tristan* to which he was supplying a companion volume.

---

[1] The French has "not, as some think, with his own hands."

[2] Aldus *Meliadus*, II, pp. 68, 68 v°. It is a little clearer in the French text, *Meliadus de Leonnoys* (1532), cap. xciii, f. cxxxi v°. Cf. Bédier, *La Mort de Tristan et d'Iseut, d'après le manuscrit Fr.* 103, p. 484; Löseth, sect. 540 (a). In Eilhart, it is not Ruvalen, but Kehenis (Kahedyn) who is the lover of the lady and is killed by the Bedalis of the French version. M. Bédier shows that Kahedyn was the original hero of the adventure.

CHAPTER VII

SOME "TRISTAN" AND "LANCELOT" FRAGMENTS

WE have seen that the first Italian Tristan romance
—as represented by the *Tristano Riccardiano*—remains a magnificent fragment. Its matter is supple-
mented by a later manuscript, the language of which
is less archaic and has traces of a western Tuscan
origin.

The manuscript in question—the Codice Panciatichiano 33 of the Biblioteca Nazionale at Florence
—was written in the earlier part of the fourteenth
century.[1] It is an Arthurian medley, made up of
five independent sections: (i) the beginning of the
Grail quest (ff. 1–38); (ii) a portion of the Tristan
romance from his birth to the false report of his
death (ff. 39v°.–116v°.); (iii) a version of a portion of
the *Mort Artu* branch of the *Lancelot* (ff. 121–146v°.);
(iv) a further instalment of the story of Tristan
(ff. 150–269v°.); (v) the last adventures and death of
Tristan (ff. 271–84). This final section was edited
by Parodi to complete the *Tristano Riccardiano*;[2]

---

[1] It is labelled "Conti·della Tavola Rotonda." There is a diplo-
matic copy of it by Biscioni in the Mediceo-Laurenziana, plut.
lxxxix, inf., cod. 62.

[2] Cf. his description of the manuscript, *op. cit.*, pp. xix–xxxvi.
Other unedited Tristan texts are the *Tristano Corsini*, which is of
no importance, and the *Tristano Veneto*. The latter in Venetian,
preserved in a MS. at Vienna dated 1487, combines a special redaction
of part of the prose *Tristan* with episodes from Rusticiano (Parodi,
pp. cxvii–cxxviii).

with thé exception of a few episodes, the other sections are still unpublished. I will deal first with the Tristan matter.

From the birth of Tristan to his going to Brittany and defeating the adversary of the king, the second section closely resembles the *Tristano Riccardiano*, and is evidently based upon the same unorthodox French redaction. But the dramatic episode of the dwarf who warns Mark against Tristan does not occur, and certain portions, such as the tournament in Ireland and the fighting in Brittany, are much condensed. From this point onwards, the manuscript follows a different version. We have the episode of the Servage, the reconciliation with Segurades (here represented as the husband of the Lady of the Thorn), the association with Lamorat in the defeat of Nabon (here called "Membruto"), the liberation of the prisoners, and the change of the name of the place to the "franchigia di Messer Tristano." Tristan and Kahedyn with Iseult of the White Hands are riding across a river, when the girl's palfrey stumbles and she laughs; pressed by her brother for an explanation, she says that she laughed because the water had been more daring than Tristan. Kahedyn thus learns that she is "pulcella," but says nothing, because he knows of Tristan's love for Queen Iseult the Fair.[1] The adventures of Tristan in the Forest Perilous and his deliverance of Arthur

---

[1] ff. 105–105 v°. The motive of the "presumptuous water"—found nowhere else in Italian—is not in the orthodox prose *Tristan*, but comes from Thomas (Bédier, I, pp. 324–5, ll. 1192–5). Elsewhere, Kahedyn takes the discovery ill and remonstrates with Tristan, who then reveals the truth.

do not occur, but, on receiving Iseult's letter, he goes straight to Cornwall. Then come the familiar episodes of Kahedyn becoming enamoured of the queen, the interchange of letters (Iseult writing with the intention of comforting him and making him realise his folly), their falling into Tristan's hands, his fury and Kahedyn's leap from the window, and Tristan's going mad.[1] Iseult orders Kahedyn to depart the realm of Cornwall under pain of death. A report is spread of Tristan's death, and Andred (now called "Andirecche") bribes a damsel to declare that she has seen Tristan slain. Iseult breaks out into a passionate lay of lamentation (the "lamento mortale," beginning "Lo sole rilucie chiaro e bello"), and threatens to kill herself with her lover's sword; but the faithful seneschal Dinas exhorts her not to believe the words of a foreign damsel, and assures her that Tristan is still living.[2] Tristan's madness develops in his wanderings, with details that do not correspond with any French text. Lamorat fights five knights and is left for dead; Gawain appears and threatens to kill him (the feud between the two houses is, of course, a commonplace in Arthurian story), but Tristan fells him and goes away. The tables are turned, but Lamorat, having Gawain in his power, spares him. Palamede comes to Cornwall,

---

[1] ff. 106–09 v°. With variations and omissions, this corresponds with Löseth, sects. 75, 76, and Malory, IX, 17, 18.

[2] Cf. Löseth, sect. 76, Malory, IX, 20. The Italian version of Iseult's "lai mortel" (ff. 110–13), though very corrupt, corresponds somewhat closely with the French text in the Cod. Vat. Reg. 727 as given by V. De Bartholomaeis, *Tristano, gli episodi principali della leggenda in versioni francesi, spagnole e italiane* (Bologna, 1922), pp. 41–2.

but cannot see the queen and leaves at her orders.
Mark and Andred rejoice over the supposed death
of Tristan, and Andred asks his uncle to make him
King of Liones, but "the king said that he wanted
to be more certain of the death of Sir Tristan, and so
the matter remained."

With the fourth section, the manuscript takes up
the story at a later stage. The reader may, perhaps,
be reminded that in the meantime, in the French
romance, Tristan has been healed of his madness
and banished from Cornwall, made a knight of the
Round Table by Arthur, called back to Tintagel
to fight with Elias the Saxon, twice treacherously imprisoned by Mark, and has finally escaped with Iseult
into Logres, where Lancelot installs them at Joyous
Gard. This section of the manuscript treats of the
great tournament held by Arthur at Lonazep
("Verzeppe") to see Queen Iseult and the chivalry
of Tristan, and the various adventures connected
with Breus, Palamede, Perceval, Dinadan, and others
that precede it, including Palamede's reporting the
death of Lamorat to Perceval, and his liberation of
the Red City. There are variants in the knights
concerned, but in the main, especially in the account
of the tournament, and the conduct of Tristan and
Palamede, Arthur and Lancelot thereat, the text is
clearly based upon a French version nearly identical
with that followed by Malory. It ends with the knights
going to report the result of the tournament to Guinevere by the sea, for she has been too unwell to be present.[1]

---

[1] This section (ff. 150–269) corresponds with Löseth, sects. 352–81,
and Malory, X, 52–81.

Again to supply a missing link. In the French romance, Mark has taken advantage of the absence of the knights of the Round Table on the quest of the Grail to ally himself with the Saxons and others for war upon Arthur. He has invaded Logres, captured Iseult at Joyous Gard and sent her to Cornwall, but has been repulsed with heavy loss from Camelot.[1] The last section of the manuscript opens with Tristan, accompanied by Hector de Maris, in Norgalles on his way to Cornwall. Hector having been wounded in an adventure on the way, Tristan meets Sagramour by the sea and they sail to Cornwall, where they are received by Dinas.[2] Iseult contrives that her lover should come to her, and the catastrophe promptly follows.

Tristan is with the queen in her chamber, while she plays on her harp and sings a song that she has made. Andred hears it, and straightway tells King Mark, who stabs Tristan in the side with the poisoned lance that Morgan has given him and goes away. Feeling himself mortally wounded and unable to pursue the king, Tristan makes his way to the castle of Dinas, where he lies in agony for a month, the physicians being helpless. While Iseult despairs and threatens to kill herself, Mark is at first delighted and sends every day to know how his nephew fares, but suddenly begins to repent bitterly and to bemoan his deed. When he feels his end is near, Tristan sends for Mark, and makes a last request that he

[1] Cf. *Tavola Ritonda*, cxxii, cxxiii (see below, p. 181). There is nothing of this in Malory.

[2] This section (ff. 271–84) was edited by Parodi, *Tristano Riccardiano*, pp. 371–406. The adventures in Norgalles correspond with Löseth, sects. 539–44.

may see Iseult before he dies. With Sagramour
and Dinas, the king and queen watch round his
bed all night. When morning comes, Tristan calls
to Sagramour to bring his sword and shield; Sagramour draws the sword out of the sheath for him to
see. Tristan bids farewell to knighthood ; sends
dying messages to Palamede, "Death is here ending
all the great strife that was between us," to Dinadan,
"Now am I more fiercely mocked than you used to
mock me," and to Lancelot; kisses his sword and
shield, which Sagramour is to present to the Round
Table, and have set in some place at Camelot where
all knights may see. He addresses Mark: "Sir, so
God save you, what think you of me? Am I now
that Tristan whom you were wont so much to fear?
Since I see that it must needs be so, I pardon you
willingly, and may God pardon you likewise."
Finally, he calls Iseult to embrace him that he may
die in her arms: "Now I reck not though I die, since
I have my sweet lady with me." The force of his
embrace overwhelms her, and the two die at the
same moment, locked in each other's arms.[1]

There is lamentation in Cornwall, with dread of a
renewal of the Irish servitude, and expectation that
Arthur and the knights of the Round Table will
avenge Tristan's death. King Mark has the bodies

[1] These scenes, which I have here summarised, closely follow the
usual French text, where, however, it is Tristan himself who is
harping and singing. Cf. Löseth, sects. 546–9; P. Paris, *Les Manuscrits françois de la Bibliothèque du roi*, I, pp. 200–8; and *The Death
of Tristan from Douce MS.* 189, edited by E. S. Murrell in *Publications of M.L.A.A.*, XLIII (1928), pp. 343–83. The corresponding
portion of the *Tristano Veneto* was published by Parodi, in the
volume *Nozze Cian-Sappa-Flandinet* (Bergamo, 1894), pp. 105–29.

brought to Tintagel to be united in death, and has a tomb made for them surpassed in richness only by that of Galehaut, who "loved Sir Lancelot of the Lake as much as any man could love another, and at the end died for Lancelot." [1] Sagramour goes back by sea to Logres. He is making his way to Camelot, when in a forest he meets a knight who tells him that Arthur and all the court are in grief, for tidings have come that Palamede and many others of the companions of the Round Table have been slain. Sagramour has his own news of woe; he shows the shield and sword, and says that Tristan of Liones is dead.

We turn to the Lancelot sections of the manuscript. The first (ff. 1–38) relates the beginning of the quest of the Holy Grail, containing the matter familiar to English readers as included in the thirteenth book of Malory: the assembly at Camelot at the vigil of Pentecost; the summons to Lancelot in the name of King Pelles, and his knighting of Galahad; the adventure of the sword in the stone, and the coming of Galahad to Arthur's court; the tournament, and the apparition of the Holy Grail; the setting out of the knights (with the beautiful motive, omitted by Malory, of their parting kiss to the king); the beginning of Galahad's quest, with the episodes of the wounding of Bagdemagus and Meliant, and the liberation of the Castle of Maidens; Gawain's con-

[1] The tomb of Galehaut was at Joyous Gard. In Italian (as even in Malory) the name of Galehaut, Lancelot's friend, is occasionally confused with that of Galahad, Lancelot's son. The Italian form for Galehaut is "Galeotto," occasionally "Galiotto" or "Galealto"; but, whereas the normal equivalent of Galahad is "Galasso," it also appears as "Galas," "Galeas," "Galeazzo," "Galeatto," and even "Galeotto" (the last two forms in the present manuscript).

fession to the hermit and refusal to do penance; Lancelot's moonlight adventure at the deserted chapel where, when the Holy Grail appears, he is unable to move or honour it, but is deprived of his arms and horse by the sick knight who has been healed; his rebuke by the mysterious voice, his confession to the hermit and vow to sin no more with Guinevere, and his departure with the fresh horse and arms. There is a lacuna of four pages, where the old man should bring Galahad to the Siege Perilous, though a small portion is inserted later; but, otherwise, the manuscript follows the *Queste* of the Vulgate cycle more closely than Malory does, and is frequently a literal translation of the French text.[1] The few minor variants are of no great significance; but there is one remarkable divergence from the French text that is of singular interest. The Holy Grail enters the hall of Arthur's palace, not so that "there was none might see it, nor who bare it," but on the horns of a white stag bound with four golden chains that are held by four men in white raiment:

Allora intrò dentro per lla grande sala del palagio una molto bella cervia biancha ch' era legata con quatro catene d' oro, e queste quatro catene teniano in mano quatro huomini con vestimenta bianche, e la cervia avea in suso le corna uno vagello codunno sciamito biancho, e vi entro si era lo Santo Gradale.[2]

---

[1] Cf. *La Queste del Saint Graal*, ed. Albert Pauphilet (*Classiques frânçais du moyen âge*), pp. 1–71; Sommer, VI, pp. 3–51.

[2] The corresponding passage in the French (*Queste, ed. cit.*, p. 15) reads: "Lors entra laienz li Sainz Graal covers d'un blanc samit; mes il n'i ot onques nul qui poïst veoir qui le portoit." Cf. Malory, XIII, 7: "Then there entered into the hall the Holy Grail covered with white samite, but there was none might see it, nor who bare it."

When they were all seated in their places, then they heard a clap of thunder so great and marvellous that them thought that the palace would be shattered beneath them. And straightway there entered a ray of the sun that made the palace brighter than it ever were and seven times more shining than it was before, and so at once were they all full of the grace of the Holy Ghost, and they began to look towards each other, for they could not see or know whence this food came to them. Not for then was there one of them that could speak or utter word with his mouth, but they were all struck dumb for a great while. So they stayed for a great while in such wise that none of them might speak, and so they gazed upon each other like dumb beasts. *Then there entered into the great hall of the palace a right fair white stag that was bound with four chains of gold, and these four chains four men in white raiment held in their hands, and the stag had upon its horns a vessel covered with white samite, and within it was the Holy Grail.* And, as soon as it had entered, there was all the palace full of a good odour, as if all the spices of the world had been there. And thus it went through the midst of the palace, and all round to the door, and, as it passed between the tables, they were all straightway filled, each knight having that food which he wished in his thought.[1]

The appearance of the white stag as bearer of the Grail occurs elsewhere in Arthurian literature. It is found, under totally different circumstances, in *Le Livre d'Artus*, edited by Dr. Sommer from the Paris Manuscript 337 of the Bibliothèque Nationale.[2] Here a company of knights with Nascien the hermit,

---

[1] ff. 7v°.–8. Cf. my article, *The Holy Grail in Italian Literature*, in *M.L.R.*, XX, pp. 443–53, where the text of this passage was printed. Three other episodes from this section of the manuscript were published by Polidori as an appendix to the *Tavola Ritonda*, II, pp. 239–53.

[2] *Vulgate Version of the Arthurian Romances*, VII, pp. 244–5. Cf. Jessie L. Weston, *Legend of Sir Perceval*, I, p. 264 n., and her *Quest of the Holy Grail* (London, 1913), p. 154. For the so-called *Livre d'Artus*, see Bruce, *Evolution of Arthurian Romance*, I, pp. 443–5.

THE COMING OF GALAHAD
Florence, Biblioteca Nazionale, Cod. Pal. 556

GALAHAD AT THE TOURNAMENT
Florence, Biblioteca Nazionale, Cod. Pal. 556

in a forest near the land of Galehaut, meet the procession of the Grail, headed by a white stag with a red cross on its forehead and lighted tapers on the horns, bearing upon its back the sacred vessel covered with a cloth of silk. It is followed by a white brachet, and a young girl leading on silver chains two white animals of the size of coneys, after which comes a weeping knight in a litter drawn by four small palfreys. The companions are so lost in gazing upon this marvel that none think to ask what it means. But the entry of this stag with the four men in white raiment, in the great scene in Arthur's hall, seems peculiar to our Italian text. It is obvious that the apparition represents Christ and the four Evangelists, and is closely related with that later episode in the *Queste*, where Galahad, Bors, and Perceval with his sister, "saw afore them a white hart which four lions led." "And at the secrets of the Mass they three saw the hart become a man, the which marvelled them, and set Him upon the altar in a rich siege; and saw the four lions were changed, the one to the form of a man, the other to the form of a lion, and the third to an eagle, and the fourth was changed into an ox." And the hermit bade them wit well: "Oft-times or this Our Lord showed Him unto good men, and unto good knights, in likeness of an hart." [1] Perhaps, rather than the legends of St. Hubert or St. Eustace, the association of the

---

[1] Malory, XVII, 9. Cf. the *Queste*, ed. Pauphilet, pp. 234–6. A similar vision of Christ and the Evangelists as a stag and four lions appears to Joseph of Arimathea and his son Josephe in the *Estoire del Saint Graal* (Sommer, I, p. 257). A stag also figures in Lancelot's vision of the Grail in the *Tavola Ritonda* (cf. below, p. 178).

stag with the Grail, in the text we are considering, suggests the story of Fescamp: the "cherf mout mervelleurs," "blanc comme nef ou comme let," that led Duke Ansegis to the tree that marked the spot for the foundation of the Abbey.[1]

In the third section, we have first some pages (ff. 121–127v°.) with unimportant matter more or less derived from the *Tristan* and an episode—apparently not found elsewhere—of the chivalrous dealings of Lancelot with the king and queen of Norgalles.[2] Then follows a fragment of the *Mort Artu* branch of the *Lancelot* (ff. 128–146v°.), beginning with the return of Bors from the quest of the Grail, and Gawain's confession that he has slain twenty knights including Bagdemagus, Palamede, and Lamorat. It includes the tournament at Winchester, the story of the Maid of Astolat, and the episode of the poisoned knight, following in the main the usual Vulgate version (not the redaction more familiar to English readers in Malory), but with omissions and variants.

Mordred, seeing the kinsmen of Lancelot going to the tournament without him, is convinced that the latter is remaining behind to carry on his intrigue with the queen. Agravaine accuses Lancelot to the king; Arthur will not believe it, but tests the charge by bidding Guinevere stay away. After an interview with the queen, Lancelot goes incognito to the tournament; Arthur, who cannot sleep, from a balcony recognises his horse as he passes at night

[1] Leroux de Lincy, *Essai sur l'Abbaye de Fécamp* (Rouen, 1840), pp. 153–154. Cf. Miss Weston, *Quest of the Holy Grail*, pp. 56–8.
[2] Cf. Parodi, pp. xxix–xxx.

on his way to lodge with the lord of Astolat, who
"had a daughter more fair than the sun." From her
Lancelot accepts the token of her scarlet sleeve to
wear at the tournament, where he goes with one of
her brothers, and is the victor as "the red knight with
the sleeve on his helmet." Gawain chances to
lodge with the lord of Astolat, Gareth and Agravaine being also there. At supper he tells the girl
of the unknown knight who has won the tournament.
In the garden Gareth draws the father aside that
Gawain may speak with her. When he makes love
to her, she rebukes him, declaring first that she is
beneath him, and then that she loves a better knight.
She shows him the shield that Lancelot left behind
him: "See here the shield of that knight whom I
love more than myself." Returning to court,
Gawain—in spite of Agravaine's accusation—assures
Arthur that Lancelot is the loyalest knight in the
world, and Arthur declares that he would not believe
him false if all the world said it. Guinevere thinks
that the victor cannot be Lancelot, for he would
never have borne a token that she had not given
him; when she hears that it was he, she tells Bors
that she will forbid him ever to appear in the court
again. One day the king and queen and Gawain
are at a window talking, and Arthur wonders where
Lancelot is. Gawain jokes about the cause of his
absence, and then, in confidence, tells the whole
story and how the girl rejected his own love. The
queen leaves the room, sends for Bors and Hector,
and bids them tell Lancelot never come to any place
where she is, on pain of death.

At Astolat the maiden throws herself at Lancelot's
feet, and implores him to accept her love, not considering her lower station. Lancelot assures her
that, if he were free to love her, he would not think
of her lineage, but he belongs entirely to another.
Afterwards he meets his kinsmen who are seeking
him; Bors tells him of the queen's anger, upon which
he swoons with grief, and his wounds break out
again. The death of the maid, the coming of her
body to Camelot with the letter, reveals the truth.
Guinevere, filled with remorse, begs Bors and Lionel
to find Lancelot and assure him that she will bear
any penance; they pretend to believe that he is
dead through her fault. Then follows immediately
the poisoning of the knight, here called Giafredi, the
brother of Mador de la Porte ("Amadore della Porta"),
by the apple which Guinevere gives him at the
banquet.[1] Mador, returning from a quest, reads the
inscription on the tomb, and appeals the queen of
treason. Lancelot hears the news, but is accidentally wounded by a party of hunters. He goes to an
abbey to be healed, sending Bors and Hector to
comfort the queen and bring him his red armour
in which he will appear as her champion. The two
knights pretend that he is dead because of Guinevere's dismissal of him, and tell her that it serves
her right if she finds no champion. "And she said:
'And will not you help me? For the love of God and
for the love of Sir Lancelot, I beseech you not to

---

[1] It is not stated by whom the fruit had been given to the queen
or for what intent. In the Vulgate and Malory it is for the purpose
of poisoning Gawain, the victim being Gaheris de Kareheu in the
one, Patrise in the other.

abandon me, for the love of God and for His sweet
Mother.'" Bors bids her not seek succour from them.
She rends her garments and throws herself at their
feet. They still refuse, even when Arthur himself
pleads. When the king has gone, they raise her up
and tell her that she will have a better champion.
Lancelot is distressed and indignant when he hears.
He bids them go back to court, and Bors to be the
queen's champion if any accident should prevent
his own appearance. The scene of Lancelot van-
quishing Mador on the day of combat is condensed
into a brief passage, and the tale ends abruptly with
Mordred and Agravaine preparing fresh snares, awaiting the moment for taking Lancelot with the queen.

Apart from small variations, and the omission of
the episode of Arthur in Morgan's palace seeing
the paintings that reveal the relations between
Lancelot and Guinevere, there is a notable difference
in the order of events when compared with the
Vulgate. The death of the Maid of Astolat precedes
the poisoning of the knight, instead of intervening
between it and Lancelot's appearing as the queen's
champion. The letter of the Maid of Astolat differs
from any other known version in the pathetic and
ingenuous reference to Lancelot's wearing her token
at the tournament:

A tutti quelli i quali vederanno questa lettera. La dami-
gella di Scalliotto salute bene aventurose. Allo Re Artù e a
la Reina Ginevera e a tutti quelli della corte del Re e a tutti
quelli della Tavola Ritonda, faccio mio compianto e mio
lamento, e voglio che voi sappiate, tutta buona gente, che io
misi lo mio cuore e lo mio amore in amare messer Lancialotto
crudelissimo e dispietato, ed io lo richiesi d' amore ch' elli

s' intendesse in me, che pure solamente m' avesse apagata di parlare ed arebemi campata la morte. Ed io non trovai in lui alcuno conforto nè pietade, ond' io ne sono venuta a morte come voi vedete. Vero è ch' elli portò mie insegne al tornia- mento, ma elli lo fece per divisarsi per non essere conosciuto, e non per amore ch' elli avesse in me. E pregovi che io sia soppellita nella grande chiesa di Camellotto, ed avante scrivete in su la tomba come io sia morta per la crudelità e durezza di messer Lancialotto.[1]

To all those who shall see this letter. The Maiden of Astolat salutation and good wishes. To King Arthur and Queen Guinevere and all those of the court of the king and all those of the Round Table, I make my complaint and my lament, and I would have you know, all good folk, that I set my heart and my love in loving Sir Lancelot most cruel and pitiless, and I besought him for love that he would be my lover, for, if he had but contented me with words, he would have saved me from death. And I found in him no comfort nor pity, wherefore I am come to death as you see. It is true that he bore my token at the tournament, but he did it to disguise himself that he might not be known, and not for any love that he had for me. And I pray you that I be buried in the great church of Camelot, and write upon the tomb how I have died because of the cruelty and harshness of Sir Lancelot.

Arthurian literature has many beautiful letters, but that of the Maid of Astolat is surely the gem. No two versions are quite identical. It seems peculiar to Malory—who first gave the Fair Maid the name of Elaine and transfers the scene from Camelot to Westminster—that the letter should be addressed to Lancelot, and that the knight should himself be at the court when the girl's body arrives; the incom- parably beautiful and pathetic form in which he gives the letter is apparently his own:

Most noble knight, Sir Lancelot, now hath death made us two at debate for your love. I was your lover, that men

---

[1] f. 143. Cf. *Mort Artu*, ed. Bruce, pp. 75–6, and above, pp. 93–4.

called the Fair Maiden of Astolat; therefore unto all ladies I make my moan, yet pray for my soul and bury me at least, and offer ye my mass-penny: this is my last request. And a clean maiden I died, I take God to witness: pray for my soul, Sir Lancelot, as thou art peerless.[1]

---

[1] Malory, XVIII, 20. It is noticeable that the version, occupying six stanzas, in the English poem, *Le Morte Arthur*, is totally different, although both Malory's eighteenth book and the poem probably trace back to the same lost French redaction of the *Mort Artu*.

CHAPTER VIII

DANTE AND THE ARTHURIAN LEGEND

THERE is a famous sentence in the *De Vulgari Eloquentia* where Dante, examining the claims to preference of the three chief romance languages (as we should now call them), admits in support of French its pre-eminence in vernacular prose, and makes express mention of the Arthurian stories: "Arturi regis ambages pulcerrimae." [1] There is some question as to the precise meaning here of the word *ambages*. It is found, a few years later, in a disparaging sense, though likewise with reference to the Arthurian romances. Raymond de Béziers, in the proem of a book dedicated to King Philip the Fair of France in 1313, speaks of the king's courtiers consuming their time in "narrationibus ambagicis" of Lancelot and Gawain. But, with Dante, we must evidently understand "the most beautiful romances of King Arthur," whether *ambages* refers primarily to their fantastic character, their windings or digressions, or to their subject matter as "wanderings" or "adventures." [2]

In his love lyrics, Dante never employs conventional

[1] *V.E.* i, 10. Cf. the line in Jean Bodel, *La Chanson des Saxons*: "Li conte de Bretaigne sont si vain et plaisant."

[2] Cf. P. Rajna, "*Arturi regis ambages pulcerrimae*," in *Studi danteschi* diretti da M. Barbi, I (Florence, 1920), pp. 91–9; P. Toynbee, *Dante Studies and Researches* (London, 1902), pp. 7, 263. The word *romanzi* is used by Dante in *Purg.* xxvi, 118.

allusions to names from the Arthurian cycle in the
fashion of the poets of the Sicilian school and their
immediate Tuscan successors; but there are motives,
in the *Vita Nuova* and in his *Rime*, that inevitably
suggest an Arthurian origin. Thus, whatever may
have been its ultimate source, the dream that is the
subject of the first sonnet of the *Vita Nuova*, the
dream in which Love makes Beatrice eat of her lover's
heart,[1] harks back to the famous lines in the *Tristan*
of Thomas, where Iseult sings of how the count gave
the heart of Guirun to his wife to eat:

> En sa chambre se set un jur
> e fait un lai pitus d'amur:
> coment dan Guirun fu supris,
> pur l'amur de la dame ocis
> que il sur tute rien ama,
> e coment li cuns puis dona
> le cuer Guirun a sa moillier
> par engin un jor a mangier,
> e la dolur que la dame out
> quant la mort de sun ami sout.[2]

Again, there seem to be in the *Vita Nuova* several
echoes of an episode in another Arthurian poem,
the *Cligés* of Chrétien de Troyes. The two sonnets,
Piangete, amanti, poi che piange Amore, and *Morte
villana di pietà nemica*, in which Dante bewails the
death of a girl whom he had seen in Beatrice's

---

[1] *V.N.*, sect. iii (son. i). Cf. E. Levi, *I lais brettoni e la leggenda di
Tristano*, pp. 5 sq.

[2] "In her chamber she sat one day and made a piteous lay of
love, how Lord Guirun was surprised and slain for the love of the
lady whom he loved above all things, and how the count then gave
the heart of Guirun by craft to his wife one day to eat, and the
grief that the lady had when she knew of the death of her friend"
(Bédier, I, p. 295, ll. 833–42).

company, and that episode, later on in the book, where
the pilgrims pass through Florence after the death of
Beatrice herself, have a singularly close resemblance
to the place in Chrétien's poem where the crowds
weep for the supposed death of the Empress, and,
in the midst of their weeping, the physicians from
Salerno come to the city.[1]

An Arthurian motive has long been recognised in
one of Dante's earliest lyrics, not included in the
Vita Nuova; the sonnet addressed to Guido Cavalcanti, in which the poet invokes for Guido and Lapo
Gianni and himself a romantic voyage in an enchanted
boat, with their three ladies: Vanna, Lagia, and she
whose name was thirtieth among the names of the
sixty fairest ladies of the city in the serventese which
Dante in the *Vita Nuova* says that he composed, and
in which the name of Beatrice could only fall on the
ninth place:

> Guido, i' vorrei che tu e Lapo ed io
> fossimo presi per incantamento
> e messi in un vasel, ch' ad ogni vento
> per mare andasse al voler vostro e mio;
> sì che fortuna od altro tempo rio
> non ci potesse dare impedimento,
> anzi, vivendo sempre in un talento,
> di stare insieme crescesse 'l disio.
> E monna Vanna e monna Lagia poi
> con quella ch' è sul numer de le trenta
> con noi ponesse il buono incantatore:
> e quivi ragionar sempre d' amore,

---

[1] *V.N.*, sect. viii (sonn. iii–iv), sect. xl [xli]; *Cligés*, ed. W.
Foerster, ll. 5789–861. Cf. M. Scherillo's notes on the latter episode
in his edition of the *Vita Nuova*, and W. W. Comfort in *Romanic
Review*, II (1911), pp. 209–10. As we have seen, the *Cligés* was
apparently known to the author of the *Intelligenza*.

e ciascuna di lor fosse contenta,
sì come i' credo che saremmo noi.[1]

Here, though without the complication of the love potion, we have the motive found in the *Mare Amoroso* —which is probably somewhat later than the sonnet. The "vasel" is unquestionably "la nef de joie" of the prose *Tristan*, rather than the "barge" of the Lady of Avalon, and the "buono incantatore" can be no other than Merlin himself.[2] But there is a curious resemblance to the description of the magic boat in *Floriant et Florete*, though it is most improbable that Dante knew this poem:

Puis vous dirai que vous ferez:
dedens une nef enterrez
que je vous ferai amener;
mès ne vous estuet riens douter,
vent ne tempeste ne orage:
car ele est de si bone ovrage
quar ele ne puet empirier,
verser, fendre ne despecier;
quar ele est toute d'ybenus . . .
La nef est fete en tel maniere
que avant, encoste et arriere,
ensi com vous commanderez,
s'en ira là où vous vorrez.[3]

---

[1] "Guido, I would that thou and Lapo and I might be taken by enchantment, and put upon a ship which under every wind should go over the sea at your will and mine; so that no storm or other evil weather could disturb us, but rather, living ever in one yearning, the desire of staying together would increase. And that the good magician would then set with us Monna Vanna and Monna Lagia, with her who is the thirtieth on the roll; and there to discourse ever upon love, and that each of them should be content, even as I believe that we should be" (*Rime*, ed. Barbi, in *Opere di Dante, testo critico*, lii; *Oxford Dante*, ed. Toynbee, son. xxxii).

[2] Cf. above, pp. 104–5.

[3] "Then I will tell you what you shall do: you will enter a ship that I will have brought you; but you have nought to fear from wind or

There is another possible allusion to Merlin, as also to Tristan, in the *Rime*. It is in the well-known sestina, *Al poco giorno e al gran cerchio d' ombra*, one of the "rime per la donna pietra":

> Ma ben ritorneranno i fiumi a' colli
> prima che questo legno molle e verde
> s' infiammi, come suol far bella donna,
> di me; che mi torrei dormire in petra
> tutto il mio tempo e gir pascendo l'erba,
> sol per veder do' suoi panni fanno ombra.[1]

These lines might, I think, be taken to mean that, only to see the shadow of his lady's dress, the poet would face the fate of Merlin who, through doting on the Lady of the Lake, was entombed in perpetual sleep in the cave, and that of Tristan who, when believing himself supplanted by Kahedyn in Iseult's favour, in his madness fed upon grass.[2]

Among the souls seen in Limbo, in the "nobile castello" of Fame, are "Tullio e Lino e Seneca morale." For "Lino," among the many alternative readings,

---

tempest or storm, for it is of such good workmanship that it cannot decay, overturn, or break up; for it is all of ebony. The ship is made in such wise that forward, around, and backward, even as you shall command, it will go wherever you will" (*Floriant et Florete*, ll. 790–8, 802–5).

[1] "But in sooth the rivers will flow back to the hills before this soft and green wood takes flame, as a fair woman is wont to do, for me, who would be content to sleep in stone all my time and go feeding on grass, only to see where her garments cast a shadow" (*Rime*, ed Barbi, ci; *Oxford Dante*, sest. i).

[2] In the *Lancelot* (the more probable form in which Dante would have known of Merlin's fate): "Ele l'enigna et le seela tout en dormant en une cave" (Sommer, III, p. 21). In the *Tavola Ritonda* (cap. lxx), Tristan in his madness "a tale si condusse e venne, ch' egli pasceva l'erba."

one manuscript at least has "Merlino." [1] It is, of
course, unthinkable even as a possible variant, but
interesting as indicating the importance of Merlin
still in the eyes of Dante's century. Dante nowhere
mentions Merlin by name, and—when we remember
how Merlin obsessed the prophetic political literature
of Italy—this silence may be significant. Salimbene
had linked the "anglicus vates" with the Sibyl and the
abbot Joachim of Flora. Now the Sibyl was sacred
for Dante, and Joachim is accepted as "di spirito
profetico dotato." [2] But Salimbene further associates
Merlin with two of his own contemporaries: Michael
Scott, whose prophecies he combines with his, and the
cobbler of Parma, Asdente, who had "a mind illumined
to understand the sayings of Merlin and the Sibyl and
the abbot Joachim, and all who had foretold anything of the future." [3] Dante condemns both Michael
Scott and Asdente together to the bolgia of the
diviners and sorcerers, but Merlin is not with them;
their only companion, apart from their prototypes in
classical antiquity, is Guido Bonatti, the Ghibelline
astronomer from Forlì of their own day.[4] The poet
had obviously a contempt and loathing for the
mediaeval supposed prophet in whose image and likeness the Joachists and their allies had created a false,
unromantic Merlin. In the letter to the Italian
cardinals, he denounces *astronomi quidam et crude
prophetantes*, "certain astronomers who crudely

[1] *Inf.* iv, 141. Cf. E. Moore, *Contributions to the Textual Criticism
of the Divina Commedia*, p. 282.
[2] *Par.* xii, 139–41.
[3] *Cronica*, ed. Holder-Egger, pp. 247, 359–60, 512, 532, 537.
[4] *Inf.* xx, 115–20.

prophesy," and he could not have been ignorant of the part Merlin's name played in such matters. Elsewhere he may, perhaps, have had one such prophecy in his mind. Brunetto Latini had written in the *Trésor*: "We find in the books of Merlin or the Sibyl that the imperial dignity is to end in Frederick." Dante, in the *Convivio*, writing before the election of Henry of Luxembourg, speaks of Frederick as "ultimo imperadore de li Romani"; but promptly qualifies the statement by adding: "ultimo dico per rispetto al tempo presente," as though the prophecy were too contemptible to deserve express repudiation.[1] We know how Dante has delivered Virgil from the mediaeval degradation that represented him as a magician. Similarly, though in an immeasurably lesser sphere, his silence in the *Inferno* preserved Merlin from the current travesty. Perhaps the poet realised that Merlin, in the Arthurian legend, was mainly a force for righteousness; at least, in the one explicit reference to him that we find in Dante's works, he remains the purely romantic figure of "il buono incantatore."

There can be no question that Dante knew his "ambages pulcerrimae" at first hand in the French romances, and the place where their influence upon him is most marked is naturally the fifth canto of the *Inferno*. Here the *Tristan* and the *Lancelot* combine harmoniously with the sixth book of the *Aeneid*. The enumeration of the lovers in antiquity or romance on Virgil's lips recalls the "mourning fields," *lugentes campi*, of his own poem, where Aeneas sees the victims of love whom "secluded paths conceal and a myrtle

[1] *Epist.* viii [xi], 3, *Conv.* iv, 3.

grove embowers"; though the Roman poet's "mourning fields," in accordance with the sterner ethics of his mediaeval successor, are transformed into "la bufera infernal che mai non resta," a region of active torment.[1] But, at the same time, it somewhat recalls a passage in the *Lancelot*, where Bors gives Guinevere a list of famous men who have been undone by love or through women.[2] As in the French romance, so in the *Inferno*, the list ends with the names of Paris and Tristan; the verse pausing on the latter, as though it gave the key to the rest of the canto: "Vedi Paris, Tristano." The typical lover of the Arthurian cycle is nowhere else mentioned by Dante, nor does the name of Iseult occur in his works; as we saw, the convention that dragged in their names as a mere empty allusion in a love poem had been abandoned by the poets of the "dolce stil nuovo," and—unlike his contemporaries, but resembling in this what was to be the attitude of Malory—Lancelot is for Dante the more significant figure. The lines that follow show at first a classical reminiscence again:

> più di mille
> ombre mostrommi, e nominommi, a dito
> ch' amor di nostra vita dipartille;[3]

---

[1] *Inf.* v, 52–67, *Aen.* vi, 440–51.

[2] He puts forward examples of Jews and Saracens. There is David and Absalom the beautiful, Solomon the wise, Samson the strong; Hector and Achilles, the patterns of chivalry among the ancients: "Hestor li preus et Acilles, ki darmes et de chevaleries orent los et pris sor tos les chevaliers del monde, en morurent et en furent andoi ocis [et plus de .C. mile avoec els] par locoison dune feme ke Paris amena par force de Gresce; et a nostre tans meesmement, na encore pas .V. ans, en morut Tristrans, li nies le roi Marc, ki si loiaument ama Iseut la blonde" (*Mort Artu*, ed. Bruce, p. 58; Sommer, VI, pp. 244–5). [3] *Inf.* v, 67–9.

"More than a thousand shades he pointed out, and named to me, whom love had parted from our life." Dante is echoing Virgil's line of the spirits in the "mourning fields":

Hic quos durus amor crudeli tabe peredit;[1]

"Here are those whom hard love consumed with cruel wasting." But, at once, the classical motive is absorbed in the atmosphere of mediaeval romance:

Poscia ch' io ebbi il mio dottore udito
nomar le donne antiche e' cavalieri,
pietà mi giunse, e fui quasi smarrito;[2]

"After I had heard my teacher name the ladies of old and the knights, compassion overtook me, and I was wellnigh bewildered."

It was Torraca who first pointed out that the romance of Tristan, no less than that of Lancelot, is woven into the story of Paolo and Francesca, which is practically an adaptation of the former to a contemporary Italian tragedy.[3] There is no trace of any previous legend or tradition concerning Francesca da Polenta, her relations with Paolo, and their fate. A few isolated documents, incidentally naming the three chief actors in the drama, are all that we find before the poem, and these documents merely enable us to infer that Gianciotto and Paolo Malatesta were brothers, that the former had a wife named Francesca, and that, after a certain year, Paolo disappears from view, while, by another year, Gianciotto has another wife. That Francesca and Paolo were lovers, and met their

---

[1] *Aen.* vi, 442. [2] *Inf.* v, 70–2.

[3] *Il Canto V dell' Inferno*, in his *Studi danteschi* (Naples, 1912), pp. 399 sq. Cf. A. Farinelli, *Dante e la Francia* (Milan, 1908), pp. 15-20.

deaths at Gianciotto's hand, is merely deduced from
Dante's lines; and the commentators, in the details
they supply, are, for the most part, simply elaborating
what they read in the *Commedia*.

> Amor, ch' al cor gentil ratto s' apprende,
>   prese costui de la bella persona
>   che mi fu tolta; e 'l modo ancor m' offende.
> Amor, ch' a nullo amato amar perdona,
>   mi prese del costui piacer sì forte,
>   che, come vedi, ancor non m' abbandona.
> Amor condusse noi ad una morte:
>   Caino attende chi a vita ci spense.[1]

Dante gives no details of their death. The allusion
to Cain, the first murderer and fratricide awaiting
his mediaeval imitator, is the only indication of the
identity of the avenger. I have ventured to adopt
the reading *Caino* (the manuscripts are divided, and
both readings were known to the early commentators),
instead of the *Caina* accepted by the "testo critico"
in the sixth centenary edition, though the alternative,
the reference to the region of ice in the ninth circle
in which the treacherous slayers of their kindred are
embedded, would be hardly less significant. In the
words, "il modo ancor m' offende," "the way afflicts
me still," there is no possible reference to the alleged
trick played upon Francesca in the substitution of
one brother for the other. That, as we shall see, is
an invention of Boccaccio.

But this love that led to one same death, and is

[1] "Love, that is swiftly caught in gentle heart, made this man
enamoured of the fair body that was taken from me, and the way
afflicts me still. Love, that dispenses no loved one from loving, seized
me so mightily with delight in him that, as thou seest, it does not
leave me yet. Love led us to one death: Cain awaits him who
quenched our life" (*Inf.* v, 100–07).

unquenched even in the infernal tempest, how did
it begin?

> Ma dimmi: al tempo de' dolci sospiri,
> a che e come concedette amore
> che conosceste i dubbiosi desiri? [1]

Inevitably, the secret lay buried in the grave with
the two lovers; to interpret it, in the answer placed on
Francesca's lips, Dante had recourse to the greatest
love-story of the Middle Ages.

> Noi leggiavamo un giorno per diletto
> di Lancialotto come amor lo strinse:
> soli eravamo e sanza alcun sospetto.
> Per più fiate li occhi ci sospinse
> quella lettura, e scolorocci il viso;
> ma solo un punto fu quel che ci vinse.
> Quando leggemmo il disiato riso
> esser baciato da cotanto amante,
> questi, che mai da me non fia diviso,
> la bocca mi baciò tutto tremante.
> Galeotto fu il libro e chi lo scrisse:
> quel giorno più non vi leggemmo avante. [2]

---

[1] "But tell me: At the time of the sweet sighs, at what and how
did love grant that you should know your unrevealed desires?"
(*Inf.* v, 118-20).

[2] "We were reading one day for pastime of Lancelot, how love
bound him fast: we were alone and without any fear. Many times
that reading drove our eyes together, and turned our faces pale;
but one moment alone it was that overcame us. When we read
how the longed-for lips were kissed by so great a lover, he, who shall
never be divided from me, kissed me on the mouth all tremblingly.
Galehaut was the book and he who wrote it: that day we read in
it no further" (*Inf.* v, 127-38).
I follow the more usual interpretation, which is that of Benvenuto
da Imola and Francesco da Buti, taking *riso* as the "smiling face,"
or "smiling lips," of Guinevere. But *il disiato riso* might also, with
Boccaccio, be understood as the delight felt by the queen (*la
disiderata letizia la qual fu alla reina Ginevra*): "When we read of the
longed-for delight of being kissed by so great a lover."

"Soli eravamo e sanza alcun sospetto." This line, condensing a single sentence from the prose *Tristan*, gives the clue to the genesis of the episode.[1] A comparison with the French text, or the *Tristano Riccardiano*, makes it clear that it is modelled upon a famous scene in the romance. One may surmise that the bare report that Paolo and Francesca had died together at the hands of Gianciotto, brother slaying brother, brought back to Dante's mind the slaying of Tristan by King Mark, nephew by uncle, and that he turned to the romance for the beginning of the story, the scene upon the ship that is bringing Tristan and Iseult from Ireland, substituting the reading of the *Lancelot* by Paolo and Francesca for the game of chess, the kiss for the drinking of the love potion by their prototypes. Nor, perhaps, is it without significance that, in some French texts of the *Tristan*, Mark's suspicions are first aroused by surprising Tristan and Iseult together, talking of Lancelot and Guinevere.[2]

"Galeotto fu il libro e chi lo scrisse." The first of the three parts into which the *Lancelot* was divided, the portion including the episode that Paolo and Francesca read, bore the title of *Galehaut*.[3] But here Dante probably means that the book and its author played the same part with the lovers of Rimini as Galehaut, the "haut prince," did with Lancelot

---

[1] "Et ilz sont tous seul a seul, si qu'ilz n'ont nul destourbier ne paour ne d'un ne d'autre" (Bédier, II, p. 342). That this line derives from the *Tristan* was first pointed out by Panizzi (cf. Toynbee, *Dante in English Literature*, II, p. 521).

[2] Löseth, sect. 45.

[3] Cf. F. Lot, *Étude sur le Lancelot en prose*, pp. 12–14.

and Guinevere in making them known to each other and prompting the revelation of their mutual love. Lancelot, after his first exploits, with the image of the queen in his heart, has been imprisoned by the Lady of Malehaut who vainly seeks his love. He has been released to succour Arthur in the war against the "haut prince," and has persuaded the latter to submit to Arthur, and Galehaut, at Guinevere's request, brings Lancelot (still disguised) to see her; the Lady of Malehaut being in attendance on the queen, while concealing her identity from her former captive. Galehaut, to let Lancelot speak freely with the queen, has withdrawn a little way and seated himself with the other ladies present. Guinevere has questioned Lancelot, and, to torment him, professes to believe that he really loves the Lady of Malehaut. The knight "being in sore anguish thereat," Galehaut returns, and begs the queen to have pity upon him and kiss him "as a beginning of true love."

Dr. Toynbee[1] has printed from a thirteenth-century manuscript of the *Lancelot* (the Lansdowne 757 in the British Museum) the portions that bear upon our subject, and I avail myself of his accompanying translation:

"Lady," quoth Galehaut, "then kiss him, as a beginning of true love." "For a kiss," quoth she, "see I now neither time nor place, but no wise doubt but that I am as fain as he. But these ladies are yonder who marvel much that we have so long talked here, and it could not be but that they would see it. Nathless, if he desire it, I will kiss him right willingly." And he was so joyful and astonied thereat that he could not

---

[1] *Dante and the Lancelot Romance* (*Dante Studies and Researches*, London, 1902), pp. 9–37.

make answer, save only, "Lady, much thanks." "Ah, lady," quoth Galehaut, "doubt not now of his desire, for he is wholly set on it. And know well that none shall perceive it, for we will all three draw together even as if we took counsel." "Wherefore should I make you to pray me?" quoth she; "more do I desire it than you or he." Then they all three drew together and made as if they took counsel. And the queen saw well that the knight dared do no further, and she took him by the chin and kissed him before Galehaut no short space, so that the Lady of Malehaut knew of a truth that she kissed him.[1]

It will, of course, be observed that, with Dante, it is Lancelot who kisses the queen:

> Quando leggemmo il disiato riso
> esser baciato da cotanto amante;

the "cotanto amante" being, perhaps, an allusion to, or echo of, Galehaut's introduction of his friend: "Lady, see here the best knight in the world" (*Dame, vez ci le meillor chevalier del monde*). There has been considerable recent discussion of this episode, turning in part upon the question whether the poet had a confused recollection of the romance, or alluded to Lancelot's answering kiss, or was acquainted with a different reading, or purposely modified the story.[2] It appears that, in certain manuscripts of the romance, the episode was entitled "the kiss of Lancelot": "How Sir Lancelot kissed Queen Guinevere the first time." The question is obviously of small significance; but

---

[1] Cf. Sommer, III, pp. 262-3.
[2] P. Rajna, *Dante e i romanzi della Tavola Rotonda*, pp. 229-32; N. Zingarelli, *Le reminiscenze del "Lancelot,"* in *Studi danteschi diretti da M. Barbi*, I (Florence, 1920); V. Crescini, *Il bacio di Ginevra e il bacio di Paolo, ibid.*, III (Florence, 1921); G. Bertoni, *Il bacio di Lancilotto (Studi su vecchie e nuove poesie e prose d' amore e romanzi*, pp. 175-81).

it may well be that Dante slightly diverged from his source to make Paolo—rather than Francesca—take the initiative. If it is not too fantastic an analogy, there is warrant for Dante thus altering what he took to be the record of a true history on psychological grounds, in his treatment of the Genesis story of Adam and Eve in the *De Vulgari Eloquentia*.[1]

Now, to all true Arthurians, the line about "Galeotto"—as usually and, I believe, rightly understood—is almost as much a stumbling-block as Dante's treatment of Brutus and Cassius was to some of the humanists of the early Renaissance. The arguments of Michele Barbi and others, that the moral type of Lancelot's friend here suggested is not that of a "turpe mezzano," but of a "cavalleresco messo d' amore," seem to me to make this line utterly colourless and to be out of harmony with the tone of the canto.[2] On Francesca's lips, like the preceding line about her slayer, "Caino attende chi a vita ci spense," it has surely the force of a bitter imprecation: "Galeotto fu il libro e chi lo scrisse!" The book had wrought their spiritual downfall even as Gianciotto had quenched their earthly life. Dante, unquestionably, knew the *Lancelot* at first hand; but, while accepting real or supposed facts that he found in his sources, he maintains considerable freedom in the moral judgment that he passes upon them, as

---

[1] *V.E.* i, 4. But Parodi (*Poesia e storia nella "Divina Commedia,"* p. 69) well notes how Francesca is the dominant spirit throughout the episode, reducing Paolo "quasi ad un' ombra della sua prepotente passione."

[2] Cf. M. Barbi, *Sul testo del "Decameron,"* in *Studi di filologia italiana*, I (Florence, 1927), pp. 53-4.

we see strikingly exemplified when his treatment of Brutus and Cassius is contrasted with their characters as portrayed by Lucan. Dante knew the noble character of the "haut prince" in the romance—but, for this particular action of his, he has deliberately branded his name as that of a pander.

There is another, somewhat perplexing, reference to the same episode of the *Lancelot* in the *Paradiso*, where Dante, after learning the knightly dignity that his ancestor Cacciaguida held in the world, addresses him with the ceremonious *voi*; "whereat Beatrice, who was a little apart, smiling, seemed like her who coughed at the first fault recorded of Guinevere":

> Onde Beatrice, ch' era un poco scevra,
> ridendo, parve quella che tossio
> al primo fallo scritto di Ginevra.[1]

Here, again, there is no reason to suppose that Dante misunderstood his source. He is not alluding to the kiss, but to where, at an earlier phase of the episode, the queen compels Lancelot to utter his love; this, or possibly her insistence upon the interview, being the "primo fallo":

"By the fealty," quoth she, "that you owe me, whence came this so great and entire love that you have placed in me?" At these words that the queen spake it came to pass that the Lady of Malehaut coughed all openly, and raised her head which she had before bent down. And the knight did hear her now, for many a time had he heard her.[2]

To me, I must confess, this image of the Lady of

[1] *Par.* xvi, 13–15.
[2] Toynbee, *op. cit.*, p. 30. We owe to Dr. Toynbee the identification of the source of the motive. Cf. Sommer, III, p. 261, and, for the cough of Guinevere, in a very different situation, Malory, XI, 8.

L

Malehaut and her cough, applied to Beatrice and her smile, is one of the few places in the *Paradiso* where Dante is less than himself. The only plausible explanation seems that of Rajna.[1] The cough of the Lady of Malehaut was intended to reveal her identity to Lancelot, to warn him that she is there and watching, and that she has now understood his secret. She is seated apart with the other ladies of the queen. Beatrice similarly "era un poco scevra," because the secular conversation between Cacciaguida and his descendant does not directly concern her allegorical part of spiritual guide; but her smile, or laugh, is to remind Dante of her presence, to warn him to keep a guard upon himself, and that she has perceived the trace of vainglory in his noble ancestry, that "poca nostra nobiltà di sangue," manifested in his use of the plural *voi* to Cacciaguida.

There is a passage in the *Purgatorio* which seems to me to have an unmistakable Arthurian ring. It is where Guido del Duca weeps when he remembers the chivalrous life of Romagna in the past, and compares it with the present degeneration:

> Le donne e i cavalier, li affanni e li agi,
> che ne 'nvogliava amore e cortesia
> là dove i cuor son fatti sì malvagi;[2]

"The ladies and the knights, the toils and the disports upon which love and courtesy set our wills, there where hearts have become so evil."

It is a lamentation for the corruption of the chivalrous ideal in a small region of thirteenth-

---

[1] *Dante e i romanzi della Tavola Rotonda*, pp. 232–4.
[2] *Purg.* xiv, 109–11.

century Italy; but it might well have been uttered
by one of Arthur's own knights in the degeneration
depicted at the close of the Arthuriad, in the approach-
ing dissolution of the Round Table, when the knights
"through too much ease let their valour decay, and
wrought other shameful things";[1] while "Sir Agravaine and Sir Mordred had ever a privy hate unto
the queen, Dame Guinevere, and to Sir Lancelot,
and daily and nightly they ever watched upon Sir
Lancelot,"[2] and Mordred already meditated the
usurpation of his father's crown.

Two of the final episodes are recorded by Dante.
We have, in the circle of the traitors in the *Inferno*,
the echo of that great battle in the west beside Salisbury, than which "never was there seen a more
dolefuller battle in no Christian land," and the
death of Mordred at Arthur's hands. Among the
souls most worthy to be embedded in the ice of
Caina is "he whose breast and shadow were cleft
with that one same stroke by the hand of Arthur":

> quelli a cui fu rotto il petto e l' ombra
> con esso un colpo per la man d'Artù.[3]

The allusion is to the last branch of the *Lancelot*:
the *Mort Artu*. I avail myself again of Dr. Toynbee's
translation:

And Mordred, who saw well that the king was minded only
to slay him, avoided him not, but turned his horse's head to
him; and the king, who came at him as straight as he might,
smote him with all his strength so sorely that he burst the
mail of his hauberk, and thrust the iron of his lance through

---

[1] *Tavola Ritonda*, p. 525.   [2] *Morte Darthur*, XX, 1.
[3] *Inf.* xxxii, 61–2.

the midst of his body. And the story says that, after the with-
drawal of the lance, there passed through the wound a ray of
sun so manifestly that Girflet saw it. Wherefore they of the
country said that this had Our Lord done because of His wrath
against him.[1]

For the last phase of Lancelot, we turn to that
most beautiful chapter of the *Convivio*, where Dante
speaks of the return of the noble soul to God in the
fourth period of life:

The noble soul dedicates herself to God in this period, and
awaits the end of this life with much desire, and it seems to
her that she is leaving the hostel and returning to her own
house; it seems to her that she is coming back from a journey
and returning to her city; it seems to her that she is issuing
from the sea and returning to the harbour. O wretched and
vile who with hoisted sails rush towards this harbour, and,
where you ought to rest, shatter yourselves by the might
of the wind, and lose yourselves in the place to which you have
made so long a voyage! Assuredly, the knight Lancelot
wished not to enter with hoisted sails, nor our own most
noble Italian, Guido da Montefeltro. Verily, these noble
men lowered the sails of wordly activities; for, in their
advanced age, they dedicated themselves to religion, putting
aside every mundane delight and work.[2]

The linking of Lancelot with Guido da Montefeltro
—upon whom he was to pass so terribly different a
judgment in the *Inferno*—shows that, for Dante, the
knight of Arthur was as real and historical a figure
as one of his own contemporaries.

---

[1] *Dictionary of Proper Names and Notable Matters in the Works of
Dante* (art. *Artù*). Cf. *Mort Artu*, ed. Bruce, pp. 243–4; Sommer,
VI, p. 378.
Sir Girflet, or Griflet, is knighted in the *Morte Darthur* (I, 21–2),
where he is "of the age of the king Arthur"; he appears occasionally
later on, but Malory represents him as one of the knights slain in the
rescue of Guinevere by Lancelot and his kinsmen (XX, 8).
[2] *Conv.* iv, 28.

It will have been observed that the romances which Dante can be shown to have known directly are the prose *Tristan*, the Galehaut branch of the *Lancelot*, and the *Mort Artu*. He could hardly have been unacquainted with the mystical element of the Arthurian legend that, for some of us, is its crowning feature; but has the quest of the Holy Grail left any traces in the *Divina Commedia*? There are traditions that place the Grail Castle on an island in the sea. The City of Sarras, the Spiritual Place, is reached by Galahad and his companions in a mystical ship in the *Queste*;[1] in that perplexing Perceval romance, the *Perlesvaus*, Perceval passes away to the region which will ultimately be the place of the Holy Grail in a ship "with the white sail and the red cross thereon, and within were the fairest folk that ever he might behold."[2] Here is, at least, some resemblance with Dante's island mountain of Purgatory, rising out of the ocean and crowned by the Earthly Paradise, and the ship guided by the white-robed and white-winged angel that bears the redeemed souls.[3] The legend of the Holy Grail was certainly associated with that of the Earthly Paradise, and Rajna has urged that "la divina foresta spessa e viva," to which

---

[1] *La Queste del Saint Graal*, ed. Pauphilet, p. 273.

[2] *Perlesvaus*, XXXV, 27. I avail myself of the translation by Sebastian Evans, *The High History of the Holy Grail*, in the "Temple Classics." The French text is in C. Potvin, *Perceval le Gallois ou le Conte du Graal*, I, p. 347. The date of the *Perlesvaus*, and its position in the cycle, is a most debatable question in Arthurian criticism. Cf. Bruce, *Evolution of Arthurian Romance*, II, pp. 145 sq., and J. L. Weston, *The Relative Position of the "Perceval" and "Galahad" Romances*, in *M.L.R.*, XXI (1926), pp. 385–9.

[3] *Purg.* ii, 13–51.

Dante comes at the end of the *Purgatorio*, with its mystical rivers, is reminiscent of the scenery round the Grail Castle in the *Perlesvaus*, and that there is a resemblance between the pageant which he beholds and the apparitions that come and go, the processions of the Grail.[1] Thus, when Lancelot approaches the Grail Castle, "he is come forth of the forest and findeth a right fair meadow-land all loaded with flowers, and a river ran in the midst thereof that was right fair and broad, and there was forest on the one side and the other, and the meadow-lands were wide and far betwixt the river and the forest." And, again, when Perceval has won the castle: "Behind the castle was a river, whereby all good things came to the castle, and this river was right fair and plenteous. Josephus witnesseth us that it came from the Earthly Paradise, and compassed the castle around and ran on through the forest." [2] But it is more probable that the Grail romance would have reached Dante in the Galahad rather than in the Perceval form, and we might, perhaps, trace a parallel between the rebuke to Lancelot in the *Queste*, for having taken upon him "the adventures of spiritual things," and that of Beatrice to Dante: "Come degnasti d' accedere al monte?" [3] To me these resemblances, interesting

---

[1] *Dante e i romanzi della Tavola Rotonda*, pp. 243–6. The attempt of Dr. L. A. Fisher, *The Mystic Vision in the Grail Legend and in the Divina Commedia* (Columbia University Press, 1917), to show that the mystical procession in *Purg.* xxix is a Dantesque rendering of a procession of the Blessed Sacrament, leaves me unconvinced.

[2] *Perlesvaus*, X, 9, XXII, 1–2; Potvin, *op. cit.*, pp. 128, 249. Cf. *Purg.* xxviii; xxxiii, 112–14.

[3] *Purg.* xxx, 73–5. Cf. *La Queste del Saint Graal, ed. cit.*, p. 61: "Lancelot, plus durs que pierre, plus amers que fuz, plus nuz et plus

and suggestive as they are, are not convincing, and I still feel doubtful as to any direct influence of the legend of the Holy Grail on the *Divina Commedia*. The mysticism of Dante seems to me to have a totally different character and colour.

despris que figuiers, coment fus tu si hardiz que tu ou leu ou li Sainz Graalx reperast osas entrer?" Also, with Beatrice's words on the promise of Dante's youth (*Purg.* xxx, 109–20), compare those of the hermit to Lancelot on his perversion of the gifts Our Lord has given him (*Queste*, pp. 68–9). Cf. Malory, XIII, 19–20.

CHAPTER IX

THE "TAVOLA RITONDA"

LORDINGS, this book tells and rehearses fair adventures and great deeds of knighthood and noble tournaments that were done in the time of King Uther Pendragon and the barons of the Old Table, three hundred years and more after the death of our Lord Jesus Christ, son of the true and living God. Also it tells and rehearses other knightly deeds that were done in the time of King Arthur and the valiant knights of the New Table, and especially of Sir Tristan and Sir Lancelot, and Sir Galahad and Sir Palamede, and generally of every knight-errant of the Table, and of knights that were foreigners and from far-off lands who at that time proved their persons in feats of arms. And also we shall set forth the destruction of the Table, which befell through the enterprise of the high quest of the Holy Grail.

Thus opens the most important Arthurian romance written in Italian: the *Tavola Ritonda*, or, to give it its full title: *Il libro delle storie della Tavola Ritonda, e di missere Tristano e di missere Lancilotto e di molti altri cavalieri*.[1] The text, as edited by Polidori, is based upon three manuscripts: the Med. Laur., plut. xliv, cod. 27, which is not earlier than the middle of the fourteenth century, a manuscript of the Biblioteca Nazionale of Florence, dated 1391, and another of the Biblioteca Comunale of Siena, dated 1468. Not even the earliest of these can be

---

[1] *La Tavola Ritonda o l' istoria di Tristano*, ed. F. L. Polidori (two vols., Bologna, 1864–5).

regarded as the prototype.[1] Although Dante is not named, the author or compiler was evidently acquainted with the fifth canto of the *Inferno*. Thus, Dinadan, rebuking Tristan, says: "Io non voglio sottomettere la ragione alla volontà." The love potion was so powerful that "gli condusse ad una morte." The scene on the ship is made to correspond more closely with that of the reading of the book, and Mark's reception of Tristan's dying message to resemble Dante's bearing after he has heard Francesca's words.[2] It is clear that the writer of the *Tavola Ritonda* had read the Francesca episode, recognised its affinity with the Tristan and Iseult story, and accordingly echoed it in the version that he proceeded to give. This does not necessitate a late date for the Italian romance, as there is documentary evidence of the circulation of this portion of the poem before Dante's death. Lines from the third and fifth cantos of the *Inferno* have been found copied in the register of a notary at Bologna in 1317.[3] We are probably safe in holding that the text, as we now have it, took shape in the second quarter of the

[1] Cf. the account of the manuscripts in Polidori's preface, also Parodi's introduction to the *Tristano Riccardiano*. The Cod. Pal. 556 of the Biblioteca Nazionale of Florence, of Venetian origin, dated 1446, mainly derived from the same source as the *Tavola Ritonda*, has a series of 289 pen drawings, valuable for the iconography of the Arthurian legend, some of which are reproduced in the present volume.

[2] *Tavola Ritonda*, pp. 276, 105, 121, 122, 498. Cf. *Inf.* v, 39, 106, 109–111, 127–38.

[3] G. Livi, *Dante, suoi primi cultori, sua gente in Bologna* (Bologna, 1918), pp. 26–7. For evidence that the *Inferno* was known even some years earlier, cf. F. Egidi, *L'argomento barberiniano per la datazione della "Divina Commedia,"* in *Studi romanzi* (1928), XIX.

fourteenth century, without excluding the possibility
that an earlier work in Italian may have been here
elaborated.

There are a number of mysterious allusions to "the
good book which is the fountain of all the stories that
are read of the Table," which had first belonged to
Count Piero of Savoy, and "is now in the possession of
Messer Garo or Gaddo de' Lanfranchi of Pisa." [1]
Mystification as to sources and authorship is in accordance with the tradition of Arthurian literature.   The
writer of the Italian text does not profess to be giving
a translation of this "good book"; he seems to treat it
as a work of reference, appealing to its authority and
occasionally making quotations from it.   Count Piero
of Savoy is presumably the personage who died in
1268; the uncle of Queen Elinor, he was frequently in
England during the reign of Henry III, who made him
Earl of Richmond.   Is this association of an Italian
prince, who had lived in England, with an Arthurian
romance (presumably French) in the possession of a
citizen of Pisa purely fortuitous?   Is it not possible
that the book is the "livre monseigneur Edouart, le
roi d'Engleterre," and that it had been brought to
England by Piero of Savoy, and ultimately passed into
the hands of Gaddo de' Lanfranchi through Rusticiano
da Pisa?

It is obvious that the opening passage is imitated
from the prologue of Rusticiano: "Si orrez toutes les
grans aventures qui advindrent entre les chevaliers
errans du temps au roy Uterpendragon jusques au

---

[1] *Tavola Ritonda*, pp. 46, 105, 115, 117, 431, 442, 495, 501, and
cf. Polidori's introduction, pp. cix-cxv.

temps au roy Artus son fils, et des compaignons de la Table Reonde."[1]   But Rusticiano does not use the phrase "Old Table," which here appears for the first time. This distinction between the "Tavola Vecchia," the "Old Table" in the days of Uther Pendragon, and the "Tavola Nuova," the "New Table" of King Arthur and his knights, is a peculiar feature of the treatment of the Arthurian legend in Italy. Its ultimate source is the episode in the prose version of the *Merlin* of Robert de Boron, where—at the prophet's bidding—Uther Pendragon founded the Round Table with fifty knights chosen by Merlin himself.[2]   The continuation of Robert de Boron presented by the *Huth Merlin*—followed by Malory—makes the Round Table pass from Uther Pendragon to the father of Guinevere, King Leodegrance, by whom it is given as his daughter's dowry to Arthur, the number of Uther's knights having been inexplicably increased from fifty to a hundred and fifty.[3]   The *Merlin* names none of the knights who held seats at the Round Table in the days of Uther, nor does it attribute adventures to them, and the conception of the "Tavola Vecchia" is practically a fusion of Robert de Boron with the *Palamède*. The latter romance gave a new list of characters, belonging in the main to a supposed earlier epoch than that of Arthur. To introduce some kind of unity into their somewhat confused adventures, the notion was adopted of making them

---

[1] Löseth, *op. cit.*, p. 423.

[2] *Merlin*, ed. G. Paris and J. Ulrich (Paris, 1886, the *Huth Merlin*), I, pp. 95–7; Sommer, II, p. 54.

[3] Cf. Paris and Ulrich, *op. cit.*, I, pp. xliii–xliv; II, pp. 61–3; Malory, III, 1–2.

centre round the Table of Uther Pendragon, even though the Table itself plays no part in their stories.[1]

The *Tavola Ritonda* represents an attempt—remotely anticipating that of Malory—to fuse several branches of Arthurian story into a consistent whole. It is the only independent Arthurian cyclic romance in Italian, and draws its matter from various sources, of which some are rehandled with considerable freedom, and others have not as yet been traced.

There is curious matter in the first eleven chapters, which are not found in the earliest of the manuscripts. The first and second relate to the "Tavola Vecchia," to which there are allusions in subsequent parts of the book, and are based upon the *Palamède*. We have the great tournament held by Uther Pendragon in the month of May, in which King Ban and King Bors, King Meliadus, Lamorat, Segurant and Hector le Brun, Brunor (later described as "il fiore della Tavola Vecchia"), and others take part, and "Februe lo Brun" overthrows Uther himself. Guiron, through the false accusation of a damsel whom he has taken from her former knight, is unjustly doomed to the cart of shame and ignominiously driven through all the field. [2]

---

[1] The "Old Table" is practically unknown in English Arthurian literature. Apart from traces in the first and third books of Malory, and in the *Avowynge of Sir Bawdewyn* (see below), the only reflection of it seems to be the short fifteenth-century poem *Sir Cleges*. Sir Cleges "in the tyme of kynge Uter" was one of the Round Table: "A dowtyar was not of dedes | Of the round tabull ryght" (in H. Weber, *Metrical Romances*, Edinburgh, 1810, I, p. 331).

[2] Cf. Löseth, *Le Tristan et le Palamède des manuscrits de Rome et de Florence* pp. 89–94, where, however, there is considerable difference in the knights who are present, and Galehaut

When the tournament is ended, the tale passes to speak of the New Table and King Arthur, to tell especially of Tristan and Lancelot, the former being "the fountain and foundation of knighthood."

A brief account of the descent and history of the kings of Cornwall and Liones, until the two crowns were united in the person of Felix, comes—with considerable variations—from the beginning of the prose *Tristan*. As in the *Tristano Riccardiano*, Mark and Meliadus are brothers. Episodes from the early history of Lancelot serve as an introduction to the marriage of which Tristan is to be the offspring. In Great Britain, only Meliadus and Galehaut refuse homage to Arthur. The latter's ally, King Ban, has died at the sight of the burning of his city of Benoic. His wife, Constance, follows him to the grave, after giving birth to Lancelot, who is brought up by the Lady of the Lake. When he is fifteen years old, the Lady of the Lake sends him to Arthur's court. On the way, he meets three knights—Gawain, Kay, and Erec—whom, in their shining armour, he at first worships as gods or angels: a motive which seems derived from some version of the story of Perceval. At the royal banquet at Camelot, a dumb damsel speaks for the only time, and reveals that the newcomer is the son of King Ban, and he is knighted with great honour. Lancelot and Queen Guinevere fall

le Brun plays the part here assigned to Segurant. The *Tavola Ritonda* throughout confuses Brunor, of the Castle of Pleur, with Branor le Brun, the "Old Knight" in Rusticiano. "Februe" is probably the son of Galehaut le Brun, but his presence at this tournament is a manifest impossibility. Lamorat ("lo Gallese," son of Pellinor) is here confused with his uncle, Lamorat de Listenois.

in love with each other, but the matter goes no
further for the present. Lancelot leaves the court to
achieve the adventure of Dolorous Gard, which he
conquers and changes its name to Joyous Gard,
building there a church called "Santa Maria del-
l' Umiltà"—a touch singularly in accord with his
character all through the Arthuriad.[1] He is at
Joyous Gard, when he hears that Arthur is hard
pressed by Meliadus and Galehaut. Hastening to
his succour in disguise, he is so absorbed at the sight
of Guinevere that he lets his horse go where it will.
The queen sends him a lance and a garland, bidding
him fight against the forces of Meliadus. His horse is
killed under him; summoned by Meliadus and Galehaut
to surrender, he accepts a new horse and lance from
the latter, undertaking to fight against Arthur's folk
until the lance is broken, on the condition that the
"haut prince" will give him a gift that he will ask.
Arthur and his army are driven from the field, when
Lancelot calls upon Galehaut to fulfil his promise by
submitting himself to the king. Meliadus consents
to make peace while preserving his own liberty.
Lancelot then reveals himself, and the peace is con-
firmed by the marriage of Meliadus with Eliabella,
who is represented as the niece of Arthur and a kins-
woman of Lancelot himself. Lancelot now becomes
the lover of Guinevere, but neither Galehaut nor the
Lady of Malehaut plays any part in the matter, though
Lancelot's imprisonment by the latter has been

[1] Lancelot's humility appears again and again, as in the coming
of Galahad and the combat at the rock of Merlin, and, characteristically, he accuses himself at the last, "mine orgule and my pride"
(Malory, XXI, 11).

previously mentioned.[1] It is noteworthy that the first part of the *Lancelot* is comparatively scantily represented in Italian, and the best-known episode in the story of Galehaut is given only by Dante.

With the marriage of Meliadus and Eliabella is woven the story of Messer Ferragunze. He is a knight of small stature who, with his beautiful wife Verseria, has previously been in charge of the bride. To the two kings he makes a "vaunt" of four things: he is of noble race; he has never feared a knight or even two; he was never jealous of his wife; he was never overcome by wine. Meliadus and Arthur put the last three vaunts to the test. Meliadus sends him on a mission to a certain castle, arranging an ambush of twenty-four knights to intercept and threaten him with death. He forces his way through, but, when reporting the result of his mission to the king, says nothing about it. His boasted sobriety is next tested at a banquet. Finally, Arthur summons him to play chess, and, in the middle of the game, bets the queen's girdle to Verseria's that he is winning. Ferragunze goes for his wife's girdle, Arthur having previously arranged that he shall find Gawain making love to her. In the meantime, the king changes a pawn on the board, to try if the knight

---

[1] Capp. v–ix. The motives corresponding with those in the prose *Lancelot* (cf. Lot, *op. cit.*, pp. 308–11, and Bruce, II, pp. 324–31) are strangely modified in the Italian, the Joyous Gard episode being completely changed. The association of Meliadus with Galehaut in war upon Arthur seems peculiar to the *Tavola Ritonda*, for the purpose of the marriage that is to make Tristan and Lancelot kinsmen. Is it possible that the Italian is derived from the *Lancelot* of the pseudo Robert de Boron cycle, the existence of which is maintained by Dr. Brugger?

will be too angry to notice it. Ferragunze finds
his lady with Gawain "in grande druderia." He
calmly says: "Dame, toss me over the key of your
wardrobe"; and, returning in high good humour to the
game, at once detects the altered position of the pawn.
Questioned by the kings, he explains the cause of his
vaunt. He has learned to have no fear of death,
because once, at the time when Uther Pendragon died
and he formed part of the garrison of Liones, he was
going secretly to speak with a lady he loved, taking a
squire behind him on his horse. The guard, whose
challenge he had ignored, hurled a lance which missed
him and killed his companion. This convinced him
that each man is appointed to live until the time deter-
mined for his death. Again, he was defending a
castle against the Saracens, having under him five
hundred and sixty knights and a thousand infantry,
with whom was one single woman. The coming of
another woman, who had been taken prisoner, so
aroused the jealousy of the first that she was with
difficulty restrained from killing her as a rival. How,
then, could he expect his wife to be content with him
alone? If she is good, he can be sure of her; if not,
jealousy will not make her good. For the rest, physical
considerations have taught him sobriety, and, as for
nobility (though himself of high lineage), "gentile
può essere ogni persona che ha belli atti e costumi, e
dolce parlare fa gentilezza." [1]

This story closely resembles an English metrical
romance of the fifteenth century: *The Avowynge of
Sir Bawdewyn.* Sir Baudwin—who is a familiar

[1] Capp. x–xi.

figure in Malory—avows that he will never be jealous
of his wife, nor dread death for any threat of king or
knight. At Kay's instigation, Arthur agrees to put
him to the proof. Kay waylays him with a band of
armed men threatening death, but Baudwin calmly
defeats them and says nothing about it to the king.
He is sent out hunting, and it is arranged that, on
his return, he shall find his lady in a compromising
position with another knight, while the king plays
chess. Baudwin is absolutely unmoved. He explains the matter to the king. In the days of Arthur's
father, he had to defend a castle against the Saracens,
with more than five hundred men and three women.
Two of the women for jealousy slew the third, and
then one of the survivors murdered the other. The
moral appears to be that it is useless to contend with
a woman's will. The castle was closely besieged.
In a sally one of the defenders turned coward
and was killed by chance, while those who fought
remained unhurt. This convinced Baudwin that
death comes to each at its appointed time, and it
is useless to try to evade it.[1] A common French
source for the Italian "vaunt" and the English

<hr />

[1] *The Avowynge of King Arthur, Sir Gawan, Sir Kaye, and Sir
Bawdewyn of Bretan*, stanzas lviii–lxxii, in *Three Early English
Metrical Romances*, edited by J. Robson (London, 1842). The title
of the poem is due to the editor. Different versions of the motive
of the men and women in the besieged castle are found in a French
fabliau (Montaiglon, *Recueil général des Fabliaux des xiiie et xiv[e]
siècles*, I, xxvi) and in the *Poetria* of Joannes de Garlandia. Cf.
Gaston Paris, *Romans en vers du cycle de la Table Ronde (Histoire
Littéraire de France*, XXX, pp. 111–13; E. A. Greenlaw, *The Vows of
Balduin*, in *Publications of the M.L.A.A.*, XXI (1906); G. L.
Kittredge, *The Avowing of Arthur*, in *M.L.N.*, VIII, pp. 502–3.
The connection was first pointed out by Parodi.

M

"avowing" seems probable, but it has not yet been traced.

The text now, for a while, follows the same redaction as the *Tristano Riccardiano* with some modifications (xii–xlvi). On his way back to Cornwall after his first visit to Ireland, Tristan is driven by winds to the shores of Liones, where he avenges the death of his father. The episode of the cloven shield is altered so as to make it refer to Tristan and Iseult, who are exalted above Lancelot and Guinevere. In the scene on the ship, it is Gouvernal who, in anger at his mistake, scatters the remains of the love potion which the dog laps up; we are told that it henceforth never left the lovers, and, after their burial, was found dead upon the grave on the third day.[1] But, at the point where Tristan, after he has been wounded with the poisoned dart, is counselled by Brangwain to go to Brittany, the tale takes a different turn, and episodes are interpolated to bring Lancelot upon the scene.

Tristan writes a letter which so moves Mark that he allows him to stay in the castle of Cornasin until Brangwain heals him of his wound, and he can ride every day to Tintagel and see from afar the tower in which Iseult is imprisoned (xlvii–xlviii). Lancelot, coming to Cornwall to see Tristan whom as yet he knows and loves only by repute, encounters him too absorbed in thinking of Iseult to return his

[1] Cap. xxxiv. So in *Sir Tristrem* (ll. 1693–4): "Thai loued with all her might | And Hodain dede al so." In the *Tristan* manuscript Fr. 103 (Bédier, *Romania*, XV, p. 509), "Heudent le chien" is found watching and mourning by the tomb, and taken by Gouvernal and Brangwain to Liones.

greeting. There is an admirable verbal altercation, followed by the inevitable combat until the two reveal their names. Lancelot induces Mark to make peace with Tristan and release Iseult from her tower in order to heal their wounds. The result is a fresh attempt on the part of the king to surprise the lovers, and its frustration by Lancelot.[1] Lancelot returns to Camelot, where he is surprised in the queen's chamber by Sir Daniel (a brother of Dinadan) and thirty knights. Guinevere is sentenced to the fire, but rescued by Lancelot and his kinsmen, who convey her to Joyous Gard where they are besieged by Arthur. This is obviously a new version of the great scene in the *Mort Artu*, introduced at this stage of the romance (and involving another siege in its proper place) for the exaltation of Tristan, who now comes to the rescue, throws himself into Joyous Gard, and (assisted by Lancelot's surely most uncharacteristic threat to hang his prisoners) induces Arthur to pardon both Lancelot and the queen. This is the first time that Tristan has met Arthur or Guinevere (l). Lancelot renounces all rights in Joyous Gard, which is given by Arthur to Tristan. Mark's fears being thereby increased, he imprisons Iseult again; Tristan's wound grows worse, and he now goes to Brittany.

The story now (li–lxii) follows the same version as the *Tristano Riccardiano*, with Tristan's exploits in Brittany, his marriage, adventures in the Forest Perilous, and deliverance of Arthur, but includes the

---

[1] Cap. xlix. Much of this seems a considerably altered version of the release of Tristan by Lancelot at a later stage in the prose *Tristan*. Cf. Löseth, sects. 289–92.

episode from Thomas, which we have already found
in the lyrics of Giacomo da Lentino, of the "salle
aux images."[1]   The two companions of the Round
Table associated with Kay in the forest are Agravaine and Gareth.[2]   In the account of the liberation
of Arthur, there is a long and voluptuous description
of the "Palagio del grande Disio" with its history; its
lady, the sorceress and would-be murderess of the
king, being "Elergia." She is the daughter of the
Lady of Vallone, "who by art had raised this palace,
thinking to repose therein with the prophet Merlin
and have him at her pleasure; but Merlin, who knew
a bit more of the art than she, deceived her and sent
her to dwell in the island of Vallone in the Syrian
sea."[3]

After the meeting with Perceval (the point at which
the *Tristano Riccardiano* broke off), we have the
friendly reception of Tristan and Kahedyn at Tintagel,
Mark's hostility having been temporarily allayed by
his nephew's marriage and letter.[4]   Then follows a
long interpolation of five chapters, ultimately derived
from Thomas, but not preserved in the extant fragments of his poem, though contained in the works
based upon it, and here naturally rehandled by the

[1] Cap. liv. Cf. Bédier, I, pp. 309–14.

[2] The writer seems fond of Agravaine, whom he has previously
(absurdly) introduced as one of Tristan's allies against Mark.

[3] Cap. lix. The "dama dell' isola di Vallone" is no doubt the
"Dame d'Avalon" of the *Prophecies de Merlin*, and the Italian
writer so freely changes characters and corrupts names that Elergia
may possibly be meant for Aglentine (Esglantine). Cf. above, p. 105.

[4] In the prose *Tristan* (Löseth, sects. 75–7), Mark is left in ignorance
of his nephew's coming, and believes that he is still in Brittany.
So in Malory, IX, 17.

Italian writer or his more immediate source. There is first the scene in the garden, followed by the ugly episode of the blood-letting, the strewing of the floor with flour, and Tristan's leap upon the queen's bed. Then the ordeal of Iseult's chastity — here in two stages: the queen's oath at the "Red Rock," and the grasping of the red-hot iron. The device by which Iseult is able to swear without perjuring herself—Tristan, disguised as a pilgrim, having helped her to disembark and held her closely embraced—is here suggested, not by herself (as in the *Saga* and other derivatives of Thomas), but by Tristan; and the writer characteristically doubles the part played by the latter, making him reappear as a madman and kiss her—a motive derived from one of the French poems of the *Folie Tristan* in which the hero comes to Mark's court as a pretended madman. At the court of a duke —here called Bramante—Tristan wins the fairy dog "Petitto Araviuto" (Petit Creu) as guerdon for slaying the giant Urgan. At the advice of Mariadoco (the Meriadoc of the Thomas derivatives, where he is the first to arouse Mark's suspicions before the garden scene), Tristan and Iseult are banished and live together in the wilderness, where Mark finds them sleeping with a sword between them, and leaves his glove on Iseult's face to defend her against the sun. Convinced of their innocence, the king slays Mariadoco and summons the lovers back to his court.[1]

This singularly incongruous interpolation of what

[1] Capp. lxiii–lxvii. Cf. Bédier, I, pp. 198–247; Loomis, *The Romance of Tristan and Ysolt*, pp. 154–82; Parodi, p. lxxxviii. The insertion of these chapters, or at least the four later ones, at this late stage of the story is, of course, dramatically absurd.

we may take as Thomas has interrupted the course of
the story. The author now returns to the prose
Tristan, portions of which he freely rehandles. We
have Kahedyn's hopeless love for Iseult and Tristan's
consequent madness. Mark discovers the madman
in the desert and has him brought to Tintagel, where
(another of the writer's characteristic reduplications)
he is recognised not only by Iseult's brachet, "which
had shared the love potion," but also by his horse.
On his recovery he is again banished from Cornwall,
Iseult giving him as a parting gift a ring that she had
received from Galehaut as a protection against
enchantment (lxviii–lxxii). Tristan is accompanied
by Dinadan (as in the French romance), and also by a
young squire, Alcardo, the brother of Iseult, a personage peculiar to this text, who now takes the place of
Gouvernal (who has been made King of Liones), and is
apparently introduced as a companion figure to the
brother of the other Iseult, Kahedyn, who is dying in
Brittany. The Italian writer takes a special delight
in the humours of Dinadan, "il savio disamorato";
the scene of the debate between him and his companions on the subject of love is excellent, and there
is a comic episode, in which he is dismayed by a
damsel who pretends to be enamoured of him, which is
in the spirit of Boccaccio and evidently a fresh invention (lxxiii–lxxv). The slaying of Osenain Cuer Hardi
(Suziano Cuore Ardito) by Tristan (lxxvii) seems
peculiar to the Italian text. From the prose *Tristan*
comes the reception of the hero by Morgan le Fay in
her castle, her giving him the shield designed to shame
Arthur and Guinevere which he is to bear at the

tournament (with the lie that it had belonged to her father, Uther Pendragon, and she does not know the meaning of the figures), Tristan slaying her paramour Onesun (Huneson, Malory's Sir Hemison), Morgan drawing the end of the lance from the wound and placing on the tomb the promise that Tristan will die a more painful death by the same weapon.[1] But an entirely new figure is introduced in the person of "Gaia Pulcella," the daughter of Morgan and Onesun, whom Tristan sees at the castle and whom her mother offers, half jestingly, to him as wife, telling him that Iseult of the White Hands is dead: "For grief at your departure she fell sick and died thereof". Tristan meets her would-be lover, Burletta della Diserta, who —with unusually gross details—relates how he had carried her off and was about to ravish her when Lancelot intervened, and, while they fought, her father had arrived and taken her away "cosìe pura com' ella era di prima." Tristan takes the quarrel upon himself, compels Burletta to become his prisoner, and the latter throws himself from his horse into a river and is drowned rather than fall into the hands of Lancelot (lxxxi). Here—as in other peculiar episodes that appear as complete in themselves in the *Tavola Ritonda*—we have probably the matter preserved of a lost popular narrative poem, of the type that in Italy preceded the cantari.

Tristan's exploits at the tournament of the "Rocca dura" where he bears Morgan's shield, his encounter with Arthur and Ivain, and the revelation of his identity to the king by Lamorat (lxxxii), do not

[1] Cap. lxxx. Cf. Löseth, sects. 190-1, and Malory, IX, 41-3.

differ, save in details and names of personages, from
the French *Tristan*.[1] A remarkable episode follows,
partly based upon one found at a later stage in the
French romance, where Tristan accompanied by
Palamede, after sundry dealings with a knight who
gives him hospitality and tries to compel him to
tell his name, comes to the "Tour du pin rond," the
lord of which has defeated many of the best knights,
and made them write their names on their shields
which he has hung round the battlements of his
tower.[2] But here Palamede does not appear, and the
unnamed knight of the tower becomes the giant
Carados—evidently the Carados of the Dolorous
Tower, in the prose *Lancelot*, who abducts Gawain,
and is slain by Lancelot. The tower is here the
"Torre vittoriosa," and Carados is represented as
"a knight of the Old Table," a most chivalrous
personage who takes his defeat at Tristan's hands in
an edifying spirit, composes a suitable inscription for
his own shield, and finally retires to the desert of
Darnantes where he becomes a monk.[3]

It is expressly stated that Carados has no "arte
d' incantamento," but things are otherwise with Lasancis, whose story is the sequel to Tristan's deliverance of Arthur from the "Palagio del grande Disio"
in the Forest Perilous, and who is "uno pro cavalier

---

[1] Cf. Löseth, sects. 192, 192a; Malory, IX, 43, X, 1.

[2] Cf. Löseth, sects. 461–66. The name of Tristan's host in the
present text, Adanain or Danain, was clearly suggested by that of
Danain le Roux in the *Palamède*.

[3] Capp. lxxxiii–lxxxvi. For the Dolorous Tower episode, cf.
Sommer, IV, pp. 112 sq., 128–37, and the brief account in Malory,
VIII, 28.

della Tavola Vecchia." Lasancis is the uncle of
Elergia and her brothers whom the king and Tristan
slew, and he has been sent from the island of Vallone
by their mother to avenge their deaths and destroy
the whole Round Table. The lady has provided
him with enchanted armour and a magic lance, the
slightest touch of which will immediately overthrow
an opponent. According to her instructions, Lasancis
takes up his quarters in the guest palace outside
Camelot for thirty days, and, beginning with Ivain,
overthrows all the flower of the Round Table, including Arthur himself and Lancelot, and imprisons
them in the hall of the palace with the intention of
burning the place and the prisoners together. But
Guinevere with four damsels goes in search of Tristan,
whom she meets on the borders of Gascony, and a
holy hermit warns him of the enchantment that he
has to face. Tristan contrives to fight Lasancis without the latter being able to use his lance, and compels
him to surrender and confession. In spite of the
protests of Arthur and Lancelot, Tristan contents
himself with destroying the lance, and having Lasancis imprisoned in the guest palace for the rest of
his life. Arthur raises a column of white marble in
commemoration, and has a new guest palace built.[1]

Tristan now returns to Cornwall (there is no
previous reconciliation with Mark at Arthur's intervention, as in the French and in Malory); he goes to
Iseult disguised as a priest, is taken with her in the

[1] Cap. lxxxvii. Here, again, we are clearly dealing with a lost
popular narrative poem, the matter of which the compiler has transformed into his own prose as he had done with portions of Thomas.

bed - chamber, and both are imprisoned (lxxxviii).
Perceval, guided by Dinas the seneschal, defeats
Andred and two other knights and Mark himself,
and compels the king to release Tristan, who—while
Mark and Andred are temporarily imprisoned in
their turn—carries off Iseult by sea. Tristan, disguised as a monk, is bringing his lady through the
kingdom of Logres, when they meet Lancelot, on his
way to the rescue, who now becomes enamoured of
Iseult, and the two knights fight until mutual recogni-
tion comes by means of Alcardo (lxxxix). Near
Camelot, in the presence of Arthur, Tristan—concealing his identity—overthrows Gawain (the motive
of whose strength becoming threefold "in fra la
sesta e la nona" is borrowed from the *Mort Artu*),
Mordred, Agravaine, and others, and is finally
brought by Lancelot to Joyous Gard, where Alcardo
is knighted and takes the name of Lantris (xc).[1]

The next nine chapters (xci–xcix) deal with various
episodes leading up to and centring round the great
tournament at Verzeppe (Lonazep). We have Pala-

---

[1] It is during this stay of Tristan in Cornwall that the prose *Tristan*
places the deliverance of Mark from Elias and the Saxons, and the
scene between Tristan and Iseult in the garden (Löseth, sect. 282).
The lovers are surprised sleeping together (sect. 285), the king
ultimately taking Tristan by means of a drugged potion (sect. 287,
cf. Malory, X, 50). The release of Tristan by Lancelot has been
already utilised in the Italian text. In the French, he is again
imprisoned and then released by Perceval (sect. 317, cf. Malory,
X, 51), and it is after this that Tristan and Iseult leave Cornwall in
the "nef de joie" (sects. 323–4), to which there is no allusion in
our text. The encounter with Lancelot is naturally peculiar to the
Tavola Ritonda, in accordance with the purpose, apparent throughout, of exalting Tristan above him. For the overthrow of Gawain
and other knights, cf. Löseth, p. 253, and Malory, X, 56.

mede pursuing the Questing Beast, the trick played
upon Perceval and Hector de Maris and Erec by Breus,
when he is flying from Blioberis, the reconciliation
of Palamede with Tristan, Iseult's practical joking
with Dinadan. The gorgeous cavalcade with which
Tristan brings Iseult to Lonazep is clearly the invention of the Italian writer, who elaborates the
real or pretènded cowardice of Dinadan, and his
japes at the expense of better knights which seem
highly appreciated by the victims; but, in the main,
these episodes are only slightly modified from the
French *Tristan*.[1] The actual tournament, however,
is considerably altered. Tristan is the hero throughout, and his final passing over to the party of Arthur
has been previously arranged with the king and
Lancelot. There is no hint of jealousy or treachery
on the part of Palamede, who acts as a loyal and
devoted friend of Tristan throughout. Guinevere
herself is present at the tournament, and thus brought
into personal relations with Iseult, the two queens
exchanging crowns and mantles in pledge of mutual
love when they part.[2] Amoroldo or Amoroldino,
the young king of Ireland who leads the party opposed
to that of Arthur, is the son of the famous Morholt;
he had been knighted by Tristan on his second visit

[1] Cf. Löseth, sects. 352, 353, 355-8, 361, 363, 364, 368-70. Lancelot finds the court mourning for news of the deaths of Lamorat and
Adriano (Driant), but the dramatic story of the former's death at
the hands of Mordred and his brothers is not given.

[2] Guinevere and Iseult never actually meet in the *Tristan* or in
Malory. See the charming passage in the latter, X, 81, where
Guinevere (who has been absent through illness) hears the results of
the tournament and delights in the praises of Iseult's beauty. For
the tournament, cf. Löseth, sects. 378-81, and Malory, X, 65-80.

to Ireland, and made heir to that kingdom,[1] and
Tristan's constant aid and protection of the son of
the man he slew is a pleasant feature of our romance.
Arthur has statues set up of Tristan, Lancelot, Palamede, and the young Irish king in the meadow in
front of Lonazep, to which afterwards that of Galahad was added. In after years Charlemagne saw
the five images, and declared that Arthur deserved
his fate since, with five such knights, he ought to
have conquered the world. Only the Danish paladin
Ogier could wield the sword of Tristan, which, having
been shortened, was called "Cortana." The Emperor
kept the sword of Galahad for himself, Oliver having
that of Lancelot, Rinaldo that of Amoroldo, while
Palamede's weapon fell to Ildusnamo of Bavaria.
This is a variation of a passage in the *Tristan* where,
however, there are only four statues (the younger
Morholt not being included), and Charlemagne takes
only the swords of Tristan and Palamede, giving
that of Tristan to Ogier, and keeping that of Palamede for himself.[2]

At intervals in our romance appears the motive
of the enmity between Lancelot and Brunor lo Bruno,
the varlet of "La Cote Male Taile" (brother of Dinadan
and Daniel), on account of the slaying of Sir Daniel.
It is now linked to a series of episodes considerably
modified from the *Tristan*. The two meet at the
court of the Duke of Dusbergo (Handebourc), and
arrange to fight within ten days. Brunor borrows

---

[1] *Tavola Ritonda*, p. 114.

[2] Löseth, sect. 440. For "Cortaine," the sword of Tristan, cf.
above, p. 15. According to the orthodox tradition, it was shortened
because even the gigantic Danish paladin found it too long.

Tristan's arms, and fights with Lancelot (letting him believe that he is Tristan) until the duke intervenes, when he returns to Joyous Gard reporting that he has been engaged with a stranger (c). In revenge, Lancelot, with Bors, Hector, and Blioberis, disguises himself and attacks Tristan at Joyous Gard, where the latter is supported by Dinadan, Palamede, and Brunor. The battle lasts until Tristan recognises Lancelot, when there is a general reconciliation—the episode fitly closing with the japery of Dinadan, for whom the conversion of Palamede to Christianity seems a fruitful theme for mirth.[1] But Gawain stirs up fresh misunderstandings between Lancelot and Tristan, with the result that, when a war breaks out between Amoroldo of Ireland and Alois of Norgalles for the possession of a castle, Lancelot with his kinsmen takes arms for the King of Norgalles, Tristan and his friends for the Irish king. There is a general engagement between the two armies, Tristan and Lancelot each bent upon slaying the other, the latter's life saved only by the succour of his kinsmen. To stop further slaughter, the King of Norgalles proposes that the issue shall be decided in single combat between him and his rival, but Tristan demands that he and Lancelot shall represent the two kings. Hector and Lionel send a messenger to Arthur, who despatches Mordred and Ivain with a large force of knights to compel the cessation of hostilities. Lancelot (who throughout is the weaker, and is glad of Arthur's intervention) and Tristan refuse to be reconciled, until the king persuades the

---

[1] Cap. ci. Cf. Löseth, sects. 478, 489, 490.

latter to send for Iseult. Iseult and Guinevere make Tristan sit between them, and induce him to agree to a full peace with Lancelot. This time it is lasting, and the two set out on adventures together.[1]

The text now leaves the *Tristan* and introduces episodes from unknown sources. The two companions meet "an ancient knight of more than a hundred and seventy years," who introduces himself as a knight of the Old Table, Segurant le Brun, whose name is familiar to Tristan as that of "the Knight of the Dragon," "the mightiest warrior that King Uther Pendragon had in his court." But he is more friendly to the younger generation than were some of his compeers, and is happy to joust with Tristan in order to know whether he is as fine a jouster as was his father, King Meliadus. Tristan and Segurant overthrow each other, horse and man; when the old knight recovers, he borrows his opponent's horse, and overthrows Lancelot, who takes it rather ill (cv). Later, we hear that Segurant is dead; "and it was believed by some that he died of the fall he received when he jousted with Tristan." [2] It is impossible to reconcile this version of Segurant's end with what we learn of him in the *Palamède* and the *Prophecies de Merlin*, and it would seem that the writer invented the episode in order to represent the best knight of the Old Table finding at last his match in Tristan.

---

[1] Capp. cii-civ. Cf. the various French versions in Löseth, pp. 342–7. The French knows nothing of the initial malice of Gawain (who acts as Arthur's peace emissary), and naturally nothing of the intervention of the two queens, whose mutual relations are peculiar to our text.

[2] Cap. cxi.

TRISTAN AND LANCELOT IN THE HOUSE OF THE LADY OF THE LAKE
Florence, Biblioteca Nazionale, Cod. Pal. 556

The long story that follows (cvi–cvii)—how the Lady of the Lake, by a series of magical devices, gets Tristan and Lancelot, Iseult and Guinevere into her power, and entertains them in her enchanted pavilion for a fortnight—is probably drawn from some lost narrative poem of the "Breton lay" or cantare type.

On the authority of the "mastri delle storie," the tale now turns to the quest of the Holy Grail. It is naturally a "Tristan form" of the Grail story that we are given, combining an abbreviation of portions of the Vulgate *Queste* with adventures of Tristan.[1] As a version of the quest, it is the least significant part of the *Tavola Ritonda*, except perhaps for one episode.

It begins with the begetting and birth of Galahad (Galasso), whose mother is "la donzella Perevida" or "Provida" (it will be remembered that the name "Elaine" is peculiar to Malory). The knighting of Galahad by Lancelot, the filling of the Siege Perilous, and the entry of the Holy Grail into the palace (it is covered with red, instead of white, samite) are much the same as in the *Queste* and in Malory, save that Tristan is present and is contrasted with Galahad as the most perfect type of mundane chivalry. Tristan is among the first to vow himself to the quest, and, when the knights separate, he accompanies Lancelot. Galahad's acquisition of the shield of Joseph of Arimathea is summed up in a few sentences (cviii–cx). The first adventures of Lancelot and Tristan introduce characters harking back to the days of the Old Table, apparently the author's own invention—like the

---

[1] Cf. J. L. Weston, *The Quest of the Holy Grail*, pp. 26–7; Löseth, pp. 278 sq.

unfortunate Gabrionello who through fear has become the liegeman of a giant (cxi, cxii). A somewhat maimed and misplaced version of the agreement of Tristan and Palamede to meet at the rock of Merlin, with the consequent combat between the former and Lancelot, leads to a remarkable episode.

Tristan and Lancelot enter the Dark Valley, where they come to the castle of the Felon Knight, a magician who has five times the strength combined of any knights with whom he engages in combat. He is small of stature, mounted upon a black horse, and fights in silence with an iron mace. He stuns Tristan, and carries off Lancelot to his castle to join his other prisoners. Tristan recovers his senses and is proceeding to the rescue, when he meets a lady on horseback who tells him that she is the daughter of Lancelot, dwelling in the forest to do penance, and has come to show him how to defeat the Felon Knight: "Before the gate there is a waste chapel where there is a small Crucifix. Do thou enter therein, and promise God to sin no more with Queen Iseult; and then go confidently to the battle, and, at every stroke that the knight shall smite upon thee, do thou straightway say: Christ crucified, help me; and, for every time that thou shalt say it, he will lose the strength of one knight." Thus instructed, Tristan overthrows the Felon Knight, spares his life on his declaration that the prisoners can only be delivered by his hands, and drags him into the castle where he appears to be dead. Mysterious hands light torches, lay a banquet, and lead Tristan— still dragging the Felon Knight with him—into a chamber where there are two rich beds of silk. Tris-

tan, fully armed, rests on one, making the Felon Knight
his pillow. He sees what appears to be the figure of
Brangwain moving about the chamber, and hears the
voice of Iseult calling him to the empty bed. He
springs up and is about to enter it, when thunder is
heard, the whole palace quakes, the bed seems all
burning, and a voice says: "Tristan, you are deceived."
The Felon Knight is on his feet again, but Tristan—
with an act of contrition and calling again upon
Christ—cuts off his hand. He spares his life on condition of his being baptised and holding the castle for
King Arthur; Lancelot and the other captives, including fourteen of the Grail questers, are released.[1]

Here the motives of the "Waste Chapel" and the
"Perilous Bed" are familiar and primitive. Lancelot's daughter, elsewhere unknown, plays a part somewhat similar to that of the hermit Ogrin in Béroul's
poem, and Tristan's repentance—however transient—
may possibly hark back to the same source.[2] I would
conjecture that we have here the matter of another
lost narrative lay, introduced and, perhaps, modified to
match the temptations endured by the regular Grail
questers, Bors and Perceval, as also Lancelot's resolution, after he has been admonished by the hermit, to
amend his life.

The two knights—after another adventure together
—part company; Tristan abandons the quest of the
Holy Grail in order to return to the queen, while

[1] Capp. cxiii–cxiv. In the Cod. Pal. 556 of the Biblioteca
Nazionale, Tristan slays the Felon Knight.
[2] Cf. Béroul, *Le Roman de Tristan*, ed. E. Muret (*ed. cit.*), ll. 1378 sq.,
2185–8, and E. Vinaver, *The Love Potion in the Primitive Tristan
Romance*, in *Medieval Studies in Memory of G. S. Loomis*, pp. 84–6.

N

Lancelot's experiences in the quest—those wonderful episodes reproduced for us from the French text by Malory—are reduced to a few colourless sentences, but with the noteworthy peculiarity that we have here again the appearance of the stag, though not as Grail bearer:

Tristan . . . was far more desirous of seeing Queen Iseult than of sitting at the Holy Table even as the twelve knights sat who were without thought of carnal sin, and without hate or pride . . . And know that the thought and desire of seeing Iseult took from Tristan the grace of beholding and of perceiving; and, but for that, he would have been, for his loyalty and courtesy, of the first to behold and to taste the grace of the Holy Vessel. And, when Lancelot departed from Tristan, he went straight to the castle of Corbenic, to be there where the knights of the Table should be; but, because he had his heart occupied with other things, the true semblance was veiled from him. Nevertheless he was at last at the spiritual palace, and there fell in a swoon and lay as a dead man twenty-four days, even as he had been in the sin of dis- ordered lust twenty-four years; and he perceived so far that he saw a stag borne by four angels; which stag became a child of human flesh, and afterwards returned into its own figure of a stag as it was at first. And, at the end of twenty- four days, Lancelot recovered his senses.[1]

We have another adventure of Tristan on his way to Joyous Gard; he has killed a young knight who challenged him to joust, is imprisoned, and about to be beheaded by the latter's father, but delivered —after some hesitation—by Palamede.[2] The story now turns to Perceval, Bors, and Galahad, whose adventures are an abbreviation of the Vulgate *Queste* with a few unimportant modifications. Perceval

[1] Cap. cxv.
[2] Cap. cxvi. A part of this story, but somewhat different, is in the *Tristan*. Cf. Löseth, sect. 445, and p. 305, n. 2.

LANCELOT AT THE CASTLE OF CORBENIC
Florence, Biblioteca Nazionale, Cod. Pal. 556

comes to the hermitage of the former Queen of the
Waste Lands—here called his sister,[1] but not confused with the maiden "suora carnale" who appears
later—from whom he hears of his mother's death
and the story of the three Tables. He is rescued
from the twenty knights by Galahad, has the adventure of the demon horse, intervenes between the lion
and the serpent, is tempted by the fiendish damsel of
the black ship, enters the white ship at the bidding
of the old man. Bors confesses to the hermit, has
the vision of the Pelican, is entertained by the
oppressed lady (whose cause, however, he does not
undertake), dreams of the two birds, refrains from
rescuing Lionel in order to save the damsel, and sees
the false semblance of his brother dead. He is
tempted by the twelve seeming damsels of the tower.
A hermit expounds these matters, and assures him
that Lionel is living. The wonderful scene of his
meeting with Lionel [2]—surely, as retold by Malory,
one of the great things of literature—does not occur.
Bors joins Perceval on the ship covered with white
samite. The tale turns to Galahad with his coming
to an abbey, and, in virtue of his pure virginity,
quenching the fires that torment a dead man.[3]
Departing thence, he meets Perceval's sister—here
called Agrestizia—who brings him to the seaboard
to the ship where Bors and her brother are waiting.
They are borne to the Ship of Solomon, where

---

[1] At least in the printed text; she is his aunt in the Cod. Pal. 556.

[2] Cf. F. Lot, *Étude sur le Lancelot en prose*, pp. 104–5. The episode
was in the archetype, as it appears in the Cod. Pal. 556.

[3] A confusion of the episode of the tomb of Simeon, here out of
its proper order. Cf. *Queste, ed. cit.*, p. 264; Malory, XVII, 18.

Agrestizia explains the wonders on board, and, with
the belt made out of her own hair, girds Galahad
with the Sword with the Strange Hangings. There is
no hint of the beautiful speech with which we are
familiar from Malory: "Now reck I not though I
die, for now I hold me one of the blessed maidens of
the world, which hath made the worthiest knight of
the world." [1] Then follows the story of the wicked
sons of Count "Erveus" (Hernolx), and the injunction,
here uttered by the count himself before his death, to
go and heal the Maimed King. The episode of the
stag and the four lions is omitted, the story passing
straight to the "Castello Aspetta Ventura" and the
self-immolation of Perceval's sister, somewhat modified from the *Queste*. The three pass to the castle
of Corbenic, the mending of the broken sword, the
gathering of the twelve at the Holy Table, the revelation of the Grail, the coming of Joseph, the issuing
of Christ from the sacred Vessel. The whole scene
in the castle follows the *Queste* fairly closely—save
that two of the chosen twelve come from Scotland
instead of Denmark. The failure of Lancelot, Hector
de Maris, and Gawain is indicated, and the slaying
of knights by Gawain in his wrath, "only because
he had been one of the first to undertake the said
quest." The body of Perceval's sister does not go
independently to Sarras, but is found on the Ship of
Solomon with the sacred Vessel at her head. What
happens at Sarras is much abbreviated. The questers

[1] Malory, XVII, 7; *Queste, ed. cit.*, p. 228 ("Certes, sire, or ne me
chaut il mes quant je muire; car je me tiegn orendroit a la plus
beneuree pucele dou monde, qui ai fet le plus preudome dou siecle
chevalier").

GALAHAD, BORS, AND PERCEVAL; THE SISTER OF PERCEVAL
Florence, Biblioteca Nazionale, Cod. Pal. 556

are not imprisoned, but the king dies on the night of their arrival, and the conclusion—the coronation of Galahad, his death after a year, Perceval's retirement to the desert as a hermit, and the return of Bors to Camelot—is barely summarised.[1]

The quest of the Grail having been achieved, our text turns to the end of the story of Tristan—the portion omitted by Malory. It corresponds with sections of the prose *Tristan*, but with welcome omission of adventitious matter, and with modifications and motives that heighten the dramatic effect.

Mark has taken advantage of the best knights of the Round Table being engaged upon the quest to ally with the King of the Saxons and two other kings who wish to be free from Arthur, to invade the latter's kingdom and besiege him in Camelot. During the siege, hearing that Lancelot and Tristan are absent, Mark lies in ambush near Joyous Gard, and carries off Iseult. In an attempted rescue Lantris (Alcardo) is killed; Brangwain, left behind at Joyous Gard, dies of grief. Iseult is sent to Cornwall. Mark and his allies continue the siege of Camelot, but are defeated by the valour of Palamede and Mordred and other knights who have come to Arthur's aid, and Mark returns to Cornwall with the small remains of his forces.[2]

---

[1] Capp. cxvii–cxxi.

[2] Capp. cxxii–cxxiii. Cf. Löseth, sects. 516–25, and p. 372, n. 5. In the French, Galahad has the chief part in the defeat of the Saxons, though Palamede is also concerned. The French knows nothing of Lantris or the death of Brangwain. In the version represented by the manuscript 103 (Bédier, in *Romania*, XV, p. 510), Brangwain marries Gouvernal and ends her days as Queen of Liones.

A messenger from Joyous Gard meets Tristan as he
is returning from his abandoned quest of the Grail, and
tells him the news. As in the French romance, he
encounters Kay and Dodinel, and, absorbed in his
grief, lets himself be overthrown by the former;
Hector de Maris, taking him on his own statement
as a mere knight of Cornwall, dishonours his shield,
and learns his error.[1]   Still as in the French, Tristan
delivers a damsel from the pursuit of Breus, but here
we find an original and dramatic modification. This
damsel has been sent by Morgan le Fay to bring to
King Mark the lance with the steel with which Tristan
slew Onesun and by the stroke of which he is himself
to die; he does not understand her mysterious explanation, and only wonders what friendship there
can be between Mark and Morgan.[2]   The episode that
follows—Breus entertains Tristan and Hector in his
castle, only revealing his name when he has raised
the drawbridge on their departure — likewise shows
marked differences from the French.   On their way to
the castle, a girl at the window of a tower sings to her
viol two "sonnets" that Tristan had made for Iseult in
the past, and Tristan himself is recognised by a damsel
of Breus when he takes the harp and sings a "sonnet"
that he composed when "he heard the dolorous news
of Joyous Gard."[3]   The adventures of Tristan and
Hector de Maris in Norgalles are mingled with

---

[1] Cap. cxxiii. Cf. Löseth, sects. 533, 535.

[2] Cap. cxxiv. A somewhat analogous episode—but far less
dramatic—occurs at an earlier stage in the *Tristan* (Löseth, sect. 191).

[3] Cap. cxxiv. It is in the farewell taunts addressed by Breus to
Tristan that we hear for the first time of Gawain being the lover of
"la Gaia Donzella." See below, Chap. XII.

episodes peculiar to the present text. A repetition of
the motive of Breus insulting a damsel of the Lady of
the Lake, who is bringing a shield to Lancelot, leads
to his death at Lancelot's hands (cxxv), and another
version of the combat between Tristan and Lancelot
at one of the "perrons" of Merlin, Lancelot being
this time mistaken for Breus instead of Palamede.
Tristan, riding by himself towards Cornwall, comes
to an empty palace where he delivers the damsel Rima
from a terrible serpent.[1] As in the prose *Tristan*, he
meets Sagramour by the sea, and the two pass to
Cornwall, where they are received by Dinas in his
castle. Peculiar to our text is Tristan going to Iseult
disguised as a girl, as also the dreams of the two lovers
presaging the end (cxxvi). The discovery by Andred,
the swift vengeance of King Mark, and the death of
the two protagonists — though the tragic effect is
marred by extraneous matter and reflections—is
substantially as in the French and in the Panciatichiano 33. But the writer places a "santa preghiera"
of contrition on Tristan's lips, and brings in a holy
archbishop and others to aid him to make a Christian
end. Also, he expressly rejects the traditional motive
of Iseult's dying through the pressure of Tristan's last
embrace.[2]

Mark has the two bodies buried in a splendid tomb
at the entrance to the cathedral of Tintagel; upon it
are carved two golden images, that of Iseult holding a

---

[1] Cap. cxxvi. This vivid little story—told in a few sentences
(p. 493), with all the aspect of a fairy tale—is again, perhaps, derived
from some lost narrative lay.

[2] Capp. cxxvi—cxxix. "Non per istretta nè per niuna forza fatta,
ma per debolezza e per proprio dolore" (p. 505).

flower, that of Tristan a sword as the deliverer of the
kingdom.   A vine springs up with two roots, one in
the heart of each lover, and overshadows their
images.[1] Sagramour, bringing the helmet and arms
of Tristan to Camelot, meets the knight (here alone
identified as Kay) who tells him of the mourning at
court for the news that Bors has brought of the death
of so many good knights in the Grail quest.   Dinadan
demands the instant invasion of Cornwall.   Arthur
agrees, but says that first comes the time for mourning, and there is an elaborate account of the lamentation, in which Dinadan takes the lead, the text adding
a quaint rumour, for which the writer will not vouch,
of a papal indulgence granted to those who prayed for
the souls of Tristan and Iseult (cxxxii–cxxxiii).

Although none of the extant orthodox texts of the
prose *Tristan* relates the end of King Mark, it is most

---

[1] Capp. cxxx-cxxxi. The detail of the vine—which seems a folklore motive—does not occur in the normal prose *Tristan*. Cf. Löseth,
p. 392 n., and Bertoni, *La Morte di Tristano, loc. cit.*, pp. 257 sq.
Though not in the poem of Thomas as it has come down to us, it
may possibly have been there originally (Bédier, I, p. 416 n.), and
is found, in various forms, in the Norse *Saga*, in the poem of Eilhart,
and in the French manuscript 103, which, as we saw, has a version
of the death resembling that of the poems.   In the *Saga*, Iseult of
the White Hands has the two lovers buried in separate tombs on
opposite sides of the chapel; a pair of trees grows up, one by the side
of each tomb, until their branches interlace upon the roof.   In the
French manuscript 103 (Bédier, in *Romania*, XV, p. 509), when the
bodies are conveyed to Cornwall, it is Mark who has Tristan and
Iseult buried, in tombs of chalcedony and beryl, on opposite sides
of the chapel; a bramble or briar rose (*ronche*) grows out of Tristan's
tomb, spreads over the roof of the chapel, and comes down to pene-
trate the tomb of Iseult.   The king has it cut down three times, but
each time it grows up again by the next day.   In Eilhart, Mark
plants a rose bush over Iseult and a vine over Tristan, and the two
plants grow together inseparably.

probable that some such close of the romance existed.
Indeed, several texts anticipate that vengeance will
be taken: "And they said that someone will yet
come who will avenge the death of Tristan. King
Arthur is not dead, nor those of the Round Table
who loved him as though he were their brother." [1]
Our text now gives an account of this vengeance for
Tristan.

Amoroldo of Ireland and Gouvernal of Liones—
the two kings who owe their crowns to Tristan—have
already laid siege to Tintagel, when Arthur with his
knights appears upon the scene and takes command.
Mark, reduced to extremities, beheads his nephew
Andred, "because he had been the beginning and
mean and end of the destruction of Tristan," and
sends a letter to King Arthur proposing one of three
courses. He will surrender and hold the city as
Arthur's subject; he will be allowed freely to depart
and leave the kingdom to Arthur; or he will come
out and give battle with his forces and himself be on
the field, on the condition that Arthur sends against
him the same number of men, but with no knights-
errant among them. Arthur chooses the third
proposal, but will only send half the number of men,
one of his against every two of Mark's, the whole
force being exclusively from Ireland (the country-
men of Iseult). When the battle is at its height,
Mark—who, in spite of his pledge, has not accompanied his troops—escapes from the city with his

---

[1] Cf. Löseth, pp. xviii, xix, 388, 422. Malory, XIX, 11, appears
to have known a peculiar version of the story. Cf. Vinaver, *Le
Roman de Tristan et Iseut dans l'œuvre de Thomas Malory*, p. 220.

treasures, but is intercepted and captured by Gouvernal. The knights of Cornwall are completely
defeated by those of Ireland and all slain, as Mark,
before leaving, has had the gates of the city closed.
The Arthurians enter Tintagel, and are lamenting
the escape of Mark, when Gouvernal and Dinas the
seneschal (who, alone among the Cornishmen, has
made common cause with the avengers of Tristan)
bring in the prisoner and present him to Arthur.
Dinadan, who, although a knight-errant, has taken
part disguised in the battle to avenge his friend,
wounds Mark in the head and would have slain him,
but Arthur interposes and is himself wounded in the
arm. Arthur declares that, although he would gladly
have Mark executed, he cannot, according to the
laws of chivalry, put his prisoner to death, and he
condemns Dinadan to be beheaded for unknightly
conduct, adding, in answer to the protests of the
two other kings and Lancelot, that he will only
withdraw the sentence if Mark will pardon the
aggressor. Lancelot induces Mark to do this:
"Would that I had thus forgiven him for whose sake
he has wounded me; for I should not be in so evil a
plight!" Mark is imprisoned in a cage on the top
of a high tower to watch over Tristan's tomb, and
fed exclusively on meat and strong wine until he
dies. Finally, Dinas the seneschal is made king of
Cornwall.[1]

We have no evidence for deciding whether this

[1] Capp. cxxxiv–cxxxvii. Amoroldo marries a sister of Gawain.
Our author, as we have seen, is fond of linking the threads of his story
by dynastic unions of this kind.

story is derived from a lost French source, but it has certain points of resemblance with one of the presumably late additions to the prose *Tristan*.[1] Dinadan, having vowed to avenge the death of Tristan, goes to Tintagel, and, with the aid of Dinas, stirs up a rebellion of the Cornish knights against Mark who is supported by Andred. The king's forces are defeated, and he tries to make his escape by sea. On board ship he is recognised by some of his former subjects, who leave him stranded on a desert island. Dinas refuses the crown of Cornwall which the vassals offer him, and sends an embassy to Arthur to ask him to give them a king. In the meantime, by deceiving a fisherman, Mark has escaped from the island. Meeting King Arthur in a forest, and being unrecognised, he represents himself as a potentate who has been unjustly driven from his dominions, and obtains his promise of aid and protection, even if he were Arthur's deadliest enemy. Then he reveals his identity. When the embassy from Cornwall arrives, Arthur compels them to take back Mark as king on the condition that, if he commits more acts of treachery, he shall be handed over to him for punishment.

From the "High Vengeance for Sir Tristan," we pass to the "Destruction of the Round Table," already foretold by Arthur when he heard of the hero's death. These closing chapters of the book (cxxxviii–cxlv) are a condensed and inferior rendering of the last branch of the story, differing considerably from both the standard Vulgate *Mort Artu* and the

[1] Analysed by Löseth, sects. 574–600, 608.

version presented by Malory. They are, perhaps, based upon a lost French redaction of the Vulgate.[1]

The knights of the Round Table have sunk into sloth and luxury, save only Lancelot who is absorbed in reckless love of the queen. The peace is broken by a renewal of the war between the King of Norgalles and King Amoroldo of Ireland, the former taking advantage of the death of Tristan. Lancelot and his kinsmen go to the aid of the King of Norgalles, Gawain and the lineage of King Lot to that of Amoroldo. The King of Norgalles falls by the hand of his rival, but his party is, nevertheless, victorious through the prowess of Lancelot, who slays Amoroldo in single combat, thereby incurring the deadly hatred of Gawain.[2] In consequence of the latter's malice, and the increasing estrangement with Arthur, Lancelot and his kindred leave Camelot and retire to Joyous Gard, from which he is recalled by a letter from Guinevere, bidding him come to her at a palace three miles beyond the gate of the city. Lancelot, with four of his knights disguised as merchants, goes to the palace where he is joined by the queen. Gawain by a stratagem discovers his presence, informs Arthur, and attacks the palace with his brothers and followers. Lancelot kills Agravaine and another of the brothers,[3] loses three of his four knights, but

[1] Cf. Bruce, *Evolution of Arthurian Romance*, I, p. 448. Rusticiano may possibly have been responsible for an unorthodox conclusion.

[2] Among the slain on Amoroldo's side is the King of the Hundred Knights. This personage—Heraut, Malaquin, or Berrant in Malory (X, 60)—appears frequently in Arthurian story, but this seems the only account of his death.

[3] Gaheris, here called Galiens or Gariens. Gareth (Gariette) is present, but not killed.

succeeds in carrying off the queen to Joyous Gard.
The ensuing siege is briefly described, Ivain ultimately inducing Lancelot to surrender the castle
and give back Guinevere to the king, who pardons
her. Gawain persuades Arthur to destroy Joyous
Gard and invade Gaul. Benoic is besieged, until
Lancelot proposes that the war shall be ended by single
combat between himself and a champion on Arthur's
behalf. Gawain, relying upon the magical, waxing
of his strength until noon, claims to accept the
challenge. In the meantime, Mordred has become
enamoured of the queen, and, finding himself loyally
deluded by her, is besieging her in the castle of Urbano,
from which she sends a message to Arthur. The
messenger arrives when the long combat between
Lancelot and Gawain has ended with the latter falling
with the wound in the head. The siege is raised.
There is no battle with the Emperor of the Romans
as in the orthodox *Mort Artu*, but Arthur's army is
attacked by a certain Turinoro, Count of Carthage
and brother of the Roman Pontiff, who is on his way
to aid Lancelot, and Gawain receives a fresh stroke,
from which he dies. Arthur summons Mordred to
leave the siege of Urbano, and the battle follows in
which almost all the knights-errant are slain:

But King Mordred was the victor; and King Arthur took
to flight, grievously wounded, and in company with Sir
Ivain and a squire; and they fled until they came to the shore
of the sea. And then Sir Ivain, who was wounded with three
wounds, fell dead, whereat King Arthur made the greatest
lamentation of the world. And then King Arthur drew forth
his sword, and put it into the hand of the squire, and bade
him cast it into the sea; and the squire withstood him, because

the sword was right beautiful, and the king bade him three times. Then the squire cast it in, and he saw that an arm came out of the water, and grasped the sword, and brandished it three times, and then drew it under the water; and never was aught known of it. And, after a little, lo there came over the sea a small boat, all covered with white, and, when King Arthur saw it, he said to the squire: "Now has come mine end." And the ship drew near the king, and from the ship came forth some arms that took King Arthur and visibly set him in the ship, and bore him away over the sea. And the squire, greatly terrified, stayed there as long as he could see the ship; then he departed, and related the marvel. And it is believed that Morgan le Fay came by art in that little ship, and bore him away to an island of the sea, and there he died of his wounds, and the Fay buried him in that island.[1]

Mordred presses on the siege of the castle, but Guinevere contrives to have a message conveyed to Lancelot. There is another tremendous battle, in which Mordred falls by Lancelot's hand. That same evening the squire arrives with the news of Arthur's fate, which he announces to Lancelot and the queen. Guinevere, believing herself the cause of the disaster, dies straightway of grief. Lancelot, having seen her nobly buried, alone and unarmed, seeks "the desert of Adernantes," where he finds Bors and Hector de Maris and Blioberis doing penance in an abbey: "And Lancelot remained with them to do penance for his sins, and he lived a year and three months, and he was a priest and sang Mass; afterwards he died and passed out of this life."

[1] Cap. cxliv. Cf. Malory, XXI, 5–6, and *Mort Artu*, ed. Bruce, pp. 244–51.

JOSEPH OF ARIMATHEA
Florence, Biblioteca Nazionale, Cod. Pal. 556

THE REVELATION OF THE HOLY GRAIL
Florence, Biblioteca Nazionale, Cod. Pal. 556

CHAPTER X

Two Italian romances of Merlin were produced in the fourteenth century, both deriving in part from the *Prophecies de Merlin*, but with matter from other sources. The earlier of these is the *Storia di Merlino* of Paolino Pieri, probably the Florentine chronicler of that name who was living at Florence in 1324, which has come down to us only in a large fragment preserved in a fifteenth-century manuscript in the Biblioteca Riccardiana.[1] The other—a much more elaborate work, divided into six books of unequal length—purports to be a translation from the French written on 20 November, 1379, and appears to have been the first Arthurian text printed in Italy, as the *editio princeps* is dated Venice, 1 February, 1480 (O.S.). There were at least five subsequent editions. The translator or compiler called it similarly the *Historia di Merlino*, but, in later editions, it bears the title *Vita di Merlino con le sue profetie*, by which it is now more usually known.[2]

[1] *La Storia di Merlino di Paolino Pieri* edita ed illustrata da Ireneo Sanesi (Bergamo, 1898).

[2] The text opens: "Incomincia il primo libro de la historia di Merlino, divisa in sei libri ne li quali si descrive prima la natività d' esso Merlino, e la vita sua, e poi molte prophetie le quale lui fece scrivere a più persone." Sanesi, *op. cit.*, pp. lii–lvi, has shown that the attribution of the work to a certain "magnifico messer Zorzi" is due to a misunderstanding of the Venetian phraseology of the

After the *Tristano Riccardiano* and the *Tavola Ritonda*, it is the most important of all the Italian prose Arthurian romances.

The first book of the *Vita di Merlino*—which occupies nearly half the work—is a free rendering, with some important variations and a large interpolation, of the prose version of the Merlin poem of Robert de Boron, which elaborates the story told by Geoffrey of Monmouth (Robert's immediate source being probably not Geoffrey himself, but Wace), carrying it on to the coronation of Arthur.[1] To counteract the harrowing of Hell and the redemption of the world, the devils conspire that another man shall be born without a human father, who shall undo the work of Christ and lead mankind to perdition. The mother is not a British princess (as in Geoffrey), but the daughter of a rich man who has been ruined with his family by diabolical machinations, and, after the downfall of her sister, the girl is watched over by her confessor, the holy hermit,

colophon at the end of the printed volume; Zorzi (Giorgio) being simply the name of the father (deceased) of the owner of the "libro autentico" from which the text itself has been printed: Pietro di Giorgio Delfin, a historical personage of the fifteenth century. At the end of the edition of 1480 (81) it is stated that it was written in Venice. I have not seen the Florentine edition of 1485; but the subsequent editions (Venice, 1507, 1516, 1539, 1554), which I have examined, with the exception of that of 1516 (where the place is not mentioned), give "in Florentia." The translation is unquestionably by a Venetian. The date mcccclxxix, assigned to it by the editions of 1539 and 1554, is clearly due to a misreading or misprinting of the Roman numerals. Miss Paton, *Prophecies de Merlin*, I, pp. 48–9, describes a manuscript of the same work in the Biblioteca Palatina of Parma, written at Venice in 1402.

[1] Sommer, *Vulgate Version of the Arthurian Romances*, II, pp. 1–88; a different text in the *Huth Merlin*, ed. Paris and Ulrich, I, pp. 1–146.

Blasio or Blaise. The child is born while the mother is imprisoned, and christened Merlin, but the diabolical plot is frustrated because, though he has supernatural knowledge to know the past, present, and future, he has received grace at baptism to use this for good. When eighteen months old, he speaks to reassure his mother, and then delivers her from sentence of death by revealing the paternity of the judge.[1] Blaise, who becomes the child's confessor, now begins to record his prophecies; but Merlin from the outset—and this does not appear in the French—dimly foresees his own end: "But I would have thee know that my body will die by deception."[2] Then follows the story of Vitiglier (Vortigern) and his tower, the history (as given by Robert de Boron) differing from that of Geoffrey of Monmouth in that, among other things, the two brothers who are the rightful heirs to the throne are not Aurelius Ambrosius and Uther Pendragon, but Uther and Pendragon. Merlin induces the king to pardon those clerks of his who sought his life, and, having foretold Vitiglier's death, returns to Northumberland. Pendragon and Uther land, Vitiglier is burned in his tower, and Pendragon becomes king. Pendragon sends for Merlin, and we have a number of scenes in which the young sage appears in different shapes to one or other of the royal brothers, whose chief adviser he becomes, and the motive—ultimately derived from Geoffrey's *Vita*

---

[1] In the Italian text (I, 29), but not in the French, the judge has his own mother poisoned when he learns the truth.

[2] *Vita di Merlino*, I, 30. In the French text, Merlin will disappear mysteriously, and Blaise is to go to the region of the Companions of the Holy Grail.

o

Merlini—of how he foretold three different modes of death, all of which were verified, for the man who tried to delude him.

At this point, where the French text speaks of the beginning of "le livre des prophecies Merlin," or "lis contes des prophecies Merlin," but does not otherwise interrupt the narrative,[1] the Italian version interpolates an independent section of twenty-five chapters: "Le profetie di Merlino le quai scrisse il santo romitto Blasio"; partly narrative, partly prophecies delivered to Blaise.[2] Some of these supplement the romance, as where Merlin speaks of his nativity and makes a full profession of the Christian faith, puts to confusion the countryman who tried to deprive the prophet's mother of her heritage, or —in a very dramatic chapter—foretells to the Saxon queen of Vortigern how she will perish at the hands of a servant of Pendragon, and then magically eludes her attempts to make him prisoner,[3] or appears upon the speaking stone to deliver a damsel from the unjust sentence of King Arginus who is stoned to death by his people.[4] The coming of Arthur is foretold in figurative fashion; there shall be a king called "Falcon," upon whom shall come the "super-falcon" with twenty-nine heads (Galehaut), who will devour them for the love of a "leopard" (Lancelot), and the leopard shall have a son called "Virgin Lion" (Gala-

---

[1] Paris and Ulrich, I, p. 85; Sommer, II, p. 48. Cf. Miss Paton, II, pp. 302–3.

[2] *Vita di Merlino*, I, 91–115.

[3] *Ibid.*, I, 104. As far as I know, this legend of Rowena (who is not named) is otherwise unknown.

[4] *Ibid.*, I, 101.

had) who shall achieve the quest of the Holy Grail.
Some of the prophecies are of the historical or pseudo-
historical kind, and appear to have been composed
at a later date than the Franco-Italian text of the
Prophecies, several seeming to refer to events in Italy
during the fourteenth century.[1] It is peculiar to
this work that Blaise, the hermit and scribe, should
himself be represented as an Italian born at Vercelli.[2]

Merlin now leaves Northumberland and the hermit,
and returns to Pendragon and Uther. Pendragon is
killed in a battle with the Saxons. Uther succeeds
and, at Merlin's advice, henceforth calls himself Uther
Pendragon. It is to make a worthy tomb for the
slain king that Merlin has the "Dance of the Giants"
brought over from Ireland to Stonehenge. Merlin
next tells Uther Pendragon the story of the Holy
Grail, and bids him found the Round Table in Carduel
with fifty knights chosen by himself. The Italian
version follows the French text fairly closely, in the
account of the foundation of the Table with the vacant
place for the achiever of the Grail, and the fearful fate
of the rash knight who tried to occupy it; but there are
two noteworthy modifications. The unnamed knight,
who is to sit in the Siege Perilous and achieve the

---

[1] Cf. Miss Paton, II, pp. 337–43.

[2] *Vita di Merlino*, I, 98. Blaise has been hypothetically identified
with the "fabulator Bledhericus" mentioned by Giraldus Cambrensis, the "Breri" referred to in the *Tristan* of Thomas, and the
"Bleheris" cited by Wauchier in his continuation of Chrétien's
Perceval—a real or fictitious conveyer of the "matter of Britain."
Cf. E. K. Chambers, *op. cit.*, pp. 148–50, 157; J. D. Bruce, I, pp. 156,
285; W. H. Schofield, *Mythical Bards and the Life of William Wallace*
(Harvard University Press, 1920), pp. 176–83. Malory only
mentions him once (I, 17).

adventure of the Holy Grail, in the French text is usually taken to be Perceval; in the Italian, though still unnamed, he is unmistakably Galahad.[1] Again, in the French text, the fifty knights who sit at the Table propose to remain stationary at Carduel; but, in the Italian, where the account of their answers to the king and Merlin is in other respects almost identical with the French, they are prepared to play the part of knights-errant: "In such manner shall we live at the pleasure of our Lord God, and, at the command of our king Uther Pendragon, we shall ride and fight in whatever place shall be most his will."[2] Here we have clearly the conception of the adventures of the knights of the "Old Table," which, as we saw, developed under the influence of the *Palamède*.

Then follows the story, elaborated by Robert de Boron from the shorter narrative in Geoffrey of Monmouth, familiar to English readers in a slightly different form in the first seven chapters of Malory, and presented in the Italian with some expansions and slight changes in the order of events. Uther Pendragon is enamoured of Igraine (Izerla), and, by Merlin's shape-shifting device, begets Arthur. There is a curious confusion about the half-sisters of Arthur. Morgan, who "was afterwards called Morgan le Fay," is represented as a bastard daughter of the Duke of Cintanel (Tintagel) and as becoming the wife of King Lot of Orkney, whereas an unnamed daughter of the duke

---

[1] I, 125, where it is stated that he will be knighted by his own father. Cf. Paris and Ulrich, I, p. 98; Sommer, II, p. 56; also Bruce, I, p. 145, n. 36.

[2] I, 124. Cf. the corresponding passages, Paris and Ulrich, I, p. 97; Sommer, II, p. 55.

and Igraine marries King Neutres of Caules (Garlot)[1].
No mystery was made about Arthur's parentage in
Geoffrey or in Godfrey of Viterbo, but here, as in the
Robert de Boron version, he is given to Merlin who
entrusts him to a good man Autor (Malory's Sir Ector)
to be brought up by his wife.   Uther Pendragon, from
his litter, wins his last victory over the Saxons and
dies, while Merlin whispers into his ear: "Thy son
Arthur shall be head of thy realm after thee by the
virtue of Jesus Christ, and it shall be he who will
complete the Round Table which thou hast founded." [2]
Merlin bids the barons wait until Christmas, when a
miracle will show them whom to elect as king.   At
the appointed time, over the sea comes the stone with
the anvil in the centre, and within it a sword fixed up
to its hilt: "He who shall draw this sword out of the
stone, shall be king by the choice of God."   None of
the two hundred barons chosen by the bishop can
draw out the sword.   Arthur with his foster-brother
Chiex (Kay) has come to the church, and the latter,
having quarrelled with a knight, asks his supposed

[1] I, 147, 148.   In Sommer's text (II, p. 73), an unnamed daughter
marries King Lot, another (also unnamed) marries King Neutres
of Garlot, and the third, Morgan, is set to learn letters, and afterwards
called "Morgue la fée."   In the *Huth Merlin* (I, p. 120), King Neutres
of Sorhaut marries the duke's illegitimate daughter named Morgan;
but she is not confused with the third who is called "Morgue la fée,"
and who in the continuation (I, p. 201), as Morgain (also called Morgue),
is married by Arthur to King Uriens of Garlot ("Gore" in Malory),
by whom she becomes the mother of Ivain.   It was apparently
Malory who gave to the wife of King Lot (the mother of Gawain and
Mordred, the most tragic figure of a woman in Arthurian story) the
name of Margawse (Morgause), and that of Elaine to the wife of King
Neutres (Nentres).   Cf. *Morte Darthur*, I, 2.
[2] I, 155.   The death scene is different in the French.

brother to fetch him a sword. Arthur easily draws
out the sword, and, without thinking, gives it to Kay,
who hides it under his coat and tells his father that he
has drawn it out.   The latter compels him to tell the
truth.   Arthur replaces the sword, and promises his
foster-father that, when he is king, he will make Kay
seneschal of all his court.   Brought before the bishop,
Arthur again draws out the sword, but, while the
people adhere to him, the barons still refuse to accept
him as king until finally won over by his nobility.
At Pentecost, all again failing, Arthur is knighted, and
the bishop bids him again draw out the sword that he
may bless it together with the crown:

Then Arthur, making three times the sign of the Cross,
set his hand to the sword and lightly drew it forth, as he had
done before, and presented it to the holy bishop. And no
sooner had he drawn forth the sword than straightway
appeared a wondrous miracle, for the stone with the anvil
rose up in the air in the sight of all the people, and went into
a place where it was never more seen.   Then the bishop said
before all: "Now has our Lord Jesus Christ shown His will,
wherefore let none of you any longer make exception to the
coronation of your king chosen by God." [1]

With Arthur's coronation, the first book of the
Vita di Merlino—like the prose version of Robert de
Boron—ends.   It is here represented as having been
written, like the prophecies, by Blaise himself as
Merlin's confessor, and Blaise "lived twenty-two days

[1] I, 165. In the French text, there is nothing about the miracle;
when they come out from the church after the coronation, they
merely find that the stone has disappeared: "Et quant il fu sacres et
la messe fu chantee, si issirent fors del moustier et esgarderent si
ne virent point le perron.   Ne ne sorent quil fu devenus" (Sommer,
II, p. 88).   Cf. Paris and Ulrich, I, p. 146.

after the coronation of King Arthur, and then passed from this life to celestial glory." [1]

There are two well-known continuations of the prose version of Robert de Boron: the Vulgate *Merlin*, in which Blaise is still living and acting as Merlin's scribe when the prophet falls into the power of Viviane or Niniane (Malory's Nimue), who is not here identified with the Lady of the Lake; and the later, pseudo Robert de Boron, the *Huth Merlin*, from which Malory drew the magnificent and pathetic story of the two brothers, Balin and Balan, which is not represented in Italian.[2] The *Vita di Merlino* follows neither of these, but presents us with a totally different "Suite de Merlin," in the form of five books according to the various scribes who succeeded Blaise, derived in part from the Franco-Italian *Prophecies*, but more coherently arranged and with a continuous narrative.[3]

The first of these scribes is Tolomeo (Tholomer, Ptolemy), a chaplain of the Pope; but he is soon made a cardinal and returns to Rome, for which reason the second book, which he writes, is shorter than the others. In fact, it only contains a few mysterious prophecies about the Venetians, after which Tolomeo resigns his bishopric in Gaul to "a wise clerk named

[1] I, 165. The modern reprint, *I due primi libri della Istoria di Merlino secondo la rarissima edizione del* 1480, ed. Ulrich (Bologna, 1884), contains only the first book of the Italian text, omitting the prophecies delivered to Blaise (capp. 91–115) and the final chapter (166), which is naturally not found in the French *Merlin*, but based upon the *Prophecies*, in which, after the death of Blaise, Tolomeo takes his place.

[2] A third continuation is the *Livre d'Artus* (Sommer, VII).

[3] Cf. Miss Paton, II, chap. ix ("The Scribes of Merlin").

Master Antonio," and receives final instructions from
Merlin as to his duties as cardinal for the reformation
of Christendom. This book is in substance in the
Prophecies.

Bishop Antonio now becomes Merlin's scribe, and
writes the long third book. Antonio having been
born in Ireland, "e volendo gran bene a quella terra,"
wishes first to know the future of that land; so the
prophecies begin with the drowning of the Irish pope
by a minister of the Dragon of Babylon—the prophecy
which stands first in the Rennes manuscript.[1] A long
series follows, in which Venice, the land of the "buoni
marinari," the March of Treviso, and the Crusades
figure largely. Most of these, though not all, can be
traced to one or other French text of the *Prophecies*,
but hardly concern our subject. Three prelates—
Bertoldo a German, Felix of Milan, and Gregorio
a Roman—come to Gaul from the Pope to examine
Merlin as to his faith, and, by his usual shape-
shifting devices, are themselves convicted of simony:
"Our Lord Jesus Christ suffered me to come into the
world for the shame and loss of our hellish foes, and
especially to tell the world the evil miracles of the
Dragon of Babylon, because no saint speaks of him,
except the Apostle and Evangelist John; and, also, I
am come into the world to reveal the evil deeds that
will be done by the clergy, of which you have already
given a sign in Gaul."[2] In the latter part of the book,
genuine Arthurian matter begins to predominate.
The presentation of Merlin's character is a striking

---

[1] *Vita di Merlino*, III, 2; *Prophecies, ed. cit.*, I, p. 57.
[2] III, 37. Cf. *Prophecies, ed. cit.*, I, p. 101.

one.   Conceived of a devil, but redeemed by the grace
of Christ, he is full of Christian orthodoxy and zeal for
righteousness, but tempted "a hundred times more
than other men of the world."   He had told Blaise:

> There never was nor shall be a man in the world so lustful
> as I shall be; for lust will be mightily enkindled upon me, and
> by no effort of mine will it depart from me, since I was the
> child of lust, and that demon who procured my birth was the
> demon set over lust.   But, by the grace of my Lord Jesus
> Christ, I was drawn out of his hands in this world, and in the
> other he will have no power over me.[1]

A damsel from Liones of marvellous beauty, under
the pretext of giving him her love, induces Merlin to
teach her how to enchant a man and a place so as to
have both in her power.   Merlin yields, but cautions
her not to try the experiment in her own country.
The damsel is the one who ensnares King Meliadus in
the *Tristan*, and we are given the story of the enchant-
ing of the king, Merlin's meeting with Queen Eliabel,
the liberation of the king and slaying of the damsel,
the death of the queen and the birth of Tristan as in
the romance.[2]   Merlin, speaking to Antonio, exalts the
wisdom of the Lady of the Lake above that of Morgan.
Is the Lady the "bianca serpente," by whom "the
half man full of knowledge" will be put to death
through the sin of lust?   God does not allow him to
see how this will happen.[3]   The same sin will cause

---

[1] I, 107.   Cf. the Pope's charge in the consistory, III, 83: "Thou
art so lustful that we may not believe that the Holy Spirit reveals
to thee the things that are to come."

[2] III, 67, 68, 72, 74.   Partly in *Prophecies, ed. cit.*, I, p. 121.

[3] III, 69, 72.   Note the curious passage, at the end of cap. 69,
where "la donzella della Roccha de li Sesni" (Saxons) and "la dami-
scella de la foresta dardante" are said to have been among Merlin's

the death of Tristan at his uncle's hands, and he will
be equally unable to save himself:

> I would have thee set in writing that he will not be able
> to guard himself, for he will not be in his own liberty, but in
> the control of lust, and for this he must needs die, and in the
> like condition shall I myself be, for through the sin of lust
> I shall die, since I cannot guard myself from it. I cannot
> see how lust will put me to death, for, did I but know it, I
> should make such a spell as would keep me right well from
> receiving death.[1]

Then comes what is represented as the triumph of
Merlin's life.   The Cardinal Gregorio, whose elevation
Merlin had foretold when he was one of the three
ministers who came to test him in Gaul, is now Pope;
Merlin goes to Rome, and, in full consistory, convicts
the hypocritical bishop Conrad who had accused him
of heresy, puts the prelates to shame, and is trium-
phantly acquitted.[2] We have a group of final
prophecies delivered to Antonio after their return, including the familiar one of the destruction of the palace
that St. Thomas built for the King of India.   Merlin
again foretells his death.   He cannot deceive the
Lady of the Lake, "so wise and pure is she"; he will
himself be deceived, but God will not let him know
how.   "I know right well that the white serpent will

loves, both of whom will be slain on account of King Arthur.
They are evidently the Camille of the *Lancelot* and the sorceress of
the Forest Perilous in the *Tristan*, Malory's Annowre. Cf. *Prophecies*,
ed. cit., I, p. 122.

[1] III, 75. The statement (III, 73), that Tristan will slay the
Questing Beast, "sarà propriamente quello che metterà a morte la
bestia gratixanit (*sic*)," is peculiar to this Italian text.

[2] III, 78–85. This episode is not in the Rennes MS., but occurs
in the 1498 edition of the French *Prophecies*. Cf. Miss Paton,
I, pp. 476–81.

go in company with the half man full of wisdom through the forest of Nartes, when the white serpent will herself return and leave the half man full of wisdom, and no more can I see." With a last prophecy of the growing evil of the world, telling Antonio that, when he hears no more tidings of him, his body will be dead, Merlin kneels before the bishop for his blessing, and makes his way into the mysterious forest where he awaits the coming of the Lady of the Lake.[1]

Here, at her bidding, by his magic art Merlin has built in a cavern a splendid dwelling-place with a tomb, a place "so hidden that, if all the knights of the world had been set to seek it in that forest, they would never have found it." Segurant le Brun will come from Abiron to see the tomb, and, if he chose to stay in these parts, no knight could sustain the honour of chivalry against him, "save only the good knight who will issue from the lineage of King Ban of Benoic, and all his virgin strength will be on the part of the heavenly chivalry."[2] The Lady of the Lake hates Merlin, because Morgan has accused her of sexual intercourse with "the half man full of wisdom." Merlin and the Lady abide here for fifteen days, while they hear Morgan and her knights hunting through the forest to find her, and she believes that

---

[1] III, 98–9. Cf. *Prophecies, ed. cit.*, I, pp. 162–4. The comparison of the Lady of the Lake with "Lucifer" in the Italian is a confusion over "Lusente," the name of the woman associated with Virgil in the French. In the Vulgate *Merlin* (Sommer, II, pp. 450–1), Merlin takes leave of Arthur and Blaise (who is still living). Note that, in the Italian "suite," Merlin is not brought into contact with Arthur after the latter's coronation.

[2] Galahad.

Merlin has made Morgan come in order to deliver
her, the Lady of the Lake, into her rival's hands.[1]
The book ends with Merlin sending to Antonio
his prophecies of the quest of the Holy Grail
and the death of Arthur at the hands of his own
evil son.

The Lady of the Lake now acts as Merlin's scribe
at the beginning of the fourth book, where the
narrative is interrupted by a series of prophecies,
partly Arthurian, partly relating to Venice and Greece.
To satisfy the Lady's desire to know the fate of her
foster-sons, Merlin foretells events from the *Lancelot*:
Lancelot's love for Guinevere, his rescuing her from
the fire and retirement from the world after her death,
the birth of Galahad, and the achieving of the Grail
the saintly end of Perceval and Bors, the death of
Lionel at the battle of Salisbury.[2]   Segurant le Brun
(here called Segurades) will conquer all pagandom
and be crowned King of Abiron, and "will generate
a lion from whom will issue many lion cubs who will
be very fervent in increasing the wings of Jesus
Christ"; but, after making the Saracens pay dear,
he will himself die young.[3]   Elia (Helain le Blanc), the
son of Bors, will be the ideal of Christian chivalry;
he will cross the sea and be crowned Emperor of

---

[1] III, 100–2. Cf. *Prophecies, ed. cit.,* I, pp. 164–7, where a totally
different reason is given for the Lady's resolution to destroy Merlin.
In the French text the catastrophe follows immediately, without
the prophecies interpolated at the beginning of the Italian fourth
book. So in the printed *Prophecies* of 1498.

[2] In the *Mort Artu,* as in Malory, Lionel falls in the subsequent
engagement at Winchester.

[3] IV, 6. There seems no suggestion of Segurant's early death in
any of the French texts or elsewhere.

Constantinople.[1] Then comes a prophecy of peculiar interest:

"My lady," said Merlin, "I would have thee set in writing that the false King Mark of Cornwall will pass the sea, and come into Great Britain after the death of the adventurous king, where that evil King Mark will devastate all that country, and then he will come to Joyous Gard, and will have the tomb opened in which he will find the bodies of Galehaut le Brun and Lancelot of the Lake, and he will have them burnt to ashes. And, having done this, he will wish to be crowned King of Logres; but this will not be suffered him, for King Bors will come out of a hermitage, and take arms, and assemble the folk of that country, and set himself against that evil king and take him, and then he will put him to death for the outrage done upon the bones of that cousin of his and those of Galehaut le Brun." [2]

There is no trace of this prediction in the French texts of the *Prophecies*. It is a unique redaction of the alternative legend of the end of King Mark, which, instead of making it a part of the vengeance for the death of Tristan before the destruction of the Round Table, places it at a later date.[3] The story is due to the pseudo Robert de Boron. The *Huth Merlin* promises a third book which should end "after the death of Lancelot, at the same point where he treats of the death of King Mark." [4] The *Palamède*

---

[1] IV, 8-9. The story of the birth of Helain—Bors is vowed to chastity, but overthrown by a magic ring—is in the *Lancelot* (Sommer, IV, pp. 250-70). Cf. Malory, XII, 9, XVI, 3 (where Bors is the white bull with the spot). Helain is a kind of replica of Galahad; but cf. R. S. Loomis, in *M.L.R.*, XXIV (1929), pp. 420-2.

[2] IV, 10. The writer has fallen into the common error of confusing Galehaut "the haut prince" (the friend of Lancelot) with Galehaut le Brun, the son of Hector. It was, of course, the former who was buried at Joyous Gard.

[3] Cf. present work, pp. 185, 263.

[4] *Merlin*, ed. Paris and Ulrich, I, pp. li-lii, 280.

incidentally alludes to the destruction and wasting
of Camelot by King Mark, on the authority of the
book of "Messer Robert de Boron my companion." [1]
The story is preserved, in what is regarded as a fragment of the pseudo Robert de Boron version of the
Queste, as a detached episode at the end of a French
manuscript of Rusticiano.   After the burial of Lancelot, Bors and Blioberis, with Meraugis de Portlesguez
(who, in the prose *Tristan*, is represented as a son of
Mark, and is killed by Gawain), join the Archbishop
of Canterbury in his hermitage.   It is now more than
seven years since the death of Tristan, and Mark
has grown old; but, hearing that Lancelot and so
many knights are dead, he invades the kingdom
of Logres, devastating and slaughtering, destroys
Joyous Gard and burns the bodies of Lancelot and
Galehaut, attacks Camelot itself and destroys the
Round Table.   He then makes his way to the hermitage to kill the four companions there, kills the
archbishop, but is himself slain by a knight of the
lineage of King Ban, named Paulart, who was seeking
the hermits.   Mark's men dare not lay him in
consecrated ground, but bury him in front of the
hermitage, and only a few of them know how he
met his death.[2]   The same story—with some variants
—occurs at the end of the Spanish *Demanda del
Sancto Grial*.   The news of Lancelot's death having
spread, Mark invades the kingdom of Logres, with

[1] B.M. Add. MS. 12228, f. 16 v°.   Cf. H. L. D. Ward, *Catalogue of
Romances*, I, p. 368.

[2] Löseth, sect. 575a (p. 409).   For the MS. (Bibliothèque Nationale,
340), see Löseth, pp. 472–3, and cf. Bruce, *Evolution of Arthurian
Romance*, I, pp. 472–3.

the purpose of not leaving a trace of Arthur's work in that realm. He takes Joyous Gard and destroys the tombs of Lancelot and Galehaut, defeats the people of Camelot who sally out against him, and destroys the Round Table. One of his knights advises him to slay Bors and his companions, as they were knights of the Table. He goes to the hermitage with a single knight, kills the archbishop who comes forward to meet him, and is himself slain by Paulart (here called Paulos) who has just arrived. Paulos binds Mark's companion to secrecy, and the hermits themselves give the king burial.[1]

It would seem that the Italian follows a redaction of the pseudo Robert de Boron different from that in the French and Spanish versions. The appearance of Bors as the saviour of what remains of Arthurian society well befits his character, nor is it inconsistent with Merlin's previous prediction that he would end his days as a hermit, for he may well have returned to the hermitage to die.

Having duly recorded these and other prophecies, the Lady of the Lake now determines to rid herself of the prophet. Under pretext of desiring to be laid in the same tomb after death, she induces Merlin to enter and lie down in it, in order that she may see her future place. Merlin has been deluded into thinking that she is not the "white serpent" through whom he is to die; because, by means of a charm learnt from him, she has let him suppose that he has "taken

---

[1] *Demanda del Sancto Grial*, ed. A. Bonilla y San Martín, capp. 452–5 (*Libros de Caballerías*, I, pp. 336–8). Summarised by Bruce in *Romanic Review*, IV, p. 429.

her whiteness from her," whereas she is still a virgin. By another charm he has taught her, she closes the tomb immovably upon him, and then taunts him with the fulfilment of his prophecy: "Merlin, thou seest that I am the white serpent." His body will decay within a month, but—though only two knights, Segurant and Meliadus "il bel cavalliero," will find the place before the Lady herself dies—his spirit will not cease to speak to all who come until the day of judgment.[1] The news spreads through Great and Little Britain. King Meliadus searches the forest to find the tomb, but is repulsed by a noise so terrible that neither heart of man nor the most powerful horse can withstand it. Queen Guinevere sends a hundred knights on the same quest, led by Galehaut ("Lord of the Distant Isles," but confused as usual with Galehaut le Brun); they seek in vain, and return to Arthur's court. Perceval alone remains behind; he comes to a hermitage where he finds the holy hermit Elia (Helias), who himself had been one of Merlin's scribes in the past, and to whom it had been foretold by an angel that the virgin son of King Oriel (Pellinor) should receive the prophecies from him and then lay him in his grave.[2]

[1] IV, 17–22, which are substantially the same as in *Prophecies*, (*ed. cit.*, I, pp. 167–72). This account of Merlin's entombment seems related with the *Huth Merlin* (which in this part derives from the lost *Conte del Brait*), where, however, the only knight who finds the tomb and speaks with Merlin is Bagdemagus. Cf. *Merlin*, ed. Paris and Ulrich, II, pp. 196–8, and Miss Paton, II, pp. 298–300. The actual coming of Segurant is apparently among the lost portions of his story, though it is mentioned again in VI, 10.

[2] IV, 27–9. In *Prophecies* (*ed. cit.*, I, p. 270), it is Merlin himself who has foretold Perceval's coming. Cf. below, p. 214.

PERCEVAL DELIVERS THE YOUNG LION FROM THE SERPENT (Malory, XIV, 7)
Florence, Biblioteca Nazionale, Cod. Pal. 556

The fifth book is composed of Elia's reminiscences
of Merlin in the prophet's early days in Northumberland, when prophecies were delivered to him, which
he now repeats to Perceval or are found afterwards
in his book.[1] The only story of Arthurian interest is
that of the ten knights from Val Brun who come to
learn from Merlin the future of their ten sons, one
of whom, Ugier (Roger), is to be the presumptuous
man who attempts to sit in the Siege Perilous in the
days of Uther Pendragon. Elia dies; and Perceval,
having seen his soul carried by angels into Paradise
and buried his body, takes the book of his prophecies
to Antonio.[2]

A genuinely romantic figure appears as the last of
Merlin's scribes in the sixth book: "il bel cavalliero,"
Meliadus the younger, the fruit of the abduction of
the Queen of Scotland by King Meliadus as told in
the *Palamède*—where, however, there is no mention
of any child. Born to his mother in captivity, he
was secretly sent to the Lady of the Lake, who
brought him up with Lancelot, Lionel, and Bors,
and now, after her victory over Merlin, takes him as
her lover. At his repeated request she brings him
to Merlin's tomb, which is guarded by a quaking

---

[1] Most of these reminiscences, which, as Miss Paton remarks, "are
designed to exemplify Merlin's power in detecting and reproving
various sins," are likewise in the French. The historical prophecies
are later additions, that of the fall of Constantinople (IV, 9) being
obviously a fifteenth-century interpolation.

[2] "Il savio clerico maestro Antonio" (V, 27). In the *Prophecies*
(I, p. 205), Antonio has renounced his bishopric and died a hermit,
appointing a "Sage Clerc" to succeed him in receiving and setting
down all reported prophecies of Merlin. The Italian text makes this
"Sage Clerc" and Antonio the same person.

P

mountain. "Meliadus, said Merlin, thou hast taken her whiteness from the white serpent better than I did, for, had I taken it as thou hast, verily she would not have shut me in this tomb." Merlin prophesies to him concerning the Albigenses and the jewels in the crown of the Dragon of Babylon, one of which will previously have been offered at the altar of the Blessed Virgin in Abiron by Segurant when about to leave his kingdom to find the tomb.[1] But he also vouchsafes some Arthurian information. Together with his brother Tristan, Meliadus will liberate his mother and avenge his father upon the King of Scotland; the Lady of the Lake will live after him, and will still be in life when "the false King Mark of Cornwall, thy uncle, will be put to death by one of the lineage of King Ban of Benoic."[2] Meliadus passes to and fro bringing the prophecies to Antonio: "In this place lies the wisest mortal man that ever was in the world. His flesh decays, but his spirit is enclosed here within, and will never issue forth until the last day." Much does Antonio yearn to speak in person with the spirit of Merlin, but this is forbidden by God. Instead, by magic art, he flies through the air on a round stone, within which is the devil who presided over the prophet's generation, sees from above the place of Merlin's entombment,

[1] VI, 10. Cf. Miss Paton, II, pp. 279–80. Whatever the original significance of this, and of other Segurant episodes, may have been, it is clearly lost.

[2] VI, 9. Here it is stated that the King of Scotland treacherously put King Meliadus to death. There is no hint of this in the *Tristan* or the *Palamède*, where the guilt is laid at Mark's door. The slayer of Mark is clearly Bors. Cf. the different account of the vengeance for Tristan in the *Prophecies, ed. cit.*, I, p. 214.

and questions the fiend on the subject of his ultimate salvation. He is delivered from the perils of this excursion by the holy prayers of Perceval, and arrives at Camelot.[1] Merlin foretells the death of Tristan at the hands of Mark, for which "the evil Morgan has already enchanted and poisoned the lance." He bears no rancour against the cause of his fate; his last words to Meliadus convey a warning to the Lady of the Lake to protect her from the treachery of Morgan who is seeking her death.[2]

Meliadus and Perceval ride together to Arthur's court, after which the former returns to the Lady of the Lake. Antonio, feeling that his end is near, summons all the ecclesiastics of Gaul, reveals the existence of the book, and appoints his chaplain Robert his successor, to spend his amassed treasures in collecting further prophecies of Merlin. After the death of the "savio clerico di Gaules," Robert begins to read the prophecies of Merlin, in which he finds the following amazing prediction that Merlin uttered to the Lady of the Lake after she had shut him in the tomb:

My lady, when you shall pass from this life, our Lord Jesus Christ will have you brought before Him and will ask you concerning me; and you will tell Him all the truth, whereat He will command me to come to you even as I shall be with the tomb. But I know for certain that the demons of Hell shall have no part within my soul. This will be because of the baptism that I had upon me; and each one who is contrite and confessed will experience the grace of the Lord God, for heaven and earth are full of His mercy.

---

[1] These extravagant adventures in the French naturally belong to the "Sage Clerc," not to Antonio, who, as a bishop, has nothing to do with necromancy.

[2] VI, 59, 60.

A knight comes from India, and assures Robert that there is much talk of Merlin in those parts. The chaplain promptly sends ten clerics to collect such prophecies to add to the book, and continues to spend the treasures in the service of Merlin.[1]

There is less Arthurian matter in the Florentine text, the *Storia di Merlino* of Paolino Pieri. The prologue tells how the Emperor Frederick, finding a prophecy of Merlin fulfilled, sent for Master Richard, who "in Syracuse or Catania" was translating this prophecy, had him come to Palermo, and "believed everything Merlin had said was a thing divine." At the Emperor's bidding, Richard translated the whole work into French, and Paolino Pieri claims to be now rendering it into Italian.[2] It is a combination of portions of the *Prophecies* with a narrative of Merlin's youth, which differs considerably from that given by Robert de Boron and followed in the *Vita*.

In the *Vita*, the mother, at the advice of Blaise, is relegated to a tower, and there forgotten by the judges, until the child speaks to her when he is eighteen months old. In the *Storia*, when Merlin is born after eight months, Blaise obtains from the judge (here named Matteo) a respite of forty days.

---

[1] VI, 64–5. All this fantastic business of Rubers le Chappelain, including Merlin's prophecy of his coming to judgment with his tomb, is in the French 1498 edition of the *Prophecies*, but not in the French manuscripts. In the French, "le Sage Clerc de Galles," who has amassed this treasure, is again a totally different person from Antonio (with whom the Italian identifies him), who is mentioned in his speech to the clergy as already dead. Cf. Miss Paton, I, pp. 486–9, II, pp. 320–2.

[2] This is told again in detail in the body of the *Storia*, ed. Sanesi, pp. 82–4, but without again naming Richard.

As in the English poem, *Arthour and Merlin*, the child utters his first words to one of the nurses, when he is brought back from being baptised (he is not yet six days old).[1] There is pathos and tenderness in the scene where the mother (Marinaia) in vain implores him to speak to her, too:

The mother held him in her arms and soothed his weeping, and said many words to him, praying him to speak to her; and he did not speak. And she said: "O my sweet son, I conceived thee, and I know not how, and I have borne thee in my body nine months with great labour, and brought thee forth with such great sorrow and fear; I pray thee, if it be possible, that thou speak to me. Thou hast spoken to Liabella; ah, why dost thou not speak to me? Thou knowest that I have no other joy in the world but thee; speak to me, if thou wilt." And the child did not speak to her, and uttered not a word. [2]

When less than three weeks old, Merlin speaks to reassure his mother, but will not speak before the bishop and the judge until, the forty days being completed, the mother is about to be condemned to death, when he reveals the judge's own paternity. The case is finally decided by the bishop laying it before the people on Sunday at Mass, and obtaining the mother's pardon because of the miraculous character of the child.

A number of episodes follow, as occuring during Merlin's childhood under the patronage of the bishop, with various prophecies written down by Blaise: the child's profession of faith in the Blessed Sacrament, when just over a year, and his rebuke of the abbot for

[1] *Storia di Merlino*, p. 11. Cf. *Arthour and Merlin*, ed. E. Kölbing (Leipzig, 1890), ll. 991–1004.
[2] *Ibid.*, pp. 11–12.

simony, the doctor of medicine and his ill-gotten gains, the hypocrite "Agresto" and his threefold manner of death, the merchant's wife and her robe in the making of which the devil had his share—which becomes an example of how the "marca amorosa" of Treviso will become "dolorosa." We have here from the *Prophecies*, what we are not given in the *Vita*, the previous history of the hermit Elia (Helias):

> On another day Merlin was in the church, and a knight was there who was very jealous of his lady, and there was that other knight whom he suspected. And that jealous one had often thought to slay him by treachery, because he firmly believed that he had lain with his wife. This other knight came before Merlin, and said: "Tell me, Merlin, for courtesy, what I should do." And he replied: "Thou shalt die a hermit in the forest of Dornates, and thy virginity shall be preserved until death." [1]

The virgin knight is here called Herbeus (his enemy Morans), but afterwards Englias; at a later stage in the story, when Merlin goes into Gaul, it is said that Blaise gave what Merlin had made him write to a hermit named Englias that he might give it to Perceval.[2] Several of the Merlin episodes, such as the merchant of Rodiana (Erediana, Heraclea) and the money-changers, told as a warning to the Romans, the wicked priest and the poor woman, the ten knights and

---

[1] *Storia di Merlino*, p. 28. Cf. *Prophecies*, I, p. 270, where the episode is related by Helias (Helians) himself to Perceval. In the French, Helias had asked Merlin "comment je devoie finer," which in the Italian is disguised as "come io debo fare." The name Helias should, perhaps, be associated with that of Helyes of Toulouse, one of Galehaut's "sages clercs" in the *Lancelot* (Sommer, IV, pp. 20–34), and that of Morans (not in the French) was, perhaps, suggested by that of Marin(s), the jealous knight in *Perlesvaus* (IV, 2–4; Potvin, pp. 49–52).

[2] *Ibid.*, p. 78.

their ten sons—related by Elia in the *Vita*—are here
recorded by Blaise.[1] Merlin has already an assured
position with the King of Northumberland before the
episode of Vortigern's tower, which differs considerably
from Robert de Boron and the *Vita*. Vortigern
(Vertaggiere) is not the seneschal of King Constantius,
but a hostile lord who has defeated and killed the
king. He sends ambassadors into the four parts of the
world to find the child who has been born without a
father. Two of these, Ruggieri and Labegues, arrive
in Ireland, and hear from a Count Richard that such a
child has been born in Northumberland. The episode
of the two boys at play does not occur. They are
shown Merlin in church, and finally meet him at table,
with the king and the bishop; and Merlin practises a
series of his shape-shifting devices, for the benefit or
edification of Vortigern, before solving the problem of
the tower. The two dragons rush to the sea, and then
turn upon each other. They fight until evening, when
the white dragon returns to its den under the tower
and the red remains at the shore. At sunrise the
white dragon goes back to the sea to fight the red,
returning at nightfall; on the third day, it kills the
red, but dies five days later of its wounds. The perpetual falling of the tower has been caused by the
renewed fighting each night of the two dragons,[2] of
which the red symbolises Vortigern himself, the white
the two sons of Constantius.

Merlin, who has been accompanied by Blaise,

[1] *Prophecies*, I, pp. 279–85, 291–3; *Vita*, V, 2–6, 10–19.
[2] So in *Arthour and Merlin*, ed. *cit.*, ll. 1459–62. In the *Vita*
(I, 51), it is caused by the movement of the dragons when they feel
the weight of the building upon them.

returns to Northumberland, and is not brought into contact with Uther and Pendragon. He delivers a number of prophecies to Blaise, mainly concerned with the March of Treviso, Lombardy, Venice, and Rome. He then goes to Gaul, takes Master Antonio as scribe, and continues these predictions, the greater part of which are contained in the *Prophecies*. The only Arthurian motives among them are the story of the submission of Galehaut to Arthur for love of Lancelot, and that of the damsel of Gaul who comes to offer her love to Merlin, and is told instead that she will become the wife of the King of Ireland and bear a son who will be crowned King of Bellistans by King Arthur.[1] The book ends abruptly in the middle of the episode of the three cardinals.

The occasional agreement between the *Storia di Merlino* and *Arthour and Merlin* led the editor of the former, Sanesi, to the conclusion that the narrative portion of the Italian text derives from the same source as the English poem: the supposed lost first form of the poem of Robert de Boron or an earlier version of the story.[2] While the resemblance in the case of the child's first words to his nurse seems too close to be a mere coincidence, the essentially different treatment of the central episode of Vortigern's tower looks more like a later rehandling of Robert de Boron.

[1] *Storia di Merlino*, pp. 86–7. The tale of the damsel of Gaul is in the *Prophecies, ed. cit.*, I, p. 60, and the *Vita*, III, 4–5. For this child, Belio, Bellic, or Belien, "King of Bellistans," we are referred to "le livre de sa vie," apparently a romance now lost.

[2] Sanesi, *op. cit.*, pp. lxxxiv–xci. Cf. J. E. Wells, *A Manual of the Writings in Middle English* (London, 1916), I, p. 42.

CHAPTER XI

THE "MATTER OF BRITAIN" IN THE POETS OF THE TRECENTO AND BOCCACCIO.

GIOVANNI DEL VIRGILIO—a poet and professor at Bologna—had exchanged poetical correspondence in Latin verse with Dante, in the last years of the exiled Florentine's life, and had drawn from him his two Eclogues. A few years after Dante's death, more precisely in 1325, he addressed a similar pastoral poem to the Paduan poet and patriot, Albertino Mussato, in which he speaks of the latter as the successor of one Lycidas who had sung the love of Iseult:

> Ysidis ibat enim flavis fugibundula tricis
> non minus eluso quam sit zelata marito
> per silvas totiens per pascua sola reperta
> qua simul heroes decertavere Britanni,
> Lanciloth et Lamiroth et nescio quis Palamedes.[1]

The fourteenth century scholiast upon these Eclogues—probably Boccaccio himself, to whose pious care their preservation is due—bids us recognise in Lycidas the Paduan Latin poet, Lovato de' Lovati, who died in 1309 and was praised by Petrarca. Six

---

[1] "For Iseult with golden tresses strayed wandering, her husband eluded not less than she was desired, she so often found alone among the woods and among the pastures, what time the Britannic heroes fought, Lancelot and Lamorat and one hight Palamede" (Wicksteed and Gardner, *Dante and Giovanni del Virgilio*, London, 1902. Carmen vi, 211–16.)

lines of his poem on Iseult have been preserved in a single manuscript:

> Turris in amplexu laticum fabricata virentem
> despicit agrorum faciem; procul exulat arbos
> sponte sua; tristi ridens patet area bello.
> Huc studio formata dei, cantata britanno,
> Hyseis ardenti totiens querenda marito,
> venerat insanos frustrans Palamedis amores. [1]

These lines hardly suggest any known episode of the story of Iseult, and throw little light upon Lovato's treatment of his theme.

Less learned poets in this same region did not esteem the "matter of Britain" so highly. A body of what is known as Franco-Italian poetry is extant, which runs from the end of the thirteenth to the latter part of the fourteenth century, and had its centre in the Veneto and the March of Treviso. The authors of the two most important of these poems, Italians writing in French (more or less Italianised), profess to scorn the Arthurian legends.

The *Entrée d'Espagne* was composed by an anonymous Paduan some time before 1320.[2] He exalts

---

[1] "The tower, reared within the embrace of waters, looks down upon a verdant stretch of country; the boat, of its own accord, glides far off; the smiling plain lies exposed to dismal war. Hither Iseult, made by divine and sung by Britannic art, so oft to be sought by her ardent spouse, had come, frustrating the mad love of Palamede." Med. Laur., plut. xxxiii, cod. 31 (f. 46). Cf. L. Padrin, *Lupati de Lupatis etc carmina quaedam* (Padua, 1887), p. 42, who reads: "despicit agrorum faciem, procul exulat arbos, | sponte sua tristi ridens patet area bello." My rather temerarious translation is intended to suggest a connection with the "nef de joie" and the tower on the "Isle de la Fontaine" (cf. Löseth, sects. 324–37).

[2] *L'Entrée d'Espagne, chanson de geste franco-italienne,* publiée d'après le manuscrit unique de Venise par Antoine Thomas (Paris, 1913). Cf. F. Torraca, *L'Entrée d'Espagne,* in his *Studi di Storia Letteraria,* pp. 164 sq.

his own "gloriose cançons" above the fables of
Arthur:

> Segnors, car escoltez, ne soit ne criz ne hu,
> gloriose cançons, c'onques sa pier ne fu;
> ne vos sambleront mie de les flabes d'Artu.[1]

But he knows these fables, and occasionally con-
descends to refer to them. Ogier the Dane is now
the wielder of the sword of Tristan:

> Tient l'espee en son poing, que fist Gallaneüs,
> qe fu al buen Tristans, le fiuz Meliadus,
> dont oncist le Morot en l'isle de Carchus,
> quant il vient au roi Mars demander le treüs. [2]

The achievement of the Holy Grail is mentioned
as an example of sustained labour;[3] and, when
Charlemagne is indignant at his supposed desertion
by Roland, this is his vow:

> Par cil Diex q'en la cros sofri paine et moleste,
> n'ala si Galaaz por le Graal en queste
> con je ferai par lui en plains et an foreste.[4]

Febus (obviously the ancestor of Guiron in the

---

[1] "Lordings, pray listen, let there be nor hue nor cry, to the
glorious song of which was never its peer: these will not seem to you
like the fables of Arthur" (*Entrée d'Espagne*, ll. 365–7).

[2] "He holds in his hand the sword which Gallan made, which
belonged to the good Tristan, the son of Meliadus, wherewith he slew
the Morholt in the island of Carchus, when he came to demand the
tribute of King Mark" (*Entrée d'Espagne*, ll. 971·1–14). Gallan, a
famous maker of swords in romance, is mentioned elsewhere in the
poem. M. Thomas (II, p. 295) suggests that "l'isle de Carchus" may
be a confusion with the "isle de Colcos en mer" of the romance of
Troie. The sword of Tristan was given to Ogier by Charlemagne.
Cf. above, p. 172.

[3] *Entrée d'Espagne*, l. 8728.

[4] "By that God who on the Cross suffered pain and anguish,
Galahad went not so on the quest for the Grail as I shall do for him
over plains and through forests" (*Entrée d'Espagne*, ll. 9229–31).

Palamède) is three times cited as an example of prodigious strength, his name coupled with those of Antaeus and Hercules.[1]

Similarly in the *Attila*, composed by a Bolognese, Nicola da Casola, about 1350, the poet declares that he will not sing of the heroes and heroines of Breton fables, but a true history:

> Nen croy vous chanter des fables de Berton,
> de Isaut, ne de Tristan, ne de Breuz li felon,
> ne de la roine Zanevre, que amor mist au baron,
> quella dame dou Lac nori iusque infançon,
> ne delle rois Artu, ne de Hector li bron;
> mes d'une ystoire verables, que n'i est se voire non,
> si cum ie ai atrué in croniche por raison.[2]

Nevertheless, the *Entrée d'Espagne* begins that approximation of the Carolingian cycle to the Arthurian which was to be the characteristic feature of Italian poetry of chivalry in the Renaissance, while the *Attila*, in some respects, anticipates the *Gerusalemme Liberata*.

The incidental mention of Arthurian personages in lyrical poetry is much less frequent than in the earlier epoch, and generally presents no novelty. Frate Stoppa de' Bostichi, a Florentine friar at Lucca, apparently in the twenties of the century, composed a ballata on Fortune and the world, with the traditional mediaeval "ubi sunt?" motive, at times

---

[1] *Entrée d'Espagne*, ll. 5428, 10088, 14917.

[2] "I think not to sing you Breton fables, of Iseult nor of Tristan, nor of the felon Breus, nor of Queen Guinevere, who set love in the baron whom the Lady of the Lake reared from childhood, nor of King Arthur nor of Hector le Brun, but a true history which is all sooth, even as I have rightly found it in the chronicle" (G. Bertoni, *Attila, poema franco-italiano di Nicola da Casola*, Fribourg, 1907, p. 6).

curiously anticipating the two famous ballads of
François Villon. Where are the heroes of Rome,
where are Alexander and Nimrod? Where is the
courteous and noble Saladin?

> Tristano e Lancialotto,
> ancor nel mondo la lor fama vale?
> li altri di Cammellotto
> per la fortuna fecer l' altrettale.[1]

Where are Charlemagne, Orlando, Oliver? Where
are those who illumined the world with their wisdom
and poetry?

> Dov' è la gran fortezza
> ch' ebber le dure braccia di Sansone?
> dov' è la gran bellezza
> di Ginevra e d' Isotta e d' Ansalone? [2]

Two other motives have, at least, some singularity.
Bruzio Visconti compares his lady's hands with those
of the maiden wife of Tristan:

> Lì non appare alcun soverchio nodo;
> ongni parte avea modo,
> sicchè la mano fu sanza magagnia,
> qual si legge d' Isotta di Brettagnia.[3]

Francesco di Vannozzo, in a long frottola against

---

[1] "Tristan and Lancelot, does their fame still avail in the world?
The others of Camelot by fortune have fared the same" (in Carducci,
Cantilene e ballate, strambotti e madrigali nei secoli xiii e xiv, Pisa,
1871, pp. 104–8).

[2] "Where is the great strength that the brawny arms of Samson
had? Where is the great beauty of Guinevere and of Iseult and of
Absalom?"

[3] "Nought stands out too much upon them; every part was meet,
so that her hand was without blemish, as we read of Iseult of Brittany" (*Liriche edite ed inedite di Fazio degli Uberti*, ed. R. Renier,
Florence, 1883, p. 233).

Venice, takes the Holy Grail as type of a lengthy romance:

> Io vegio ben ch' io canto   e troppo zanzo;
> toe frasche son d' avanzo
> da farne un pien romanzo   e un Sangradale.[1]

We find a singularly interesting treatment of Arthurian matter in the poetry of a contemporary of Petrarca and Boccaccio: Fazio degli Uberti. In his famous canzone in the name of Italy, denouncing Charles of Luxembourg, he invokes upon the degenerate Cæsar the fate of Mordred:

> Come a Mordret il sol ti passi il casso;

"May the sun pass through thy chest as it did to Mordred"; [2] the reference, of course, being to the famous episode in the *Mort Artu* which Dante had used in the *Inferno*. But far more noteworthy than the occasional allusions in Fazio's lyrics are the Arthurian passages in his poem in terza rima, the *Dittamondo* (begun about 1350 and left unfinished at his death, which occurred shortly after 1368). Here he represents himself as led by the classical geographer Solinus over all the countries of the known world, ending with the Holy Land.[3] In a discourse on the history of Rome, his guide tells him that, at the time of Theodoric, talk was already heard

---

[1] "I see well that I sing and talk too much; thy follies are more than would make a full romance or a Holy Grail" (*Le Rime di Francesco di Vannozzo*, ed. A. Medin, Bologna, 1928, p. 161).

[2] *Liriche edite ed inedite di Fazio degli Uberti*, ed. cit., canz. xiv, 5.

[3] The editions of the *Dittamondo* all present an unsatisfactory text: Vicenza 1474, Venice 1501, Venice 1820 (*Parnaso Italiano*), Milan 1826 (ed. Monti). In my quotations I have collated—and, in one important detail, emended—the text, with the two fifteenth-century MSS. in the British Museum: Add. 10318 and Add. 10424.

of Uther Pendragon and of Merlin, and of the Round
Table, and he mentions the conquests of Arthur:

> In questo tempo già parlar s'udia
> di Uterpandragon e di Merlino,
> e del lavor che sfondato sparia.
>
> .   .   .   .   .   .
>
> Artù, benigno, largo e franco in guerra,
> con l'alta compagnia Francia conquise,
> Fiandra, Norvegia, e ciò che quel mar serra.[1]

The atmosphere becomes more romantic when the
poet with his guide arrives in Brittany, "la minor
Brettagna":

> Io fui in Gannes, dove ancor s' accerta
> la morte di Dorens, e la donzella
> che i livrier lassò al re della diserta.
> E fui ancora dove si novella
> che combattendo Artù Froles conquise,
> acquistando i due regni e le castella.[2]

In the *Lancelot*, Claudas, the king of "la terre
deserte" ("la terre del regne Claudas estoit apelee
deserte"), has usurped both Benoic, the kingdom of
Ban, the father of Lancelot, and Gannes, the kingdom

---

[1] "In that time already talk was heard of Uther Pendragon and
of Merlin, and of the work which, broken, disappeared . . . Arthur,
benign, generous and valiant in war, with his high fellowship
conquered France, Flanders, Norway, and what that sea encloses"
(*Dittamondo*, II, 15).

[2] "I was in Gannes where the tale is believed still of the death of
Dorins, and the damsel who left the greyhounds to the King of the
Desert. And I was there, too, where they tell that Arthur conquered
Frolle in combat, winning the two kingdoms and the castles" (IV, 22).
The difficulty of the first allusion, which mystified Graf (*Artù nell'Etna*,
p. 345), is simply due to the corruption of the text in the printed
versions: "che il curier lassò al re de la deserta" (1474 and 1501),
or "che il corrier lassò al re di là deserta" (1820 and 1826). Both the
MSS. I have examined read: "chel virier lascia al Re della diserta";
the word being "levriers" in the French text.

of Bors, the brother of Ban.   He detains at his court
the children of the latter, Lionel and the younger
Bors.   These two boys kill Dorins, the only son of the
king, and the latter is pursuing them when Saraide,
the damsel of the Lady of the Lake, transforms them
into greyhounds, leaving two real greyhounds under
the enchanted appearance of the children for Claudas
to seize.   At a later stage in the romance, Arthur, with
Lancelot and the sons of Bors, invades Gaul which is
claimed by Frolle d'Alemaigne who is allied with
Claudas.   Arthur kills Frolle in single combat, upon
which Claudas surrenders Gannes; the two kingdoms
here mentioned are Benoic and Gaul.[1]

Fazio now turns from the *Lancelot* to the *Tristan*:

> Poi vidi l' isoletta dove uccise
>   Tristano l' Amoroldo, e dove ancora
>   Elias di Sassogna a morte mise.
> In Tintoille udi' contar allora
>   d' un' ellera che dello avello uscia
>   là dove il corpo di Tristan dimora,
> la quale abbarbicata se ne gia
>   per la volta del coro, ove trovava
>   quello nel quale Isotta par che sia.
> Per le giunture del coperchio entrava,
>   e dentro l' ossa tutte accolte avea,
>   e come viva fosse l' abbracciava,
>   e ciò di nuovo trovato parea.[2]

---

[1] Sommer, III, pp. 55–6, V, pp. 373–7. Cf. Bruce, *Evolution of
Arthurian Romance*, I, pp. 439–40, II, pp. 325–6, 358. In Geoffrey
of Monmouth, *Historia*, IX, 11, Frollo is the Roman ruler of France
who is killed by Arthur on an island in the Seine outside the walls
of Paris.

[2] "Thereafter I saw the island where Tristan slew the Morholt, and
where again he put Elias of Saxony to death. I heard then told of
an ivy in Tintagel which came forth from the tomb where the body
of Tristan lies, and, taking root, went on through the vault of the
choir, where it found that in which it seems that Iseult is. Through

The story of how the Saxons with "a great number
of men of arms and an hideous host," under a leader
named Elias, invaded Cornwall to demand the truage
that had been previously (before the slaying of the
Morholt) paid to Ireland, and how finally Tristan slew
Elias in single combat, is told in the prose *Tristan* and
by Malory [1]; it does not occur in the *Tristano Riccardiano* nor in the *Tavola Ritonda*. The picturesque
detail of the plant springing up and uniting the tombs
of the two lovers—elsewhere a vine or a wild rose—
we have found already in Italian in the *Tavola Ritonda*.

The poet now passes into "Great Britain," and his
lines take on the true note of Arthurian romance.

> Noi fummo a Londres, e vidi la torre
>   dove Ginevra il suo onor difese,
>   e il fiume di Tamis che presso corre.
> E vidi il bel castel, ch' a forza prese
>   con gli tre scudi il franco Lancilotto,
>   l' anno secondo che a prodezza intese.
> Vidi guasto e disfatto Camelotto;
>   e fui là dove l' una e l' altra nacque,
>   quella di Corbenich e di Scalotto.[2]

Guinevere's defence of the Tower of London against
Mordred, the stories of the daughter of the "Fisher

the joinings of the cover it entered, and within had gathered up all
the bones, and embraced them as though it were alive; and this seemed
newly found" (IV, 22).

[1] Löseth, sects. 270–8; *Morte Darthur*, X, 28–30.

[2] "We were at London, and I saw the tower where Guinevere defended her honour, and the river Thames that flows hard by. I
saw the fair castle which brave Lancelot took by force with the three
shields, the second year that he wrought deeds of prowess. I saw
wasted and ruined Camelot; and I was there where the one and
other damsel was born, she of Corbenic and she of Astolat" (IV, 23).

I take it that the line about Camelot refers to its destruction by
King Mark, which Fazio, no doubt, had found mentioned in the
Palamède (cf. above, p. 206).

Q

King" of Corbenic (who becomes the mother of Galahad) and the maiden of Astolat, are, of course, obvious, as also the allusion to the tale, told at length in the *Lancelot*, how the hero at the beginning of his career, when he was the anonymous white knight, took the Castle of Dolorous Gard with the aid of the three shields shown him by the damsel of the Lake.[1]

> Vidi il castello dove Arech si giacque
>   con la sua Nida, e il peron di Merlino,
>   che per amor altrui veder mi piacque.
> Vidi la landa e la fonte del pino,
>   là dove il cavaliero al nero scudo
>   con pianto e riso guardava il cammino;
> io dico, quando il nano acerbo e crudo
>   dinanzi a gli occhi di messer Galvano
>   battendo il menò via con grande studo.[2]

The castle in question, in the *Erec et Enide* of Chrétien de Troyes, is probably that of Penevric where Erec recovers of his wound and the lovers forget their grief.[3]   The rock of Merlin (*perron Merlin*) is, of course, not his tomb, but the "perron," which he set up in the meadows near Camelot, where Tristan and Lancelot fought; for love of them, the poet rejoiced in the sight.   In the *Lancelot*—an episode omitted by the *Tavola Ritonda* and Malory—at the fountain under the pine a knight with a black shield, who weeps and laughs alternately, overthrows several knights of the

[1] There is no reference to the three shields in the unorthodox version presented by the *Tavola Ritonda*, cap. viii.

[2] " I saw the castle where Erec lay with his Enide, and the rock of Merlin which for another's love I liked to see.   I saw the meadow and the fountain by the pine, where the knight with the black shield guarded the road with tears and laughter; I mean, when the harsh and cruel dwarf, before the eyes of Sir Gawain, with stripes led him away with eager zest " (IV, 23).

[3] *Erec et Enide*, ed. Foerster, ll. 5187–250.

Round Table in the presence of Gawain, but is himself
taken away with stripes by a dwarf of whose daughter
he is enamoured. He turns out to be Hector de
Maris, Lancelot's half-brother.[1]

> Vidi la valle, che acquistò Tristano,
>   quando il gigante uccise allo schermire,
>   traendo di prigion qual v' era strano.
> E vidi i campi, ove fu il gran martire
>   in Saglibier, quando rimase il mondo
>   voto d' onor, di piacer e d' ardire.[2]

Here, in accordance with the *Palamède*, the poet
places Tristan's slaying the giant Nabon and deliverance of the captives in the Servage in a valley on the
mainland, instead of, as in the *Tristan*, on an island.
The list ends appropriately with the last great battle
from the *Mort Artu*; but, in the next canto, the poet's
guide speaks again of Arthur, when he gives an account
of the kings of Britain. More than four hundred and
sixty years had passed from the Incarnation when
Uther Pendragon, by the counsel of Merlin, became
lord of the whole island. His son and successor,
Arthur, "was so feared and loved by his people that,
long while after his death, it was expected that he
would return":

> Tanto da' suoi fu temuto ed amato,
>   che lungamente dopo la sua morte
>   ch' ei dovesse tornar fu aspettato.[3]

The poet has still a couple of Arthurian sites to

---

[1] Sommer, III, pp. 277–80.

[2] "I saw the valley which Tristan won, when he killed the giant
in sword-play, drawing from prison the strangers there. And I saw
the plains where was the great slaughter near Salisbury, when the
world remained bereft of honour, of delight and daring" (IV, 23).

[3] IV, 24.

notice before his English travels are completed; the scenes of the two great combats in the *Palamède*, between Meliadus of Liones and the Saxon prince Ariohan, and between Guiron and Danain le Roux:

> Tanto mi dilettava il ragionare
> accorto e bello della scorta mia
> che andando in fretta non mi parea andare.
> E noi trovammo un fiume per la via
> sopra 'l qual pose campo il re Artù
> con la sua grande e ricca compagnia;
> io dico, quando gran battaglia fu
> da Aroan a quel di Leonois,   .
> credo che 'l sai, però non dico più.
> Poi trovammo la fonte in Sorelois,
> dove fu l' altra non men aspra e grave
> tra Danain e Guron lo Cortois.[1]

Boccaccio naturally felt the allurement of the Arthurian story, and dealt with it after his own fashion. In the *Amorosa Visione*, in a hall of the castle of Mundane Life, he sees painted the triumph of glory, where, after the heroes of ancient Rome, appears the cavalcade of the knights of the Round Table. Arthur himself is riding at their head, followed by the three Grail questers—Bors, Perceval, and Galahad.[2]

---

[1] " So much did the wise and fair discourse of my guide delight me that, though we were going in haste, I heeded not the going. And we found a river by the way over which King Arthur camped with his great and goodly company; I mean, when the great battle was made by Ariohan on him of Liones; I believe thou knowest it, and therefore say no more. Then we found the fountain in Sorelois where was the other, not less fierce and grim, between Danain and Guiron the Courteous" (IV, 26). For "Aroan," the modern editions read "Caraon." Cf. above, pp. 53, 57.

[2] *Amorosa Visione*, canto xi. I quote from *Opere volgari di Giovanni Boccaccio*, ed. Moutier, vol. XIV. The text differs considerably from the earliest editions, the Venetian of 1521 and the Giolito of 1549. Boccaccio calls Galahad "Galeotto," perhaps for sake of the rhyme, but the real Galehaut appears in his proper place.

Lancelot is riding with Guinevere, attended fittingly
by the faithful Galehaut, Boccaccio already showing
his admiration for the figure of the "haut prince":

> Non molto dietro ad esso con gran cura
> seguiva Galeotto, il cui valore
> più che altro di compagni si figura.[1]

Then come "Chedino," Hector de Maris, "Messer
Suano," the Morholt of Ireland, Agravaine, Palamede,
Lionel, Pellinor, Gawain, Mordred, and Dodinello.[2]
Tristan and Iseult are clasping hands as they ride,
while she timidly prays him to turn that she may see
his face, and behind them comes Brunor, "rubesto e
fiero," the lord of the Castle of Pleur, with whom the
list of those named concludes. Lancelot and Guinevere, Tristan and Iseult, are figured again, further on
in the poem, in the pageant of the lovers.[3]

Madonna Fiammetta, when deserted by Panfilo,
"measuring her sufferings with those of many ladies
of olden time," inevitably thinks of Iseult:

I remember to have read in the French romances, if any
faith can be placed in them, how Tristan and Iseult loved each
other more than did any other lovers, and passed their youth
in delight mingled with many adversities, and because, while
at the full tide of their mutual love, they came to one end,
it seems to be believed that, not without very great grief of
both, did they leave their earthly delights. This may easily
be granted, if they departed from the world with the belief that
these delights could not be had elsewhere; but, if they thought
to be elsewhere as they were here, we must deem that, as they

---

[1] "Not far behind him with great heed Galehaut followed, whose
worth is shown beyond any of his companions."

[2] For "Suano," the editions of 1521 and 1549 read "Ivano," which
seems plausible, unless it is Osenain Cuer Hardi who is called
Suziano in the *Tavola Ritonda*. For Dodinello (Dodinel le Sauvage),
see below, p. 258. "Chedino" is, perhaps, Kay rather than Kahedyn.

[3] *Amorosa Visione*, canto XXIX.

died, joy rather than sorrow was given them by the death that they received, which, though held by many most cruel and hard, I do not believe was so. . . . In the arms of Tristan was his death and that of his lady, and if, when he clasped her, she had suffered, he would have opened his arms, and the pain would have ceased. And, besides, though it may be called most grievous, what grievousness shall we reasonably say can be in a thing that only happens once and occupies a very small space of time? Assuredly, none. Both Iseult and Tristan, then, ended at one moment their delights and their sorrows; but for me has remained a long time in incomparable sorrow beyond the delights that I have had.[1]

In the *Corbaccio*, the satire against women that Boccaccio wrote at a later epoch, Arthurian allusions become cynical or licentious. The lady esteems her lover a Lancelot, a Tristan, or even a Morholt of Ireland according to his power of corresponding with her desires. To contradict her fables and lies, is to enter upon a wordy conflict for which she is only too ready, "deeming that in might she surpasses Galehaut of the Distant Islands or Febus." Her prayer-books and rosaries are the French romances; "in which she reads of Lancelot and of Guinevere, of Tristan and of Iseult, and their feats and their loves, and the jousts and tournaments and assemblies. She is all thrilled when she reads of Lancelot or Tristan or someone else forgathering secretly and alone in the chambers with their ladies." Her lover would destroy the nobleness of his mind, if he had as much "as had of old the lineage of King Ban of Benoic."[2]

Boccaccio's commentary on the fifth canto of the

---

[1] *La Fiammetta*, cap. viii. Cf. *Tavola Ritonda*, p. 505.

[2] *Il Corbaccio*, in *Opere volgari di G.B.*, ed. Moutier, vol. V, pp. 219, 221, 233, 246.

Inferno shows that he knew the Tristan and Lancelot stories at first hand in these "romanzi franceschi," though now—in his old age—he prudently remarks that they contain "cose, per quel ch' io creda, più composte a beneplacito che secondo la verità." This applies in some measure, perhaps, to his own remarkable elaboration of the tragedy of Paolo and Francesca. He tells us, in what is practically a novella in the spirit of the *Decameron*, though accepted as sober history by later commentators in his steps, how Paolo went to Ravenna to woo Francesca by proxy for his brother, and, lest she should be repelled by the grim personality of Gianciotto, her father had Paolo pointed out to her as her future husband—the deception not being laid aside until the wedding night at Rimini when Gianciotto was substituted for Paolo.[1] Torraca first pointed out the impossibility of this story from the historical point of view, and suggested that Boccaccio was simply adopting the story of Tristan and Iseult: Tristan wooing Iseult by proxy for King Mark, her father urging him to plead for himself (in the *Tavola Ritonda*, the Irish king at first lets her suppose that Tristan himself is her destined bridegroom), the substitution of Brangwain for Iseult on Mark's wedding night.[2] Other details may be similarly matched; the catastrophe being brought about by the servant, who sends word to Gianciotto, is paralleled in the betrayal of the lovers to Mark by Andred. If this is so, we must suppose that Boccaccio's critical insight

---

[1] *Il comento alla Divina Commedia e gli altri scritti intorno a Dante*, ed. D. Guerri (Bari, 1918), II, p. 137–9, 144–5.

[2] *Studi danteschi*, I, pp. 413 sq.

led him to recognise the Arthurian atmosphere of the canto and the correspóndence of its culminating passage with the Tristan story, and that, to complete it, he turned back to Dante's source and carried the correspondence further.

It is noticeable that Petrarca places the lovers of Rimini alone with those of the "dim Arthuriad" in the *Trionfo d'Amore*, though with a characteristic note of contempt for such purely popular literature:

> Ecco quei che le carte empion di sogni:
> Lancilotto, Tristano, e gli altri erranti,
> ove convien che 'l vulgo errante agogni.
> Vedi Ginevra, Isolda, e l' altre amanti,
> e la coppia d'Arimino, che 'nsieme
> vanno facendo dolorosi pianti.[1]

Boccaccio with his commentary did not reach the canto in which Mordred appears, but he had already dealt faithfully with that "nefarius homo" in the Latin prose of his chapter on King Arthur in the *De Casibus Virorum Illustrium*—the chapter in virtue of which Caxton, who knew the work only at third hand through the medium of Lydgate, was to appeal to the authority of "Bochas" in testimony to the historicity of the national hero of Britain.[2] Having succeeded

---

[1] "Here are those who fill the pages with dreams: Lancelot, Tristan, and the other knights-errant, for which it is meet that the erring vulgar herd yearn. See Guinevere, Iseult, and the other lovers, and the couple of Rimini, who go together uttering mournful laments" (*Triumphus Cupidinis*, iii, or, as edited by Appel, ii, 79-84). Petrarca mentions Arthur ("Ov' è un re Arturo?") in the *Triumphus Famae*, ii, 134.

[2] Lib. VIII, cap. xix: "De Arthuro Rege Britonum." Boccaccio composed two redactions of the *De Casibus*, which are represented by the Strasburg edition of 1475 (and the Paris probably of 1507) and the Augsburg edition of 1544 respectively. Cf. A. Hortis,

his father Uther Pendragon as king, Arthur took advantage of the fallen state of the Roman Republic to conquer Ireland, the Orkneys, Dacia, Gothland, Norway, and parts of Gaul. Contented with his achievement, lest valour should decay through ease, he founded the Round Table, "by the counsel, it is said, of Merlin the prophet who flourished at that time." This was the law for all the companions of the Table: "Not to lay down arms; to seek out monsters; to defend, when called, the right of the weak with all their power; to do violence to no one; not to injure each other; to combat for the safety of friends; to risk life for their native land; to seek for themselves nought but honour; on no account to break faith; most diligently to practise religion; to offer hospitality freely to all according to their means; to relate events, whether redounding to the honour or shame of the reporter, with entire fidelity and truth to those in charge of the annals." Thus, and by the might of his fellowship of knights (none of whom are named by Boccaccio), the name of the king came to such glory that, in spite of adverse fortune and the long course of years, it has lasted to our time. Arthur refused to pay tribute to Rome, crossed into Gaul, defeated the consul Lucius, and was proceeding to further conquests, when he was recalled to Britain by the rebellion of Mordred, "his son by a concubine," whom he had left in charge of his kingdom, and who, after

Studi sulle opere latine del Boccaccio (Trieste, 1879), pp. 117-54; H. Hauvette, *Recherches sur le "De Casibus Virorum Illustrium" de Boccace* (in *Entre Camarades*, Paris, 1901, pp. 279 sq.); H. Bergen, *Lydgate's Fall of Princes*, IV (Washington, 1927), pp. 125-7, 327-9 (text of the Arthurian chapter).

ingratiating himself with the people and refusing his father supplies, had produced forged letters to the effect that the king was dead. There is no mention of Guinevere. Arthur landed, and, after the engagement on the shore, Mordred retreated to Cornwall. Here the last great battle was fought, the valour of Arthur's knights being unable to prevail against the overwhelming numbers on the other side. Almost all the king's men had fallen, when Arthur urged his horse against his son, and pierced his breast with his lance. Mordred, mortally wounded, smote his father on the helmet with his sword, the stroke penetrating to the brain. As Arthur withdrew his lance from the dying man's breast, "they say that the wound was so widened that the rays of the setting sun passed through it." The king, feeling the end of his days at hand, had himself conveyed in a boat to the island of Avalon, where he died, leaving the kingdom and the vengeance to be executed to his nephew Constantine. But—whether the death of Arthur was concealed by his successor, or, because of the perturbation of the times, few knew that he was dead and he was buried without ceremony—the Britons believe that he is not dead, but still secretly alive, and assert that, when his wounds are healed, he will assuredly return. Thus, by the daring of one infamous man, the kingdom of Arthur with his life was taken from him; the Round Table, all its noble heroes slain, was deserted and broken, and became a fable for the common folk, the whole history being a lesson for mortals that nought in the world save humility can endure.

The story here presented follows Geoffrey of Mon-

THE ROUND TABLE

From Boccaccio, *De casibus virorum illustrium* (French translation by Laurent de Premierfait). B.M., Add. MS. 35321

mouth, but substitutes the founding and rules of the Round Table for Geoffrey's account of the coronation of Arthur. The business of the refusal to pay tribute and the defeat of the Roman consul is again Geoffrey; but the details of Mordred's rebellion, particularly the motive of the forged letters, is adopted from the *Mort Artu* branch of the *Lancelot*, as also the fact that Mordred is the king's son, though there is no hint of his incestuous birth—a motive which seems to have been unknown to all the early commentators on Dante.[1] It agrees with Geoffrey in placing the last battle in Cornwall, instead of near Salisbury, but has drawn from the French romance the account of the death of Mordred at Arthur's hands, with the fantastic detail of the ray of sunlight passing through the wound. The conclusion is practically that of Geoffrey, but with the usual added motive of Arthur's expected return, and the rationalising explanation of how the tale may have originated.

We find an almost precisely similar, but somewhat fuller, version given by Boccaccio's disciple, Benvenuto da Imola, in his commentary on the thirty-second canto of the *Inferno*.[2] He gives further details: Arthur's preliminary struggle with the Saxons, the list of eastern kings whom Lucius summons to the support of the Romans, Mordred's impious marriage

---

[1] The motive in question appears in the *Estoire del Saint Graal*, the Vulgate *Merlin*, and the *Huth Merlin*, which precede in the order of narrative; but Bruce has argued that the story originated with the author of the *Mort Artu*, which was composed earlier. See J. D. Bruce, *Mordred's Incestuous Birth*, in *Medieval Studies in Memory of G. S. Loomis*, pp. 197–208.

[2] *Comentum super Dantis Aldigherii Comoediam*, ed. Vernon and Lacaita, II, pp. 497–501.

with Guinevere, his being besieged by the king in Winchester, and the date of Arthur's passing; all of which are manifestly from Geoffrey of Monmouth. But, whereas Boccaccio vaguely refers to "the Britons in their annals," Benvenuto cites as his authority "Gualterius anglicus in sua chronica quae britannica vocatur," in which "he mingles many false things with true for the exaltation of his native land," and he points out the historical impossibility of Lucius the consul "having with him many eastern kings, to wit, the kings of the Greeks, the Medes, the Parthians, Libya, Egypt, Babylon, Bithynia, Phrygia, Crete, and many others," at the time of Arthur.[1] It has been suggested that this "Walter the Englishman" should be identified with Walter Map, the reputed author of the *Lancelot* and other Vulgate romances [2]; but, save for the few motives that Boccaccio, too, had drawn from the *Mort Artu*, Benvenuto's main source is unquestionably Geoffrey of Monmouth. The reference is surely to an earlier holder of the archdeaconry of Oxford than Walter Map—the "Walterus Oxenefordensis archidiaconus," whose mysterious "liber Britannici sermonis" Geoffrey professed to be translating into Latin.[3] It is, perhaps, possible that Boccaccio and Benvenuto had before them some *Brut* in which Geoffrey was confused with Walter of

---

[1] Cf. Geoffrey of Monmouth, X, 1.

[2] P. Toynbee, *Index of Authors quoted by Benvenuto da Imola* (Boston, 1901), p. 24.

[3] Geoffrey of Monmouth, I, 1, XI, 1. The colophon in the Welsh text, of which Mr. Griscom has published a translation (*op. cit*, p. 536), seems to me to prove that redactions of the *Historia Regum Britanniae* were current under the name of Walter of Oxford.

Oxford, and the story of the Round Table, together with the motives from the *Mort Artu*, already woven into the narrative.

There are occasional Arthurian echoes, or analogues, in the *Decameron*. The twin daughters of Messer Neri degli Uberti are named "Ginevra la bella" and "Isotta la bionda." The story of the daughter of the Soldan of Babylon has been traced by Bruce to the same oriental source as that of the hero's ancestress Chelinde in the prose *Tristan*, while that of the Marquess of Saluzzo and Griselda inevitably invites comparison with the *Erec et Enide* of Chrétien de Troyes.[1] More significant for our purpose is the somewhat notorious sub-title, where, at the beginning and end of the book, we read: "Il libro chiamato *Decameron*, cognominato *Principe Galeotto*." Understanding the name "Galeotto" in the sinister sense made traditional through Dante's line, Hauvette suggested that it was an addition of Boccaccio's own in later life, after his conversion, as a repudiation or a warning in the spirit of his letter to Mainardo Cavalcanti, where he urges his friend not to allow the women of his family to read the book.[2] Massèra, in spite of the almost unanimous testimony of the manuscripts, uncompromisingly rejects it as an interpolation, on the grounds that, if we take "Galeotto" as type of a mere pander or go-between, Boccaccio would never have been guilty of casting such a stigma upon his own

---

[1] *Decameron*, X, 6; II, 7; X, 10. Cf. J. D. Bruce, *A Boccaccio Analogue in the Old French prose Tristan*, in *Romanic Review*, I (1910), pp. 384 sq.; E. Philipot, in *Romania*, XXV, p. 264.

[2] H. Hauvette, *Principe Galeotto*, in *Mélanges offerts à M. Émile Picot* (Paris, 1913), I, pp. 505—10.

work, and that, if we accept the character of the "haut prince" as given in the French romances, and take him as "simbolo dell' amore cortese," his name would be in flagrant contradiction with the nature of the book.[1]   Michele Barbi has, however, shown good reasons for holding that the sub-title is, in all probability, due to Boccaccio himself, and that the character of Galehaut, not as a "turpe mezzano," but as the "cavalleresco messo d' amore," the helpful friend of Lancelot in need, is thoroughly in accordance with the purpose that the writer himself professes in the *Decameron*.[2] The prefix "principe," given to Galeotto, shows that Boccaccio had in mind, not primarily Dante, but the original romance, which his commentary on the fifth canto of the *Inferno* shows that he knew directly.   That "li sires des Lontaines Illes," the builder of the castle of the "Orgueilleuse emprise," should thus have given his name to the *Decameron* is among the more curious reflections of the Arthurian legend in Italy.

[1] *Il Decameron* a cura di A. F. Massèra (Bari, 1927), II, pp. 351–2.
[2] *Sul testo del "Decameron,"* in *Studi di filologia italiana*, I, pp. 53–4. As already stated, I disagree with Barbi's interpretation of Dante's allusion in a similar sense.

CHAPTER XII

FRANCESCO DA BUTI, in his commentary upon Dante written between 1380 and 1390, passes lightly over the references to Lancelot and Guinevere in the fifth canto of the *Inferno*, on the grounds that it is a familiar story: "come dicono i cantari." The cantari were popular narrative poems, recited or sung to the people in the public squares of Italian cities by professional reciters or singers, "cantastorie," the successors of the old "giullari." The Florentine "cantastorie" were famous all over the peninsula, but more or less similar conditions prevailed elsewhere. St. Francis of Assisi had heard recitations about Charles the Emperor and his paladins that were perhaps of this character,[1] and we have documentary evidence of these "cantastorie" at Bologna—where they were known as "cantatores franciginorum," and spoken of as those who "cantant de domino Rolando et Oliverio"—in the second half of the thirteenth century. There is the record of a process at Bologna in 1307, when a wineseller is accused of having abused the Guelf Party and wounded a disputant in a certain street, but pleads an alibi, calling witnesses to prove that he was in another part of the city, listening to a minstrel who was singing "about

---

[1] *Intentio Regulae*, ed. L. Lemmens, p. 92; *Speculum Perfectionis*, ed. Sabatier, cap. 4.

a Frenchman or a paladin." Under cross-examination one witness does not remember what Frenchman it was, but another deposes that the singing was about William of Orange. At a later date, in the Quattrocento, the humanist Poggio tells how a citizen of Milan, after listening to one of these singers, came home in tears, and, to the exhortations of his wife to console himself with supper, could only answer: "Roland is dead, who was the sole defence of Christendom." These examples point to the legends of the Carolingian cycle having been more popular; but that the Arthuriad was likewise appreciated, may be gathered from Franco Sacchetti's story of the blacksmith, who sang something of Dante's "come si canta uno cantare," and, when rebuked by the poet, henceforth, if he wanted to sing, "sang of Tristan and of Lancelot, and let Dante be." [1]

From the twenties of the fourteenth century, these lyrical narratives begin to come down to us in ottava rima, the earliest cantare preserved being apparently that of Fiorio and Biancofiore, the French story retold in prose and at inordinate length by Boccaccio in his *Filocolo*. It was probably written between 1320 and 1330; that is, before Boccaccio with the *Filostrato* and the *Teseide* had made the ottava rima a literary, as well as a popular, measure.[2] But it must be borne

[1] See the masterly monograph by Ezio Levi, *I cantari leggendari del popolo italiano nei secoli XIV e XV*, issued as Supplement 16 of the *G.S.L.I.* (Turin, 1914). It is a companion to the collection that he is editing in the *Scrittori d' Italia: Fiore di Leggende*, cantari antichi editi e ordinati da E. Levi (*Serie prima: cantari leggendari.* Bari, 1914).

[2] *Il cantare di Fiorio e Biancifiore*, ed. V. Crescini (Bologna, 1899); *Il cantare di Fiorio e Biancofiore*, ed. G. Crocioni (Rome, 1903).

in mind that we only possess the cantari in what is, so to speak, their final stage of evolution. They present close analogies with the northern ballad. As in the ballad, much of the matter "seems to be ancient or even primitive," whereas the actual metrical form is comparatively new.[1] The poets— who, with the exception of Antonio Pucci, are anonymous—are fond of appealing to a "libro" or a "scrittura"; but their actual sources can very seldom be definitely traced, for, as Ezio Levi finely puts it, "behind the cantari spreads out in its immensity the whole literature of the Middle Ages."

The cantari that deal with the "matter of Britain" fall into two classes: those that more or less represent the so-called "Breton lays," only incidentally connected with the main Arthurian story, and in which the motive of the knight and his fairy mistress frequently occurs; those which retell in verse the episodes of the Arthurian legend familiar in the prose romances.

In the *Tavola Ritonda*, we have already met "la Gaia Pulcella," or "la Gaia Donzella," the daughter of Morgan le Fay and her paramour Onesun (Huneson), who is rescued from Burletta by Lancelot, and taken away by her own father; a pathetic little figure with nothing supernatural or "gay" about her.

[1] Cf. W. P. Ker, *On the History of the Ballad*, in *Form and Style in Poetry*, ed. R. W. Chambers (London, 1928), especially pp. 21–34. It is noteworthy that Antonio da Tempo, in his *Summa artis rithimici* written in 1332 (*Delle rime volgari trattato di A. da T.*, ed. G. Grion, Bologna, 1869), does not include the ottava rima as a recognised form of vernacular rhythm. The earliest Italian poems of this kind were probably in the "lassa ottonaria," like the famous *Cantilena del giullare toscano*.

R

We hear no more of her until at a later stage of the
romance, where Breus tells Tristan that he will
trust no enamoured knight:

> How can a man trust you, who have many times taken
> Queen Iseult from King Mark? and Lancelot, brother of that
> traitor there, has done the like to King Arthur; and also it is
> not long since Gawain took the Gaia Donzella from Morgan le
> Fay.[1]

This story appears in one of the earliest extant
cantari—dating probably from the middle of the
fourteenth century—that of the *Pulzella Gaia*.[2]

In the court of King Arthur, Messer Troiano—who
figures incidentally in the *Tavola Ritonda* where he
is killed by Tristan in a tournament[3]—makes a
"vaunt" with Gawain, each to stake his head that
he will bring back a better trophy of the chase than
any other knight. Troiano takes a white doe, which
he presents to Guinevere. Gawain is worsted in a
fight with a horrible serpent, which—when, after at
first pretending to be Lancelot, he reveals his name
—becomes a girl, "più bella che una rosa di verzieri,"
who tells him that she has long desired him, and that
she is "Pulzella Gaia," the daughter of Morgan.
In her arms he suddenly remembers his pledge and
that he must return to die. She gives him a ring
which will bring him all he desires, including herself,
but which will lose its power if he reveals the joy he
has had. She returns to the serpent's form, while
he—obtaining from the ring a charger, a whole troop

---

[1] *Tavola Ritonda*, cxxiv (p. 487). The "traditore" is Astor
(Hector) de Maris, who is in Tristan's company.

[2] Ed. E. Levi, *Fiore di Leggende*, II.

[3] *Tavola Ritonda*, xc (p. 346).

of captive knights, and a wonderful monster as trophy
of his hunting—makes his way back to the court,
where he is hailed as victor, and Troiano departs dis-
comfited. The ring brings Pulzella Gaia to Gawain's
embraces, and she once more warns him not to
reveal their love. Guinevere—who appears throughout in an odious light—makes advances to him which
he rejects. She summons a tournament at which
each has to make a vaunt of his or her greatest
treasure. Gawain is at first silent, but at length,
stung by the queen's taunts, forgets his oath:

> Allor messer Galvan disse: Io mi vanto,
> e d' esta cosa i' mostrerò certanza:
> io son avventuroso di cotanto
> più d' ogni cavalier che porti lanza;
> e chi cercasse il mondo tutto quanto,
> non troveria una sì bella amanza
> come è la mia gentile damigella;
> e quella è il fiore d' ogni donna bella.[1]

The queen then proclaims that whoever cannot
prove his vaunt on the third day shall lose his head.
In vain does Gawain appeal to the ring to summon
Pulzella Gaia; it has lost all its power. He is
sentenced to death by King Arthur, and all the pre-
parations for the execution are made; but, as he
kneels before the block, Gawain declares that he has
deserved his doom and will die content, if he may
only see his lady again. At this the Pulzella comes
to the rescue with a whole army from Fairyland,

---

[1] "Then Sir Gawain said: 'I make my vaunt, and of this thing I
shall show the proof; I am far more fortunate than any other knight
that bears lance; and whoso should search through all the world would
not find so fair a love as is my gentle damsel; of every fair lady she
is the flower' " (stanza 32).

rebukes him for his disloyalty, and goes away,
declaring that her own fate will be worse than death:

> O dislial, perchè m' hai palesata?
> Mala ventura a chi ti cinse spada!
> La più gentil donzella hai ingannata
> che si trovasse per ogni contrada;
> onde per te io sono imprigionata;
> ben vo' morir, dappoi ch' ella t' aggrada
> Mia madre mi darà prigion sì forte,
> che meglio mi saria aver la morte.—
> E l'uno e l'altro sì forte piangia,
> e intrambi duo sì si abbracciava.
> Lo re, tutta la corte li vedia, ·
> di suo' bellezze si meravigliava.
> E la Pulzella Gaia in quella dia
> dal buon Galvano sì s' accombiatava,
> e disse: Amanza ti convien trovare:
> più non potra' mi veder nè parlare.[1]

Pulzella Gaia returns to her mother, who casts her
into a subterranean dungeon up to her waist in water.
Gawain, rebuked by Arthur, wanders through the
world to find his lost love. A knight challenges him,
and reveals himself as **Breus**:

> Io vo cercando Tristan, Lancilotto,
> messer Galvano e 'l buon Astor di Mare,
> Palamidès, Galasso tanto dotto,
> Troiano e Lionel vorria trovare;

---

[1] "'O disloyal one, why hast thou revealed me? Ill luck to him who
girded on thy sword! The most gentle damsel hast thou deceived
who might be found throughout the lands; wherefore through thee
am I imprisoned; fain would I die, since thou wouldst have it so;
my mother will give me a dungeon so harsh that better for me would
it be to have death'.

"And both wept bitterly, and each embraced the other. The king,
all the court, saw them; they marvelled at her beauty. And Pulzella
Gaia that day took leave of good Gawain, and said: 'Needs must
thou find another love; me thou shalt not see nor speak with more'"
(stanzas 49–50).

messer Ivano e Artù di Camellotto,
e Lionbordo ancor per tale affare;
e tutti li altri cavalieri erranti,
chè impiccar li vorria tutti quanti.[1]

Gawain overthrows him at the first stroke, and
goes his way. After six months wandering, he
comes to a castle, where he is well entertained, but
hears damsels lamenting the captivity of the Pulzella Gaia and cursing his own disloyalty—a motive
perhaps suggested by the bewailing for the unasked
question in the story of Perceval. Before another
castle, a lady invokes maledictions on all knights
for his sake, and, when he declares himself a friend
of Gawain, summons a hundred armed knights to
take and slay him. He easily defeats them, and,
moved by the valour of the "povero cavaliere," as he
calls himself, the lady becomes enamoured of him,
and directs him to the city of "Pela Orso" (the
"Pellaus" or "Palaus" of the *Tavola Ritonda*), where
the Pulzella is imprisoned. Gawain attempts to enter
as a merchant; when that fails, he conquers the
surrounding country, and besieges the city for four
years. He takes it at last, but the castle is impreg-
nable, until—aided by a letter which the Pulzella
has conveyed to him — he obtains an entry ·by

---

[1] "I go seeking Tristan, Lancelot, Sir Gawain, and the good Hector
de Maris, Palamede, Galahad so skilled, Troiano and Lionel I would
fain find; Sir Ivain and Arthur of Camelot, and Lionbordo, too, for
this business; and all the other knights-errant, for I should like to
hang them every one" (stanza 56). Liombordo or Liombardo appears
in the *Tavola Ritonda* (vii, pp. 18, 19) as an enemy of the knights
of the Round Table, who is unhorsed by Lancelot and sent as prisoner
to the queen; later, he joins Arthur against Lancelot in the siege of
Joyous Gard (l, pp. 184, 185).

disguising himself and a band of his followers as the Lady of the Lake and her women. The Pulzella is liberated, Morgan imprisoned in her stead, and the lovers return together to Camelot, where they are received with universal rejoicing.

The carrying off of the Pulzella Gaia from Morgan by Gawain, the appearance of Breus in the story, the names of Troiano and Lionbordo, the title of Morgan's castle, all show a close connection with the *Tavola Ritonda*, or one of its unidentified sources. But the Pulzella, who is there a mere human girl, helpless and evidently simple, becomes attached in the first part of the poem to a story of another kind. The cantare here takes its place with a class of French poems, presumably founded on "Breton lays," represented more particularly by the *lai* of *Graelent*, and the *lais* of *Guingamor* and *Lanval* of Marie de France. In each, the knight rejects the love of a queen, wins that of a fairy maiden, infringes an injunction that she lays upon him, but is ultimately reunited to her.[1] In *Graelent* and *Guingamor*, the court is that of an unnamed king of Brittany, though Guingamor is his nephew (as Gawain is of King Arthur); in *Lanval*, the setting is Arthur's court, and the queen, though not named, is obviously Guinevere. The *Pulzella Gaia* differs from the French lays of this type in that the hero is not ultimately conveyed to the mysterious

---

[1] Cf. W. H. Schofield, *The Lay of Guingamor*, in *Studies and Notes in Philology and Literature*, V (Boston, 1896), and *Lays of Graelent and Lanval*, in *Publications of the M.L.A.A.*, XV (1902); J. L. Weston, *Guingamor, Lanval, Tyolet, Le Bisclaveret* (London, 1910); Levi, *op. cit.*, pp. 36–45; T. P. Cross, *The Celtic Elements in the Lays of Lanval and Graelent*, in *Modern Philology*, XII (Chicago, 1915).

land of his bride, but draws her permanently into the
world of the living at Arthur's court.

This characteristic of the Italian poem—the lover
finally bringing his mistress into the mortal world,
instead of himself being transferred to hers of Avalon
or some such supernatural region—is found in two
other cantari of the same class: the *Bel Gherardino*
and *Liombruno*; the former dating from the middle,
the latter from the third quarter of the century.[1]
Here, too, we have the motive of the love of a mortal
for a fairy, the Fata Bianca and Aquilina respectively,
the revelation of the secret, and ultimate reunion
after a series of adventures; but neither of them
connects the tale in any way with the Arthurian cycle.

A remarkable composition, set in an Arthurian
frame, is *Gismirante*, in two cantari, by that
versatile Florentine poet, Antonio Pucci, who died
in 1388.[2] He shows from the outset a peculiar
complacency in his theme; it is "una storia novella";
his audience have perhaps never heard one so beautiful.
A knight, "il cavalier Cortese," who has left the court
of King Arthur and is dying at Rome, bids his young
son go to the court, and commend himself to Tristan,
Lancelot, and Calliano (Gawain). This son is Gismirante. He wins the favour of the king and the love
of all his knights. He has been seven years at the
court, when it befalls that, for two days, neither
king nor baron can touch food because no news of
fresh adventures has come.[3] Gismirante calls upon

---

[1] *Fiore di Leggende*, I and III. Cf. Levi, *op. cit.*, pp. 26–36, 46–57.
[2] *Ibid.*, VII.
[3] This custom of Arthur's on certain high festivals, not to sit at
his meat until he has seen some adventure, occurs constantly. Cf. the

Arthur to knight him, and sets forth to find the
required adventure to save the court from starvation.
He meets a wise fairy, "una saputa fata," who comes
from a realm where the most beautiful girl in the
world, the daughter of a king, goes once a year on
the vigil of St. Martin, naked ("sanza pondo") to
the church, anyone who looks upon her as she passes
being sentenced to beheading. She gives the knight
a hair from the head of this princess, with which he
returns to court. When they have eaten, the
wonderful hair, "ch' era duo braccia e parea d'oro
fino," is presented to the king, after which Gismirante
sets out to see the princess herself. Levi suggests
analogies with the story of Lady Godiva, and the
motive, in some of the Tristan poems, of the golden
hair of Iseult which the swallow brought from Ireland
to Cornwall.[1] Gismirante delivers a gryphon from a
dragon, feeds a starving eagle, liberates a hawk. A
fairy (not the previous "fata saputa") gives him a
magic horse which conveys him to the city of the
dangerous beauty, where he penetrates into the
church, and, when the princess comes, arranges to
escape with her. They are pursued by her father and
his knights. The girl has given him a magic wand,
with which he can dry up a river and make the water
return again. She passes in this fashion, but he

Queste del Saint Graal (ed. cit., p. 5); Morte Darthur, XIII, 2;
and the poems summarised by Bruce, Evolution of Arthurian
Romance, II, pp. 209, 246. But it is nowhere suggested that the
custom was carried out to such an extent as is implied in Pucci's
poem.

[1] In Eilhart von Oberge and the Folie Tristan poem. Cf. G.
Schoepperle, op. cit., pp. 86-8; Bédier, I, pp. 103-13, II, pp. 213-33;
Bruce, Evolution of Arthurian Romance, I, p. 190.

remains, until he has fought and conquered the
pursuers. While they are sleeping at a fountain,
"un uomo selvaggio," apparently a kind of giant,
carries off the lady. Gismirante seeks the fairy, but
is confronted by an unpassable river, in which he
is about to drown himself when the gryphon, whom
he had delivered from the dragon, appears and bears
him across. The fairy directs him to the enchanted
castle of the giant, where forty-three ladies are held
in captivity, and where he must learn from his love
the secret of where their captor keeps his heart. The
girl entices the giant to reveal that his heart is guarded
by a terrible boar, "il porco troncascino," who infests
Rome; within the boar is a magic hare, and, within
the hare, a living swallow who keeps the heart in
safety. After further consultation with the fairy,
the knight makes his way to the court of the Emperor,
and slays the boar. The hare escapes, but is caught
by the eagle whom Gismirante had fed, and the
swallow similarly by the hawk whom he had freed.
The giant is now very ill in consequence of these
proceedings; the fairy bids Gismirante enter the
castle in the guise of a physician, and, as soon as he
has crossed the threshold, kill the swallow. He does
so, the giant instantly dies, and the captives are
delivered. The fairy, after a final test of his fidelity,
allows him to return to King Arthur with his lady
and her companions, and gives what we may take
as the moral of the story:

> Ed ella disse: Po' che in tuo paese
> vo' ritornare, una cosa t' impongo,
> che contro a ogni gente sie cortese,

> e spezialmente a que' c' hanno bisogno.
> Ch' io sono istato a tutte tuo' difese,
> benchè di dirlo alquanto mi vergogno,
> per quel che tue facesti a' tre uccelli,
> conciosiecosachè son mie' fratelli.[1]

The poem ends with the marriage of Gismirante to his princess of the golden hair in the presence of Arthur and Guinevere and all the court. We have here, in an Arthurian framework, a medley of several well known fairy stories, notably the Fair with the Golden Locks, and the three grateful beasts or birds which is common to the folklore of many peoples.[2]

A much shorter cantare, probably also by Antonio Pucci, is *Bruto di Brettagna*, which was first published by Ezio Levi.[3] It consists of forty-six stanzas, the first being identical with the opening of *Gismirante*. Bruto of Britain is a young knight enamoured of a lady, who promises that she will content him with her love, if he will procure for her what she desires:

> Disse la donna: Or vedi, cavaliere,
> là dove fa lo re Artù dimoro,
> ha nella sala un nobile sparviere
> che sta legato ad una stanga d' oro.

---

[1] "And she said: 'Since to thine own land thou wouldst return, one charge I lay upon thee: Be courteous towards all folk, and especially to those who are in need. I have defended thee all through, although I am somewhat ashamed to tell it, because of what thou didst to the three birds, for they are my brothers'" (ii, stanza 56).

[2] Cf. Levi, *op. cit.*, pp. 92–100; A. Wesselofsky, *Le tradizioni popolari nei poemi di Antonio Pucci* (in *Ateneo Italiano*, I, Florence, 1866, pp. 227–9). The poem presents notable analogies with the story of *Kulhwch and Olwen* in the *Mabinogion*, the "porco troncascino" being inevitably suggestive of the "porcus Troit" of Nennius. Cf. E. K. Chambers, pp. 70–1, and J. Loth, *Les Mabinogion* (Paris, 1913), I, pp. 243–346.

[3] *Fiore di Leggende*, VIII.

Appresso quell' uccel, ch' è sì maniere,
due bracchi stan che vaglion un tesoro,
la carta de le regole d'amore,
dove son scritte 'n dorato colore.[1]

He undertakes to bring her these gifts. In a forest
a golden-haired damsel appears to him, evidently of
the race of the fairies. To gain what he seeks, he will
have to make a "vaunt," and prove by combat,
that he has the love of a more beautiful lady than
any other knight. But first, to enter Arthur's palace,
he must have the hawk's glove, which he can only
obtain by overcoming two giants who guard it. She
graciously permits him to regard herself as this lady
of peerless beauty, gives him a kiss and a horse as
swift as the wind. At a bridge of gold over a great
river he defeats the two giants, and, in a meadow
full of flowers, finds a repast prepared, which he is
enjoying when a third giant appears, whom he dis-
ables and compels to lead to the glove. Bruto pro-
ceeds to the sumptuous palace of King Arthur, where,
at the sight of the glove, the twelve guardians allow
him to pass. In the great hall, before the king, he
makes his vaunt, and slays a baron who accepts the
challenge. The hawk, the scroll, and the two brachets
are now his. He takes leave of Arthur, and rides
away to the "donna selvaggia," the lady of the wood,
who, after kisses and embraces, bids him return to
his "donna verace."

---

[1] "The lady said: 'Now see, knight; there where King Arthur dwells
is in the hall a noble hawk which is bound to a perch of gold. Near
that bird, which is so tame, are two brachets which are worth a
treasure, and the scroll of the laws of love where they are written in
colour of gold'" (stanza 5).

The poet cites as his source "un libro che mi par degli altri il fiore," which Levi shows to have been the *De Amore* of Andreas Capellanus, that curious Latin treatise written in France at the end of the twelfth century, which had so great an influence on the courtly love of the Middle Ages, and was generally known in Italy as "Gualtieri," or "il libro di Gualtieri," from the name of the person to whom it is addressed. Pucci, if he is the author, has condensed and somewhat modified the story, which, in the original, is merely intended to introduce the famous thirty-one rules of love.[1]   Indeed, the British knight is there only suffered to have the hawk on the condition that he takes these rules and reveals them to all lovers, and the tale ends, in Andreas Capellanus, with the calling of a solemn assembly and their promulgation through all the world in the name of the King of Love. They have no significance in the poem, which has, perhaps, come down to us without its proper conclusion.

One of the most important poems of this class, to which students of comparative literature have devoted some attention, is *Carduino*, in two cantari, tentatively attributed to Antonio Pucci, and probably dating from the seventies of the century.[2]

---

[1] *Andreae Capellani regii Francorum de Amore libri tres*, recensuit E. Trojel (Havniae, 1892) ,II, viii: "De regulis amoris" (pp. 295–312). Cf. Levi, *I cantari leggendari*, pp. 101–13; P. Rajna, *Tre studi per la storia del libro di Andrea Cappellano*, in *Studi di filologia romanza*, V (Rome, 1891); T. F. Crane, *Italian Social Customs of the Sixteenth Century* (Oxford, 1920), pp. 27–37.

[2] *I cantari di Carduino giuntovi quello di Tristano e Lancielotto quando combattettero al petrone di Merlino*, per cura di Pio Rajna (Bologna, 1873).

Carduino is the son of a great baron of Arthur's court at Camelot, named Dondinello, who has been treacherously poisoned for envy of the king's favour. The young widow flies into the forest with the little child, who grows up among the wild beasts—his mother telling him that he has no father save God, and that there are no folk in the world save she and he and the beasts. He finds two spears left in the forest by a hunting party, and his mother tells him that they are a present from God, his father. Later, he sees the king himself hunting with his train (they chase him as a "wild man"), and resolves to go out into the world. To content him, his mother settles in a city, where his new associates bid him go to the court of Arthur: "Ongnun mi dicie di questo re Artue"; "Everyone talks to me of this King Arthur." Then his mother reveals to him the real story of his father's death; he was killed by Mordred and his brethren. He goes to Arthur's court, tells the king that he does not know who his father was, but that his mother was of lowly origin and has sent him to serve him. The barons wonder at his strength and appetite: "per più di sei baroni avie mangiato." A lady with a dwarf appears, demanding a champion to deliver an enchanted city and rescue her sister Beatrice from an evil baron, who, with magic arts, has turned her people to beasts and is compelling her to become his wife. In spite of the protest of the dwarf, the king bids Carduino undertake the adventure.

They come to the castle of a duchess, a mistress of magic art, whose "usanza" is to force visitors to accept her love for a night, and then delude them. Carduino accepts her invitation, but, though desirous of her, does not obey her injunction to do the contrary of whatever she says. Her chamber becomes a vast river appearing before him, over which he is hung up by the arms by four giants, "as was the custom." The enchantment vanishes with the morning, when the dwarf takes it all as a matter of course ("questa pena è avenuta a più giente"), and the three go on their way. They meet a knight, Agueriesse (Guerrehes), the brother of Gawain. He demands the surrender of the damsel at the price of Carduino's head, but the latter kills him with one of his two spears:

> Il nano disse: Omè! che à' tu fatto?
> Quest' è nipote dello re Artue;
> ma in far tradimenti egli era adatto,
> senpre in tradire mettea suo virtue;
> e vo' ti dir di lui a questo tratto
> quel c' una volta da lui fatto fue:
> un cavaliere e' fecie avolenare
> che Dondinello si facie chiamare.
>
> E Carduin diciea: I' lodo Iddio.
> Sanza dir nulla pensò fra suo cuore:
> Quest' è quegli ch' ucise il padre mio,
> chella mie madre men disse il tinore.
> A nulla rispondea il baron pio,
> se non che disse: Questo traditore
> questa donzella ci volea furare,
> ma io gliel' ò fatta conperare.[1]

---

[1] "The dwarf said: 'Alas, what hast thou done? This is a nephew of King Arthur; but he was an adept in treachery, always setting his skill in betraying; and I will tell thee now what was once done by him: he had a knight poisoned who was called Dondinello.'

"And Carduino said: 'I praise God.' Without other words he thought in his heart: This is he who slew my father, for my mother

While they are resting for the night in a wood, piteous cries for succour to the Blessed Virgin are heard, and Carduino rescues a girl from the hands of two giants. At last they come to the enchanted city, where the dwarf instructs him how to act. Carduino enters; the roaring of the beasts and their rush to meet him terrifies his horse, but they are friendly. In the square a great chained serpent, beauteous in aspect, is moving round and round, striving to speak, but can only utter the words: "Baron, fa che sia ardito e dotto." At Carduino's summoning shout, the gigantic knight magician comes out of the palace, fully armed and mounted upon a swift charger. Carduino slays him, cuts off his head, and in his girdle finds a ring which he at once breaks. As soon as this is done, all the beasts of the city rush upon the dead body and tear it to pieces. Carduino rides back to the chained serpent, which comes towards him with leaps, "like an eagle when it goes to strike":

> E Carduino non s'ardia apressare,
> ma 'l suo cavallo sì ebe fermato.
> La serpe allui facie grand' afoltare,
> e 'l suo cavallo è forte inpaurato;
> ma gli sproni il facieno oltre andare;
> non sa che farsi il cavalier pregiato;
> in sè diciea: I' nolla vo' baciare.
> Egli à paura e non sa chessi fare.
>   Ma pur del suo caval fu dismontato
> e ricordossi del detto del nano,
> e colla ispada i' mano ne fue andato
> presso a la serpe il cavalier sovrano.

told me the tale thereof. No answer made the faithful baron, but only said: 'This traitor would have stolen the damsel from us, but I have made him pay it dear'" (ii, stanzas 24-5).

Nella man destra il brando à inpugnato;
la serpe istava allora umile e piano;
e Carduino la basciava in bocca:
odi quie chenn' avien com' e' la tocca.
De! odi quie una nuova novella:
chè come quella serpe fu basciata
ella sì diventò una donzella
legiadra e adorna e tutta angielicata:
del paradiso uscita pare ella,
d' ongni bellezza ell' era adornata;
e draghi e leoni e serpenti
diventar come prima, ch' eran gienti.
Aparve nella terra un ta' romore,
come saetta che da ciel si parte,
quando la dama tornò in suo valore,
perchè l' era conpiuta e guasta l'arte.
Ella ringrazia Cristo Salvatore,
e Carduin da lei non si diparte.
Ella tenea il braccio a Carduino,
diciendo: Tu sarai l' amor mio fino.[1]

The adventure thus accomplished, Carduino announces that he will not return to court, because

[1] "And Carduino did not dare approach, but had checked his horse's
course. The serpent was springing towards him, and his horse is
sorely afeared, but the spurs made it go on; the gallant knight
knows not what to do, but said in himself: 'I will not kiss her.'
He fears, and knows not what to do.

"But, nevertheless, he dismounted from his horse and remembered
the words of the dwarf. With sword in hand, the noble knight has
drawn near the serpent. In his right hand he has grasped the steel;
the serpent then stayed meek and quiet, and Carduino kissed her on
the mouth. Hear now what befell when he touched her.

"Ah! hear now a new tale; for, when that serpent was kissed, she
became a damsel, winsome and fair and of angelic mien; she seemed
come forth from Paradise, with every beauty was she adorned; and
dragons and lions and serpents became the folk they erst had been.

"There arose in the city an uproar like a thunderbolt departing from
the sky, when the lady returned to her beauty, for the charm was
completed and broken. She thanks Christ the Saviour, and Carduino
departs not from her. She stretched out her arms to Carduino,
saying: 'Thou shalt be my perfect love' " (ii, stanzas 62-5).

he wishes to avenge the death of his father. Arthur
sends ambassadors, and, for the love of the king,
Carduino consents to make peace. Gawain and all
his surviving brothers beg pardon for the death of
Dondinello, "although Guerrehes slew him," and
there is a complete reconciliation. Arthur gives
Beatrice to Carduino for wife, and assigns the disen-
chanted city to his care. The mother returns;
Carduino and his bride show themselves wiser than
Merlin, "as the script relates"; he becomes Arthur's
most valiant knight, and soon has a little son who
grows up a mighty man of arms.

Carduino is the Italian representative of a group of
poems to which belong the French *Guinglain* or *Li
Biaus Descouneus* of Renaud de Beaujeu, the German
Wigalois, and the English fourteenth-century *Sir
Libeaus Desconus*.[1] It is usually held that the
English and French poems are independent of each
other, but go back to a common original, whereas
the Italian in some features represents an earlier
tradition. In all the other versions, the "Fair Unknown" turns out to be a son of Gawain; but the
account of his youth resembles that of Perceval,
and Dr. Schofield and Miss Weston urged that the
two were originally identical. The Italian poem
seems to show the influence of the prose *Tristan*,
where Pellinor, the father of Lamorat and Perceval,

---

[1] Besides Rajna's introduction, cf. W. H. Schofield, *Studies on the
Libeaus Desconus* (Vol. IV of *Studies and Notes in Philology and
Literature*, Boston, 1895); Jessie L. Weston, *Sir Cleges and Sir
Libeaus Desconus* (New York, 1902), and her *Legend of Sir Perceval*
and *Legend of Sir Lancelot du Lac*; F. Lot, *Étude sur le Lancelot en
prose*, pp. 180–1; Bruce, *Evolution of Arthurian Romance*, II, pp. 194-8.

s

is slain by Gawain and Gaheris in the feud between the two houses.[1] Thus the Italian version, substituting a new name for that of Perceval, finds a father for the hero in Dondinello; but Dr. Brugger has recently argued that the names of father and son have become interchanged, and that, whatever its ultimate source, we have here the story of the youth of the knight who makes a fitful appearance in Arthurian romance as Sir Dodinel, or Dodinas, le Sauvage.[2] The motive of the "daring kiss" (*fier baiser*), familiar in folklore, is assigned to Lancelot in the German poem *Lanzelet*. That the enchantment should be broken by the knight, and not (as in the French and English poems) the serpent herself, giving the kiss, is one of the aspects of the story in which *Carduino* probably represents the more primitive version.

Another poem, comparatively insignificant in itself, which might have been expected to appear as a cantare, takes the form of a canzone and is called by its anonymous author a "morale."[3] It télls how, "at the time of the Round Table, the good Sir Gawain

---

[1] Cf. Löseth, sects. 302, 306–8; Malory, X, 24.

[2] E. Brugger, *Bliocadran, the Father of Perceval*, in *Medieval Studies in Memory of G. S. Loomis*, pp. 162–171, where the name Carduino is identified with Bliocadran, the name given to the father of Perceval in a single French text. Carduino, in the poem, grows up with the wild beasts, and is so hairy that "a vedere parea unuon selvagio," which, Dr. Brugger observes, is "the very epithet of Dodinel." But, in the Vulgate *Merlin* (Sommer, II, p. 171), Dodinel is the son of King Belinans of Sorgales and Eglente, daughter of King Machen de l'Île Perdue, and is called "le Salvage" because of his passion for hunting. This Vulgate *Merlin* is a late text.

[3] P. Rajna, *Intorno a due canzoni gemelle di materia cavalleresca*, in *Zs. f. rom. Phil.*, I (1877), pp. 381–7.

found himself in a country so strange that there was
nothing to eat or drink":

> Al tempo de la Tavola Ritonda,
> si ritrovò il buon messer Chalvano
> in paese sì strano
> che no v' avea da mangiar nè da bere.

He sees a castle, and is told by a rustic that it belongs
to a courteous baron who welcomes every comer on
his arrival, but has him beaten when he departs.
Gawain is hospitably received, waited upon by the
baron himself, sumptuously fed, and put to sleep in
a rich bed, his host next day holding his stirrup for
him to mount, and accompanying him on his road.
After they have parted, Gawain turns back and asks
an explanation. The baron explains that previous
guests have tried to prevent or outdo him by what
is intended for courtesy, refusing to drink unless he
drinks with them and the like, thus taking from him
the lordship of his own castle, whereas Gawain has
accepted everything without demur. Among the
poems of Antonio Pucci is a canzone giving another
version of the same theme.[1] Here the Arthurian
setting has disappeared; Gawain is changed to "un
gentiluom di Roma," and, in addition to other
variations, the host's courtesy extends to making his
guest enter the bed in which is his own wife, though
he ultimately places himself between them. We
have here the motive of the "imperious host," found
also in the Middle English romance of the *Carle of*

---

[1] No. viii among the poems of Antonio Pucci, in Carducci, *Rime di M. Cino da Pistoia e d'altri del secolo xiv.* Rajna holds that both poems are by Pucci, the second being a later version.

Carlisle, or *Sir Gawain and the Carle of Carlisle*, the two Italian and the English poems ultimately being derived from a lost French poem of the Breton lay type. In the two Italian poems, what was originally a test or temptation (a trace of which is preserved in the detail of the wife in the second) has been reduced to a mere "moral," not to contend in courtesy with our host, but accept his hospitality without ceremonious protest, probably because they derive from the French poem not directly, but through a Latin *exemplum*.[1]

We are back in the regular Arthurian cycle with the short cantare of forty-two stanzas, dating likewise from the latter part of the fourteenth century, of the combat between Tristan and Lancelot: *Quando Tristano e Lancielotto combattettero al petrone di Merlino*.[2] Tristan, hearing that Hector de Maris is in prison, sets out from Cornwall to deliver him. Night comes, and he is resting on the ground, when Palamede arrives; not seeing Tristan, he pours out his lamentations that his rival has taken Iseult from him, and threatens vengeance. In the morning they fight; Palamede would have been slain, but for the arrival of Lionel, who stops the duel in the name of King Arthur. Tristan compels his opponent, in Lionel's presence, to swear that he will come and end the battle within eight days at the Rock of Merlin. His wounds prevent Palamede from keeping the

[1] G. L. Kittredge, *A Study of Gawain and the Green Knight* (Harvard University Press, 1916), pp. 85–106, 304, 305. Cf. G. Paris, in *Romania*, XXIX (1900), p. 597; Rajna, *Fonti dell' Orlando Furioso* (2nd edition), p. 425, n. 2.

[2] Edited by Rajna, together with *Carduino*, in the volume cited.

appointment. Lancelot comes to the Rock; he reads
an inscription that the two best knights of the world
must fight there, thinks that they may be his own
son, Galahad, and Tristan, and decides that, if so,
he will separate them. Tristan arrives, takes Lancelot for Palamede, and insults him. They fight until
they can do no more, Tristan taunting his supposed
rival about "the queen," whom Lancelot naturally
supposes to mean Guinevere. At length, seeing his
opponent growing weary, Tristan says: "Henceforth I hold thee of no account, for I see well thou
dost not love Iseult." Lancelot draws back, and
again suggests an exchange of names. Tristan insists
that his opponent is Palamede and only mocking him,
and reminds him of the tournament in Ireland when
Palamede bore the two swords:

> E sì diciea allora: I' son Tristano,
> settù non ti ricordi ben del nome,
> e tu sì se' Palamides pagano,
> a cui convengo caricar le some.
> E Lancielotto udendo il sir sovrano
> trasesi l' elmo, e mostrogli il come,
> diciendo: Lancielotto è tuo pregione.
> Or fa di me ciò che vuoi, barone.[1]

They embrace, and go together to the castle of
Dinasso (Sir Dinas the seneschal), where they find
Palamede, "and all the three made complete peace."
The episode is a familiar one, occuring in the
prose *Tristan* and in Rusticiano; but the poem,

---

[1] "And then he said: 'I am Tristan, if thou dost not in sooth
remember the name, and thou art Palamede the pagan, to whom I
must give his deserts.' And Lancelot, hearing the sovereign knight,
drew off his helmet, and showed him who he was, saying: 'Lancelot
is thy prisoner; now do with me what thou wilt, baron'" (stanza 41).

while somewhat resembling the latter version, seems
independent. Rusticiano has nothing about the
imprisonment of Hector de Maris, and it is not Lionel,
but Brandelis, the son of Lac, who causes the post-
ponement of the combat. Tristan arrives at the
Rock of Merlin before Lancelot, and there is no mention of the inscription.[1] Peculiar to the poem is the
latter detail, with the characteristic touch that
Lancelot, when he reads it, never for a moment
imagines that one of the two best knights may be
himself. Similarly, when Galahad has achieved the
adventure of the sword, and the damsel bids Lancelot
not ween from henceforth that he is the best knight
of the world: "As touching unto that, said Lancelot,
I know well I was never the best." [2]

Two other notable Tristan cantari, *La Morte di
Tristano* and *La Vendetta*, preserved in a Milanese
manuscript of 1430, but composed in the fourteenth
century, are still unpublished.[3] The former follows
the general lines of the prose *Tristan* in its account
of the death of the two lovers, with some curious
variations; Tristan's cousin and accuser is not called
Andred, but "Alebruno," and it is Tristan himself

[1] *Girone il Cortese, ed. cit.*, cap. vii. Cf. Löseth, sects. 196–7,
202–3.

[2] Malory, XIII, 5. Cf. *Queste, ed. cit.*, pp. 12–13.

[3] Biblioteca Ambrosiana, Cod. 95 sup., a rehandling of an originally
Tuscan text by a Milanese scribe. The first poem exists also in a
fourteenth-century manuscript of the Biblioteca Nazionale of Florence, where it is preceded by another, in a fragmentary condition,
relating the adventures of Tristan with Hector de Maris and Breus,
as in the *Tavola Ritonda*, capp. cxxiii–cxxiv. See G. Bertoni, *La
Morte di Tristano, loc. cit.*, pp. 244–56. I understand from Professor
Bertoni that a critical edition of the *Morte* is in preparation.

who brings the lance of Morgan le Fay, which he leaves outside the door of the queen's chamber and which thus passes into the hands of King Mark. The poem ends with Lancelot's vow of vengeance: "Darò la morte allo re Marcho con dolore."

This vengeance is related in the second poem: *La Vendetta che fe meser Lanzelloto de la morte de miser Tristano*.[1] A hundred and seven knights of Britain, who have vowed vengeance for the death of Tristan, led by Lancelot, don mourning attire and invade Cornwall. They ravage the country and finally, still concealing their identity, besiege Tintagel. King Mark, who is here represented as no coward, wishes to sally out in person against them, but is overruled by his barons. A portion of his army goes forth without him. They sound trumpets and other instruments, but Lancelot has ordered no music on the part of his black-robed knights, the "cavalier de la morte." The Cornish knights are defeated and driven back to the city, Alebruno—"he who accused Tristan and Iseult"—being slain by Lancelot. Mark now sends ambassadors to the invaders, upon which Lancelot reveals his identity and that of his companions. There is dismay in the royal council, until one of the barons urges that it is better to die in battle with honour than stay within the walls with shame. The king with all his forces issues out of the city, a number of his barons being attired like himself, and a great battle ensues, Mark—who fights

---

[1] Biblioteca Ambrosiana, Cod. 95 sup., ff. 255–64. The opening stanzas of this poem, as also of the *Morte*, were printed by Polidori in the appendix to the second volume of the *Tavola Ritonda*. I propose to publish the complete text of the *Vendetta* separately.

like a brave knight—being finally killed, unrecognised,
by Lancelot:

> E lo re Marcho, nobel persona,
> combateva como nobel chavaliere;
> de Lanziloto lo libro rasona
> che andava rompando le schiere,
> e poy in ver de lo re Lanziloto sprona,
> nol cognosando, ferillo volentera,
> e per sì gran forza un colpo li presta
> che dal busto li taiava la testa.[1]

Tintagel is captured, and, Mark not being discovered among the royally dressed barons when they
are disarmed, search is made for him until he is
found among the dead, and honourably buried.
Lancelot and the others visit the tomb of Tristan,
after which they repair for repose and healing of their
wounds to the castle of Dinas, who is oddly described
as the brother of Sagramour. Before returning to
Britain, they make Sagramour lord of Cornwall.[2]

It is the fashion with the composers of cantari to
refer to alleged sources. Consequently, in the present
poem, we read phrases like "como lo libro si novella"
(f. 261), "lo libro rasona" (f. 264), though, as in the
majority of such compositions, the source is unknown.
But there are passages in the prose *Tristan* where

---

[1] "And King Mark, that noble person, fought like a noble knight;
of Lancelot the book relates that he went shattering the bands, and
then he spurred towards the king; not knowing him, he smote him
zealously, and gave him a stroke with such great might that he clove
his head from its trunk" (f. 264).

[2] Here, as in one Spanish version of the Tristan story, Sagramour
is represented as a knight of Cornwall; but the real Sagramour le
Desirous, in the orthodox tale, was a Greek prince who came from
Constantinople to be a knight of the Round Table (cf. Sommer,
II, pp. 179, 253), and could not have been any relation of Dinas.

Lancelot solemnly swears to King Mark that, if he harms Tristan, he will die by his hand.[1] Apart from the curious feature of the final rehabilitation of Mark, we may possibly here have to deal with a genuine ending, elsewhere lost, of the Tristan romance.

There is a somewhat similar version in a Venetian prose text of the fifteenth century already mentioned, the *Tristano Veneto*. Here, a year after the death of Tristan, Lancelot resolves to execute vengeance. He assembles a company of a hundred knights, and makes them swear to be of one mind and will to go against King Mark, "to destroy him and his city, and deal a mighty vengeance for the death of Sir Tristan." They waste the country round about, and besiege Tintagel. Mark sallies out, and is slain after a fierce battle. The walls are destroyed so that not a stone remains upon stone, and then all the houses of the city are burnt, "in such wise that there remained neither dog nor cat. And whoso would know this history, let him read the book of Sir Lancelot in which is written all this history in well ordered wise and with most beautiful verses." [2] Is this "libro de miser Lanciloto," to which the author refers, our poem, or one of those lost Franco-Italian texts, the supposed intermediaries between French and Italian Arthurianism?

The longest, and, in some respects, the most important, of these poems directly connected with the Arthurian cycle, is the seven *Cantari di Lancellotto*

---

[1] Cf. Löseth, sects. 252a, 261.
[2] Parodi, *Tristano Riccardiano*, introduction, pp. cxxv–cxxvi.

or *La Struzione della Tavola Ritonda*.[1] Dating from
the end of the fourteenth or beginning of the fifteenth
century, it covers the same ground as the practically
contemporaneous English stanzaic poem, *Le Morte
Arthur*. While closely connected with the Vulgate
Mort Artu, it introduces characters from the prose
Tristan; the details and order of events differ, here
and there, from the other versions, and it may be
preserving a primitive feature of the story in representing Mordred as merely the nephew of Arthur and
making no allusion to the motive of his incestuous
birth.

There is no mention of the previous quest of the
Holy Grail, the story being simply the destruction
of the Round Table through the guilty love of Lancelot for the queen and the treason of Mordred. It is
the latter, supported by Kay and Dodinel, who accuses
the lovers to the king, Agravaine playing a merely
subordinate part in the poem. The tournament at
Winchester is summoned at the suggestion of the
three accusers, in order to incriminate Lancelot if
he stays away. We have the love of the Maid of
Astolat for Lancelot, his wound at the hand of Bors
at the tournament where his presence dispels the
suspicions that Mordred had instilled into the king's
mind, and Gawain's advances to the Maid repulsed
by her showing him Lancelot's shield. After Gawain
has told the queen, Lancelot's enforced absence from

---

[1] *Li Chantari di Lancellotto*, edited by E. T. Griffiths (Oxford,
1924). It was first edited by C. Giannini, *Lancilotto, poema cavalleresco* (Fermo, 1871), and there is a poor edition by W. de Gray
Birch (London, 1874). Mr. Griffiths' introductory remarks on the
sources, pp. 48–75, are noteworthy.

the second tournament increases her wrath, while confirming Arthur's belief in his innocence. Bors having reported Guinevere's resentment to Lancelot and obtained his pardon for the wound, the latter sets out on his wanderings; but the coming of the boat with the Maid's dead body and her letter reveals the truth to the queen. The episode of the poisoned apple comes after, instead of before, the death of the Maid. Làncelot reappears as the queen's champion in the guise of the black knight at the ordeal by combat, which is followed by the renewal of their guilty intercourse, the fresh accusation, the attack upon Lancelot in the queen's chamber, the ambush and rescue from the fire with the death of the three brothers of Gawain—Agravaine being here slain by Bors. In his account of the siege of Joyous Gard, which occupies the fourth cantare, the poet casts his net wide to find allies for the besieged; not only do Pellinor and Dinas from the *Tristan*, and a hundred knights whom Lancelot had delivered from the Valley of False Lovers appear, but King Pelles and his daughter, "who was mother of the strong Galahad," send aid;[1] and there is a curious motive where Astor (Hector de Maris), going by sea to collect reinforcements, arranges to hoist red banners on his return if successful.[2]

---

[1] iv, 10. Galahad is here called "Ghaleatto." In reality, his mother had died long before the siege of Joyous Gard. Cf. *La Queste del Saint Graal, ed. cit.*, p. 259, and Malory, XVIII, 16.

[2] iv, 15. Mr. Griffiths, p. 67, suggests that this motive is "inspired by the very beautiful conception of the final scenes of the Tristan poetic tradition." I think this improbable, as the story of the two sails seems elsewhere unknown in Italian literature.

The last three cantari relate the invasion of Lancelot's French dominions by Arthur, to appease Gawain's desire of vengeance for the death of his brothers, the treachery of Mordred and the battle with the Romans in which Gawain meets his end, the slaying of Mordred and the passing of Arthur, the death of Lionel in the rising of the sons of Mordred, and Lancelot's end as a hermit. The differences from the Vulgate are mainly in details and order of events. In Arthur's dream, the soul of Gawain is alone; he has been saved by the prayers of the poor whom he befriended in life, but is not accompanied by them as in the French text.[1] As in the *Tavola Ritonda*, Morgan le Fay and the queens do not appear; but Arthur is lifted into the boat by mysterious hands. Lancelot and Guinevere do not meet again.[2] In the account of the burial of Lancelot there are three tombs, and the text is manifestly corrupt. I believe the right reading to imply that Lancelot was buried by the side of Galahad (Galeatto), on the other side of whom lay Galehaut (Galeotto) the "haut prince"; the poet (or his source), knowing little of the quest of the Grail, was misled by the inscription on the tomb in the *Mort Artu* into supposing that Galahad, as well

---

[1] vi, 16–18. In the *Mort Artu*, Gawain is accompanied by the souls of the poor, and it is they, not Gawain, who tell the king that they have conquered the house of God for their benefactor (Sommer, VI, p. 360; ed. Bruce, p. 218). In Malory, he appears with the ladies for whom he did battle in righteous quarrel; in the stanzaic *Morte Arthur*, with lords and ladies.

[2] The final interview between Lancelot and Guinevere is peculiar to Malory and the stanzaic English poem, though he is present at her death in the *Tavola Ritonda*.

THE DEATH OF GUINEVERE
Florence, Biblioteca Nazionale, Cod. Pal. 556

LANCELOT ENTERS THE HERMITAGE
Florence, Biblioteca Nazionale, Cod. Pal. 556

as his father and Galehaut, was buried at Joyous Gard.[1]

Another long poem, of a somewhat earlier date, is the so-called *Febusso e Breusso* in six cantari. The title seems due to its editor, the author evidently calling it *Febusso il forte*. It is a popular rendering of the story in the *Palamède*, of how Breus, cast down into the cavern by the treacherous damsel, met the grandfather and father of Guiron, and heard from the former the history of Febus.[2] In some details it differs from the orthodox version. The damsel is not the one previously delivered by Guiron, but has been taken from a knight to whom Breus has left another whom he had intended to kill. The dying Febus has to intervene to protect the princess and her father from the threats of his kinsmen. There is a curious stanza in which Febus, before he has seen the princess, is assured that her beauty surpasses that of all others including Helen, Dido, Blanchefleur, and "la donzella figlia di Morghana," who is evidently Pulzella Gaia.[3]

We saw that, about the end of the thirteenth century, the *Mare Amoroso* supplied a kind of reper-

---

[1] "Chi gist Galehos, li sires des Lontaines Illes, et avoec lui si gist Lanselos del Lac, ki fu li miudres chevaliers ki onkes entrast el roiame de Logres, fors seulement Galaas, sen fil" (*Mort Artu*, ed. Bruce, p. 262). In the poem, vii, 47–8, I would read: "E soppelliro messer Lancelotto | in un sepolcro a Galeatto allato. | Eravi quello prenza Galeotto . . . Quella di Galeatto i' mezo stava, | e Lancelotto e 'l prenza eran dal lato." Cf. *M.L.R.*, XX, pp. 215–6.

[2] *Il Febusso e Breusso*, edited by Lord Vernon with an essay by F. Palermo (Florence, 1847), with a fragment of an early translation of *Gyron le Courtoys*. Palermo was under the erroneous impression that this was the earliest "poema cavalleresco" in Italian.

[3] iii, 13.

tory of the imagery used by the early lyrical poets.
For the cantari, we have an analogous work in the
shape of the remarkable poem edited by Rajna, which
he called *Il Cantare dei Cantari*, and would date
somewhere between 1380 and 1420.[1] It consists of
fifty-nine stanzas, in which the anonymous poet
enumerates all the subjects upon which he is prepared to write, sing, or recite, from the Creation
through the whole course of sacred or profane history
and literature. Nine stanzas (39–47) enumerate
subjects from the Arthurian cycle. He begins by
offering to lovers, young and old, "the fair treatise
of Lancelot and Sir Tristan." But would his audience prefer first to be told of the founding of the
Round Table and of the arts of Merlin, the exploits
of the knights-errant at the time of Uther Pendragon? If so, he has four hundred cantari of the
Old Table—the best knights that ever were, and all
their adventures; fountains, pines and meadows,
gracious damsels, and all usages of chivalry. Or
give the poet just a hint, and he will come to the
New Table at Camelot; he will tell what was written
of King Arthur, of Guinevere and Sir Lancelot,
of Iseult and Tristan of Liones, of Blioberis and
Sir Agravaine, "and of Lamorat, the sovereign
knight." He will sing of the birth of Sir Perceval,
and every tournament at Lonazep, of the feats in
jousts of Brunor and Gareth, of the race of
King Ban and the crimes of Breus, and the famous
deeds of many others, of Hector de Maris, of

---

[1] *Il Cantare dei Cantari e il Serventese del Maestro di tutte l'Arti*,
in *Zs. f. rom. Phil.*, II (1878), pp. 425–37.

Bors and Dinadan, "and then the treacheries of Gawain."[1]

> Di Tristan canterò la falsa morte,
> e po' la morte vera e dolorosa,
> e 'l nascimento, e come venne a corte,
> dell' Amoroldo d' Irlanda ogni cosa;
> di messer Lasansissa, el pro e 'l forte;
> molte battaglie alla Guardia Gioiosa;
> come Ginevra fu falsificata
> da la Donna del Lago inamorata.[2]

The "falsa morte" of Tristan is obviously the report of his death, when wandering in madness, spread by Andred. We have already met Lasancis in the *Tavola Ritonda*, where the epithet "pro" is likewise, somewhat inappropriately, given to him ("uno pro cavalier della Tavola Vecchia"); this is the only other mention of his name that I have found. The curious allusion to the "falsification," or "counterfeiting," of Guinevere may, perhaps, refer to the episode in the *Lancelot*, of which we have heard an echo in a thirteenth-century Italian lyric: Morgan le Fay making Lancelot see a false dream of the queen in the arms of another knight.[3] If so, the poet has confused Morgan with the Lady of the Lake. But it is vaguely suggestive of a previous episode in the same romance, unknown elsewhere in Italian, where the false Guinevere, the queen's half-sister, passes

---

[1] The allusion is to Brunor "le valet à la cotte mal taillée," not to the father of Galehaut. Cf. Mallory, IX, 1–9.

[2] "Of Tristan will I sing the false death, and then the true and dolorous one, and his birth, and how he came to court, and everything of the Morholt of Ireland; of Sir Lasancis, the brave and strong; many battles at Joyous Gard; how Guinevere was counterfeited by the enamoured Lady of the Lake" (stanza 44). For *falsificare* in this sense, cf. Dante, *Inferno*, xxx, 44.

[3] Sommer, IV, p. 151. Cf. above, p. 33.

herself off as the real wife of Arthur.[1] The true Lady of the Lake displays no hostility to Guinevere in Arthurian story.

The poet has the whole story of the Holy Grail ready, and the birth of Galahad, for whom he expresses a special predilection. In fact, there is no adventure or fair quest of which he is not prepared to sing. Just tell him what you want, and he will straightway begin "la vecchia e nuova tavola a cantare"; there is only one tale that he will not face:

> Un conto sol di costor mi dispiace
> di leggere, o di dire, o di cantarlo,
> el quale ancora so ch'a voi non piace:
> la tavola distruger di cu' parlo.[2]

This poem has affinities with the traditional minstrel "vaunt," of which we have Italian examples in the serventese of Ruggieri Apuliese as well as the *Mare Amoroso*. But the poet is not himself a *cantastorie*, but a man of classical feeling, who, instead of the usual pious invocation at the beginning, calls on Apollo. He professes to have composed a poem on Theseus in continuation of the *Teseide* of Boccaccio, and, with the Renaissance sense of the "romanità" of Italy, boasts that he has in store more than a thousand subjects from the history of Rome, "con verità d' ogni cantare il fiore."

---

[1] Sommer, IV, pp. 12, 44 sq. There is no other allusion to the story of the false Guinevere in Italian, until we come to the sixteenth-century translation of the French printed *Lancelot*, where she represents herself as having been imprisoned in a castle near a lake. The whole story is ignored by Malory.

[2] "One sole tale of these I like not to read or tell or sing, which I know, too, does not please you: the destruction of the Table of which I speak" (stanza 49). He is evidently alluding to the extant Lancelot poem which we have already considered.

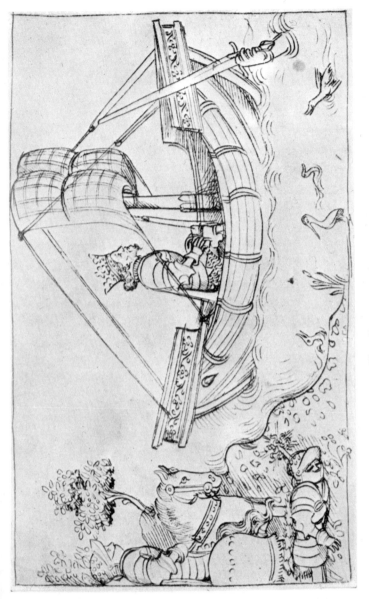

THE PASSING OF ARTHUR
Florence, Biblioteca Nazionale, Cod. Pal. 556

CHAPTER XIII

THE ARTHURIANISM OF BOIARDO AND ARIOSTO

BOCCACCIO in the *Amorosa Visione* and the writer of the *Cantare dei Cantari* pass, somewhat similarly, from the Arthurian to the Carolingian cycle; from the "materia di Brettagna" to the "materia di Francia." The former declares that he will name no more of the knights:

> Ma io, la vista mia
> dopo la lunga schiera discendendo,
> conobbi più mirabil baronia; [1]

for he sees robed in purple Charlemagne riding forward, with Orlando and Oliver and Rinaldo. The writer of the *Cantare* bids his hearers leave in peace the tale of the destruction of the Round Table:

> Però ch' i' sento aparecchiato Carlo
> imperador, figliuol de re Pipino,
> e 'l conte Orlando, e ogni paladino.[2]

The triumph of romantic poetry in Italy in the earlier part of the Renaissance was the fusion of the two cycles, achieved at Ferrara by the two great poets of the court of the house of Este.[3]

At Ferrara, as in other north Italian courts, men

[1] "But, my eyes passing down after the long band, I recognised a more wondrous array of barons."

[2] "For I perceive ready the Emperor Charles, son of King Pepin, and Count Orlando, and every paladin."

[3] The subject has been dealt with more particularly in the now classical work of P. Rajna, *Le Fonti dell' Orlando Furioso* (second edition, Florence, 1900), and the more recent volumes of G. Bertoni, *Nuovi studi su Matteo Maria Boiardo* (Bologna, 1904) and *L' Orlando furioso e la Rinascenza a Ferrara* (Modena, 1919).

and women of the reigning house frequently bore
Arthurian names: Lionello, Meliaduse, Gurone, Isotta,
Ginevra; and there was a passion for Arthurian and
kindred romances. The registers of the palace
library in the fifteenth century show scholars and
courtiers eagerly borrowing such works, both "in
lingua gallica" and "in vulgare," and the inventories
give the titles of a large number of Arthurian items,
in both languages, almost all of which have now
disappeared. We find Duke Borso himself, in 1470,
writing to Count Ludovico di Cuneo: "We have now
finished reading all the French books that we have
in our possession. So we send you this mounted
messenger of ours expressly to ask you to send him
back laden with as many French books as you can,
to wit, some of those of the *Tavola Vecchia*, for we
shall receive more pleasure and content therefrom
than from the acquisition of a city." [1]

It was for this society that the Count of Scandiano,
Matteo Maria Boiardo, wrote the *Orlando Innamorato*.
Chronologically, Boiardo was a younger contemporary
of our Sir Thomas Malory. The *Orlando* was begun
about 1475, some few years later than the completion
of the *Morte Darthur* in 1469 or 1470; but the pub-
lication of the two works was practically simul-
taneous. The first two parts of Boiardo's poem
were printed at Reggio in 1484,[2] the first edition

---

[1] Bertoni, *L' Orlando furioso*, pp. 92–4. Cf. also his *Nuovi studi su
M. M. Boiardo*, pp. 173–81, and *La Biblioteca Estense e la coltura
ferrarese ai tempi del duca Ercole I* (Turin, 1903), appendici II² and III.

[2] See G. Reichenbach, *Le prime edizioni dell' Orlando Innamorato*,
in *G.S.L.I.*, LXXXIV (1924), pp. 68–74. There were three editions
before the complete edition of 1506.

of Malory's prose epic was printed by Caxton in 1485.

In one of those admirable preludes prefixed to his cantos, Boiardo contrasts the two cycles, the "materia di Brettagna" with the "materia di Francia":

> Fo glorïosa Bertagna la grande
> una stagion per l'arme e per l'amore,
> onde ancora oggi il nome suo si spande,
> sì che al re Artuse fa portare onore,
> quando e' bon cavallieri a quelle bande
> mostrarno in più battaglie il suo valore,
> andando con lor dame in aventura;
> et or sua fama al nostro tempo dura.
> Re Carlo in Franza poi tenne gran corte,
> ma a quella prima non fo sembïante,
> benchè assai fosse ancor robusto e forte,
> et avesse Ranaldo e 'l sir d'Anglante.
> Perchè tiene ad Amor chiuse le porte,
> e sol se dette alle battaglie sante,
> non fo di quel valore e quella estima
> qual fo quell' altra che iò contava in prima.[1]

But, notwithstanding this personal preference, Boiardo did not write an Arthurian poem. Instead, he transformed the matter of the Carolingian cycle by an infusion of the Arthurian spirit. Taking his

---

[1] "Britain the great was glorious once with arms and love, whence still its name resounds so that it brings honour to King Arthur, when the good knights in those regions showed their worth in many battles, going on adventure with their ladies; and now its fame lasts to our time.

"King Charles afterwards held high court in France, but it was not like that former one, albeit it, too, was right strenuous and strong, and had Rinaldo and the lord of Anglante; because it kept the gates closed to love, and only engaged in holy battles, it was not of such worth and such renown as was that other of which I first told" (O.I., II, xviii, 1–2). I quote the edition of F. Foffano, *Orlando Innamorato di M. M. B. riscontrato sul codice trivulziano e su le prime stampe* (Bologna, 1906–7).

heroes from the familiar and popular figures of the cycle of Charlemagne, he gave them characteristics and assigned them adventures drawn from, or resembling those of, the cycle of Arthur, converting the grim paladins of the Emperor into knights-errant like those of the Round Table, and making love the lord of all. Thus the terrible Roland himself, the thunder of whose horn at Roncesvalles rolls through the literature of the Middle Ages to find an echo still in Dante's *Inferno*, becomes "innamorato"—like a Lancelot or a Tristan, though on a far lower plane:

> Non vi par già, Signor, meraviglioso
> odir cantar de Orlando inamorato,
> chè qualunche nel mondo è più orgoglioso,
> è da Amor vinto, al tutto subiugato;
> nè forte braccio, nè ardire animoso,
> nè scudo o maglia, nè brando affilato,
> nè altra possanza può mai far diffesa,
> che al fin non sia da Amor battuta e presa.[1]

The opening scene shows the transformation and sets the key-note. We are at the great banquet given by Charlemagne at Paris for the tournament to be held at Whitsuntide:

> Imperò che ogni principe cristiano,
> ogni duca e signore a lui se afronta
> per una giostra che aveva ordinata
> allor di maggio, alla pasqua rosata.[2]

---

[1] "Deem it not marvellous, lordings, to hear sung of Orlando enamoured; for whoso in the world is most orgulous is utterly conquered and subdued by love; neither strong arm nor courageous daring, nor shield or mail, nor sharpened sword, nor other might can ever withstand, but at the end it is beaten and captured by love " (*O.I.*, I, i, 2).

[2] "He bade every Christian prince, every duke and lord to come before him for a joust that he had then ordained on Pentecost in May " (*O.I.*, I, i, 8).

This inevitably suggests the customs of Uther Pendragon, and, more particularly, the holding of the
high feast of Pentecost by his son, when "all manner
of strange adventures came before Arthur as at that
feast before all other feasts."[1] Charlemagne himself
"se fu posato alla mensa ritonda."[2] And, like the
damsels and the rest who appear in the Arthuriad on
such occasions, so here comes Angelica with the four
giants and her brother Argalia, to enamour all present
with her beauty, and challenge all and each to
encounter the latter:

> Fuor de la terra lo venga a trovare,
> nel verde prato alla Fonte del Pino,
> dove se dice al Petron di Merlino[3];

her person to be the prize of the victor.

The "fonte del pino" and the "petron di Merlino"
are traditional Arthurian localities, while the main
features in the situation are derived from two distinct
Arthurian sources. It is clearly modelled upon the
episode of Branor le Brun, at the beginning of the
compilation of Rusticiano da Pisa, where at Camelot,
"per un dì di pasqua di maggio," this gigantic old
knight of Uther Pendragon appears at Arthur's
court with his niece and esquires, and similarly
challenges all the knights to do battle with him and
win the damsel as prize.[4] But Branor would scorn
to use enchantment, so Boiardo has fused this episode

---

[1] Malory, VII, I.   [2] *O.I.*, I, i, 13.

[3] "Let him come to meet him outside the city on the green meadow
at the Fountain of the Pine, where the Rock of Merlin is said to
be" (*O.I.*, I, i, 27).

[4] Löseth, sect. 621; *Girone il Cortese*, ed. F. Tassi, cap. i. Cf. Bertoni, *Nuovi studi su M. M. B.*, cap. viii, and G. Razzoli, *Per le fonti
dell' Orlando Innamorato* (Milan, 1901).

with that of Lasancis in the *Tavola Ritonda*. Even
as Lasancis has been sent by his sister, with enchanted
armour and the magical lance which instantly un-
horses whom it touches, to destroy the Round Table,
so Angelica and Argalia have been sent by their
father to overthrow the power of Charlemagne;
Argalia has enchanted armour and a magic lance
with the same properties. In the *Tavola Ritonda*,
the situation is redeemed by Tristan, who, by a
stratagem, deprives the knight of his lance and takes
him prisoner; in the *Orlando*, the plot is similarly
rendered ineffective by the lance passing accidentally into the hands of Astolfo, the English paladin,
who—unlike Tristan—uses it though unconscious of
its powers, with results that give one of the most
delightfully comic episodes of Boiardo's poem.[1]

For the rest, the *Orlando Innamorato* reads at
times like a partly cynical, partly humorous,
always absolutely unmystical Arthuriad under its
Carolingian disguise; these

> strane aventure e battaglie amorose,
> quando virtute al bon tempo fioriva
> tra cavallieri e dame grazïose.[2]

As a rule, it is merely motives that Boiardo adopts
and usually transforms. The magic fountain at
which Rinaldo drinks, his love for Angelica becoming
thereby turned to hate, is associated with the story
of Tristan:

> Questa fontana tutta è lavorata
> de un alabastro candido e polito,

---

[1] *O.I.*, I, i, 37 *sq.*; ii, 18; iii. Cf. *Tavola Ritonda*, lxxxvii.
[2] "Strange adventures and amorous battles, when virtue in the good
time flourished among knights and gracious ladies" (*O.I.*, III, i, 4).

e d' ôr sì riccamente era adornata,
che rendea lume nel prato fiorito.
Merlin fu quel che l' ebbe edificata,
perchè Tristano, il cavalliero ardito,
bevendo a quella lasci la regina,
che fu cagione al fin di sua ruina.
Tristano isventurato, per sciagura,
a quella fonte mai non è arivato;
benchè più volte andasse alla ventura,
e quel paese tutto abbia cercato.
Questa fontana avea cotal natura,
che ciascun cavalliero inamorato,
bevendo a quella, amor da sè cacciava,
avendo in odio quella che egli amava.[1]

Though the orthodox *Tristan* tells us nothing of
such a device on Merlin's part, this may possibly
have been suggested by a passage in the *Vita di
Merlino*, where the prophet declares that it will be
impossible to save Tristan from death at his uncle's
hands, because he will not be free, but under the
control of passion.[2] The episode of Origille harks
back to the *Palamède*. Orlando comes upon a woman
hanging by her hair to a pine and lamenting bitterly.
An armed knight warns him not to help her, and
tells the story of her treachery for which she is

[1] "This fountain is all wrought of white and polished alabaster,
and was so richly adorned with gold that it shone in the flowery
meadow. Merlin was he who had built it, in order that Tristan,
the daring knight, drinking of it, might leave the queen who was
at the end the cause of his ruin.

"Hapless Tristan, unfortunately, never came to that fountain,
although many times he went on adventure and searched all that
land. This fountain had such nature that every enamoured knight,
by drinking at it, drove love from himself, and hated her whom
he was wont to love" (*O.I.*, I, iii, 33-4).

[2] *Vita di Merlino*, III, 75: "Et Merlino disse: Voglio che metti in
scritto, che lui non si potrà guardare, imperochè non sarà in sua
libertà, ma in libertà della lussuria, e per quella convenirà morire."

condemned to this punishment. Orlando nevertheless undertakes her cause, overthrows the knight
and three others in succession, releases the woman,
and is promptly tricked by her and robbed of his
horse.[1] In the romance Guiron finds two knights
who have bound a lady and another knight naked
to a tree in the snow. One of the knights similarly
bids him not to interfere with the course of justice,
and relates the crime of the two prisoners; but
Guiron believes their protestation of innocence,
defeats the would-be avengers, only to be himself
presently dealt with treacherously in the same fashion,
not by the woman, but by the man, Helin le Roux.[2]
The Valley of the False Lovers, from the prose
Lancelot, reappears, transformed and elaborated, as
the realm of Morgana at the bottom of the enchanted
lake, with Orlando playing the part of Lancelot in
the release of the prisoners, though Morgan le Fay
of Arthurian story is hardly recognisable in the
"bella fata" of the Italian poet.[3] Friendship between man and man is always nobly rendered by
Boiardo, and the friendship between Orlando and
Brandimarte seems to repeat that between Lancelot
and Galehaut, even though this may not be its source.
The most beautiful love scene in the poem, the first
meeting of Ruggiero and Bradamante, has naturally
no Arthurian prototype; the maiden warrior found
no place amongst the chivalry of the Round Table.[4]
But three admirable stanzas—among the most truly

---

[1] *O.I.*, I, xxviii–xxix.
[2] Löseth, p. 463; *Girone il Cortese*, cap. lxxii.
[3] *O.I.*, II, vii–ix.   [4] *O.I.*, III, v.

romantic in the poem—bring us back to the true
Arthurian world:

> Il vago amor che a sue dame soprane
> portarno al tempo antico e' cavallieri,
> e le battaglie e le venture istrane,
> e l' armeggiar per giostre e per tornieri,
> fa che il suo nome al mondo ancho rimane,
> e ciascadun lo ascolti volentieri;
> e chi più l' uno, e chi più l' altro onora,
> come vivi tra noi fossero ancora.
> E qual fia quel che, odendo de Tristano
> e de sua dama ciò che se ne dice,
> che non mova ad amarli il cor umano,
> reputando il suo fin dolce e felice?
> che, viso a viso essendo e mano a mano
> e il cor col cor più stretto alla radice,
> ne le braccia l' un l' altro a tal conforto
> ciascun di lor rimase a un ponto morto.
> E Lancilotto e sua regina bella
> mostrarno l' un per l' altro un tal valore,
> che dove de' soi gesti se favella,
> par che de intorno il celo arda de amore.
> Traggase avanti adunque ogni donzella,
> ogni baron che vol portare onore,
> et oda nel mio canto quel ch' io dico
> de dame e cavallier del tempo antico.[1]

---

[1] "The fair love that knights bore to their sovereign ladies in the
olden time, and the battles and the strange adventures, and the
combating in jousts and tourneys, makes its name still last in the
world, and each one gladly hears of it; and one honours more
one and another more another, as though they were yet living
among us.

"And is there a man that, hearing of Tristan and his lady the tale
that is told, is not moved in his heart to love them, deeming their
end sweet and happy? For, face to face, and hand to hand, heart
joined to heart in close embrace, in each other's arms thus comforted
they died together at one moment.

"Lancelot, too, and his lovely queen showed each for each such
worth, that, where we speak of their deeds, it seems that the sky

Boiardo originally intended to call his poem the *Innamoramento d' Orlando*, after the fashion of the "cantastorie," and the *Orlando Innamorato* may be regarded as an artistic elaboration of the popular cantari, of which its separate cantos retain some of the typical characteristics. He largely developed the system of "entrelacement," the weaving together of episodes, the interruption and then taking up again of threads and motives, found already in the cantari and, before them, in the French prose romances of the Arthurian cycle and their Italian imitations.[1] This device was employed with consummate art by Ariosto. Messer Ludovico speaks of himself as "continuando la invenzione del conte Matteo Maria Boiardo," but the *Orlando Furioso*—while continuing the matter of its predecessor—is in a different spirit and represents another aesthetic ideal. Ariosto accepts the fusion of the Carolingian and Arthurian legends that Boiardo had effected, but is writing a romantic poem which—as far as the nature of the subject permits—should approximate to classical standards.

The opening lines echo a passage of Dante's *Purgatorio*, and hark back naturally to the "arma virumque cano" of the *Aeneid*; but, as Rajna observes,

around burns with love. Let every damsel then come forward, every baron that would gain honour, and hear in my song what I say of ladies and knights of the olden time" (*O.I.*, II, xxvi, 1–3).

Boiardo also mentions Galahad (Galasso), not in connection with the Grail, but merely coupled with Tristan as a type of a strenuous "cavallier della ventura" (I, xxvii, 29).

[1] Cf. A. Gaspary, *La letteratura italiana del Rinascimento*, ed. V. Rossi (Turin, 1900), I, p. 267, and F. Lot, *Étude sur le Lancelot en prose*, pp. 17–28.

they "could have been written at the head of any romance of the Round Table":

> Le donne, i cavallier, l' arme, gli amori,
> le cortesie, l' audaci imprese io canto.[1]

In like manner, the title of the poem—*Orlando Furioso*—suggests a classical source, the *Hercules Furens* of Seneca; but the madness of the hero is manifestly an elaboration of that of the lover of Iseult in the prose *Tristan*. In each case, the madness is brought about by jealousy; unfounded in the case of Tristan, with good cause in that of Orlando. The initial motive is analogous: Tristan finds the letter which Iseult, "unadvised," had written to comfort Kahedyn; Orlando reads the inscription in which Medoro had blessed the scene that witnessed his union with Angelica. Not a few of the details of their frenzies are alike; the throwing away of the armour, the "brasting down the trees and boughs," the wandering naked in the forest or wilderness, the encounter with shepherds, feats of prodigious strength, and so on.[2] But, with Ariosto, though the treatment of Orlando's madness is serious and pathetic, the solution—the recovery of his lost wits through Astolfo's fantastic journey to the Moon—

---

[1] "The ladies, the knights, the arms, the loves, the courtesies and daring deeds I sing" (*O.F.*, i, 1). I quote throughout from the recent critical edition of Professor S. Debenedetti in the *Scrittori d'Italia: Ludovico Ariosto, Orlando Furioso*, a cura di Santorre Debenedetti (Bari, 1928).

[2] *O.F.*, xxiii, 102–36; Löseth, sects. 76, 101–3; *Tavola Ritonda*, lxx–lxxi; Malory, IX, 17–21. Cf. Bertoni, *L' Orlando furioso e la Rinascenza*, p. 105. In the following pages I am largely indebted to Rajna and Bertoni, who have, indeed, left little more to be gathered in this field.

is sheer comedy; for, throughout the poem, the Comic Muse will not let her tragic sister too far out of her sight.

Ariosto's main sources for Arthurian matter were manifestly the *Tristan* for the "Tavola Nuova," and the *Palamède* as representing the "Tavola Vecchia"; the prose *Lancelot* and the Italian *Vita di Merlino* seem also to have been laid under contribution, but to a far lesser extent. In his Arthurian dealings the poet usually takes some general features and motives, and transforms them into a new episode, frequently fusing elements from several such sources. He utilises Arthurian matter more extensively than Boiardo had done.

One of the most Arthurian episodes of the poem— and here the direct source is obvious—is where Rinaldo, who has been sent by Charlemagne to Britain ("Bretagna che fu poi detta Inghilterra"), is driven by the wind on to the coast of Scotland:.

> dove la selva Calidonia appare,
> che spesso fra gli antiqui ombrosi cerri
> s' ode sonar di bellicosi ferri.[1]

Under its classical name, this "selva Calidonia" is the romantic "forest de Darnantes," and, the poet continues, it is the scene of the exploits of the famous knights of the two Tables:

> Vanno per quella i cavallieri erranti,
> incliti in arme, di tutta Bretagna,
> e de' prossimi luoghi e de' distanti,

---

[1] "Where the Calidonian wood appears, which often among the overshadowing ancient oaks is heard to resound with steel weapons of war" (*O.F.*, iv, 51). Similarly, in Geoffrey of Monmouth, IX, 3, the Saxons make their stand against Arthur "in nemore Colidonis."

di Francia, di Norvegia e de Lamagna.
Chi non ha gran valor, non vada inanti;
che dove cerca onor, morte guadagna.
Gran cose in essa già fece Tristano,
Lancilotto, Galasso, Artù e Galvano,
    et altri cavallieri e de la nuova
e de la vecchia Tavola famosi:
restano ancor di più d' una lor pruova
li monumenti e li trofei pomposi.[1]

The poet is here transferring to Rinaldo the
adventure of Tristan in the "Forest Perilous," "la
forest de Darnantes." Tristan, with his companions,
is driven ashore on a wild and desert region of the
kingdom of Logres, where, the pilot tells him, is "the
garden of the Round Table, and it is called the desert
of Andernantes, which is so renowned for strange and
high adventures." Thus the *Tavola Ritonda*.[2] Hearing that this is the place where all the knights-errant
tested their valour, Tristan sends Gouvernal and
Brangwain to Cornwall, while he goes his way—
with Kahedyn and their two squires—through the
desert or forest in quest of adventures. Rinaldo bids
the pilot go and await him at Berwick, while he pro-
ceeds alone:

Senza scudiero e senza compagnia
va il cavallier per quella selva immensa,

---

[1] "Through that wood go the knights-errant, illustrious in arms,
of all Britain, and of places near and far away, of France, of Norway,
and of Germany. Whoso has not great valour, let him not adventure; for, where he seeks honour, he wins death. Great deeds in it
wrought of old Tristan, Lancelot, Galahad, Arthur, and Gawain,
"and other famous knights both of the New and of the Old Table;
of many of their feats the monuments and blazoned trophies still
remain" (O.F., iv, 52–3).
[2] Capp. lv–lvii. Cf. above, pp. 79–84.

> facendo or una et or un' altra via,
> dove più aver strane aventure pensa.[1]

Tristan and his companions come to a hermit's cell,
Rinaldo to an abbey of monks; in very similar words,
each asks where he can meet knightly adventures.
But their respective hosts have a different adventure
to suggest. The hermit proposes to Tristan the
search for King Arthur, who has been lost in the
desert, the "Forest Perilous." The enterprise which
the monks urge upon Rinaldo is the defence of the
daughter of their king, who is condemned to the
fire unless she finds a champion:

> E se del tuo valor cerchi far prova,
> t' è preparata la più degna impresa
> che ne l' antiqua etade o ne la nova
> giamai da cavallier sia stata presa.[2]

Here we come to one of the most famous episodes
of the poem: the story of Ginevra, which was—perhaps
through the medium of Bandello—to supply Shakespeare with part of the plot of *Much Ado about Nothing*.
Ariosto himself drew that part of the story—the
accusation of infidelity through the girl being counterfeited by her maid—from a Spanish source, the *Tirant
lo Blanch* of Johanot Martorell—but the motive has
become immeasurably purified and ennobled in his
hands.[3] The condemnation to the fire, and the
appearance of the true lover at the last moment as the

---

[1] "Without squire and without company, the knight goes through
that immense wood, taking now one and now another way, where
he thinks most to have strange adventures" (*O.F.*, iv, 54).

[2] "And, if thou dost seek to test thy worth, there is prepared for
thee the most worthy enterprise that was ever undertaken by knight
in ancient time or new" (*O.F.*, iv, 57).

[3] Cf. Rajna, *op. cit.*, pp. 149–63.

TRISTAN AND KAHEDYN AT THE FOREST OF DARNANTES
Florence, Biblioteca Nazionale, Cod. Pal. 556

TRISTAN AND THE HERMIT
Florence, Biblioteca Nazionale, Cod. Pal. 556

champion (Ariodante is there before Rinaldo arrives),
are clearly reminiscent of Lancelot's rescue of Guinevere when accused by Sir Mador de la Porte. And it
was from the Lancelot romance that Ariosto chose the
name "Ginevra." [1]

Another thoroughly Arthurian episode, or series of
episodes, is that of the "Rocca di Tristano," in a
later canto. Bradamante meets a lady, afterwards
called Ullania, attended by three kings, who is bearing
a golden shield from the Queen of Iceland to be
awarded by Charlemagne to the best knight of his
court. The maiden warrior lets them pass, with the
reflection that this shield will cause "discordia e rissa
e nimicizia immensa" in France, if Charlemagne has
to make the decision. Seeking shelter for the night,
she asks a shepherd for guidance. He tells her of a
castle near at hand, called the "Rocca di Tristano,"
but adds that he who seeks to lodge there has to joust
for his place with previous occupants, whatever their
number; and further, if a dame or damsel comes, and
then another arrives, there is a similar contest of
beauty, and the less lovely has to go. Bradamante
undertakes the enterprise, finds the three kings with
Ullania already in possession, overthrows the three
with her enchanted lance, and is courteously received
by the lord of the castle. When she takes off her
helmet, her flowing golden tresses reveal her sex:

> La donna, cominciando a disarmarsi,
> s' avea lo scudo e dipoi l' elmo tratto;
> quando una cuffia d' oro, in che celarsi

---

[1] There is explicit mention of Guinevere (xliii, 28) with reference
to the enchanted horn sent to Arthur by Morgan in the prose *Tristan*.

soleano i capei lunghi e star di piatto,
uscì con l' elmo; onde caderon sparsi
giù per le spalle, e la scopriro a un tratto
e la feron conoscer per donzella,
non men che fiera in arme, in viso bella.[1]

In answer to her questions, her host explains the origin of this "usanza." The castle belonged in old days to Clodion, son of King Pharamond of France, who jealously guarded his lady there with the company of ten knights. One evening Tristan arrived with a lady whom he had just rescued from a giant. Clodion, not to allow any stranger to enter while his lady was there, refused him admission. Tristan challenged him, overthrew him and his knights, and shut them out. To punish Clodion for his discourtesy, he sent out the lady whom he had brought, as being less beautiful, to bear him company, and, while keeping loyal to Iseult (for the love potion, "la pozïon che già incantata bebbe," was still efficacious), let Clodion suppose that he himself was making love to the lady who remained in the castle. In the morning, everything was cleared up. Tristan reminded Clodion that love is no excuse for churlishness:

ch' Amor die' far gentile un cor villano,
e non far d' un gentil contrario effetto.[2]

Clodion consigned the castle to a friend with the

----

[1] "The lady, beginning to disarm, had drawn off her shield and then her helmet, when a golden coif, in which her locks were wont to be hidden and lie concealed, came off with the helmet; whereat they fell loose down her shoulders, and straightway revealed her, and made her known as a damsel not less lovely in face than fierce in arms" (*O.F.*, xxxii, 79).

[2] "For love should make a churlish heart noble, and not work the contrary effect on a noble one" (*O.F.*, xxxii, 93).

pact that this usage was ever afterwards to be
observed:

> che 'l cavallier ch' abbia maggior possanza,
> e la donna beltà, sempre ci alloggi;
> e chi vinto riman, vòti la stanza,
> dorma sul prato, o altrove scenda e poggi.[1]

Supper has been brought in, when the lord of the
castle suddenly remembers the second condition: that
the more beautiful woman must stay and the other go.
It is decided that Bradamante surpasses the other in
beauty as she had surpassed the three kings in might;
but she declares that, whether more or less beautiful,
she has come, not as a woman, but as a warrior, so
that her rival must be allowed to stay.

All this, as Rajna has shown, is a fusion of
several different episodes from the *Tristan* and the
Palamède.[2] Ullania, bringing the golden shield from
the Queen of Iceland to Charlemagne—though the
shield has now another significance, and the purpose is
not the same—is the damsel of the Lady of the Lake
who bears the "écu fendu" to Guinevere.[3] The meeting
of Bradamante with the shepherd, and the jousting for
lodging, come ultimately from an episode in the *Tristan*
familiar to English readers in Malory:

> Then Sir Tristram and Sir Dinadan rode forth their way
> till they came to the shepherds and to the herdmen, and there

---

[1] "That the knight who has the greater prowess, and the lady
beauty, should ever harbour here; and whoso remains vanquished,
should sleep on the meadow, or go down and rest elsewhere" (*ibid.*, 94).

[2] *Op. cit.*, pp. 479-502.

[3] Löseth, sect. 37. The part of Breus sans Pitié, in taking away
the shield, is repeated in that of Marganorre in canto xxxvii, with
which cf. *Tavola Ritonda*, cxxv. In the *Palamède* (Aldus *Meliadus*,
II, cap. cv), a damsel brings a crown to Arthur's court, which the
king gives to Meliadus and he in turn to Guinevere.

U

they asked them if they knew any lodging or harbour there nigh hand. Forsooth, sirs, said the herdmen, hereby is good lodging in a castle; but there is such a custom that there shall no knight be harboured but if he joust with two knights, and if he be but one knight he must joust with two. And as ye be therein, soon shall ye be matched.[1]

But the story of Clodion, with which it is blended, is an adaptation from the *Palamède*, where it has no connection with Tristan. There it is Guiron and Danain who, after rescuing a damsel from a giant, come to a castle and have to joust for their lodging with Lac and Breus, who are already there and whom they defeat. As in Ariosto, the story is told by the castellan; but, instead of Clodion, we have Uther Pendragon, and, for Tristan, an unknown knight of very small stature. Uther, who has been newly knighted, has come privily to the castle to see a lady of the country whom he loves. The diminutive knight, arriving with his damsel, demands lodging, and is told that there is not room for more than one knight. He promptly answers that the other is not a knight, upon which the then castellan (the father of the narrator) bids Uther go out and show that he is one. The king is defeated, and has to spend the night outside. Next morning, he reveals his identity to the castellan, and pledges him to establish the custom, in honour of his opponent, that only he who proves himself the better knight shall be allowed to stay.[2] The motive of jealousy does not enter, nor

---

[1] Malory, IX, 24. Cf. Löseth, sect. 109.

[2] This story, for which see Löseth, *Le Tristan et le Palamède des manuscrits de Rome et de Florence*, pp. 96–8, only appears in certain texts of the *Palamède*, and is not in Rusticiano.

the second condition—the contest of beauty. Here ultimately, though entirely transformed by the poet, we have again the story, from the prose *Tristan*, of the evil custom of the Castle of Pleur that was destroyed by Galehaut after his combat with Tristan. Ariosto has rejected the barbarous and primitive element in the story: the beheading of the unfortunate lady who fell short in the comparison.

A notable feature is the part played by Merlin in the *Orlando Furioso*. Ariosto has returned to the practice of the Italians in the preceding centuries, of combining the purely romantic figure of the Arthurian sage with that of a prophet of the events of their own day. His Merlin is particularly concerned with the history of Italy in the sixteenth century, and with the fortunes of the princes of the house of Este to spring from the marriage of Brada-mante and Ruggiero. To introduce the theme, Ariosto adopts the motive of Breus and the cavern of the ancestors of Guiron from the *Palamède*. Pina-bello, one of the treacherous family of Maganza, who is unwillingly bearing Bradamante company, induces her to descend into a cave, by the story of a beautiful and richly attired damsel who is in need of help below, and then hurls her down to her supposed death by loosing hold of the bough with which he pretends to be aiding her descent. It is the same device by which the lady in the romance attempts to destroy Breus.[1] But, instead of the grandfather of Guiron

---

[1] *O.F.*, ii, 67–75; *Girone il Cortese*, cap. xxxviii. Ariosto has also drawn upon the story of the love of Febus for the princess of Northumberland in his episode of Lidia and Alceste (*O.F.*, xxxiv, 11–43), but has altered the conclusion.

and his long discourse, the "maga" Melissa appears, and leads Bradamante to the tomb that holds the soul and bones of Merlin:

> Questa è l' antiqua e memorabil grotta
> ch' edificò Merlino, il savio mago
> che forse ricordare odi talotta,
> dove ingannollo la Donna del Lago.
> Il sepolcro è qui giù, dove corrotta
> giace la carne sua; dove egli, vago
> di sodisfare a lei, che glil suase,
> vivo corcossi, e morto ci rimase.
> Col corpo morto il vivo spirto alberga,
> sin ch' oda il suon de l'angelica tromba
> che dal ciel lo bandisca o che ve l' erga,
> secondo che sarà corvo o colomba.
> Vive la voce; e come chiara emerga,
> udir potrai da la marmorea tomba,
> che le passate e le future cose
> a chi gli domandò, sempre rispose.[1]

Ariosto's source is evidently the Italian *Vita di Merlino*, with its motive of "il profetico spirto" continuing to speak to all comers after his entombment [2]—Melissa guiding Bradamante as the Lady of the Lake did the younger Meliadus. We saw that,

---

[1] "This is the ancient and memorable cave that Merlin built, the wise magician whom thou perchance dost sometimes hear recalled, where the Lady of the Lake deceived him. The sepulchre is here below, where his flesh lies corrupt; where he, eager to satisfy her who persuaded him, lay down alive, and there dead remained.
"With the dead body the living spirit dwells, until it hear the sound of the angel's trumpet to banish it from heaven or raise it thereto, according as he will be raven or dove. His voice lives; and how clear it comes forth thou shalt hear from the marble tomb, for, to all who asked him of past and future things, he ever replied" (*O.F.*, iii, 10–11).

[2] "Madonna, disse Merlino, la carne mia sarà marza infino ad uno mese, et il spirito mio non fenirà di parlare a tutti quelli che veniranno quivi" (*Vita di Merlino*, IV, 22. Cf. VI, 16).

in the *Vita*, Merlin professed himself assured of
ultimate salvation; Ariosto leaves his final lot in
uncertainty, perhaps to correspond with the mediaeval
tradition as to the doubtful fate of Solomon in the
other world. From the tomb the living voice informs
Bradamante of her high destiny as ancestress of the
house of Este, and the images of her descendants
pass in spectral pageantry before her eyes, like those
of Banquo before Macbeth in the witches' cavern.
Again, further on, we are shown the fountain which
"Merlino, il savio incantator britanno," made in
the time of King Arthur, sculptured with images
of things to come: the monster, who seems to be at
once the Questing Beast of Arthurian legend and
Dante's "lupa" of avarice, pursued and slain by the
European princes of the poet's own day.[1] This is
mere adulation; typical of the less worthy aspect of
the *Orlando Furioso*. A higher note is struck in
a later canto. Here, on the wall in the Rocca di
Tristano, Bradamante sees depicted the story, traced
through the centuries to the poet's own day, of the
French invasions of Italy and their result. The
pictures were wrought by the magic art of Merlin
for King Pharamond, who had been dissuaded by
Arthur from his design of attempting the conquest
of the peninsula:

> Artur, ch' impresa ancor senza consiglio
> del profeta Merlin non fece mai,
> di Merlin, dico, del demonio figlio,
> che del futuro antivedeva assai,
> per lui seppe, e saper fece il periglio
> a Fieramonte, a che di molti guai

---

[1] *O.F.*, xxvi, 30–9.

o

porrà sua gente, s' entra ne.la terra
ch' Apenin parte, e il mare e l' Alpe serra.
　Merlin gli fe' veder che quasi tutti
gli altri che poi di Francia scettro avranno,
o di ferro gli eserciti distrutti,
o di fame o di peste si vedranno;
e che brevi allegrezze e lunghi lutti,
poco guadagno et infinito danno
riporteran d' Italia; che non lice
che 'l Giglio in quel terreno abbia radice.[1]

Here Merlin becomes, as it were, the exponent of
Ariosto's own national sentiment; the long series of
stanzas that follow, move the reader's imagination
like the music heard by De Quincey in his opium-
dream, that "gave the feeling of a vast march, of
infinite cavalcades filing off, and the tread of in-
numerable armies."

[1] "Arthur, who never yet undertook an enterprise without counsel
of Merlin—of Merlin, I say, son of the demon, who foresaw much of
the future—knew through him, and made Pharamond know, the
peril of many woes to which he will expose his folk, if it enters the land
that the Apennines divide and the sea and the Alps enclose.
"Merlin made him see that wellnigh all the others, who shall thereafter bear sceptre in France, will see their armies destroyed by steel,
or by famine, or by pestilence, and that short joys and long griefs,
little gain and infinite loss will they bring back from Italy; for it is
not suffered that the Lily take root in that soil" (O.F., xxxiii, 9–10).

CHAPTER XIV

LATER TREATMENT OF ARTHURIAN MATTER IN ITALY

ARTHURIANISM in Italy culminated in this poetic fusion of the "matter of Britain" with the Carolingian cycle that Ariosto received and developed from Boiardo. But there remain a number of works not undeserving of some consideration.

In addition to the *Meliadus* and the later editions of the *Vita di Merlino*, three other prose Arthurian romances appeared in the sixteenth century published at Venice: *I due Tristani, Parsaforesto*, and *Lancillotto dal Lago*.

Of these the first-named is, on several accounts, the most interesting.[1] If we accept Professor Northup's theory, that the resemblance between the Spanish and Italian *Tristans* is due, not to the Italian and Spanish versions being descended independently from a common unidentified French source, but to the Spanish texts being derived directly from an Italian original or originals, the romance before us is, in part, bringing back to Italy what Spain had received from her.[2]

The *Due Tristani* is a translation of a Spanish

[1] *L'opere magnanime dei due Tristani cavalieri della Tavola Ritonda.* Venice, Michele Tramezzino, 1555. In two volumes.
[2] G. T. Northup, *Italian Origin of Spanish prose Tristan versions*, in *Romanic Review*, III, and *El Cuento de Tristan de Leonis*, edited from the unique MS. Vaticano 6428 (Chicago, 1928). Cf. W. J. Entwistle, *The Arthurian Legend in the Literatures of the Spanish Peninsula*, pp. 115–29, and in *M.L.R.*, XXIV, pp. 230–3.

romance published at Seville in 1534, and retains
or italianises the Spanish forms of the names of the
characters: Mares (Mark), Isea (Iseult), Gorvalan
(Gouvernal), Brangilla (Brangwain), Quedino (Kahedyn), and so on. Save for a long interpolation, the
first book reproduces the well-known Spanish version,
Don Tristan de Leonis.[1] The earlier portions of the
story, up to the encounter with Galehaut and the
destroying of the evil custom of the Castle of Pleur
(i–xxii), correspond closely with the *Tristano Riccardiano* (i–lxv), with modifications in detail and some
elaboration. For instance, the motive of the dog
lapping up the remains of the love potion on the ship
does not occur; on the island of Pleur, Tristan refuses
to behead Brunor's wife, and orders one of the
inhabitants to do it.

Then comes the long interpolation (xxiii–lvii), of
a more diffuse and elaborate character, suggesting a
totally different atmosphere, which is evidently the
invention of the sixteenth-century Spanish author.
Galehaut and the King of the Hundred Knights
return to the mainland, where the latter—whose city
is apparently Piacenza—marries his friend's sister,
here called Riccarda. Galehaut, who has lost all
traces of his original character, makes an edifying
end in a monastery of St. Bernard, where he is buried.
Tristan and Iseult spend two years on the island of

---

[1] *Libro del esforzado caballero don Tristan de Leonis*, ed. A. Bonilla
y San Martín, in *Libros de Caballerías*, I (Madrid, 1907). The *Cuento
de Tristan de Leonis*, edited by Northup, contains portions of a
different text apparently derived ultimately from the same redaction.
The Spanish original of the *Due Tristani* is entitled *Coronica . . . del
buen cauallero don Tristan de Leonis y del rey don Tristan de Leonis
el Joven, su hijo.*

Pleur, where they have two children, a boy and a girl, to whom they give their own names. Floris-delfa, a sorceress who has been taught by Merlin, becoming enamoured of Tristan, sends him a herd of horses by magic over the sea (their coming is the best scene in this part of the story), and follows in a crystal tower upon a chariot drawn by two elephants breathing fire from their eyes and mouths, but dashes herself down from the loggia of the castle at the sight of Iseult's beauty. Tristan and Iseult finally decide that they must proceed to Cornwall; they leave the children in the charge of their foster-parents, after revealing their identity to a few chosen knights, who swear to have young Tristan as their lord, or, failing him, his sister.

The story now returns to the version given by *Don Tristan de Leonis*. From the arrival at Tintagel to the deliverance of Arthur in the Forest Perilous (lviii–lxxviii), the general lines of the narrative resemble the *Tristano Riccardiano*, but there are many divergences. There is, for instance, a curious account of Palamede. He is descended from a pagan king who bore a red-crossed shield that had belonged to Joseph of Arimathea, became secretly a Christian, was imprisoned by his subjects and miraculously fed in prison. His children were banished; Palamede, of their race, though he believes in part, has not been baptised, because his mother has told him that, if he is baptised, he will not recover the kingdom.[1] The

---

[1] I, lx, pp. 142-3. We are referred to "il libro di Merlino"; but Palamede's ancestor, "Ebalato," is clearly a combination of Esclabor n the *Palamède* with Evalac (Mordrain) in the *Estoire del Saint Graal*.

wounded knight, who alone ventures to attempt the
rescue of Iseult from Palamede, is Sagramour, who
plays a leading part subsequently as Tristan's friend
and supporter in Cornwall, taking the place that
properly belongs to Dinas.[1]   The treacherous damsel,
the mistress of Andred, figures more prominently in
the betrayal of the lovers to King Mark.   Iseult of
Brittany tries to retain Tristan by a love potion,
which he destroys.   The events leading up to the
deliverance of Arthur are somewhat different.   As in
Rusticiano, it is Brandelis, not Hector or Blioberis,
who intervenes between Lancelot and Lamorat, and
a further indication of the influence of Rusticiano,
or the *Palamède*, is seen in the damsel of the Lady of
the Lake naming the Knight without Fear as one of
the possible champions that she is seeking.   A horn
sounds, after which fifty armed men bring out the
king, the sorceress dragging him to the ground by
his hair, exclaiming: "Will you have me for wife,
King Arthur, and escape?"   There is no combat
between Tristan and Perceval, though the latter is
evidently the unnamed "red knight" who is following
the Questing Beast.

From this point onwards, where the *Tristano
Riccardiano* broke off, the remainder of the first book
differs considerably from any extant French text of
the *Tristan*, while, here and there, agreeing with
the *Tavola Ritonda*, or drawing from Rusticiano.

---

[1] In the *Cuento*, he is Segris, the Sigris or Sagris of the *Tristano
Riccardiano* and *Tavola Ritonda*. Sagramour was popular with the
Arthurians of the Spanish Peninsula, and is the hero of a sixteenth-
century Portuguese romance, the *Triunfos de Sagramor* of Jorge
Ferreira de Vasconcellos. Cf. Entwistle, *op. cit.*, p. 213.

Sagramour reconciles Tristan temporarily with King Mark, who, however, sets him to guard the passage of Tintagel for a year, in the hope that some knight-errant may kill him. The episode of Kahedyn's love for Iseult and Tristan's madness does not occur. The lovers escape to Joyous Gard, and, as in the *Tavola Ritonda*, the two queens become fast friends —though Arthur thinks fit to rebuke Iseult for her conduct towards her husband (lxxxix).[1] The Knight without Fear takes part in the great tournament at Lonazep. King Mark comes to Camelot, and the motive of Tristan and Iseult found sleeping with the naked sword between them, transferred from its forest setting, becomes a somewhat unedifying comedy, devised by Dinadan with the participation of Lancelot for the benefit of the two kings (xcvi–xcvii). Tristan is made a knight of the Round Table to occupy the seat of the Morholt, and, at this point, the adventure of the old knight, Branor le Brun, is introduced from Rusticiano (ci–cvi). But Lancelot, to Guinevere's consolation, is too ill to joust, and the old knight himself refuses to fight Arthur. Morgan le Fay makes an unsuccessful attempt first to capture and then to seduce Tristan, but we are not given the episode of the slaying of her lover Hemison. Tristan and Palamede go seeking adventures together until entertained by the King of the Hundred Knights, after which they separate, Palamede and their host to share in the quest of the Grail, Tristan to return to Cornwall. The death of

---

[1] The *Cuento* breaks off at the visit of Arthur and Lancelot to Tristan's tent during the tournament.

Tristan follows in the main the lines of the French romance, but with some notable Spanish embroidery (cxi–cxiv). Iseult, with Gouvernal and Brangwain, watches all night in the church of Our Lady—the queen praying before the Crucifix that, since the fault was hers, she may die for Tristan. Morning comes, and she returns to Tristan's chamber, to find that he has confessed and received the Blessed Sacrament: "Ah, God, it hath pleased Thee that I should die in this fashion, and Thou hast not willed that I should be in the holy quest of the Holy Grail." He bids Gouvernal and Brangwain marry, and administer his kingdom in the name of young Tristan, his son. He dies in Iseult's embrace, with a last prayer to God and the Blessed Virgin, and the queen's heart breaks, seeing him dead in her arms. This version has a power of its own, but the contrast between the religious note and the traditional dying embrace is too strident.

The second book, the story of the younger Tristan, seems entirely the invention of the sixteenth-century Spanish author. It is a curious medley of fantastic episodes and courtly scenes, in which the characters have lost their original features; the Arthurian knights have become elaborately ceremonious, even Galahad appearing as little more than a courteous, if somewhat austere, member of Arthur's court with a tendency to edifying talk; but some of the adventures are interesting, and the young hero himself is well portrayed as a noble and chivalrous personage.

Sagramour, in whose castle Tristan had died, can do nothing against Mark as he is his vassal; but

Kahedyn stirs up the people of Liones, and an army, under the command of Palante, a cousin of Tristan, invades Cornwall.[1] Mark's army having been defeated and various cities taken, Palante and Kahedyn advance on Tintagel. Andred and his mistress try to escape, but are captured, recognised by Kahedyn, and compelled to confess that they had advised Mark to kill Tristan. They are burned alive in front of the city, the walls lined with the citizens, and Mark himself watching from a window. A truce having been arranged, Mark shuts himself up in a tower. In the meanwhile, Lancelot has gone with Gouvernal and Brangwain to fetch young Tristan from the island of Pleur. With all sorts of strange manifestations, the good enchantress Sargia brings her son Felice to enter Tristan's service. Tristan, as King of Liones, arrives in the harbour of Tintagel with his sister Iseult · and Lancelot. Mark, dismayed at hearing that Lancelot is there, and supposing that the young people must be the children of Iseult of the White Hands, sends for Gouvernal, tells him that he has seen the guilty parties punished before his eyes (adding that he ought to have done it himself), and he would now resign the kingdom to young Tristan as a penance for the crime he committed against his father. It is agreed that Tristan shall pardon his uncle, accept the kingdom, but leave Mark in possession of it for his lifetime. With many pious sentiments, Mark crowns young Tristan King of Cornwall. News comes that the father of Kahedyn is dead, and he is now King of

---

[1] In reality, Kahedyn had died for love of Iseult before the death of Tristan. Cf. Löseth, sect. 100.

Little Britain. Hearing of the beauty of the younger Iseult, Palamede (still "the pagan") appears at Liones, attempts to carry her off in the presence of her brother, and is killed in combat with Palante.[1] Shortly afterwards, King Mark makes a most edifying end, young Tristan arriving in time to receive his dying blessing, and Cornwall is merged into Liones to form one kingdom.

To Liones comes the Duchess of Milan, who is married with great pomp to Palante. The Queen of the Amazons likewise appears with her hundred maidens, and secretly forces her love upon Tristan; against his will, for the young king is resolved to keep himself chaste for the bride whom God will give him. Lancelot and Galahad present themselves, and the former summons Tristan to come and be knighted by King Arthur, and take the seat of his father at the Round Table. Queen Guinevere becomes desperately enamoured of him, and makes her love known when she girds on the sword at the investiture; but Tristan "prayed ever to God that He would keep him from Queen Guinevere, and turn her heart from her evil intention," for he would die rather than be disloyal to King Arthur. He is victorious in the tournament, and Lancelot, unwittingly, enables him to escape the queen's seductions. The author has

---

[1] II, cap. xxxiv. This invention is an outrage upon the memory of one of the most attractive figures in the Arthuriad. Palamede was duly baptised after his last fight with Tristan, joined in the quest of the Holy Grail, after being admitted to the Round Table, and was then murdered by Gawain. Cf. Löseth, sects. 560, 563-5. His death at Gawain's hands is mentioned in the Cod. Panciatichiano 33, f. 128v°, but there seems no detailed account of it in Italian.

pitifully degraded the character of Guinevere, but the
whole of this part of the story is vivid and powerfully
told.[1] The romance now deteriorates. There is
much slaying of giants by Tristan, and magical intervention on the part of the enchantress Sargia. Tristan undertakes the adventure of Florinca, an Irish
lady married to a comic braggart of a Portuguese. He
delivers the Queen of the Amazons from the King of
the Idumeans and his giants, but departs without
revealing his identity to her. Finally, he goes to
Spain as an unknown knight, enters the service of
King Juan of Castile, and delivers the Infanta Maria
from the Moors. It is arranged that Tristan shall
marry the Infanta, and Don Juan wed Iseult. The
comparatively modern atmosphere of these last
chapters is rudely dispelled by the sudden irruption,
during the jousts at Liones, of a giant of the kin of
Palamede. He is duly slain by Tristan, after which
the book ends with King Juan and Queen Iseult
departing for Castile, leaving Tristan and Maria
to reign together in Liones.

The *Parsaforesto* is a translation of the French
romance of *Perceforest*, which was published by
Galliot du Pré at Paris in 1528 and reprinted in
1531.[2] The original is a vast composition which, as
Gaston Paris observes, links the fabulous history of
Alexander with that of the Holy Grail, and, by an
extraordinary leap, unites the Macedonian conqueror

---

[1] II, capp. lxiv–lxvii.

[2] *La dilettevole historia del valorosissimo Parsaforesto Re della gran
Brettagna, con i gran fatti del valente Gadiffero Re di Scotia, vero
essempio di Cavalleria.* Venice, Michele Tramezzino, 1556–8. In
six books, which form seven volumes in the British Museum copy.

with Arthur and covers the space of eight centuries in three generations.[1]   Written in imitation of the prose Arthurian romances, its purpose is to go back, beyond the *Palamède* and the Old Table, to the mythical history of early Britain and the forebears of characters in the *Tristan* and Vulgate cycle.

The brothers Parsaforesto (Perceforest) and Gadiffero (Gadifer)—the ancestors of Arthur—are made Kings of Britain and Scotland respectively by Alexander the Great.   Parsaforesto (originally Bétis, Betide) wins his name by penetrating the enchanted forest, and slaying the magician Darnante from whom it was called.   There is a profusion of tournaments (which Alexander introduced into Britain), adventures of knights-errant, distressed damsels, and the like, of the usual Arthurian type.   Gadiffero marries the wise Queen Fay ("la Reina Fata"), and, incurably wounded by a magic boar (the "porco cornuto"), becomes the "re magagnato," an obvious imitation of the "maimed king" of the Grail story; while Parsaforesto builds a temple to the Supreme God, and founds the order of the "Cavalieri del Franco Palagio," in anticipation of the Round Table.   The latter's son Betide marries "la bella Circe romana," and she, through her lover Lucio, invites the Romans

---

[1] Gaston Paris, *Le conte de la Rose en vers et en prose dans le roman de Perceforest*, in *Romania*, XXIII (1894), pp. 78 sq.   According to him, it was composed shortly before the middle of the fourteenth century; but a later date has sometimes been assigned to it.   Cf. Ward, *Catalogue of Romances*, I, pp. 377–8, and Dunlop-Wilson, *History of Prose Fiction*, I, ch. iv.   H. Vaganay, in *Rivista delle Biblioteche e degli Archivi*, XVI (Florence, 1905), pp. 14–15, shows that the Italian text is mainly an abridgement, with omissions, of the French edition of 1531.

to Britain under Julius Caesar. The two kings have
resigned their crowns to their sons; but Parsaforesto
returns to share in the great battle in which the
knights of the Franco Palagio are annihilated by the
Romans, and the palace itself reduced to ruins. The
king, left for dead, is mysteriously conveyed from
the battlefield to join his brother. Throughout the
romance flits the strange figure of Zefiro, "the subtle
spirit that so loves the realm of Britain," one of the
fallen angels apparently, but who believes that God
has still power to pardon him. He has entrusted to
the care of Morgan le Fay a lad named Passaleone,
who is the lover of Morgan's daughter and the ancestor
of Merlin. Gallaffaro (Gallafar), son of the "maimed
king" and the "Queen Fay," is now the hero of the
romance; he becomes King of Britain, restores the
Franco Palagio, and renews the chivalrous life of the
land which had been destroyed by the Romans. By
his wife Alessandra, a descendant of Alexander the
Great, he has two sons: Olofer and the younger
Gallaffaro. These two lads are carried off by Zefiro
in the form of a great bird, to save them from the
destruction brought upon Britain by a host of Germanic invaders. King Gallaffaro alone escapes in the
slaughter of his army, and is conveyed by Zefiro to the
Island of Life. The Sicambrian, Scapiolo, becomes
King of Britain, and is led by Zefiro in the guise of a
stag to Gerne, the daughter of Gallaffaro, whom he
marries. From this marriage is descended Lucius,
the first Christian King of Britain. Olofer is made
Duke of Cornwall, and slays the "porco cornuto."
In a boat drawn by a white swan, he is conveyed to

x

the Island of Life, where he is met by his father, and, with an ointment prepared from the marrow of the boar's tusks, heals Gadiffero and Parsaforesto of their wounds. Olofer then returns to the world, but is slain by the Questing Beast.

Now the Holy Grail comes to Britain. Olofer's brother, the younger Gallaffaro, an astronomer who had first lived as a recluse adoring the Unknown God, has become king of a simple folk in a land called Forania, but is stricken by an incurable disease. The Christian faith is being preached, when Alain, the keeper of the Grail, comes to Forania, converts Gallaffaro, and gives him the name Arfarano at baptism. Arfarano, as he is now called, is healed by the touch of the sacred vessel, gives his daughter as wife to Alain's brother Josue, and builds a chapel for the Grail in his castle of Corbenio (Corbenic). With the priest Natael or Nathaniel, who had been with Joseph of Arimathea at the time of the Crucifixion, Arfarano is brought by Zefiro over the sea to the Island of Life; where in extreme old age his father Gallaffaro, Gadiffero, Parsaforesto, and the Queen Fay are praying and awaiting the coming of the Son of the Virgin. Arfarano preaches the faith to them, and they are baptised by Natael. They now desire only death, and, since in this island human nature cannot die, ask to be conveyed to some other land. A sea captain, who has had a vision of Christ, is awaiting them at the shore with his ship. They reach an unknown port, where the sailor and his crew are baptised; the pilgrims from the Island of Life die, and are buried in tombs found miraculously prepared.

Arfarano will return and abide there; but, in the meantime, he goes back to Corbenic, where Gamael has been made bishop. In the chapel he sees Gamael draw out the holy vessel covered with red samite and officiate at Mass, where a figure, lying on a rich bed with covered face but crowned, receives Communion. Alain tells the story of the coming of the Grail, the imprisonment of Joseph and his companions, and how they were miraculously fed. The wounded king is Mordrain, who sought to see too much of the mystery; his bed is to be in the chapel, where he is to lie until the holy coming of the valiant knight who will heal him, "the good messenger of the lineage of Nascien, who shall openly behold the secret of the Holy Grail and fulfil the adventures."[1]

The third of these romances, *Lancillotto dal Lago*, in three books (the first ending with the death of Galehaut), includes versions of the *Lancelot* proper, the *Queste del Saint Graal*, and the *Mort Artu*. It is a translation of the French printed *Lancelot du Lac* published at Paris in 1533, and offers no points of fresh interest, save in so far as it thus represents some sections of the Vulgate in an accessible Italian form.[2]

A few insignificant poems, in which Arthurian characters figure, have come down from the fifteenth century. Forty stanzas have been preserved of a

---

[1] Much of this concluding portion of the romance is obviously adapted from the *Estoire del Saint Graal* (which is otherwise unrepresented in Italian), Arfarano being Alphasem, the leper king Kalafe of the "Terre foraine," but with fresh figures introduced and the beautiful invention of the aged band in the Island of Life.

[2] *L' illustre et famosa historia di Lancillotto dal Lago.* Venice, Michele Tramezzino, 1558-9. The British Museum copy is bound as six volumes.

Venetian poem to which its editor gives the title of
Galasso dalla scura valle.[1]   But this Galahad seems to
have no connection with the Grail.   He is living as a
hermit in the "dark valley," sustained and consoled
by the visits of an Angel of God.   He shelters a
damsel, slays the giant Fieragrasso, is anointed by
the angel, who sends him against three other giants
and a pagan host which he destroys.   Returning to
his cell to die, he sends his horse and arms to his father
(who is apparently not Lancelot), is attended in death
by the angel, and his body is watched over by the
beasts of the forest until found by King Arges and his
barons.   A worthless poem of the cantare type, *La
Battaglia de Tristano e Lancelotto e della Reina Isotta,*
printed in 1492, relates how Galahad and Lancelot
delivered Tristan from the castle of the giant Barba-
folta.[2]   In the early years of the Cinquecento, several
Arthurian poems were composed in imitation of the
cantari.   Thus Matteo Fossa of Cremona, who died in
1516, wrote the *Innamoramento di Galvano,* retelling
the story of Gawain and Pulzella Gaia.   Nicolò degli
Agostini—the Venetian continuator of Boiardo—
produced an *Innamoramento di messer Tristano e di
madonna Isotta* (1520), and an *Innamoramento di
Lancilotto e di Ginevra,* which was continued by
Marco Guazzo (1521–6).   These poems lack the fresh-
ness and charm of the early cantari, and are of small
literary value, for the most part substituting new

---

[1] A. Moschetti, *Frammento d'un poemetto veneto su "Galasso dalla
scura valle,"* in *Miscellanea di Storia Veneta* edita per cura della
R. Dep. Veneta di Storia Patria, serie II, tom. ii (Venice, 1894).

[2] P. Rajna, *I Cantari di Carduino,* pp. xli–xliv.   Rajna notes
elements drawn from the Carolingian cycle.

inventions for the orthodox legends.[1] Thus Nicolò degli Agostini rejects the famous scene on the ship, and makes Iseult give Tristan the love potion intentionally; in the third book of the poem, Arthur and the knights of the Round Table ineffectually intervene to save King Mark from the vengeance wreaked upon him by the friends of Tristan and the father of Iseult, who, in defiance of Arthurian chronology, is represented as still reigning in Ireland when his daughter and her lover died. In his other poem, the figure of Guinevere is subordinated to that of Pulzella Gaia, here called Gaggia, who has entirely changed since she appeared in the fourteenth-century cantare; restored from serpent's form to that of a woman by the kiss of Gawain, she nevertheless compels Lancelot to become her lover.

More noteworthy are the two long Arthurian poems of Luigi Alamanni: the Florentine who in his youth had caught republican fire from the discourses of Machiavelli, and who died, an exile at the French court, in 1556. The first of these, *Gyrone il Cortese*, in twenty-four books, was undertaken at the bidding of King Francis I, and published with a dedication to Henry II in 1548.[2] In a somewhat lengthy preface on

---

[1] Cf. F. Foffano, *Il poema cavalleresco* (Milan, 1911), pp. 56–7, 122–4; P. Verrua, *Studio sul Poema "Lo Innamoramento di Lancilotto e di Ginevra" di Nicolò degli Agostini* (Florence, 1901); G. Malavasi, *La materia poetica del ciclo brettone in Italia* (Bologna, 1903).

[2] *Gyrone il Cortese di Luigi Alamanni, al Christianissimo et invittissimo Re Arrigo secondo* (Paris, 1548); *Girone il Cortese*, etc. (Venice, 1549). A third edition, in two small volumes, was published at Bergamo in 1757. Cf. H. Hauvette, *Un exilé florentin à la cour de France au xvie siècle, Luigi Alamanni, sa vie et son œuvre* (Paris, 1903), pp. 303–32; F. Foffano, *op. cit.*, pp. 150–1.

the chivalrous customs of King Arthur's court,
Alamanni sets forth Guiron as the perfect type of
knighthood, whom the young knights of the present
day may well take as an example.   The poem is
mainly a rendering, into rather monotonous Italian
octaves, of the printed French text of the prose
romance, *Gyron le Courtoys*, which, as we saw, came
through Rusticiano from the *Palamède*; but Alamanni
freely omits and condenses episodes (generally to
the advantage of the poem), expands or modifies, and
perhaps, as Foffano suggests, somewhat heightens the
moral tone of the original, whereby duty and sacrifice,
rather than love, become the soul of the chivalrous
world that he depicts.   He discards Rusticiano's
opening tale of Branor le Brun, as also the early
history of his hero (which he could have found
elsewhere), and begins at once with Guiron on
his way to Malehaut.[1]   The slight motive of Guiron
being imprisoned and compelled to reveal his
name, after the slaying of the giants, is transformed
into the charming episode of the Castle of the
Maidens, where he is made captive by the forty
girls whom he has delivered.[2]   The passion of the
Lady of Malehaut, and Guiron's struggle with his own
conscience after the tournament, are considerably
elaborated; the dramatic force and poignancy of the
great scene with the sword of Hector le Brun, and that
other, where Danain, believing the false report of his
betrayal, confronts the repentant lovers, are some-

---

[1] The opening of the poem corresponds with cap. viii of the Italian
prose *Girone il Cortese*.

[2] Cf. Book i, stanzas 93 sq., with the Italian prose, cap. ix, p. 72.

what weakened by the lengthened speeches placed
upon the lips of the actors—though these are noble in
their kind, as, for instance, the five stanzas of Guiron's
address to his sword which expand the brief prose
sentences of the original.[1] The adventures of Breus
in the cavern of the ancestors of Guiron occupy three
books (xii–xiv), and here Alamanni slightly modifies
the story in honour of his royal patrons. Pharamond
is not, as in the prose romance, a freedman who has
obtained the crown of France by treachery, but a
cousin to whom Guiron's grandfather has given it
with the consent of the people, and stanzas are
introduced in exaltation of the French kings, his descendants, down to Francis and Henry. The great
combat with Danain, and the subsequent rescue of
the latter from the giant (xvii–xviii), are somewhat
differently related, with the purpose of setting Guiron's
courtesy in stronger relief, and the reconciliation
between the two friends is complete.

The abbot of the monastery, to which the wounded
Danain is conveyed, has been one of the squires of the
King of Estrangorre, and he relates to Guiron the
story of the Good Knight without Fear falling into the
hands of Nabon in the "val du Servage."[2] Guiron now
sets out to deliver the Good Knight, and we have the
episode of Helin le Roux (but without the horrible
tale of his origin), Danain's reappearance and rescue

---

[1] Books iii, v, vi.

[2] Books xviii–xx. In the prose text, where the story is in
direct narration, there is no suggestion that the squire who accompanies the Good Knight became a monk. Here, by making him
relate the whole story to the hero, Alamanni has contrived to improve
the structure of the romance.

of Guiron and Bloia. Guiron's lady is left with a
widow at a castle, while the two friends depart
together, separating, as in the prose romance, at the
parting of the roads of "wrath" and "false pleasure."
But, from this point onwards, the poem becomes
mainly Alamanni's own invention. Both Danain and
Guiron achieve their adventures without mishap.
Danain passes on to the valley of the Servage, where
he is compelled to fight the Good Knight without
Fear whom he has come to rescue, and, desperately
wounded, becomes the captive of Nabon (xxi).
Guiron, after defeating Galinan, converts him to a
better life, and deals in the same way with his even
more churlish brother; the latter episode, which takes
the place of his imprisonment and the death of Bloia,
being apparently devised to emphasise the power of
the hero's courtesy. After a visit to the Lady of
Malehaut, Guiron penetrates the Servage, defeats the
forces that Nabon sends against him, but—by the
devices of the false damsel who had previously
betrayed the Good Knight—is captured by treachery
(xxii–xxiii).

The close of the poem (xxiii–xxiv), while taking
motives from the *Meliadus* and the printed *Tristan*,
is, again, in great part Alamanni's own. Nabon, now
that he has the flower of chivalry in his hands, sends
ambassadors to King Arthur, announcing that he will
put the prisoners to death unless the king consents to
become his vassal. The envoys are shown the chapel
in which the shields of the knights-errant are sus-
pended, including that of Balin le Sauvage ("Balaan
gigante"), who, like Palamede, alone bears two

swords.[1] To save the lives of the prisoners, Arthur consents to dissemble; Lancelot, Tristan, Palamede, and Segurant are to go to Nabon, ostensibly as ambassadors, in reality to draw him out to battle and release the captive knights. In various adventures by the way, the Arthurians delude Nabon's envoys into supposing that they are unwilling to fight. Nabon orders a magnificent tournament, to impress them with his power. The four knights profess to enter with reluctance, and then, according to a prearranged plan, suddenly assail the tyrant's forces, who are defeated after a prolonged battle, Nabon himself and his son Nathan being slain by Tristan. The prisoners—a vast number including knights from various regions—are set at liberty. Guiron refuses the crown of the country, saying that it should be given to Arthur, and Segurades, one of the released prisoners, is appointed to rule in the king's name.[2]

The *Gyrone* had been written hastily and to order, and the result was little more than the versification of a mediaeval prose romance; but, at the end of the preface, Alamanni promised another "new work of poetry," less unworthy of his royal patron, "composed according to the ancient manner and pattern,

[1] This (xxiii, 72), which occurs also in the preface, seems to be the only allusion in Italian to that pathetic figure (from the *Huth Merlin*) that we know so well in the pages of Malory. But these stanzas (xxiii, 65-84) are derived from the "Devise des armes de tous les chevaliers de la Table Ronde," prefixed to the French editions of *Gyron le Courtoys* (cf. Hauvette, *op. cit.*, p. 316), where Alamanni would have found Balin mentioned: "Brallain quon disoit le chevalier aux deux espees."

[2] Segurades, the husband of the Lady of the Thorn, in the prose *Tristan* and Malory. Hauvette, *op. cit.*, p. 317, n. 2, has confused him with Segurant.

in imitation of Homer and Virgil." This poem is the *Avarchide*, in twenty-five books, begun about 1549, and finished shortly before the author's death, though not published until many years later (1570) by his son Battista, Bishop of Macon.[1]

Here we have a serious attempt to accomplish one of the great literary aspirations of the century, the quest of what Tasso called the "idea del perfettissimo poema"[2], or, as Ker puts it, "the learned ambition to embody the abstract form of Epic in a modern vernacular work."[3]   Alamanni, as his son writes in the dedicatory epistle, had set himself to imitate Homer and thus compose a "Tuscan Iliad": "Egli con ogni studio e diligenza si è ingegnato di volere quasi una Toscana Iliade formare."   For this purpose, he adopts the curious device of attaching the story of the *Iliad* to the "matter of Britain," with Avaricum (Caesar's name for Bourges) substituted for Troy.[4] Boiardo and Ariosto had fused the Arthurian and Carolingian cycles, by taking Carolingian heroes and giving them the characteristics and adventures of

---

[1] *La Avarchide del S. Luigi Alamanni, alla Sereniss. Madama Margherita di Francia, Duchessa di Savoia e di Berrì*, Florence (Giunti), 1570.   A modern reprint, in two small volumes, Bergamo, 1761.   Cf. Hauvette, *op. cit.*, pp. 357–400, and O. Renda, *L'elemento brettone nell' Avarchide di L. Alamanni* (Naples, 1899).

[2] *Discorsi del poema eroico*, in *Le prose diverse di Torquato Tasso*, ed. C. Guasti (Florence, 1875), I, p. 121.

[3] *Collected Essays of W. P. Ker*, ed. C. Whibley (London, 1925), I, p. 14.

[4] It is tempting to think that Alamanni was influenced by his French contemporary, Joachim du Bellay, whose *Deffence et Illustration de la Langue françoyse* appeared in 1549: "Choysi moy quelque un de ces beaux vieulx romans francoys, comme un *Lancelot*, un *Tristan*, ou autres: et en fay renaitre au monde un admirable *Iliade* et laborieuse *Eneïde*" (ed. H. Chamard, Paris, 1904, pp. 235–6).

knights of the Round Table; Alamanni, without
effecting any real fusion, combines the motive, from
the earlier part of the *Lancelot*, of the war waged
by Arthur and Lancelot upon King Claudas for the
latter's usurpation of the dominion of King Ban, with
the Homeric poem by taking Arthurian figures and
making them, with frequent modifications and some
interchange of roles, play the part of personages in
the *Iliad*:

> Canta, o Musa, lo sdegno e l' ira ardente
> di Lancilotto, del Re Ban figliuolo,
> contra 'l Re Arturo, onde sì amaramente
> il Britannico pianse e 'l Franco stuolo.[1]

Arthur appears as Agamemnon, Lancelot (who is
represented as the ancestor of the French kings) as
Achilles with Galehaut, the Lord of the Distant Isles,
as Patroclus; Tristan and Bors alternately act as Ajax
and Diomede, Gawain is usually Menelaus, Maligante
(Meliagrance, the son of King Bagdemagus) most
inappropriately is Ulysses; while Viviana, the Lady
of the Lake, naturally assumes the functions of
Thetis—and gives a curious and unorthodox account
of her relations with Merlin and her motive for delud-
ing him.[2]   The part of Priam is sustained by King
Claudas (Clodasso), and his young son Clodino—the
person who makes that strange appearance at the
table of the Grail in the *Queste*—occasionally takes
that of Paris.   The Arthurian army is mainly composed of Britons and French, whereas the besieged in

---

[1] "Sing, O Muse, the wrath and burning rage of Lancelot, son of
King Ban, against King Arthur, wherefrom the British and the
French host had bitter cause to wail" (i, 1).

[2] i, 96–103.

Avaricum are Germanic pagans. Palamede, who is
represented as an Irishman, is fighting on their side,
together with some other Arthurian personages like
Dinadan (who shows no trace of his Arthurian
character); but so are Theodoric and Odoacer, and
even Nabon (here said to have been the son of Alaric
and Rosmunda) seems to have returned to life for the
same purpose. The *Lancelot* is not the only source;
the *Tristan*, *Meliadus* and *Gyron* have also been laid
under contribution. King Lac, now very old, is the
Nestor of Arthur's camp, and, for the Hector of the
poem, appears no less a personage than Segurant le
Brun (Segurano), who has become King of Ireland by
slaying the Morholt in single combat.[1] With him is
Galinan, the son of Guiron, but the poet gives no
hint of his traditional bad qualities. Segurant differs
from his classical prototype in being the son-in-law
of Claudas, and has been brought into the defence
of the city as the husband of the king's daughter
Claudiana, who combines the parts of Andromache and
Chryseis. She has been released by Lancelot in spite
of Gawain, who himself desired to marry her, and it is
the acceptance by Arthur of his nephew's accusations
that causes "lo sdegno e l' ira ardente" of Lancelot
from which the poem starts, the son of King Ban and his
faithful Galehaut retiring from the war in consequence.

The Arthurian element in the poem is comparatively superficial, being confined to the borrowing
of names and allusions to past episodes in the first
part of the *Lancelot* (Alamanni ignores all the later

---

[1] ix, 69–72. Alamanni makes Segurant the son of the elder
Hector and brother of Galehaut le Brun.

portions) and, in a minor degree, the *Meliadus* and
the *Gyron*. In the main, it is a somewhat uninspired
imitation of the *Iliad*, with the intervention of the
Gods omitted. The sense of romance is almost
entirely lost, and the characters are no longer knights-
errant. As M. Hauvette puts it, the Tristan of the
poem appears never to have known Iseult, and Lancelot has lost all remembrance of his love for Queen
Guinevere.[1] Alamanni has, not unhappily, adapted
from the *Meliadus* the motive of the anxiety of the
Lady of the Lake that Lancelot and Segurant should
not meet in combat. There the reason is not given;
here it is that Merlin had told her that the Knight of
the Dragon was destined to die by her foster-child's
sword; with the result that, while Lancelot, in
obedience to the oath she made him swear, has always
turned from the encounter, Segurant is bent upon
fighting him.[2] In spite of the valour of Tristan and
Bors, the Arthurians are hard pressed by the prowess
of Segurant. Finally, when they are being worsted,
Arthur himself and Bors with many other leaders
wounded, Lancelot consents to Galehaut, clad in his
armour, leading their united forces to the rescue. The
Lord of the Distant Isles kills Nabon; but, in spite
of Lancelot's injunctions not to fight Palamede or
Segurant, he encounters and is himself slain by the
latter, who takes the enchanted armour. Like
Thetis in the *Iliad*, Viviana brings Lancelot new arms

[1] *Op. cit.*, p. 390. But there are allusions to Lancelot's chivalrous
devotion to the queen in i, 52, and xx, 10. In xiv, 63, in imitation
of Achilles in the *Iliad*, Lancelot refuses Arthur's offer of Guinevere's
sister Lodaganta as bride.

[2] viii, 55–9. Cf. the Aldus *Meliadus*, II, cap. lxxxviii.

obtained from Merlin at his tomb, with a shield upon
which are engraved the future exploits of the kings
of France. Lancelot refuses to fight Galinan; but
slays Dinadan, Palamede, and young Clodino. The
final combat does not reproduce the Homeric model;
Segurant does not flee three times round the walls of
Avaricum as Hector round those of Troy, and the
conduct of Lancelot is more chivalrous than that of
Achilles; he would spare the life of his wounded
adversary and restore him to the city, if he will but
accompany him to do honour to the dead body of
Galehaut:

> Piacciavi oggi trovar l' albergo mio,
> del quale e poi di me vi fo signore,
> ivi al Re Galealto umile e pio
> domandar sol la pace, e fargli onore;
> e vi prometto qui, se son degn' io
> d' esser da voi creduto, che 'n brevi ore
> vi renderò in Avarco; e non vogliate
> ch' io spenga sì gran lume a questa etate.
>
> Che potete veder c' omai m' è dato
> sovra voi questo dì certa vittoria,
> la qual non mia virtù, ma vostro fato
> stimerò sempre, e di noi par la gloria;
> ma lassar senza onore in tale stato
> non potrei fuor di biasmo la memoria
> d' un Re sì grande, e sì leale amico,
> ch' ogni essempio avanzò moderno e antico.[1]

---

[1] "Let it please you to-day to visit my lodging, of which and then
of myself I make you lord, there solely to ask peace of King Galehaut,
humbly and devoutly, and do him honour; and I here promise you,
if I am worthy of your trust, that in a few hours I will restore you to
Avaricum; and do not have me quench so great a light for this age.

"For you can now see that this day a sure victory is given me over
you, which I shall ever deem not my might, but your fate, and our
glory equal; but I could not without blame leave unhonoured in such
a state the memory of so great a king, and a friend so loyal, that
surpassed every modern and ancient example" (xxiii, 145-6).

But Segurant bids him use the power fate has given him, for he had rather die a thousand deaths than receive his life from Lancelot, and forces his opponent to slay him. As victor, Lancelot refuses all honours save that of knighthood at Arthur's hands. The apparition of the spirit of Galehaut to his friend in a dream, before the funeral rites and games, christianises the corresponding scene in the *Iliad*, and has a Petrarcan intonation.[1] Claudas does not himself come to Lancelot's camp, but sends King Vagor, who is guided by Tristan, and naturally finds the hero all reverence and gentleness, the poem closing with the obsequies of Segurant and Clodino in Avaricum.

The *Avarchide* is less significant as a contribution to Arthurianism than as a point, in the evolution of the heroic poem in Italy, between the *Italia liberata dai Goti* of Trissino and the *Gerusalemme Liberata* of Torquato Tasso. Tasso thought highly of Alamanni's two poems. "Love," he writes, "is described more nobly and with greater constancy by the Spanish than by the French poets; unless an exception should be made for Guiron the Courteous, who so heavily punishes his own amorous frailty at the fountain; but, certainly, it is more praiseworthy to have the mind so disposed that no passion can take arms against reason. Therefore, the friendship between Guiron and Danain would have been more perfect, if it had not been disturbed by love." He adds, however, that, "if Guiron had not been so near to committing the sin, his virtue would, no doubt, seem greater to us, but the poem would not be so pleasing in that part." [2]

[1] xxiv, 42–6.   [2] *Discorsi del poema eroico, loc. cit.*, p. 120.

The *Avarchide* he considered as having the best woven
plot in Italian poetry, and as having shown him the
road upon which he himself was to follow in the
Gerusalemme Liberata.[1] Motives from the *Merlin*,
the *Lancelot*, the *Tristan*, and *Perceforest*, have been
traced in the *Gerusalemme*, though they are somewhat
remote.[2] But there is an Arthurian element in
Tasso's earlier poem, the *Rinaldo*, where the paladin,
more seriously than with Boiardo and Ariosto, has
become a knight-errant.[3] In the third canto, Rinaldo
and his Spanish companion Isoliero come upon two
bronze statues of armed warriors:

> Qui già 'l gran Lancillotto e 'l gran Tristano
> fer paragon de le lor forze estreme;
> quest' aere, questo fiume e questo piano
> de' lor gran colpi ancor rimbomba e geme.
> Questi guerrier che da maestra mano
> impressi in bronzo qui veggonsi insieme,
> sono i ritratti lor; tali essi furo
> quando fero il duello orrendo e duro.
>   Queste le lance fur, ch' a scontro acerbo
> reggendo, si restar salde ed intere,
> per ciò che tutte son d' osso e di nerbo
> d'alcune strane inconosciute fere.
> Io per due cavalier qui le riserbo,
> ch' abbian più di costor forza e potere.
> Chi non fia tale, altrui lasci la prova,
> che nulla invan l' avventurarsi giova.[4]

---

[1] *Discorsi del poema eroico, loc. cit.*, p. 104: *Del Giudizio sovra la sua Gerusalemme da lui medesimo riformata, ibid.*, p. 509.

[2] Thus Dunlop suggested that the tomb miraculously rising to receive the body of the Danish crusader Sveno (viii, 39) derives from the entombment of the pilgrims from the Island of Life in *Perceforest*.

[3] *Poemi minori di Torquato Tasso*, ed. A. Solerti (Bologna, 1891), Vol. I. Cf. E. Proto, *Sul "Rinaldo" di Torquato Tasso* (Naples, 1895), p. 298.

[4] "Here of old the great Lancelot and the great Tristan matched their full strength; this air, this river, and this plain still echo and

Rinaldo, who has already heard of this adventure, tells his companion that these two statues were made and set up by Merlin after the deaths of the two heroes, together with the lances he had given them, until two stronger knights should come and take them from their hands. The Spaniard attempts to take Tristan's lance, and is promptly struck to the ground; but, when Rinaldo approaches, the statue yields the weapon, and bows its head as to a knight of greater worth than he who had wielded it.

Tasso's older contemporary, Erasmo da Valvasone, began a poem on "i lunghi errori e i peregrini affanni" of Lancelot.[1] It is little more than a series of episodes, the writer's own invention, loosely linked together. Lancelot is imprisoned by Morgan in an enchanted island, and sought for by various knights including Galeodin (a nephew of Galehaut) and Galahad. Tristan and Iseult escape from the court of King Mark, who stirs up Breus to execute his vengeance upon them, and they are rescued from their pursuers by Gawain. But the same poet handles Arthurian matter more attractively in his chief poem, *La Caccia*, where, in the fourth canto, we find the

moan with their mighty strokes. These warriors, here seen together fashioned by a master hand in bronze, are their portraits; such were they when they fought their terrible fierce duel.

"These were the lances that, sustaining the grim encounter, remained firm and whole, for they are all of the bone and sinew of some strange unknown beasts. Here I reserve them for two knights who shall have more strength and power than these. Whoso is not such, let him leave the test to another, for it boots nothing to adventure himself in vain" (iii, 59–60).

[1] *I primi quattro canti di Lancilotto*, Venice, 1580. Cf. F. Foffano, *Ricerche letterarie* (Leghorn, 1897), pp. 102–6; V. Cremona, *Erasmo da Valvasone* 1523–93 (Monteleone, 1919), pp. 41–51.

delightful fable of the Hind of the Fays, "La Cerva delle Fate." [1]

The observant hunter, following his craft by night, may haply see many strange things:

> Ed oh se ti traesser mai le stelle
> a ritrovar la gran Cerva d' Arturo,
> ch' ha tutte di rubin le corna belle,
> l'unghie di ferro risonante e duro,
> e simile al monton di Frisso e d' Elle
> il vello d' oro rilucente e puro!
> Oh se dal Ciel già mai ti fosse dato
> passar dove si cela, o te beato. [2]

King Arthur once, out hunting in a great wood, found himself lost. Night came on, and he suddenly saw the hind with the shining horns, which he pursued by the light of its golden hide. Following it into a cave, he finds it fawning like a dog upon a nymph to whom he reveals his identity, and who tells him that he is on his way to Morgan. He passes through caves in the depths of the earth, where precious stones give light, and the "terrene ninfe" are carrying out the hidden work of nature. He hears the sound of the sea and enters the cavern of Demogorgon, where the guiding nymph leaves him to follow the gleam of the horns of the stag, which brings him up again to the light of day on a mountain. There, upon a plain covered with flowers, is the palace of Morgan le Fay.

---

[1] First published in 1591. I quote from the Milanese edition of 1808, *La Caccia, poema di Erasmo da Valvasone*, in the *Classici Italiani*. The episode occupies stanzas 141–219 of the canto.

[2] "And oh, if the stars ever drew thee to find again the great hind of Arthur, that has its fair horns of ruby, its hoofs of sounding and hard iron, and, like the ram of Phrixus and Helle, its fleece of shining and pure gold! Oh, if it were given thee to pass where it hides, O happy thou."

From the roof of the palace the king beholds "all the immense aspect of the heavens," the stars and the planets, and then, from a balcony, the sea, all the idle and fruitless work of men on earth, and the dangers and cares that beset kings. Morgan then tells him that it is time to return; he has learned about heaven and earth, and can draw norms for his future conduct. She gives him a sword, the hilt of which is made of the shed horns of the hind. In this sword he will mirror himself every day of his life, will see his own defects and how to amend them, thus triumphing over his foes and himself. But how will Arthur find the hind again, if he needs Morgan's counsels? Morgan answers that a wise fay does not dwell in one single place, nor is her palace always there. The hind, which only appears to noble men, wanders here and there at its pleasure, and, when found, always leads to the nearest fay, since it belongs to and knows them all. She adds to her gift a little dog that has the power of detecting the hind's presence. Arthur retires to rest, and is awakened next morning by the neighing of his horse:

> Ma poi che bianco il volto e 'l crine aurato
> in Oriente il nuovo dì mostrossi,
> ecco e 'l proprio destrier nitrir a lato
> sentissi, ed a quel suon desto levossi;
> e seppe pur di non aver sognato,
> sebben nel verde prato egli trovossi,
> onde entrò pria nel sotterraneo speco,
> perchè il don di Morgana avea pur seco.[1]

---

[1] "But, when the new day showed its white face and golden hair in the east, lo, he heard his own horse neighing at his side, and rose awoken at the sound; and he knew in sooth that he had not dreamed,

This beautiful little fable is clearly a blending of Cicero's *Somnium Scipionis* with a romantic motive. The white stag or hind is, of course, common in Arthurian story. There is one that leads Floriant to Morgan's palace in *Floriant et Florete*. In *Graelent* a white doe, pursued by the hero, guides him to his fairy love, and it is in the form of a white stag that Zefiro brings the Sicambrian king to Gerne in *Parsaforesto*. In the *Cerva Bianca* of Antonio Fregoso—an allegorical poem published in 1510 and frequently reprinted in the sixteenth century—a nymph whom Diana has changed into a white hind, pursued by the hounds of desire and thought, leads the hunter through various perils and adventures into the City of Love and to Love's eternal throne.

In the next canto, Erasmo da Valvasone asks by whom and when hawking was invented, and suggests that it may have been introduced into Great Britain in Arthurian times:

> E forse in quella età famosa e magna
> d' Arturo, a cui sì come i fiumi al mare
> da tutti i liti che Nettuno bagna,
> tutte l' arti correan pregiate e rare,
> questa anco entrò ne la maggior Bretagna,
> poi che ne' gesti de gli erranti appare
> del cavalier Britone il nobil vanto,
> ch' acquistò lo sparvier regale e 'l guanto.
>   D' oro era il guanto, e lo sparvier legato
> era a pertica d' oro, e d' ogni parte
> d' uomini e d' arme il loco era guardato,
> e ben mille custodie avea cosparte.

---

although he found himself on the green meadow whence he had first entered the subterranean cavern, for he still had with him the gift of Morgan."

Il gagliardo Britone innamorato
superò tutto il faticoso Marte,
e fatto d' alta preda altero erede
a la sua nobil donna in don la diede.[1]

The allusion is obviously to the story, in the *De
Amore* of Andreas Capellanus, of the young British
knight who wins his lady's love by bringing her the
hawk from Arthur's palace, to obtain which he has
first to achieve the adventure of the glove.   We have
already had an Italian version in the cantare, *Bruto di
Brettagna*, of Antonio Pucci.

After the Renaissance, Italian literature more
rarely touches Arthurian matter.   Merlin, however,
makes a fresh appearance on the scenes as a fore-
runner and prophet of Galileo, in a seventeenth-century
epic: the *Venetia edificata* of Giulio Strozzi.[2]   At the
time of the invasion of Italy by Attila, Merlin—
erroneously believed the offspring of an aerial spirit
and a nun, but, in reality, of royal British lineage—is
living as a hermit in a cave in Tuscany.   Here he has
invented a telescope, "a wonderful and divine instru-
ment that brings the distant object near," by means
of which he has seen all the movements of the celestial
bodies and destroyed fabulous opinions.   But he does

---

[1] "And, perhaps, in that famous and great age of Arthur, to whom,
as the rivers to the sea from all the shores that Neptune bathes, all
rare and esteemed arts sped, this also entered into the greater Britain,
since among the gests of the knights-errant appears the noble vaunt
of the British knight who won the royal hawk and the glove.

"Of gold was the glove, and the hawk was bound to a perch of gold,
and on every side the place was warded, and full thousand guards
there were around.   The valiant enamoured Briton overcame all
the laborious strife, and, become the proud holder of lofty spoil, gave
it as gift to his noble lady" (*La Caccia*, v, 14–15).

[2] *La Venetia edificata poema eroico di Giulio Strozzi* (Venice, 1624)..

not announce his great discoveries; for men are not yet
adapted to receive them, and might even be led into
grievous error by thinking that the earth, instead of
being the centre of the universe, goes round the sun.
However, a time will come:

> che dell' Etruria il più pregiato ingegno
> i vetri miei rinovellando illustri,
> mentre che rifiorir gli studi e l' arti
> là si vedran nell' Antenoree parti.[1]

He preaches the Christian faith and the immortality
of the soul to the young hero Gelderico, and foretells
the future glory of Venice.[2]

In the latter part of the eighteenth century,
Giuseppe Parini, in one of those passages of the
Giorno that anticipate the romantic movement, makes
satirical use of an Arthurian comparison for the knot
that his young nobleman's mistress has hung upon the
hilt of his sword:

> Tal del famoso Artù vide la corte
> le infiammate d' amor donzelle ardite
> ornar di piume e di purpuree fasce
> i fatati guerrieri, onde più ardenti
> gisser poi questi ad incontrar periglio
> in selve orrende, tra i giganti e i mostri.[3]

When the romantic school arose in Italy in the early
years of the nineteenth century, its first propagandist,

---

[1] "When the most renowned genius of Tuscany will renew and
glorify my glasses, at the time when studies and arts will be seen
flourishing again in the Paduan region" (canto vii, 49–57).

[2] Canto xiv, 1–47.

[3] "Even so the court of famous Arthur saw the damsels, love
enkindled, dare to deck the destined warriors with plumes and purple
bands, whereat these went more daringly to encounter peril in
dreadful woods among giants and monsters" (*Il Mattino*, ll. 823–8).
"Fatati" may mean "enchanted," rather than "destined."

Giovanni Berchet, gave a literal translation of two of the three oldest Spanish ballads on the "matter of Britain," as *Tristano e Isotta* ("Don Tristano egli è ferito") and *Lancilotto e Ginevra* ("Cavalier sì ben servito").[1] But the principles, as also the national colour of romanticism in Italy, impelled writers to seek inspiration in mediaeval traditions other than those of Arthurian story.

Leopardi's adoption of the name Tristano in one of the dialogues (written in 1832) of the *Operette morali* might, possibly, hark back to the characterisation of Tristan as a bearer of sorrows in Henricus of Settimello. But the poet had previously paid tribute to the "matter of Britain," and begun a romantic tragedy in a pastoral setting entitled *Telesilla* (1821), based upon the story of Guiron, Danain, and the Lady of Malehaut, of which he had read in Luigi Alamanni.[2] In the actually written first part, a gathering of shepherds is alarmed by the appearance of an armed knight, Danaino, his spear still red with the recently shed blood of a foe. He charges one of the shepherds to tell the news to a young warrior and a lady who will presently pass, his wife and friend on their way to Malehaut, and to add that he will return on the morrow. There is a pastoral interlude, and then Girone and Telesilla appear on the scene, and mutually

---

[1] *Vecchie romanze spagnuole*, xlvii and xlviii, in *Opere di Giovanni Berchet*, ed. E. Bellorini (*Scrittori d'Italia*), I, pp. 285-7. On the Spanish originals, cf. Entwistle, *op. cit.*, pp. 2, 22, 111, 252.

[2] In *Scritti vari inediti di Giacomo Leopardi dalle Carte Napolitane* (Florence, 1906), pp. 59-92. Cf. G. A. Levi, *Inizi romantici e inizi satirici del Leopardi*, in *G.S.L.I.*, XCIII (1929), pp. 335-6. It has been suggested that the *Consalvo* was inspired or influenced by the scene of Tristan's death; this seems to me altogether improbable.

reveal their love. The lady is not the temptress, and they resist their passion. The situation is left uncertain; but, in the fragment of the second part, after an interlude of hunters, Girone appears again, and it is clear that he has betrayed his friend's confidence, as he expresses his remorse. Leopardi's additional notes, for the completion of the drama, seem to show that Danaino would have slain his wife, and then fallen by Girone's hand in single combat. There is an allusion to "la parlata di Girone alla spada" in Alamanni, but it is not clear how it could have been worked into such a complete transformation of the original story.

Carducci, that "scudiero dei classici," paid his tribute also to the Arthurian legends. Like the mediaeval poets he links Iseult with Helen, but gives her back to King Mark in the Island of the Blessed:

> Elena e Isotta vanno pensose per l' ombra de i mirti,
> il vermiglio tramonto ride a le chiome d' oro:
> Elena guarda l' onde: re Marco ad Isotta le braccia
> apre, ed il biondo capo su la gran barba cade.[1]

In more recent years, some interesting dramas on Arthurian themes have appeared in Italy from the pens of poets who, as playwrights, should rank, I take it, as followers of Gabriele D'Annunzio: the *Tristano e Isolda* (1910) of Ettore Moschino; *La Regina Ginevra* (1925) and *Merlino e Viviana* (1927) of Domenico Tumiati. An Italian poet is naturally not

---

[1] "Helen and Iseult move pensively through the shade of the myrtles, the red sunset smiles on their golden hair: Helen gazes on the waves: King Mark opens his arms to Iseult, and her fair head sinks on his great beard" (*Presso l'urna di Percy Bysshe Shelley* in *Odi barbare*). See also his sonnet on the death of Mordred (*Mito e verità*) in *Rime nuove*.

overshadowed by the tradition and authority of Malory, as an Englishman is in like case, and these dramas, from the standpoint of strict Arthurianism, are as unorthodox in their free rehandling of the legends as were the poems of Nicolò degli Agostini. All three have appreciable dramatic qualities, particularly *La Regina Ginevra* with its very striking presentation of the figure of Galeotto, and those of us who are old enough to remember Irving's production of the *King Arthur* of Comyns Carr will realise that, if similarly mounted, this tragedy would be profoundly impressive upon the stage.

The Arthurian legend came to Italy, as John Herschel said the molecule came to man's knowledge, with "the essential character of a manufactured article." But it contained within it elements that are lost in the lands where it originated, and, on Italian soil, it entered into fresh combinations, with rich results in the literature of the closing Middle Ages and the Renaissance, and touched finely to fine issues the two greatest poets of the nation: Dante and Ariosto.

APPENDIX

AN UNPUBLISHED ROMANCE OF THE OLD TABLE

THE importance attached to the "Tavola Vecchia" in the *Tavola Ritonda*, in the *Cantare dei Cantari*, and by Ariosto, might seem to imply the existence of more matter on the subject than we find actually preserved in Italian. In a sonnet by Gillio Lelli, a Perugian poet of the earlier half of the fourteenth century, there is a noteworthy allusion to the chivalrous customs of the court of Uther Pendragon: "As was custom in the olden time at the great court of Uther Pendragon for two champions to joust together when there was contest of love between them; each maintained his lady the more beautiful, wherefore they were brought to the test of mortal battle on the arena, until one as conquered surrendered":

> Come nel tempo anticho si solea
> a la gran corte d' Uterpandragone
> prender la giostra fra dui champione,
> quando d' amor tra lor si contendea;
> ciascun sua donna più bella dicea,
> onde si conduceano al parangone
> de la mortal batalglia in sul sabione
> in fin che l' un per vinto si rendea.[1]

Here, however, there is no explicit mention of the Table In a fifteenth-century inventory of the library of the Duk of Ferrara, we read of an item entitled *Cavalieri de la Tavola Vecchia,* together with others suggestive of the same cycle, all of which have disappeared.[2] As far as my present know-

[1] Monaci, *Dai Poeti antichi perugini del Cod. già Barber. XLV*–130, *ora Vat.* 4036 (Rome, 1905), p. 19. My attention was called to this sonnet by S. Debenedetti, in *G.S.L.I.*, XCV, p. 168. For Gillio Lelli, see Massèra, *Sonetti burleschi e realistici*, p. 109.

[2] Cf. Bertoni, *Nuovi studi su Matteo Maria Boiardo*, pp. 173-81.

ledge goes, the only extant romance in Italian that expressly
proclaims itself a tale of the Old Table is a curious work—
still unpublished—contained in a fifteenth-century manuscript
in the Biblioteca Nazionale of Florence, with the title: "The
Vengeance that the descendants of Hector, the son of King
Priam of Troy the Great, with the aid of King Uther Pendragon and other kings and barons and knights-errant of the
Old Table, took upon the Greeks":

> Questo libro chonta della vendetta chome i desciendenti d' Atorre,
> figluolo de Re Priamo di Troia la grande, coll' aiuto de Re Uter
> Pandragone e degli altri re e baroni e chavalieri erranti della Tavcla
> Vecchia, feciono la vendetta sopra de' Greci.[1]

Troas, a descendant of Hector, is king of Thessaly, where
the Trojans form a small ruling caste, the population being
native. He has three sons: Hector, Troiano, and Laomedon.
Hector has a son named Troilus; Troiano two sons, Palamede
and Hector the Little ("Ettor lo Pitetto"). Troiano, hearing
of a great tournament to be held in Britain, secretly leaves
his father's court. The ship lands at Troy, where he sees
the ruins, hears the story of its fall, and learns his own descent.
He is told that King Meliadus of Liones is the best knight
that bears arms among the knights-errant. Continuing his
journey, the Trojan prince meets Meliadus on his way to the
tournament, and is accepted as one of his squires. During
the night at an abbey, Troiano, wearing the armour of
Meliadus, fights with the Good Knight without Fear. He
is knighted by Meliadus, takes the name of the "cavalier del
gran duolo," and encounters a knight in golden armour who
turns out to be "the good King Galehaut" (uncle of Galehaut
le Brun). At the tournament, Troiano challenges Uther Pendragon on behalf of Meliadus (who has a grievance over the

---

[1] Biblioteca Nazionale, Cod. II, III, 332 (Magl. cl. XXIII, num. 113).
As I am here concerned only with the narrative, I have generally
made the proper names conform with the more usual versions where
the persons indicated are familiar figures in Arthurian story. The
manuscript is eccentric both in nomenclature and in the relationship
of some of the characters.

truage paid to the King of Ireland). Uther's forces are
driven back into Camelot; and a company of twelve knights
is formed: Meliadus, Troiano, King Galehaut, Galehaut le
Brun, Guiron the Courteous, Danain le Roux (here called
"Daniello"), the Good Knight without Fear, King Ban, Lanbengues,[1] Febus le Brun ("Febusse lo Pitetto," represented
as the nephew of Guiron), Segurant and his nephew.

Ambassadors from King Remus of Rome, "una bella
baronia," pass the palace where the companions are resting.
They are on their way to invite Uther Pendragon to ally
with Rome in a war to take the Empire from the Greeks and
restore it to the Romans. Troiano persuades them first to
induce the companions to join the enterprise. The companions separate, to meet again at the end of two months.
Troiano tells Meliadus who he is, goes back to Troy, where
he finds countryfolk in the ruined city and neighbouring
villages still faithful to the name of Priam, and returns to his
father to prepare for war when the Romans come. Hector
and Laomedon go to secure allies and stir up rebellion against
the Greeks in Asia Minor and elsewhere, the latter gaining
over the Queen of the Amazons. Nauser, Emperor of Greece,
anticipates matters by invading Thessaly, where the natives,
incited by a descendant of Achilles, rise, but are defeated.
The Romans arrive on the scene, and an indecisive battle
is fought.

While the descendants of the Greek kings and heroes of the
Iliad assemble in Thebes to support the emperor, Uther
Pendragon and the knights-errant join Remus and the
Trojans. Uther makes peace with Meliadus and his friends,
and is appointed commander-in-chief of the whole army.
Among the leaders of the bands are King Uriens (Uriel) and
Esclabor, the father of Palamede. The twelve companions,
clad in black armour, keep together, and are joined by Ettor
lo Pitetto, supposed too young to fight, but who performs

---

[1] King Galehaut is a personage otherwise unknown. I take it
that Lanbengues is Lambegues, the tutor of Lionel and Bors in the
Lancelot (cf. above, p. 74 n).

terrific feats with his axe. In the ensuing battle, Febus and Laomedon are among the killed, but the Greeks are defeated, the hideous atrocities perpetrated on the prisoners and the women, in vengeance for what happened to the Trojan women at Troy, exciting the indignant horror of Uther and the knights-errant. Further atrocities accompany the surrender of the city in which the vanquished Greeks had taken refuge, Nauser and the Greek kings being kept alive for future judgment. Ettor lo Pitetto, who has been knighted by Uther, with an admonition to restrain his cruelty, takes the lead in the work of butchery.

Laudach, King of Constantinople, who is a rival claimant to the Empire, now comes upon the scene. Although cautioned that his gods have no power against those of the Christians, and that the Britons have a diviner who warns them of all dangers (we hear no more of Merlin in the story), he resolves to conquer Rome and Britain, with the aid of King Rions and his giants. His forces go to Thessaly, capture the unguarded Roman fleet, and sail to Italy, where they surprise Rome itself, which is taken and burned. A portion of his army invades Great Britain, while another besieges the city of Gaunes, which is defended in the name of Uther by the citizens headed by Nasciens, a knight of the Old Table and descendant of Febus the Strong. Refugees from Populonia, the only Italian city still holding out, reach Greece, and inform Remus and Uther. The two kings, finding their return prevented by the loss of their fleet, press on the war with renewed fury until the conquest of Greece is complete. In the meanwhile, the refugees from Populonia go in their ship to Great Britain, cut out the Greek fleet in the port of Gaunes, and bring it to Uther. The Romans and Trojans, after killing their prisoners, embark for Gaunes, where a terrific battle takes place. Rions is killed in single combat with Ettor lo Pitetto, while Palamede (the son of Troiano) and Troilus are among the slain on the Trojan side. The Greeks are finally defeated, and the victors enter Gaunes. A council is held to decide the fate of the prisoners, at which the only voice raised for mercy is that of King Aramante (Armant, Hermance) of the Red City—he whose murder is avenged by Palamede in the prose *Tristan* and in Malory. Guiron himself beheads one of the captives in vengeance for the death of Febus. Troiano delivers a long speech, recording the whole history of Troy, its two destructions at the hands of the Greeks; to prevent a repetition of such events, he demands that all the prisoners should be put to death at once, Laudach being given into his hands to be dealt with later. They are all, except the King of Constantinople, slaughtered in the square of Gaunes; "E così nobilmente fu fatta la vendetta di Troia la grande." Remus goes home and rebuilds Rome more beautiful than before; Troas returns to Thessaly, where Laudach is put to a cruel death "per vendetta dello nobile re Priamo."

This curious work is obviously a combination of the *Palamède*, from which the majority of the Arthurian personages are taken, with the *Roman de Troie*. Like all other Italian prose romances dealing with the "matière de Bretagne," it is full of Gallicisms, especially in the names. The earlier portions, with the adventures of Troiano at the court of Uther Pendragon, have a certain romantic colour; but all the rest is of an unrelieved brutality. It stands among Italian romances of the Arthurian cycle as *Titus Andronicus* among the dramas of Shakespeare.

INDEX I

ARTHURIAN NAMES AND MATTERS [1]

ABIRON, eastern kingdom of Segurant, 46, 203, 204, 210
Adriano, see Driant
Aglentine (Esglantine), the Lady of Avalon, 105, 106, 164 n
Agravaine (Agravano), son of King Lot of Orkney and nephew of Arthur, 124, 125, 127, 164, 170, 229, 266; killed by Lancelot, 188, or by Bors, 267
Agrestizia, sister of Perceval, 179, 180
Agueriesse, see Guerrehes
Alain le Gros, son of Bron and keeper of the Grail, 306, 307
Alcardo (afterwards Lantris), brother of Iseult the Fair, 166, 170, 181
Alisandre le Orphelin, son of Boudwin and nephew of King Mark, 65 n
Alixandre, son of the Greek emperor, 108
Alois (Alodois), King of Norgalles, 173, 188
Amadore della Porta, see Mador
Amoratto, see Lamorat
Amoroldo, the elder, see Morholt
Amoroldo, the younger (Amoroldino), son of the Morholt and King of Ireland, 171–3, 185, 188
Analida (Laudine de Landuc), bride of Ivain, 108
Andred (Andret, Adriette, Andirecche, Ghedin, Alebruno), nephew of Mark and betrayer of Tristan, 75–6, 90, 116–18, 170, 183, 185, 187, 231, 263, 298, 301; is beheaded by Mark, 185, or slain by Lancelot, 263, or burned alive, 301
Angelica, in Boiardo and Ariosto, 277–8, 283
Anguish, King of Ireland, see Languis
Annowre (Elergia), sorceress beheaded by Arthur, 82–4, 164, 169, 201 n
Antonio (Maistre Antoine), bishop of Gaul and third scribe of Merlin, 95, 200–4, 209–12, 216
Apollo, ancestor of Tristan, 62 n
Aramante, see Vagor
Arfarano (Alphasem), see Gallaffaro
Arginus, British king, 194
Argistres (Aristers, Agresto), hypocrite unmasked by Merlin, 95, 214
Ariohan, son of Frolle and ancestor of Ogier, 52, 53, 228
Arthur (Artusius, Artusus, Arthurus, Arturius, Artus, Artù, Artur, Artuse, Artue), King of Britain, son of Uther Pendragon and Igraine, 1; occurence of name in Italy, 2, 3; in the Modena Archivolt, 4, 5; early allusions to him in Italy, 6–10; in the Otranto mosaic, 11; legendary connection with Etna, 12–15; 19, 22, 32, 33; in the *Palamède*, 47–53, 59–61; letter from Galehaut, 73; deliverance by Tristan in the Forest Perilous, 79–84; relations with Galehaut, 85–8; 94, 102, 106, 109, 117, 118, 120; relations with Lancelot and Guinevere, 124–8; allusions by Dante, 130, 142, 147; in the *Tavola Ritonda*, 152, 155–64, 166–74, 177, 181; his vengeance for Tristan, 184–7; his fall and death, 187–90; his birth, youth, and coronation in the *Merlin*, 194, 196–7; his sisters, 197; the "adventurous king," 205; the attempted destruction of his memory by King Mark, 205–7; 216, 219, 220; allusions in the *Dittamondo*, 223–4, 227–8; in the *Amorosa Visione*, 228; in Petrarca, 232 n; treatment of his history by Boccaccio and Benvenuto da Imola, 232–7; in the "cantari leggendari," 242–54, 257, 260; in the *Cantari di Lancellotto*, 266, 267; his dream of Gawain and passing, 268; 270, 271; allusions by Boiardo, 275, 277; by Ariosto, 285, 293; in the *Due Tristani*, 297–300, 302; by Nicolò degli Agostini, 309; by Alamanni, 312, 313; plays Agamemnon in the *Avarchide*, 315–19; his pursuit of the Hind of the Fays in *La Caccia*, 322–5; allusion by Parini, 326

---

[1] Some associated names from the Carolingian cycle are included. In the Italian prose romances, the French forms of Arthurian names are frequently reproduced with very slight or practically no modifications.

Astolat (Ascalot, Escalot, Scalot, Scalliotto, Scalotto), the fair maiden of (Elaine in Malory), 93, 94, 108, 124–9, 225–6, 266–7; Italian texts of her letter, 94 n, 127–8

Astolfo, English paladin, 278, 283, 294–5

Astore, see Hector de Maris

Autor (Antor, Ector), foster-father of Arthur, 197

Avalon (Avalona, Vallone), island or valley, 7, 14, 105–6, 164, 169, 190, 247; the Lady of, 105, 106, 133, 164

Avarco (Avaricum, Bourges), capital of kingdom of Claudas, 314

Bagdemagus (Bademagu, Bando di Mago), King of Gorre and father of Meleagant, 88 n, 120, 124 (killed by Gawain), 208 n, 315

Bagotta, name of mother of Galehaut, 86 n

Balin le Sauvage (Balaan), 199, 312, 313 n

Ban (Bando), King of Benoic and father of Lancelot, 156, 157, 203, 206, 210, 223, 230, 315, 333

Basille (Girida), mistress of Andred, the treacherous damsel, 75, 298, 301

Baudwin of Britain (Bawdewyn, Ferragunze), 160, 161

Beatrice, the bride of Carduino, 253–7

Bedalis, husband of Gargeolain, 111, 113

Belinans, King of Sorgales and father of Dodinel, 258 n

"Bel Inconnu" ("Biaus Descouneus," the "Fair Unknown"), 257

Bellicies, daughter of King Pharamond, 67, 68

Bellistans, King of (Bellic, Bellien), 216

Benoic, kingdom of Lancelot's father, 157, 223–4

Bercilak (Bernlak), the Green Knight, 5

Bertoldo (Bertous), German cardinal associated with Merlin, 200

Betis (Betide), first name of Perceforest, 304

Betis (Betide), son of the above, 304

Biaus Mauvais, a knight in the *Palamède*, 102

Blaise (Blasio, Biagio), hermit of Northumberland and first scribe of Merlin, 193–5, 198, 199, 201, 212–16

Blanchefleur, mother of Tristan in Thomas, 36

Blanchefleur, in *Floire et Blanchefleur*, 36, 108, 240, 269

Blanchefleur, beloved of Perceval in Chrétien de Troyes, 36

Blanor de Gaunes (Blamor de Ganis), knight of the Round Table and brother of Blioberis, 69

Bledhericus (Bleheris, Breri), conveyer of the "matter of Britain," 195 n

Blioberis de Gaunes (Bleoberis, Bliomberis, Briobris, Briobisse), knight of the Round Table and kinsman of Lancelot, 69, 81 n, 171, 173, 190, 206, 270, 298

Bliocadran, name of father of Perceval, 258 n

Bloia, beloved of Guiron, 55, 57, 58, 312

Bors (Bohort, Bohors, Bordo), the elder, King of Gaunes (Gannes) and brother of King Ban, 156, 224

Bors (Bohort, Bohors, Bordo, Beorzo), the younger, son of the above and cousin of Lancelot, 74 n, 123, 124–7, 137, 173; in the Quest of the Grail, 178–81; 184, 190, 204; father of Helain le Blanc, 204, 205 n; avenger of the Arthuriad on King Mark, 205, 206, 207; 209, 210, 224, 228, 266, 267; as Ajax and Diomede in the *Avarchide*, 315, 317

Boudwin (Pernam), brother of King Mark, 65 n

Bradamante, sister of Rinaldo, 280, 287–9, 291–3

Brandelis, son of King Lac, 44, 81 n, 262, 298

Brangwain (Bragwaine, Brangien, Brangain, Brandina, Braguina, Brangilla), Iseult's gentlewoman, 70, 74, 76–80, 162, 177, 181 (her death in the *Tavola Ritonda*), 231, 285, 296, 300–1

Brandimarte, friend of Orlando, 280

Branor le Brun, the "Old Knight," uncle of Segurant, 49, 50, 156 n, 277, 299, 310

Breus sans Pitié (Brehus, Breusso), 56, 57, 69, 117, 171, 182–3 (killed by Lancelot), 220, 242, 244–6, 262 n, 269, 270, 289 n, 290, 291, 311, 321

Brun, family of, 44, 48, 58 n, 62; see Branor, Febus, Hector, Galehaut, Segurant; valley of, 209

Brunor (Breunor), lord of the Castle of Pleur and father of Galehaut, 71, 72, 86, 87, 156, 229, 296; confused with Branor, 156

Brunor lo Bruno (Brunor le Noir), the "valet à la cotte mal taillée," son of the Good Knight without Fear and brother of Dinadan, 172, 173, 270

Bruto, di Brettagna, winner of the scroll of the laws of love, 250–2, 325

Burletta della Diserta, would-be lover of Pulzella Gaia, 167, 241

"Burmaltus," in the Modena Archivolt, 4, 5

Caliburnus (Excalibur), Arthur's sword, 12 n

Calidonian wood (Nemus Colidonis), 284

Calogrenant, knight of the Round Table, 19

Calvano, see Gawain
Cameliard, kingdom of Guinevere's father, 53
Camelot (Camellotto), Arthur's capital, 42, 49, 94, *et passim*; besieged by King Mark, 118, 181; apparition of Holy Grail at, 120-2, 175; destruction by Mark, 206, 207, 225
Camille, Saxon sorceress, 84 n, 202 n
Canterbury, Archbishop of, 206-7
Carados of the Dolorous Tower, 5, 168
Carduel, foundation of the Round Table at, 195-6
Carduino, the "Fair Unknown," son of Dodinel, 253-7; suggested identification with Bliocadran, 258 n
Cariados, rival of Tristan in Thomas, 77
"Carrado," in the Modena Archivolt, 4
"Chaedino," see Kahedyn.
Charlemagne, 1, 219, 221, 273, 275-8, 284, 287; takes the swords of Arthur's knights, 172
Charrette, episode of the Cart, 92-3
"Che," in the Modena Archivolt, 4
Chelinde, ancestress of Tristan, 237
Chiesso, see Kay
Childeric the Saxon, ally of Mordred, 12
Claudas (Clodasso), king of "la terre deserte," 51, 223-4; as Priam in the *Avarchide*, 315-6, 319
Claudiana, daughter of Claudas, 316
Cleges, knight of Uther Pendragon, 156 n
Clodino (Claudins), son of Claudas, 315, 318-19
Clodion, son of Pharamond in the *Orlando Furioso*, 288, 290
Constance (Gostanza, Elaine, Clarine), mother of Lancelot in the *Tavola Ritonda*, 34, 35, 157
Constantine, nephew and successor of Arthur, 234
Constantius (Costanzo), father of Uther Pendragon, 215
Corbenic (Corbeniche, Corbenio, Carbonek), Castle of the Grail, 178, 180, 225, 226, 306, 307; damsel of (Elaine, Perevida, Provida), daughter of King Pelles and mother of Galahad, 175, 225-6, 266
Cornwall (Cornovaglia), kingdom of Mark, *passim*

Danain le Roux, friend of Guiron and husband of the Lady of Malehaut, 44, 54-5, 57-8, 60-2, 103, 168 n, 228, 290, 310-12, 319, 327-8, 333
Daniel, brother of Dinadan in the *Tavola Ritonda*, 163, 172
Darnante, magician in *Parsaforesto*, 304
Darnantes, forest or desert of, the "Forest Perilous" (Nerlantes, Nartes, Dornates, Adernantes, Andernantes), 79-84, 109, 163-4, 203, 208, 214, 284, 285, 304
Dialicies, giant of the Castle of Pleur, 71
Dinadan, son of the Good Knight without Fear, 41, 44, 117, 119, 153, 163, 166, 171-3, 184-7, 271, 289, 299, 316, 318
Dinas, the Cornish seneschal, 116, 118-19, 170, 183, 186-7, 261, 264, 267, 298
Dodinel (Dondinello, Dodinas, Oddinello) le Sauvage, knight of the Round Table, 76 n, 182, 229, 253-4, 258, 266
Dorins (Dorens), son of Claudas, 223-4
Driant (Adriano, Landriano), brother of Lamorat, 107, 171 n

Eglente, mother of Dodinel in Vulgate *Merlin*, 258 n
Elaine, see Constance, Astolat, Corbenic
Elergia (Annowre), see Avalon, Lady of
Elia, see Helain, Helias
Eliabel (Heliabel, Eliabella), wife of Meliadus and mother of Tristan, 50, 65, 66, 158, 159, 201
Elias the Saxon, slain by Tristan, 117, 170 n, 224-5
Enide (Enida, Enidia, Nida), beloved of Erec, 31, 108, 226
Erec (Arech, Arecco, Erecche, Ereccho), son of King Lac, 19, 31, 44, 108, 157, 171, 226
Esclabor (Scalabrone), the Babylonian, father of Palamede, 44, 50, 297 n, 333
Estrangorre, King of, see Good Knight without Fear
Evalac, see Mordrain

False Lovers, Valley of, 101-2, 267, 280
Fata Morgana, 13-14, and see Morgan le Fay
Fata Reina, wife of Gadiffero in *Parsaforesto*, 304-6
Febus the Strong (Phebus le Fort, Febusso), ancestor of Guiron, 56, 57, 62, 219, 220, 230, 269, 334
Febus le Brun (Febusso, Februe, Febusse lo Pitetto), son of Galehaut le Brun, 57, 156, 333-5

Felix, King of Cornwall, 65, 157
Felix, Milanese cardinal associated with Merlin, 200
Felon Knight (Cavallier Felone), in the *Tavola Ritonda*, 176–7
Ferragunze, Italian counterpart of Bawdewyn of Britain, 159–62
"Fier baiser," motive, 258
Florisdelfa, sorceress in the *Due Tristani*, 297
Forania, "terre foraine," realm of the leper king, 306
Forest Perilous, see Darnantes
Franco Palagio, order of chivalry in *Parsaforesto*, 304–5
Frolle (Frollo, Froles, Flores), German prince slain by Arthur, 52, 223–4

Gabrionello, Old Table knight in *Tavola Ritonda*, 176
Gadifer (Gadiffero), the "maimed king" in *Parsaforesto*, 303–6
Gaheris (Gariesse, Gariens), son of King Lot of Orkney and nephew of Arthur, 68, 81, 188 n
Gaheris de Kareheu (Giafredi, Patrise), the poisoned knight, 126
Gaia (Gaia Pulcella, Gaia Donzella, Pulzella Gaia, Gaggia), daughter of Morgan le Fay, 167, 241–7, 269, 308, 309
Galahad (Galasso, Galas, Galeas, Galeazzo, Galeatto, Galeotto), son of Lancelot by the daughter of King Pelles, first mention in Italian, 66; confused with Galehaut, 120 n, 228 n, 269; in the Grail quest, 120, 123, 149, 150, 175, 178–81; prophecies concerning him in the *Vita di Merlino*, 194, 195, 203, 204; 219, 226, 228, 244, 267–9, 272, 282 n, 285, 307, 321; Venetian poem on him or namesake, 308
Galegantis, knight of Arthur, 87 n
Galehaut (Galahalt, Galehot, Galehoth, Galeotto, Galealto), son of Brunor and the giantess, the "haut prince," Lord of the Distant Isles, first mention in Italian, 33; confused with Galehaut le Brun, 44 n; at the Castle of Pleur, 71–4; his youth, 85–7; his castle of the "Orgueilleuse emprise" and death, 88; treatment by Malory, 88 n; love for the lady of Malehaut, 108; 123; Dante's allusion to him, 141–5; in the *Tavola Ritonda*, 157–9; 166; in the *Vita di Merlino*, 194, 205–7 (desecration of his body by Mark), 208; 216; Boccaccio's allusions to him, 229, 230, 237, 238; 280; in the *Due Tristani*, 296; as Patroclus in the *Avarchide*, 315–19; in recent Italian drama, 329; his sister (Dalis, Riccarda), 72, 86 n, 87, 296
Galehaut le Brun, son of Hector le Brun, 44, 54, 57, 59; confused with the "haut prince," 205, 208; 316 n, 333
Galehaut, King, in romance of Old Table, 332–3
Galeodin, nephew of the "haut prince," 321
Galeschin, knight in the *Lancelot*, 5
Galinan, castellan in the *Palamède*, 58, 312
Galinan (le Noir), son of Guiron, 58, 62 n, 316, 318
Gallaffaro, son of Gadifer in *Parsaforesto*, 305–6
Gallaffaro the younger (Kalafe, Arfarano, Alfaran, Alphasem), the leper king, 305–7
Gallan (Gallaneus), maker of swords, 219
"Galvaginus" (Gawain), in the Modena Archivolt, 4
"Galvariun," in the Modena Archivolt, 4
Gamael, priest of the Grail, 307
Gareth (Gaheriet, Gariet, Gariette), son of King Lot and nephew of Arthur, 81, 83, 164, 188 n
Gargeolain, wife of Bedalis, 111, 113
Gaunes (Gannes), kingdom of the elder Bors, *passim*
Gawain (Galvaginus, Galvanus, Walwanus, Gauvain, Galvano, Calvano, Calliano), son of King Lot and nephew of Arthur, 3, 4, 5, 19, 51, 52, 68, 108, 116; in the Quest of the Grail, 120, 121, 124; 125, 130, 159, 160, 170, 173, 180, 188–9; lover of Pulzella Gaia, 182 n, 241–6; 247, 257, 258; in the "imperious host" story, 259–60; 266–8; Arthur's vision of, 268; in later poems, 271, 285, 308, 315–16 (as Menelaus in the *Avarchide*), 321
Gerne, daughter of the elder Gallaffaro, 305, 324
Giddefor (Gondefors), King of India, 95
Girflet (Griflet, Girfrette, Gilflette), knight of Arthur, 148
Gismirante, son of "il Cavalier Cortese" and knight of Arthur, 247–50
Good Knight without Fear (Le bon Chevalier sans peur), King of Estrangorre, father of Dinadan, 41, 44; in the *Palamède*, 50–3, 58–9, 61; in the *Cento novelle antiche*, 89–90; in the *Due Tristani*, 298–9; 311–12, 332–3
Gouvernal (Gouvernail, Governale, Gorvalan), companion of Tristan, afterwards King of Liones, 66, 67, 70, 76, 80, 162, 166, 181 n, 185–6, 296, 300–1
Grail, the Holy (Saint Graal, Sangradale, Sangreal), 1, 13; early allusions in Italy, 18–20, 32; Italian echoes of the Perceval version, 29–31, 103, 245; Italian version of the Vulgate *Queste*, 114, 120–4; alleged influence of legend upon Dante, 149–51; version in the *Tavola Ritonda*, 175–81; allusions in the *Vita di Merlino*, 195, 196, 204; later allusions, 219, 222, 228, 272, 299, 300

Grail, Castle of the, in the Perceval version, 30, 149–50; in the Galahad version, 178, 180, 225
Guenloie, Queen in *Yder*, 4
Guerrehes (Agueriesse), brother of Gawain and slayer of Carduino's father, 254, 257
Guinevere (Guenever, Guenièvre, Guanhumara, Guenhuvera, Ginevra, Ginevara, Zanevre, Jennifer), daughter of King Leodegrance and wife of Arthur, 4, 34, 48, 53, 60, 73, 81–4, 88, 92–3, 108–9, 121, 124–8; allusions by Dante, 140–6; the Round Table her dowry, 155; in the *Tavola Ritonda*, 157–8, 162–3, 166, 169, 171, 174, 188–9; her death, 190; 204, 208, 220–1, 225; allusions in Boccaccio, 229–30, 234, 236; in the Cantari, 239, 242–3, 246, 250, 261, 266–8, 270–2; later allusions, 281, 287, 299, 302–3, 308–9, 317, 328, 329
Guinevere, the false, 271–2
Guingamor, nephew of Arthur, 246
Guiron the Courteous (Gyron, Girone, Gyrone, Guarone, Gurone), great-grandson of Febus the Strong, 44, 53–62; his death, 63; in the *Tavola Ritonda*, 156; 219, 269, 291; in Alamanni's poem, 310–13; 333, 335
Guirun, in the *Tristan* of Thomas, 62, 131
Gwron, bard of Britain, 62

Hargodabran, Saxon giant, 92 n
Hector de Maris (Hector des Mares, Astorre di Mare, Ector, Estorre), illegitimate son of King Ban and half-brother of Lancelot, 83, 118, 125–6, 171, 173, 180, 182, 190, 227, 229, 242, 244, 260, 262, 267, 270, 298
Hector le Brun, father of Galehaut le Brun, 44, 54, 55, 156, 205 n, 220, 310, 316 n
Hector le Brun, nephew of the above, 44 n
Helain le Blanc (Elia, Helin), son of Bors by the daughter of King Brangor, 204, 205 n
Helias (Elia, Helians, Herbeus, Englias), hermit and scribe of Merlin, 208, 209, 214, 215
Helin le Roux, treacherous knight in the *Palamède*, 57, 58, 280, 311
Helyes of Toulouse, "sage clerc" of Galehaut, 214 n
Hemison, see Onesun
Hermeux de Rugel, knight in the *Palamède*, 103
Hernolx (Erveus), count, in the *Queste*, 180
Hierna, see Igraine
Hodain, dog given by Bellicies to Tristan and by him to Iseult, 67, 70–1, 162, 166
Hoel (Howell), King or Duke of Brittany, father-in-law of Meliadus, 66
Hoel (Howell, Olise, Gilerchino), the younger, King or Duke of Brittany, father of Iseult of the White Hands, 61, 76–9, 301
Hundred Knights, King of (Beraint, Heraut, Malaquin), vassal of the "haut prince," 68, 72, 73, 87; his death, 188 n; 296, 299

Igraine (Igerna, Hierna, Izerla), wife of Duke Gorlois of Tintagel and after-wards of Uther Pendragon, mother of Arthur, 7, 196, 197
Ildusnamo (Duke Naimes of Bavaria), takes sword of Palamede, 172
"Imperious host," motive, 259–60
Ireland, kings of, see Amoroldo, Languis; Tristan in, 68–70; Merlin's prophecies concerning, 200, 216
"Isdernus" (Yder), in the Modena Archivolt, 4, 5, 6 n
Iseult (Iseut la bloie, La Beale Isoud, Isotta, Isaotta, Isolda, Ysolt, Isea), daughter of King Languis (Hanguin) of Ireland and wife of King Mark, early allusions in Italian, 10, 21–29, 32, 34, 36, 37; description of her beauty, 39–40; 41–3, 48, 62; in the *Tristano Riccardiano*, 68–79, 82; in a novella, 90–1; allusions, 104–7, 109; in the two versions of Tristan's death, 110–11; her rebuke of Kahedyn and "lai mortel," 116; 117; her death, 118–20; her lai of Guirun, 131; analogy with Francesca da Rimini, 141, 153; in the *Tavola Ritonda*, 162–6, 170, 171 (relations with Guinevere), 174–8, 181, 183–4 (death and tomb); 217–18, 220–1, 224; allusions by Boccaccio, 229–31; by Petrarca, 232; 242, 248, 260–3, 270, 279, 283–4; in the *Due Tristani*, 296–300; 309, 317, 321, 328
Iseult (Iseut aux blanches mains, Isoud la Blanche Mains, Isolda, Isotta di Brettagna, Isaotta Blanzesmano), daughter of King Hoel of Brittany and wife of Tristan, 25, 76–7, 79, 108, 110–13, 115, 166; her death, 167; 184 n, 221, 298
Iseult (Isea), daughter of Tristan and the first Iseult, 297, 301–3
Island of Avalon, see Avalon; Island of the Fountain, 105, 218 n; Island of Life, 305–7, 320 n; Isola senza Aventura (île de Saint-Sanson), 68, 224
Ivain (Yvain, Ivano, Uwaine le Blanchemains), son of King Uriens and Morgan le Fay, 41, 167, 169, 173; his death, 189; 197 n, 229 n, 245

Joseph of Arimathea, 19, 71, 54, 123 n, 175, 180, 297, 306–7
Josephe, his son, 123 n
Josephus, supposed historian of the Grail, 150
Josue, brother of Alain le Gros, 306
Joyous Gard (Guardia Gioiosa), originally Dolorous Gard, Lancelot's castle, 38–9, 117, 158, 159 n, 163, 170, 181, 188–9, 225–6, 271; destruction by Mark, 205–7; tombs at, 120, 268–9

Kahedyn (Kehenis, Kehydius, Ghedino, Chedino, Quedino), son of King Hoel and brother of Iseult of Brittany, 76, 78–9, 80, 106, 110–13, 115–16, 164, 166, 229, 283, 285, 296, 301
Kalafe, the leper king, see Gallaffaro
Kay (Che, Keu, Chiesso, Chiesi, Chiex, Gheus), foster-brother of King Arthur and seneschal, 4, 19, 81, 83–4, 102, 157, 161, 164, 182, 184, 197–8, 229, 266

Labegues, in Storia di Merlino, 215
Lac, King, father of Erec and Brandelis, 44, 54–5, 60–1, 103, 262, 290, 316
Lady of the Lake (Dama del Lago, Viviana), 34, 35, 46, 59, 69, 108, 134, 157, 175, 183, 199; the "bianca serpente" and scribe of Merlin, 201–8; her love for the younger Meliadus, 209–11; 220, 224, 271–2, 289, 292; as Thetis in the Avarchide, 315, 317
Lambegues (Lambegus, Lambegant), husband of the Lady of the Thorn in Italian Tristan versions, 69, 77; champion of Iseult in French and Malory, 74 n, 76 n; in romance of Old Table, 333
Lamorat de Listenois, brother of King Pellinor, 157 n
Lamorat le Gallois (Lamorak de Galis, Amoratto, Lamoratto, Amorotto), son of King Pellinor and lover of the Queen of Orkney, 49, 50, 75, 80–1, 107, 115–17, 124, 156, 167, 217, 257, 270, 298
Lance, the Bleeding, in the Grail pageant, 30, 32
Lancelot del Lac (Launcelot du Lake, Lancellotto, Lancilotto, Lancielotto, Lancialotto, Lansalotto), son of King Ban of Benoic and foster-child of the Lady of the Lake, 16; earliest allusions in Italian, 27, 32–4, 42; in Rusticiano, 49, 59–61; in the Tristano Riccardiano, 66, 71–3, 80–2, 84; friendship with Galehaut, 85–8; charrette and maid of Astolat episodes in Cento novelle antiche, 92–4; conquers Valley of False Lovers, 101–2; 108–9, 117, 119, 120; in Grail quest, 121; tournament at Winchester and maid of Astolat episodes, 124–9; allusions in Dante, 137, 140–6, 148, 150; Tavola Ritonda version of his early history, 157–9; in the Tavola Ritonda, 162–3, 167–78, 180–1, 183, 186; relations with Guinevere and death, 188–90; Merlin's prophecies concerning, 194, 196 n, 204; Mark's outrage on his body, 205–7; 209, 216–17, 220–1, 224–7; allusions by Boccaccio, 229, 230; by Petrarca, 232; 238–9, 240, 242, 244, 247, 258; his combat with Tristan, 260–2; his vengeance for Tristan, 263–5; in the Cantari, 266–8; his tomb, 268, 269 n; 270–1; in Boiardo, 280–1; in Ariosto, 285, 287; in the Due Tristani, 298–9, 301–2; 309, 313; as Achilles in the Avarchide, 315–19; 320, 321, 327
Languis (Hanguin, Anguish), King of Ireland and father of Iseult, 68–70, 231, 309
Lasancis (Lasancisse, Lasancissa), brother of the Lady of Avalon, 168–9, 271, 278
Leodegrance (Leodagan), King of Cameliard (Carmelide), father of Guinevere, 53, 155
Lionbordo (Liombardo), knight in the Tavola Ritonda, 245–6
Lionel (Lionello), son of King Bors of Gaunes and foster-child of the Lady of the Lake, 126, 173, 179; his death, 204; 209, 224, 229, 244, 260, 262, 268
Liones (Léonis, Leonois, Leonnoys), city and kingdom of Meliadus, passim
Lodaganta, sister of Guinevere in the Avarchide, 317 n
Logres (Longres), realm of Arthur, passim
Lonazep (Louvezerp, Louvrezep, Verzeppe), castle of Arthur, scene of great tournament, 117, 170–2, 270
Lot (Loth, Lotto), King of Orkney and brother-in-law of Arthur, 107, 188, 196, 197 n
Lucius, first Christian King of Britain, 305
Lucius, consul of the Romans, 233, 235
Ludinas, knight of Norgalles, 58

Mabon le Noir, wizard in the Tristan, 105
Machen de l'Ile Perdue, father of Dodinel, 258 n
Mador de la Porte (Amadore), the accuser of Guinevere, 126–7, 287
"Maimed King" (Roi mehaignié, Re magagnato), 30, 180, 304
Malehaut (Maloaut, Maloant, Maloalto, Maloanto, Mimalto), Lady of, wife of Danain le Roux, 48, 54–5, 60, 310, 312; in the Lancelot, 108, 142–3, 145–6,

158; mention by Dante, 48, 145–6; called Telesilla in Leopardi's tragedy, 327–8

"Mardoc," in the Modena Archivolt, 4

Mariadoco (Meriadoc), accuser of Tristan, 165

Marinaia, name of mother of Merlin, 213

Mark (Marco, Mares), son and successor of King Felix of Cornwall, 22–3, 51, 60, 65–78, 87, 90–1, 111–20, 137 n, 141, 153, 162–6, 169, 170, 181–7, 202, 211, 225 n, 231, 242, 263–5, 296, 298–302, 309, 321, 328; different versions of his end, 185–7, 205–7, 210, 263–5, 300–2, 304

Meliadus (Meliodas, Meliadusse), King of Liones, brother of Mark in Italian *Tristan* versions, his brother-in-law in the French and Malory, 41, 44, 47–8, 50–4, 59, 60, 62 n, 65–6, 89, 90, 112–13, 156–9, 174, 201, 208–9, 219, 228, 289 n, 332–3

Meliadus the younger, son of King Meliadus and the Queen of Scotland, half-brother of Tristan, 208–11, 292

Meliagrance (Meleagant, Melegaunt, Meliagans, Meliagus, Maligante, Malgaretes), son of King Bagdemagus of Gorre, 4, 16, 81, 88 n, 93, 315

Meliant (Melias de Lile, Mellidanse), son of the King of Denmark, 120

Menion (Mecion, Nanowne), knight of the Round Table, 61

Meraugis de Portlesguez, son of Mark, 206

Merlin the Prophet (Merlino), occurrence of name, 3; in Godfrey of Viterbo, 6–7; as political prophet, 16–17; early allusions, 29, 32, 36–7; prophecies, 45–6, 51; in the Tristan story, 65–6; in the Novelle, 94–5; in *Sapientes*, 97–100; his magic boat and the Lady of Avalon, 104–6; 180–9; Dante's treatment, 132–6; foundation of Round Table, 155; birth, relations with Vortigern and Uther Pendragon, 192–7; procures succession of Arthur, 197; his scribes, prophecies, and deception by the Lady of the Lake, 199–211; another version of his childhood and early life, 212–16; later allusions, 223, 226 (Fazio degli Uberti), 227, 233 (Boccaccio), 257, 262, 270, (Cantari), 277, 279 (Boiardo); presentation by Ariosto, 291–4; 297, 305, 315, 317–18, 321; as a prophet of Galileo, 325–6; 334

Morans (Marins), jealous knight in *Merlino* and *Perlesvaus*, 214

Mordrain, previously Evalac, King of Sarras, 297 n, 307

Mordred (Mordret, Modredus, Mordarette), son of Arthur by the Queen of Orkney, 4, 12, 124, 127, 147–8, 170, 173, 181, 189–90, 197 n, 222, 225, 229, 232–6, 253, 266, 268, 328 n

Morgan le Fay (Morgain, Morgue la fée, Fata Morgana), daughter of Duke Gorlois of Tintagel, half-sister of Arthur, wife of King Uriens of Garlot, 13, 33–6, 50, 75, 101–2, 105–6, 109, 118, 127, 166–7, 182, 190, 196, 197 n, 203–4, 211, 241–2, 244, 246, 271, 280, 287 n, 299, 305, 321–4

Morholt, the (Amoroldo, l'Amoroldo, Marhaus), brother of the Queen of Ireland and uncle of Iseult, 15–16, 50, 60, 65–8, 91, 171, 219, 225, 230, 271, 299, 316

Morholt, the younger, see Amoroldo

Nabon le Noir (Membruto), giant, lord of the Servage, 58–61, 115, 311–13 316–17

Nadriano (Andrieus), 106–7

Nascien(s), the hermit, 122

Nascien(s), ancestor of Galahad, 307

Nascien(s), of Gaunes, knight of the Old Table, 334

Natael (Nathaniel), companion of Joseph of Arimathea, 306

Nathan, son of Nabon, 59, 313

Neutres (Nentres), King of Garlot, 197

Nicodemus, in the Grail legend, 19

Nimue (Niniane), mistress of Merlin, 199

Norgales (Northgalis), King of, 124, 173, 188

Northumberland, King of, in Merlin story, 215

Northumberland, princess of, loved by Guiron, 56–7, 269, 291 n

Ogier the Dane (Ogier le Danois, Ugieri), descendant of Ariohan and holder of Tristan's sword, 53, 172, 219

Ogrin, hermit in Béroul, 177

Oliver, paladin, receives Lancelot's sword, 172, 273

Olofer, son of Gallafar and Duke of Cornwall, 305–6

Onesun (Huneson, Hemison), paramour of Morgan, 167, 182, 241

"Orgueilleuse emprise," castle of Galehaut, 88, 238

Orkney (Organia), Queen of (Mawgawse, Morgause), wife of King Lot and half-sister of Arthur, mother of Gawain and Mordred, 81, 107, 196, 197 n

Orlando (Roland), paladin, nephew of Charlemagne, 41, 172, 221, 239–40, 273 (lord of Anglante), 275–7, 280; his madness based on that of Tristan, 283

Osenain Cuer Hardi (Ozana, Suziano Cuor Ardito), knight of the Round Table, 167, 229

Palamede (Palamedes, Palomides, Palamides, Pallamidesse), the pagan, son of Esclabor of Babylon and rival of Tristan, 37–9, 44, 49, 50, 58–62, 68, 74, 80 n, 106, 108, 116–20, 124, 152, 168, 171–3, 176, 178, 181, 183, 217–18, 229, 244, 260–1; travestied in the *Due Tristani*, 297–9, 302; 313, 316–18, 335
Palante, kinsman of Tristan, 301–2
Parsaforesto (Perceforest), King of Britain, 304–6
Passaleone, ancestor of Merlin, 305
Patrise, the poisoned knight, 126 n
Paulart (Paulos), kinsman of Lancelot in Spanish Grail version, 206–7
Pelles (le Roi Pescheor, Piles Pescaor), father of the mother of Galahad, 120, 267
Pellinor (Pillinoro, Pellinoro, Polinoro, Oriel), King of Listenois and temporarily of Galles (Gaul), father of Lamorat and Perceval, 50–3, 80 n, 107, 208, 229, 257, 267
Pendragon, elder brother of Uther Pendragon, 193–5, 216
Penevric, castle in *Erec et Enide*, 226
Perceval le Gallois (Percivale de Galis, Prezzivalle, Princivallo, Prenzivalle, Percivalle, Parzival, Peredur, Perlesvaus), son of the widow lady in Chrétien de Troyes, son of King Pellinor in the prose *Tristan*, the original Grail quester, 19, 29–31, 36; his birth to Pellinor. 52; 59; pursuit of Questing Beast in *Tristano Riccardiano*, 80, 84; 102–3, 117, 149–50, 157, 164, 170–1; in Vulgate version of Grail quest, 177–81; 196, 204; in the *Vita di Merlino*, 208–11, 214; 228, 245, 257–8, 270, 298
Pernam (Perneham, Boudwin), brother of Mark, 65
Perron (Petrone, Rock of Merlin), 50 n, 66, 183, 226, 260–2, 277
Petit Creu (Petitto Araviuto), fairy dog, 165
Pharamond (Faramon, Ferramonte, Fieramonte), King of France, 50–1, 52 n, 56, 67, 288, 293–4, 311
Pleur(s) (Proro, Pluere), castle of the evil usage, 71–3, 85–7, 229, 296–7, 301 "Porco troncascino" ("porcus Troit"?), 249, 250 n
Pulzella Gaia, see Gaia
Pulzella laida ("pucièle laide," loathly maiden), 30, 102–3

Questing Beast (Beste Glatissant, Bestia Grattisante, Bestia Grattigiante), 80, 84, 171, 202 n, 293, 298, 306

Rinaldo (Ranaldo, Renaud de Montauban), paladin, has the sword of Amoroldo, 172; 273, 275, 278; as Tristan in the *Orlando Furioso*, 284–7; 320–1
Rions, King of the Giants, 334
Rivalen, father of Tristan in Thomas poem, 36
Robert (Rubers) the chaplain, collector of Merlin's prophecies, 211–12
Rocca di Tristano, in Ariosto, 287–91, 293–4
Roger (Ugier) le Brun, the presumptuous knight, 209
Rosenna, see Soredamors
Rowena (Renwein), wife of Vortigern, 194
Ruggiero, lover of Bradamante, 280, 291
Ruvalen, brother of Kahedyn, 111, 113

Sage Clerc (Savio Clerico), scribe of Merlin, identified with Antonio, 209 n, 211–12
Sagramour (Sagramore le Desirous, Sagremor le desrée, Sagramoro, Sagrimon), son of the Emperor of Constantinople and knight of the Round Table, 19, 76 n, 118–20, 183–4, 264, 298–300
Salisbury (Salebieres, Saglibier), scene of the last battle, 204, 227, 235 "Salle aux images," in the *Tristan* of Thomas, 25, 164
Saraide, damsel of the Lady of the Lake, 223–4
Sargia, enchantress in the *Due Tristani*, 301, 303
Sarras, city of, 149, 180
Scapiolo, Sicambrian King of Britain, 305, 324
Scotland, King of, 50–2, 68, 210
Scotland, Queen of, loved by King Meliadus, 48, 50–2; mother of the younger Meliadus, 209–10
Segurades (Segwarides), husband of the Lady of the Thorn, 61, 69, 77 n, 115, 313
Segurant le Brun (Sigurans, Segurano, Segurades, Segurans), the Knight of the Dragon, son of Hector le Brun, 44, 46, 50, 59, 156, 174, 203–4, 208, 210, 313; conflicting stories of his death, 174, 204; as Hector in the *Avarchide*, 316–19; 333
Sentaille (Sentraille), follower of Tristan, 76 n
Servage, valley or island, realm of Nabon, delivered by Tristan, 58–61, 77 n, 115, 227, 311–13
Shield, the cloven ("écu fendu"), 69, 162, 289
Siege Perilous, 121, 175, 195, 209
Sigris (Sagris lo Pitetto, Segris), knight-errant, 74, 76 n, 298 n
Simeon (Symeu), companion of Joseph of Arimathea, 179 n

Soredamors (Rosenna d'amore), sister of Gawain, 108
Sorelois, kingdom of Galehaut, 57, 87–8, 228
Stag or hind, white, as bearer of the Grail, 121–3; elsewhere in Arthurian stories, 178, 322–4
Sword, of Arthur, 12 n, 197–8, 189–90; of Tristan, 15, 119, 172, 219; those of other knights taken by the paladins, 172; with the Strange Hangings ("l'Espee as estranges renges," "Spada Strinces Ranges"), 180; of Hector le Brun, 54–5, 310–11, 328

Table, Round (Tavola ritonda, rotonda), early allusions in Italy, 9, 10, 19, 32, 47; 94, 109, 127; foundation, 155, 195–7, 223, 233, 235, 270; destruction, 205–7, 272, 234; arms of the companions, 312, 313 n; the Old Table (Tavola Vecchia), origin of the conception, 155–6; allusions, 169, 174–5, 270, 285, 331, 332
Telesilla, Leopardi's name for Lady of Malehaut, 327–8
Tintagel (Tintoille, Cintanel), city of Duke Gorlois, 196; capital of King Mark, passim; various sieges, 51, 185–6, 263–5, 301
Tolomeo (Tholomer), scribe of Merlin, 199
Tor, son of King Pellinor, 81 n
Tristan (Tristano, Tristram, Tristrem), son of Rivalen and Mark's sister Blanchefleur in the Thomas version, son of King Meliadus of Liones and Mark's sister Heliabel in prose Tristan (in Italian versions Meliadus is brother to Mark, and Eliabella is of undefined parentage or of the house of King Ban), 36, 65, 157; first mention in Italy, 8; occurrence of similar names, 11; his sword, 15–16; early allusions and forms of legend, 19, 21–7, 32, 37–43; in the Palamède, 49–52, 59–61, 62 n; first Italian version of story from his birth to the deliverance of Arthur in the Forest Perilous (Tristano Riccardiano), 67–84; in the Galehaut conto, 85, 87; in the Cento novelle antiche, 90–2; poetic allusions, 104–6, 107–10; versions of his death, 110–13; madness and other episodes in Panciatichiano MS, 115–17; death, 118–19; echoes of story in Dante, 131, 133, 134, 135–41, 153; in the Tavola Ritonda, 157, 162–75; adventures in the Grail quest, 175–8; death, 181–3; tomb, 184; vengeance for his death, 185–7; in Merlin's prophecies, 201–2, 210; in fourteenth-century poets, 219–21, 224–6; in Boccaccio, 229–31; in Petrarca, 232; in Cantari, 240, 247, 260–2 (combat with Lancelot), 262 (death), 263–5 (vengeance), 270–1; in Boiardo, 278–9, 281; madness and adventures utilised by Ariosto, 283–91; in the Due Tristani, 296–300; in later poems, 308–9, 313; as Ajax or Diomede in the Avarchide, 315–19; later allusions, 320, 321, 327, 328
Tristan the younger, in the Due Tristani, son of Tristan and Iseult, 297, 300–3
Troas (Troasse), King of Thessaly, 332–5
Troiano, knight in the Tavola Ritonda, 242–4
Troiano, hero of romance of the Old Table, 332–5

Ullania, as damsel of Lady of the Lake in Ariosto, 287–9
Urbano (London), in the Tavola Ritonda, 189
Urgan, giant slain by Tristan, 165
Uriens, King of Garlot, husband of Morgan le Fay and father of Ivain, 41, 51, 52, 197 n, 333
Uther Pendragon (Uterpandragone), son of Constantine in Geoffrey of Monmouth, of Constant (Constantius, Costanzo) in the Merlin, King of Britain and father of Arthur, 6–7, 47–9, 54, 152, 154–6, 160, 167, 174; relations with Merlin, foundation of Round Table, and death, 193–7; 223, 227, 270, 277, 280, 290, 331; in romance of Old Table, 331–5.

Vagor (Armant, Hermance, Aramante), King of the Red City, 319, 335
Verseria, wife of Ferragunze, 159
Verzeppe, see Lonazep
Viviana, see Lake, Lady of,
Vortigern (Vortegirnus, Vitiglier, Vertaggiere), King of Britain, 6, 7 n, 99, 100, 193–4, 215–16

Walwanus, see Gawain
"Winlogee," in the Modena Archivolt, 4

Yder ("Isdernus"), lover of Queen Guenloie, 4, 6 n

SUBSIDIARY AND GENERAL

Agostini, Nicolò, poems on Tristan and Lancelot, 308–9, 329
Alamanni, Luigi, *Gyrone il Cortese*, 309–13, 320; *Avarchide*, 313–19, 320
Aldus, edition of the Italian *Meliadus*, 48 n
Angiolieri, Cecco, 42
Ansegis, founder of Fescamp, 124
Antonio da Tempo, 241 n
Ariosto, Ludovico, adoption of Arthurian matter in the *Orlando Furioso*, 46, 282–94, 295
Arthour and Merlin, 213, 215 n, 216
Asdente, cobbler of Parma, 135
Attila, Franco-Italian poem, 220
Avowynge of Sir Bawdewyn, 156 n, 160–2

Barbi, Michele, 134 n, 144, 238
Bari, sculptures at, 5, 11
Bédier, J., 2, 21, 25, 77 n, 91 n, 111 n, 112 n, 113 n, 115 n, 141 n, 162 n, 165 n, 184 n, 248 n
Bel Gherardino, cantare, 247
Bellay, Joachim du, 314 n
Benedetto, L. F., 47 n
Benedict of Peterborough, 12 n
Benvenuto (de' Rambaldi) of Imola, 140 n, 235–6
Berchet, Giovanni, 327
Bergen, H., 233 n
Béroul, *Roman de Tristan*, 22, 90, 177
Bertaux, E., 11–12
Bertoni, Giulio, 6 n, 29 n, 52 n, 86 n, 110 n, 143 n, 184 n, 220 n, 262 n, 273 n, 274 n, 277 n, 283 n, 331 n
Biagi, G., 88 n
Boccaccio, Giovanni, 1, 10 n, 96, 139, 166, 217; *Amorosa Visione*, 228–9; *Fiammetta*, 229–30; *Comento alla Divina Commedia*, 231; *De Casibus*, 232–6; *Decameron*, 237–8; *Filocolo*, 240; 273
Bodel, Jean, 130 n
Boiardo, Matteo Maria, use of Arthurian matter in the *Orlando Innamorato*, 274–82, 320
Bonagiunta Orbicciani, 40
Bonatti, Guido, in the *Inferno*, 135
Boncompagno da Signa, 9, 10
Bonilla y San Martin, A., 40 n, 207 n, 296 n
Boron, Hélie de, reputed author of the *Palamède*, 22 n, 45
Boron, Robert de, *Merlin*, 46, 155, 192–3, 196–9, 212, 215–16; pseudo, 159 n, 199, 205–7
Borso d'Este, Duke of Modena and Ferrara, 274
Breton Lays, 29 n, 62, 110 n, 131 n, 167, 177, 183 n, 241, 246
Brienne, Jean de ("lo Re Giovanni"), 23–6
Bruce, J. D., 6 n, 11 n, 18 n, 50 n, 94 n, 112 n, 122 n, 128 n, 149 n, 188 n, 207 n, 235 n, 237 n
Brugger, E., 159 n, 258
Bruto di Brettagna, cantare, 250–2, 325

Caesarea, taken by the Genoese, 17, 18
Caesarius of Heisterbach, 12–13, 17 n
Campbell, K., 96 n, 97 n
Cantari, 239–41; *Cantare dei Cantari*, 270–3
Capellanus, Andreas, *De Amore*, 252, 325
Capitò, G., 14 n
Carducci, Giosue, 221 n, 328
Carduino, cantare, 252–8
Carr, Comyns, *King Arthur*, 329
Casella, M., 23 n
Casini, T., 31 n, 42 n
Cavalcanti, Guido, 43, 132
Cavalcanti, Mainardo, 237
Caxton, William, 1, 232, 275
Cento novelle antiche, 84–95
Cerchiari (Zirclaria), Tomasino, *Der Wälsche Gast*, 19
Chambers, E. K., 3 n, 7 n, 8 n, 195 n, 250 n
Chambers, R. W., 241 n
Charles of Luxembourg, Emperor, 222
Chiaro Davanzati, 35, 37
Chrétien de Troyes, 2, 19 n; *Chevalier au Lion*, 41; *Chevalier de la Charrette* (*Lancelot*), 16, 92–3; *Cligés*, 108, 131–2; *Erec et Enide*, 31, 108, 226, 237; lost *Tristan*, 22; *Perceval le Gallois*, 30–1, 32, 36, 102–3
Cino da Pistoia, 43
Cleges, Sir, 156 n
Colfi, B., 6 n
Comfort, W. W., 93 n, 132 n
Compagni, Dino, 107
Compiuta Donzella, 34–5
Conti di antichi cavalieri, 85–8
Crane, T. F., 252 n
Cremona, V., 107
Crescini, V., 143 n
Cross, T. P., 246 n

D'Ancona, Alessandro, 96, 98, 100
Dante Alighieri, 14, 29 n, 40, 48; on the "ambages pulcerrimae," 130; Arthurian motives in *Vita Nuova* and *Rime*, 113–4; attitude towards Merlin, 135–6; Arthurianism of fifth canto of *Inferno*, 136–44; his "Galeotto," 144–5; on Guinevere and the Lady of Malehaut, 145–6; Arthurian note in *Purgatorio*, 146–7; on Mordred and Arthur, 147; on Lancelot in *Convivio*, 148; alleged influence of Grail legend on the *Divina Commedia*, 149–51; echoes in *Tavola Ritonda*, 153; 159, 217, 222, 231–2, 235, 237–40, 271 n, 276, 282, 293, 329
Dante da Maiano, 36
Davidsohn, R., 18 n
De Bartholomaeis, V., 15 n, 32 n, 116 n
Debenedetti, Santorre, 107, 108, 283 n, 330 n
Delfin, Pietro di Giorgio, 192 n
Detto del Gatto Lupesco, 14–15

Due Tristani, 295–303
Dunlop, J., 304 n, 320 n
Durmart le Gallois, 5

Edward I, King of England, his "book," 46, 49, 154
Egidi, F., 153 n
Eilhart von Oberge, *Tristrant*, 111, 113 n, 184 n, 248 n
Elinor, Queen of England, 154
Entrée d'Espagne, Franco - Italian poem, 218–20
Entwistle, W. J., 13 n, 27 n, 40 n, 294 n, 298 n, 327 n
Etna (Mongibello), legend of Arthur in, 12–15
Evans, Sebastian, 149 n

Faral, E., 3 n
Farinelli, A., 138 n
Febusso il Forte (*Febusso e Breusso*), cantare, 269
Ferrara, centre of Arthurianism, 273–4
Fescamp, abbey, 19, 124
Fiamma, Galvano, 15
Fieschi, Cardinal Luca, 19 n
Filippo da Messina, 26
Fisher, L. A., 150 n
Floire et Blanchefleur, 36, 108, 240
Floriant et Florete, 2, 13, 105, 133, 324
Foerster, W., 6 n, 93 n, 132 n, 226 n
Foffano, F., 275 n, 309 n, 310
Folgore da San Gimignano, 42
Folie Tristan, 165, 248 n
Fossa, Matteo, poem on Gawain, 308
Francesca da Rimini, 138–41, 144, 153, 231–2
Francesco da Buti, 140 n, 239
Francesco di Vannozzo, 221–2
Francis of Assisi, Saint, 9–10, 92, 239
Francis I, King of France, 309, 311
Frederick II, Emperor, 9, 16–17, 21, 23, 37, 44, 45, 136, 212
Fregoso, Antonio, *Cerva Bianca*, 324

Gaddo (Garo) de' Lanfranchi, 154
Gaetano da S. Teresa, 18 n
Galasso dalla scura valle, 308
Gaspary, A., 282 n
Gast, Luce de, reputed author of prose *Tristan*, 22 n
Gawain and the Green Knight, 5; *Gawain and the Carle of Carlisle*, 260–1; Italian analogue of latter, 158–9
Genoa, "sagro catino," 17–18
Geoffrey of Monmouth, *Historia Regum Britanniae*, 2, 5, 7, 11, 16, 99, 100, 192–3, 224 n, 234–6; *Vita Merlini*, 14, 95 n
Gervaise of Tilbury, 12–13
Giacomo da Lentino, 24–6
Gillio Lelli, Perugian poet, 331
Giovanni del Virgilio, 217
Giraldus Cambrensis, 195 n
Girone il Cortese (*Gyron le Courteois*), prose romance, 47–50, 53–9
Gismirante, cantare, 247–50
Godfrey of Viterbo, *Pantheon*, 6–8
Gottfried von Strassburg, *Tristan*, 22, 28
Gradalis, occurrence of name, 3
Graelent, lai, 246, 324
Graf, Arturo, 12, 16 n, 225 n

Greenlaw, E. A., 161 n
Griffiths, E. T., 266 n, 267 n
Grion, G., 19 n
Griscom, A., 2 n, 7 n, 267 n
Guazzo, Marco, 308
Guido delle Colonne, 35
Guido da Montefeltro, coupled by Dante with Lancelot, 148
Guillem de Torrella, *La Faula*, 13
Guinglain, see Renaud de Beaujeu
Guinicelli, Guido, 42–3
Guittone d'Arezzo, his Arthurian allusions, 27–31

Hauvette, H., 233 n, 237 n, 309 n, 313 n, 314 n, 317
Henricus of Settimello, *Elegia*, 8, 327
Henry II, King of France, 309, 311
Henry III, King of England, 154
Henry VI, Emperor, 17
Henry VII (of Luxembourg), Emperor, 136
Herod of Rome, in *Sapientes* story, 97–8
Herschel, John, 329
Hortis, A., 232 n
Hubert, St., 123

Iliad, the, adaption by Alamanni to the Arthuriad, 314–19
Inghilfredi, early Italian poet, 26–7
Intelligenza, 107–10, 132 n
Intentio Regulae (*S. Francisci*), 10 n, 239 n
Irving, Henry, 329

Jacopo da Voragine, 18
Janot, Denis, French publisher, 47
Joachim of Flora, 16, 17, 135
Johannes de Garlandia, 161 n

Kerr, W. P., 93, 241, 314
Kittredge, G. L., 161 n, 260 n
Krappe, A. H., 96 n, 100 n
Kulhwch and Olwen, 250 n

Lancelot, the prose, 5, 22 n, 33, 46, 48, 74 n, 84 n, 85, 87 n, 92, 102, 108, 124, 134 n, 137, 141–6, 159, 168, 205 n, 223–7, 236, 271–2, 280, 284, 307, 315–16; *Lancellotto* (cantari), 265–9; *Lancillotto dal Lago*, 88, 272 n, 307; *Lanzelet*, 258; see also Chrétien de Troyes
Lapo Gianni, 132–3
Lapuccio Belfradelli, 33
Latini, Brunetto, 14, 32, 37, 39–40, 106, 136
Leo, Friar, 9
Leonardo del Guallacca, 36
Leopardi, Giacomo, 327–8
Leroux de Lincy, 124 n
Levi, Ezio, 29 n, 110 n, 131 n, 240 n, 241, 242 n, 246 n, 247 n, 250
Levi, G. A., 327 n
Libeaus Desconus, Sir, 257
Liombruno, cantare, 247
Livi, G., 153 n
Livre d'Artus, 122, 199 n
Loomis, R. S., 4–6, 14 n, 15 n, 22 n, 24 n, 62, 165 n
Löseth, E., 22 n, 39 n, 45 n, 47 n, 48 n, 50 n, 54 n, *et passim*

Lot, F., 85 n, 102 n, 141 n, 159 n, 179 n, 257 n, 282 n
Loth, J., 250 n
Louis of Taranto, husband of Queen Giovanna of Naples, 45 n
Lovato de' Lovati, 217–18
Lucca, Santo Volto, 19
Lydgate, John, 232

Mabinogion, 31, 62, 250 n
Malavasi, G., 309 n
Mâle, E., 5
Malory, Thomas, 1, 2, 7, 38, 41, 61, 65–74, 76–81, 84 n, 88 n, 92, 106, 107 n, 116–18, 120–6, 128–9, 145 n, 147, 148 n, 151 n, 155–6, 158 n, 167 n, 168 n, 169–71 n, 175, 179, 180, 185 n, 188, 190 n, 195 n, 197 n, 199, 204 n, 205 n, 225–6, 262 n, 267 n, 268 n, 271 n, 272 n, 274–5, 277, 283, 289–90, 313 n, 329
Map, Walter, reputed author of the Lancelot, 236
Marco Polo, 47
Mare Amoroso, 101–6, 133, 269, 272
Marie de France, Guingamor and Lanval, 246
Marigo, A., 8 n
Martorell, Johanot, Tirant lo Blanch, 286
Massèra, A. F., 29 n, 37 n, 42 n, 237, 331 n
Medin, A., 222 n
Meliadus, prose romance, 45 n, 47–9, 50–4, 59–61, 112–13, 289, 316–17, et passim
Merlin, Robert de Boron, 155, 192–8; Huth (pseudo Robert) continuation, 155, 197 n, 199, 205, 208 n, 235 n; Vulgate continuation, 197 n, 199, 203 n, 235 n, 258 n; Prophecies de, 45–6, 95 n, 105–6, 174, 191–2, 195, 199–205, 208–211, 212, 214–16; Storia di Merlino, 191, 212–15; Vita di Merlino, 191–212, 279, 284, 292–3
Michael Scott, 17, 135
Mistruzzi, V., 107 n
Modena, Archivolt, 4–6, 11
Monaci, E., 23–7, 34–6, 38 n, 41 n, 331 n
Monte Andrea, Florentine poet, 34, 37
Mort Artù (last branch of the Lancelot), 22 n, 93–4, 114, 124, 128, 137, 147–9, 163, 170, 188–90, 235–7, 266, 268 n, 307; Italian versions: Panciatichiano, 124–8; Tavola Ritonda, 187–90; Cantari, 266–8
Morte Arthur, English stanzaic poem, 129 n, 266, 268 n
Morte Darthur, see Malory
Moore, E., 135 n
Moschetti, A., 308
Moschino, Ettore, 328
Muret, E., 90 n, 177 n
Murrell, E. S., 119 n
Mussafia, A., 96
Mussato, Albertino, 217

Nennius, 7 n, 250 n
Niccolò, sculptor at Modena, 5
Nicola da Casola, Attila, 220
Normans, in southern Italy, 11, 14
Northup, G. T., 64, 69 n, 76 n, 295, 296 n

Orlanduccio Orafo, 37
Ortiz, R., 11 n, 103 n, 106 n
Otranto, mosaic, 11–12

Padua, Arthurian names at, 3
Palamède, romance, 44–7, 58 n, 60, 62, 103, 156, 174, 209, 205–6, 225 n, 227–8, 269, 279, 284, 289–90, 291, 298, 335
Palermo, F., 269 n
Pallamidesse di Bellindote, 37–9
Panizzi, Antonio, 141 n
Pantaleone, worker in mosaic, 11
Papa, P., 86 n
Parini, Giuseppe, 326
Paris, Gaston, 96 n, 155 n, 161 n, 192 n, 205 n, 208 n, 260 n, 303–4
Paris, Paulin, 17, 119 n
Parma, defeat of Frederick II at, 9
Parodi, E. G., 64, 92 n, 114, 118 n, 119 n, 144 n, 153 n, 161 n, 165 n, 265 n,
Parry, J. J., 14 n, 95 n
Paton, L. A., 45, 46 n, 84 n, 95 n, 106 n, 192 n, 194 n, 199 n, 202 n, 208 n, 209 n, 210 n, 212 n
Pauphilet, A., 121 n, 123 n, 149 n, 150 n, 179 n, 180 n, 267 n
Pavia, Arthurian names at, 3
Pellegrini, F., 30 n
Perceforest (Parsaforesto), romance, 295, 303–7, 320
Perceval le Gallois, see Chrétien de Troyes
Perceval, prose, 102
Perlesvaus, romance, 149–50, 214 n
Peter of Blois, 8 n
Petrarca, Francesco, 217, 222, 232
Piccoli, R., 107 n
Pieri, Paolino, Storia di Merlino, 191, 212
Pitrè, G., 14 n
Polidori, F. L., 122 n, 152–4, 263 n
Porter, A. K., 6 n
Potvin, C., 31 n, 103 n, 149 n, 150 n
Pré, Galliot du, 47, 303
Proto, E., 320 n
Pucci, Antonio, 247, 250, 252, 259, 325
Pulzella Gaia, cantare, 241–6

Rajna, Pio, 1–3, 14 n, 48 n, 58 n, 97, 103 n, 105, 143 n, 146, 149, 252 n, 257 n, 258 n, 259 n, 260 n, 270, 273 n, 282, 283 n, 286 n, 289, 308 n
Raymond de Béziers, 130
Razzoli, G., 277 n
Reichenbach, G., 274 n
Renaud de Beaujeu, Li Biaus Descouneus (Guinglain, Le Bel Inconnu), 257–8
Renda, O., 314 n
Renier, R., 221 n
Richard Cœur de Lion, 12 n
Richard of Ireland (Maistre Richart), 45, 46 n, 212
Robert, King of Naples, 18 n
Rudolf of Hapsburg, Emperor, 37
Ruggieri Apuliese, 32, 272
Rusticiano (Rustichello) of Pisa, 47–50, 60, 62, 114 n, 154–5, 157 n, 188 n, 206, 261–2, 277 n, 290 n, 298–9, 310

Sacchetti, Franco, 240
Saint Graal, Estoire del, 123 n, 235 n, 307 n; *Queste del*, 22 n, 32, 121, 123, 149–51, 175, 179, 180; Italian versions: Panciatichiano, 120–4; *Tavola Ritonda*, 175–81; Spanish text: *Demanda del Sancto Grial*, 206–7
Salimbene of Parma, 16–17, 23, 45, 135
Sanesi, I., 3 n, 191 n, 216
Sanzanome, Florentine chronicler, 9
Sapientes, see *Setti Savi*
Savoy, Count Piero of, 154
Scherillo, M., 132 n
Seneca, *Hercules Furens*, 283
Sennuccio del Bene, 29 n
Sette Savi di Roma, 95–100
Shakespeare, 286, 293, 335
Schoepperle (Loomis), Gertrude, 112 n, 248 n
Schofield, W. H., 199 n, 257
Sicardi, E., 88 n
Sicily, Arthurian connections, 2, 12–15, 21–7, 45, 112, 212
Sommer, O., 122 *et passim*
Sommer-Tolomei, E., 43 n, 92 n
Somnium Scipionis, 324
Sordello, 29
Spanish Arthurian texts, 40, 64, 69 n, 76 n, 80 n, 206–7, 295–303, 327
Speculum Perfectionis, 10 n, 239 n
Stonehenge, 195
Stoppa de' Bostichi, Frate, 220–1
Storia di Stefano, 97, 99 n
Strozzi, Giulio, *Venetia edificata*, 325–6
Sudre, L., 27 n
Swinburne, A. C., 81 n

Tancred, King of Sicily, 12 n
Tasso, Torquato, on Alamanni, 319; *Rinaldo* and *Gerusalemme*, 320–1
Tavola Ritonda, 35 n, 54 n, 74 n, 76 n, 86 n, 107 n, 118 n, 123 n, 134 n, 147; text, date, and sources, 152–6; treatment of "Old Table," 154–5; early history of Lancelot, 157–9; the "vaunts" or "avowings," 159–61; Tristan adventures, 162–4; preserves episodes from Thomas, 164–5; Tristan adventures, 166–75; version of Grail quest, 175–81; end of Tristan story, 181–4; vengeance for Tristan, 185–6; unique version of *Mort Artù*, 187–90
Tennyson, A, 31
Thomas, *Roman de Tristan*, 21, 22, 24, 25, 28, 36, 62, 77, 85, 90, 110–12, 115 n, 131, 164–6
Thomas, Antoine, 218 n, 219 n
Torraca, F., 32 n, 104 n, 138
Torrigiano, Maestro, 34

Toynbee, Paget, 130 n, 141 n, 142, 145, 147, 236 n
Treviso, March of, 3, 4, 45, 200, 216, 218
Tristan, prose romance, 22, 37–9, 44–7, 64–5, 105, 110–13, 119, 133, 141, 162 n, 289, *et passim*; Italian prose versions: *Tristano Riccardiano*, 64–84 *et passim*; *Tristano Panciatichiano*, 114–20; *Tristano Veneto*, 114 n, 119 n, 265; Cantari: *Tristano e Lancielotto*, 260–2; *Morte di Tristano*, 262–3; *Vendetta*, 263–5; Spanish versions: *Don Tristan de Leonis*, 40, 64, 296–7; *El Cuento de Tristan*, 64 n, 69 n, 295 n, 296 n, 298 n, 299 n; Norse saga, 21–2, 184 n; see also Béroul, Thomas, Eilhart, Gottfried
Tristrem, Sir, 22 n, 71 n, 85, 162 n
Tumiati, Domenico, 328–9

Uberti, Fazio degli, 222; *Dittamondo*, 222–8
Ulrich, J., 199 n, and see Paris, G.

Vaganay, H., 304 n
Valvasone, Erasmo da, *Lancilotto*, 321; *La Caccia*, 321–5
Venice, in prophecies of Merlin, 45, 200, 204, 216, 326
Verard, Antoine, publisher of the *Gyron*, 47
Vercelli, 105
Verrua, P., 309 n
Vinaver, E., 2 n, 22 n, 69 n, 70 n, 75 n, 112 n, 177 n, 185 n
Virgil, 136–8, 203 n, 282, 314
Visconti, Bruzio, 221

Wace, *Brut*, 10 n, 192
Walter, Archdeacon of Oxford (Gualterius anglicus), 236
Ward, H. L. D., 206 n, 304 n
Warren, F. M., 11 n
Wauchier de Denain, 102, 195 n
Wells, J. E., 216 n
Weston, J. L., 6 n, 103 n, 122 n, 124 n, 149 n, 175 n, 257
Wicksteed, P. H., 217 n
Wiligelmus, sculptor at Modena, 5
William II, King of Sicily, 12
William of Orange, 240
William of Tyre, 17

Zingarelli, N., 112 n, 143 n
Zorzi (Giorgio Delfin), 191 n, 192 n
Zorzi, Bartolomeo (Bertolome), 31